Where to Stay and Eat in Scotland

Please contact:
Advertising Sales Department: advertisingsales@theAA.com
Editorial Department: lifestyleguides@theAA.com
AA Hotel Scheme Enquiries: 01256 844455

AA Media Limited would like to thank the following photographers, companies and picture libraries for their assistance in the preparation of this book. Abbreviations for the picture credits are as follows: (t) top; (b) bottom; (l) left; (r) right; (c) centre; (AA) AA World Travel Library.

Cover photos:
Front: (t) The Gleneagles Hotel; (bl) Plumed Horse, Edinburgh; (br) Loch Ness Lodge, Abriachan Back: (b) AA/S Day

Every effort has been made to trace the copyright holders, and we apologise in advance for any accidental errors. We would be happy to apply any corrections in the following edition of this publication.

Printed and bound by Graficas Estella, Spain
This directory is compiled by AA Lifestyle Guides; managed in the Librios Information Management System and generated by the AA establishment database system.

Published by AA Publishing, a trading name of AA Media Limited, whose registered office is Fanum House, Basing View, Basingstoke, Hampshire RG21 4EA.
Registered number 06112600

A CIP catalogue record for this book is available from the British Library
ISBN-13: 978-0-7495-6424-7
A04297

Maps prepared by the Mapping Services Department of AA Publishing.

Maps © AA Media Limited 2010.

Information on National Parks in Scotland provided by Scottish Natural Heritage.

This product includes mapping data licensed from Ordnance Survey® with the permission of the Controller of Her Majesty's Stationery Office.
© Crown copyright 2010. All rights reserved.
Licence number 100021153.

Contents

WELCOME TO THE GUIDE

Welcome to the first edition of Where to Stay and Eat in Scotland.

This book includes all the Scottish establishments currently held in our database. These Hotels, B&Bs, Restaurants and Pubs all belong to our rating schemes (see page 6) or appeared in the 2010 editions of the AA Hotel Guide, AA B&B Guide, AA Restaurant Guide or AA Pub Guide.

The guide is arranged in county order, with the Scottish Islands as a section in their own right at the end.

In order to make the guide easier to use, we have in some cases combined our Hotel or B&B guide entry (concerned mostly with describing the establishment's accommodation), with their Restaurant or Pub guide information (concerned chiefly with describing the food).

Throughout the guide you will notice that Star ratings for Hotels and Guest Accommodation, and Rosette awards which are given for food. Although pubs are not rated, they are chosen for having good beer, excellent food, a wonderful location or a combination of all three.

We hope you will find this guide useful when exploring Scotland's many beautiful and historic towns and regions. Scottish hospitality is renowned, and amongst the establishments in this book are some of the best hotels and restaurants in Britain.

Please note: Hotels appear first within a location, in order of star rating. If they have Rosettes for their restaurant (see page 10) then their restaurant details will appear with the Hotel entry. If their restaurant is known by its own name in the AA Restaurant Guide we'll include this. Next in sequence are Restaurants with Rooms, followed by Guest Accommodation (including Rosetted restaurant information if appropriate) then stand-alone Restaurants, and finally Pubs.

If the establishment name appears *in italics*, this means we did not receive updated information from the establishment for 2010. With restaurants, limited details (usually just opening times) also indicate that we did not receive an update. It is always a good idea to telephone an establishment in advance of your visit to ensure that your expectations will be met.

LOCATION	Map reference

Name of Establishment

★★★★★ ACCOMMODATION TYPE DESIGNATOR

◉◉ Cuisine Type V ⅃NOTABLE WINE LIST ✍

Strapline giving a brief summary (restaurants only)

☎ telephone number ▤ fax number
Address, including postcode for SatNav
e-mail: emailaddress@establishment.com
web: www.establishment-website.com
dir: Directions to help you reach the establishment, provided by the establishment themselves.

A description of the establishment which will usually include information on the location and area, the type of building, the bedrooms and some of their facilities, the food operation and representative dishes, and anything else that may be relevant.

[Hotel/Guest Accommodation Information]
Rooms Number of bedrooms (1 GF)=1 room on Ground Floor, (1 fmly)=1 family room; **S** Single room price range **D** Double room price range **Facilities** offered by the establishment **Conf** Information on conference facilities **Services** such as Lift or Air Con **Parking** number of parking spaces available to guests/customers **Notes** Other information which may be useful

[Restaurant Information]
Chef Name of chef **Owner** Name of owners **Restaurant Times** When restaurant is open during the year, and times it is open during the day **Prices** A guide to meal prices **Wines** Number of bottles under £20 and how many available by the glass **Notes** other relevant information including Vegetarian menu **Seats** number of covers **Children** Special facilities for children including own menu

[Pub information]
Open Times that pub is open during the day and during the year **Bar Meals** Serving times for lunch and dinner in the bar, average cost of main course **Restaurant** Serving times for lunch and dinner in the restaurant, average cost of 3 course à la carte ⊕ OWNER/BREWERY ◂▪ Principal Beers and ♂ Ciders ♀ Number of wines available by the glass **Facilities** offered by the establishment

★	Black stars
★	Red stars = AA Inspectors' Choice
★	Yellow stars = Highly Commended
⚜	AA Rosettes = AA award for food
	For full explanation of AA ratings and awards see page 6
V	Vegetarian menu
✍	Indicates the use of local and regional produce. More than 50% of the restaurant food ingredients are produced within a 50-mile radius. Suppliers are mentioned by name on the menu.
NOTABLE WINE LIST	Notable wine list (see page 10)
%	Inspector's Merit score (see page 7)
A	Associate Establishments
U	Star rating not confirmed
☎	Phone number
📄	Fax number
🔔	A very special breakfast, with an emphasis on freshly prepared local ingredients (Guest accommodation only)
🍽	A very special dinner, with an emphasis on freshly prepared local ingredients (Guest accommodation only)
fmly	Number of family rooms available
GF	Ground floors rooms available
rms	Bedrooms in main building
smoking	Number of bedrooms allocated for smokers
pri facs	Bedroom with separate private facilities (Restaurant with Rooms & Guest Accommodation only)
S	Single room
D	Double room (2 people sharing)
*	2009 prices
fr	From
incl. bkfst	Breakfast included in the price (Hotels only)

TVL	Lounge with television
FTV	Freeview television
STV	Satellite television
Wi-fi	Wireless network connection
⊜	Credit cards not accepted
tea/coffee	Tea and coffee making facilities
Etr	Easter
Air con	Air conditioning
🏊	Heated indoor swimming pool
🏊	Outdoor swimming pool
🏊	Heated outdoor swimming pool
🎵	Entertainment
Child facilities	Children's facilities (see page 10)
Xmas New Year	Special programme for Christmas/New Year
🎾	Tennis court
🏏	Croquet lawn
⛳	Putting green
Conf	Conference facilities
Thtr	Number of theatre style seats
Class	Number of classroom style seats
Board	Number of boardroom style seats
⊗	No dogs allowed (guide dogs for the blind and assist dogs should be allowed)
No Children	Children cannot be accommodated. If this is followed by a number (e.g. 11 yrs) this means that children under 11 cannot be accommodated.
RS	Restricted opening times
Civ Wed	Establishment licensed for civil weddings (+ maximum number of guests at ceremony)
LB	Special leisure breaks available
Spa	Hotel has its own spa
☿	If this appears by the pub name it means that more than 6 wines by the glass are available
🍺	Principal beers served by the pub
🍷	Principal ciders served by the pub
⊕	Owner or brewery

AA RATINGS EXPLAINED

AA Accommodation Classifications

AA Assessment

In collaboration with VisitBritain, VisitScotland and VisitWales, the AA developed Common Quality Standards for inspecting and rating accommodation. These standards and rating categories are now applied throughout the British Isles.

Any hotel or guest accommodation establishment applying for AA recognition receives an unannounced visit from an AA inspector to check standards. The establishments with full entries in this guide have all paid an annual fee for AA inspection, recognition and rating.

If an establishment changes hands, the new owners must reapply for classification, as standards may change.

AA inspectors pay as a guest for their inspection visit, they do not accept free hospitality of any kind.

HOTELS

★ One Star

Polite, courteous staff providing a relatively informal yet competent style of service, available during the day and evening to receive guests
- At least one designated eating area open to residents for breakfast
- If dinner is offered it should be on at least five days a week, with last orders no earlier than 6.30pm
- Television in bedroom
- Majority of rooms en suite, bath or shower room available at all times

★★ Two Star

As for one star, plus
- At least one restaurant or dining room open to residents for breakfast (and for dinner at least five days a week)
- Last orders for dinner no earlier than 7pm
- En suite or private bath or shower and WC

★★★ Three Star

- Management and staff smartly and professionally presented and usually uniformed
- A dedicated receptionist on duty at peak times
- At least one restaurant or dining room open to residents and non-residents for breakfast and dinner whenever the hotel is open
- Last orders for dinner no earlier than 8pm
- Remote-control television, direct-dial telephone
- En suite bath or shower and WC

★★★★ Four Star

- A formal, professional staffing structure with smartly presented, uniformed staff anticipating and responding to your needs or requests Usually spacious, well-appointed public areas
- Reception staffed 24 hours by well-trained staff
- Express checkout facilities where appropriate
- Porterage available on request
- Night porter available
- At least one restaurant open to residents and non-residents for breakfast and dinner seven days per week, and lunch to be available in a designated eating area
- Last orders for dinner no earlier than 9pm
- En suite bath with fixed overhead shower and WC

★★★★★ Five Star

- Luxurious accommodation and public areas with a range of extra facilities. First time guests shown to their bedroom
- Multilingual service
- Guest accounts well explained and presented
- Porterage offered
- Guests greeted at hotel entrance, full concierge service provided
- At least one restaurant open to residents and non-residents for all meals seven days per week
- Last orders for dinner no earlier than 10pm
- High-quality menu and wine list
- Evening service to turn down the beds. Remote-control television, direct-dial telephone at bedside and desk, a range of luxury toiletries, bath sheets and robes. En suite bathroom incorporating fixed overhead shower and WC

★ Inspectors' Choice

Each year we select the best hotels in each rating. These hotels stand out as the very best in the British Isles, regardless of style.

Merit Score (%)

AA inspectors supplement their hotel reports with an additional quality assessment of everything a hotel provides, including hospitality, based on their findings as a 'mystery guest'. This wider ranging quality assessment results in an overall Merit Score which is shown as a percentage beside the hotel name. When making your selection of hotel accommodation this enables you to see at a glance that a three star hotel with a Merit Score of 79% offers a higher standard overall than one in the same star classification but with a Merit Score of 69%. To gain AA recognition, a hotel must achieve a minimum score of 50%.

Types of hotel

A 'designator' is used to tell you more about the style of establishment. Most hotels choose the Hotel designator; other categories are listed below.

TOWN HOUSE HOTEL A small, individual city or town centre property, which provides a high degree of personal service and privacy

COUNTRY HOUSE HOTEL These are quietly located in a rural area

SMALL HOTEL Has fewer than 20 bedrooms and is owner-managed

METRO HOTEL A hotel in an urban location that does not offer an evening meal

Budget Hotel These are usually purpose built modern properties offering inexpensive accommodation. Often located near motorways and in town or city centres

NB Although AA inspectors do not stay overnight at Budget Hotels they do carry out regular visits to verify standards and procedures.

AA RATINGS EXPLAINED

Guest Accommodation

AA Stars classify guest accommodation at five levels of quality, from one at the simplest, to five offering the highest quality. In order to achieve a one or two Star rating an establishment must meet certain minimum entry requirements, including:

• A cooked breakfast, or substantial continental option is provided.

• The proprietor and/or staff are available for your arrival, departure and at all meal times.

• Once registered, you have access to the establishment at all times unless previously notified.

• All areas of operation meet minimum quality requirements for cleanliness, maintenance and hospitality as well as facilities and the delivery of services.

• A dining room or similar eating area is available unless meals are only served in bedrooms.

Our research shows that quality is very important to visitors. To obtain a higher Star rating, an establishment must provide increased quality standards across all areas, with particular emphasis in four key areas:

• Cleanliness and housekeeping

• Hospitality and service

• Quality and condition of bedrooms, bathrooms and public rooms

• Food quality

There are also particular requirements in order for an establishment to achieve three, four or five Stars, for example:

★★★ Three Stars and above

• access to both sides of all beds for double occupancy

• bathrooms/shower rooms cannot be used by the proprietor

• there is a washbasin in every guest bedroom (either in the bedrooms or the en suite/private facility)

★★★★ Four Stars

• half of bedrooms must be en suite or have private facilities

★★★★★ Five Stars

• all bedrooms must be en suite or have private facilities

Guests can expect to find the following minimum standards at all levels:

• Pleasant and helpful welcome and service, and sound standards of housekeeping and maintenance

• Comfortable accommodation equipped to modern standards

• Bedding and towels changed for each new guest, and at least weekly if the room is taken for a long stay

• Adequate storage, heating, lighting and comfortable seating

• A sufficient hot water supply at reasonable times

• A full cooked breakfast. (If this is not provided, the fact must be advertised and a substantial continental breakfast must be offered)

When an AA inspector has visited a property, and evaluated all the aspects of the accommodation for comfort, facilities, attention to detail and presentation, you can be confident the Star rating will allow you to make the right choice for an enjoyable stay.

★ Highly Commended

Yellow Stars indicate that an establishment is in the top ten percent of its Star rating. Yellow Stars only apply to 3, 4 or 5 Star guest accommodation establishments.

TYPES OF GUEST ACCOMMODATION

A 'designator' is used to tell you more about the style of establishment.

B&B

A private house run by the owner with accommodation for no more than six paying guests.

GUEST HOUSE

Run on a more commercial basis than a B&B, the accommodation provides for more than six paying guests and there are usually more services; for example staff as well as the owner may provide dinner.

FARMHOUSE

The B&B or guest house accommodation is part of a working farm or smallholding.

INN

The accommodation is provided in a fully licensed establishment. The bar will be open to non-residents and can provide food in the evenings.

RESTAURANT WITH ROOMS

This is a destination restaurant offering overnight accommodation, with dining being the main business and open to non-residents. The restaurant should offer a high standard of food and restaurant service at least five nights a week. A liquor licence is necessary and there is a maximum of 12 bedrooms.

GUEST ACCOMMODATION

Any establishment that meets the minimum entry requirements is eligible for this general category.

Other useful information

A These are establishments that have not been inspected by the AA but which have been inspected by VisitScotland. An establishment marked as "Associate" has paid to belong to either the AA Associate Hotel Scheme or the AA Associate Guest Accommodation Scheme and therefore receives a limited entry in the guide. Descriptions of these establishments can be found on the AA website.*

U A small number of establishments in the guide have this symbol because their Star classification was not confirmed at the time of going to press. This may be due to a change of ownership or because they have only recently joined the AA rating scheme.

* Check the AA website theAA.com for current information and ratings

AA ROSETTES & WINE AWARDS

AA Rosette Awards

Out of the many thousands of restaurants in the UK, the AA identifies over 1,900 as the best. The following is an outline of what to expect from restaurants with AA Rosette Awards.

❀ Excellent local restaurants serving food prepared with care, understanding and skill, using good quality ingredients.

❀❀ The best local restaurants, which aim for and achieve higher standards, better consistency and where a greater precision is apparent in the cooking. There will be obvious attention to the selection of quality ingredients.

❀❀❀ Outstanding restaurants that demand recognition well beyond their local area.

❀❀❀❀ Amongst the very best restaurants in the British Isles, where the cooking demands national recognition.

❀❀❀❀❀ The finest restaurants in the British Isles, where the cooking stands comparison with the best in the world.

The AA Wine Awards

The AA Wine Awards feature annually in The AA Restaurant Guide. In the 2010 edition the awards were sponsored again by T&W Wines, and attracted a huge response from all the AA recognised restaurants, with over 1,000 wine lists submitted for judging.

Three national winners were chosen – The Old Bridge Hotel, Huntingdon, England, The Cross at Kingussie, Scotland, and The Bell at Skenfrith, Wales. The Old Bridge Hotel at Huntingdon was selected as the Overall Winner, and a member of their wine team wins an all-expenses-paid trip to Willi Opitz's vineyards at Illmitz in Austria's Burgenland.

All 2,000 or so Rosetted restaurants in last year's Restaurant Guide were invited to submit their wine lists. From these the panel selected a shortlist of around 170 establishments throughout the country.
Of these, around around XX appear in this guide, highlighted with the Notable Wine List symbol

 NOTABLE WINE LIST

The shortlisted establishments were asked to choose wines from their list (within a budget of £70 per bottle) to accompany a menu designed by Martin Lam, owner of Ransome's Dock, London, the 2009 England and Overall Winner.

The final judging panel included Simon Numphud, AA Hotel Services Manager, Martin Lam, proprietor of Ransome's Dock, Trevor Hughes, Managing Director of T&W Wines (our sponsor), Brian St Pierre from Decanter magazine and Fiona Sims, an independent wine journalist.

Notable Wine Lists

What makes a wine list notable?
We are looking for high-quality wines, with diversity across grapes and/or countries and style, the best individual growers and vintages.

The list should be well presented, ideally with some helpful notes and, to reflect the demand from diners, a good choice of wines by the glass. What disappoints the judges are spelling errors, wines listed under incorrect regions or styles, split vintages (which are still far too common), lazy purchasing (all wines from a country from just one grower or negociant) and confusing layouts. Sadly, many restaurants still do not pay much attention to wine, resulting in ill considered lists.

To reach the final shortlist, we look for a real passion for wine, which should come across to the customer, a fair pricing policy (depending on the style of the restaurant) an interesting coverage (not necessarily a large list), which might include areas of specialism, perhaps a particular wine area, sherries or larger formats such as magnums.

The AA Wine Awards are sponsored by T&W Wines Ltd, 5 Station Way,
Brandon, Suffolk, IP27 OBH
Tel: 01842 814414
email: contact@tw-wines.com
web: www.tw-wines.com

AA WINE AWARD WINNER FOR SCOTLAND 2009-2010

The Cross at Kingussie ⊛⊛⊛
Kingussie, Highland (page 140)

A textile mill it may once have been, but there's nothing tweedy about David and Katie Young's classy restaurant with rooms. The stone building sits in four idyllic acres of grounds, with the Gynack Burn bubbling by a delightful terrace. The mill has been lovingly restored, its rough stone walls and heavy beams blending seamlessly with modern artworks and natural wood tables with quality glassware in the spacious dining room. Wild mushrooms are foraged locally and Scotland's finest materials are showcased in compact daily-changing menus of modern British dishes, while the wine list balances serious quality with fair pricing.

Judges' comments: A list that has a good sense of humour combined with a real passion for wine, its personal approach draws you in and overall it ticks all the right boxes. Good quality choices throughout combine with some food matching suggestions.

ADDITIONAL INFORMATION

AA Awards

Every year the AA presents a range of awards to the finest AA-inspected and rated establishments from England, Scotland, Wales and the Republic of Ireland. See who won the Scottish awards on page 14.

Rooms

Each entry shows the total number of rooms available (this total will include any annexe rooms). All hotel rooms should be en suite, for guest accommodation the number of en suite rooms is shown. The total number may be followed by a breakdown of the type of rooms available, i.e. the number of annexe rooms; number of family rooms (fmly); number of ground-floor rooms (GF); number of rooms available for smokers.

Bedrooms in an annexe or extension are only noted if they are at least equivalent in quality to those in the main building, but facilities and prices may differ. In some establishments all bedrooms are in an annexe or extension.

Prices

Prices are per room per night (and include breakfast in the case of Guest Accommodation) and are provided by the proprietors in good faith. These prices are indications and not firm quotations. ✳ indicates 2009 prices.

Perhaps due to the economic climate at the time we were collecting the data for this guide, fewer establishments than usual were able to tell us their room prices for 2010. Many places have introduced special rates so it is worth looking at theAA.com or their own websites for the latest information.

Payment

As most establishments now accept credit or debit cards we only indicate if a place does not accept any cards for payment. Credit cards may be subject to a surcharge – check when booking if this is how you intend to pay. Not all establishments accept travellers' cheques.

Children

Children's facilities may include baby intercom, baby sitting service, playroom, playground, laundry, drying/ironing facilities, cots, high chairs or special meals. In some places children can sleep in parents' rooms at no extra cost – check when booking.

If 'No children' is indicated, a minimum age may be also given e.g. No children 4yrs would mean no children under 4 years of age would be accepted.

Some establishments, although accepting children, may not have any special facilities for them so it is well worth checking before booking.

Leisure breaks

Some hotels and guest accommodation offer special leisure breaks, and these prices may differ from those quoted in this guide and the availability may vary through the year.

Parking

We indicate the number of parking spaces available for guests. This may include covered parking. Please note that some establishments make a charge to use their car park. We found when producing this guide that the number of spaces quoted for a hotel/guest accommodation and restaurant on the same site may differ. If this was the case, we have quoted the number given by the hotel.

Civil Weddings (Civ Wed)

Indicates that the establishment holds a civil wedding licence, and we indicate the number of guests that can be accommodated at the ceremony.

Conference Facilities

We include three types of meeting layouts – Theatre, Classroom and Boardroom style and include the maximum number of delegates for each. The price shown is the maximum 24-hour rate per delegate. Please note that as arrangements vary between an establishment and a business client, VAT may or may not be included in the price quoted in the guide. We also show if Wi-fi connectivity is available, but please check with the establishment for further details.

Dogs

Although many establishments allow dogs, they may be excluded from some areas of the building and some breeds, particularly those requiring an exceptional licence, may not be acceptable at all.

Under the Disability Discrimination Act 1995 access should be allowed for guide dogs and assistance dogs. Please check the establishment's policy when making your booking.

Entertainment (♫)

This indicates that live entertainment should be available at least once a week all year. Some hotels provide live entertainment only in summer or on special occasions – check when booking.

Map references

Each town is given a map reference – the map page number and a four-figure map reference based on the National Grid. For example: **MAP 05 SU 48:**

05 refers to the page number of the map section at back of the guide

SU is the National Grid lettered square (representing 100,000sq metres) in which the location will be found

4 is the figure reading across the top or bottom of the map page

8 is the figure reading down at each side of the map page

Restricted service

Some places have restricted service (RS) during quieter months, usually during the winter, and at this time some of the listed facilities will not be available. If your booking is out-of-season, check with the establisment and enquire specifically. Don't forget that in some parts of Scotland the ski season is very busy.

Smoking regulations

If a bedroom has been allocated for smokers, the establishment is obliged to clearly indicate that this is the case. If either the freedom to smoke, or to be in a non-smoking environment is important to you, please check with the establishment when you book.

Spa

For the purposes of this guide the word Spa in an entry indicates that the hotel has its own spa which is either managed by themselves or outsourced to an external management company. Facilities will vary but will include a minimum of two treatment rooms. Any specific details are also given, and these are as provided to us by the establishment (i.e. steam room, beauty therapy etc).

The AA's Scottish Award Winners 2009-2010

THE GLENEAGLES HOTEL
★★★★★ ◉◉◉◉

AUCHTERARDER, PERTH & KINROSS (p169)

World famous Gleneagles is a 5-star resort set in 850 acres of glorious Scottish countryside and probably best known for being home to three championship golf courses and a wide range of exhilarating outdoor pursuits. Everything here is at the top of its game from the luxury bedrooms and suites through to the choices of restaurants. There are 26 individually designed, sumptuously appointed suites in addition to the 232 luxury bedrooms. Guests are spoilt for choice when it comes to eating – there's Andrew Fairlie's eponymous restaurant, awarded 4 AA Rosettes, Strathearn Restaurant with 2 Rosettes and the smart new Deseo 'Mediterranean Food Market' eaterie. Not to mention the Clubhouse and the many bars. In addition to the golf there's an almost never ending list of leisure activities and country pursuits to enjoy. The ESPA Spa at the hotel has received many accolades, and it's no wonder as once through the doors the calm atmosphere ensures relaxation, and the endless list of the very latest treatments cannot fail to restore the body and soul.

PLUMED HORSE ◉◉◉

EDINBURGH (p89)

The brain-child of chef-proprietor Tony Borthwick, the Plumed Horse makes the most of its relocation from Castle Douglas to Leith by using locally landed fish and seafood. The rather sedate looking Georgian building sits in the middle of a mainly residential area and, once inside, the grandeur of its heritage comes to the fore via the many sympathetically restored original features and is enhanced by the formal table settings. Service is professional and genuinely friendly. Imaginative cooking is executed with precision and plenty of land-based local produce joins that sparkling seafood on the menu. Start perhaps with a twice-baked parmesan and truffle soufflé with tomato and cucumber salad before moving onto fillet of monkfish with curry spices, gratin of Jerusalem artichokes, green beans and orange and vermouth sauce before pushing the boat out with fudge and ginger parfait, ginger beer, vanilla, lime and 'Sailor Jerry' sorbet.

THE INN AT INVERBEG

LUSS, ARGYLL & BUTE (p38)

Situated just off the A82 and commanding stunning
views across Loch Lomond and its surrounding hills,
this is Scotland's first boutique inn. Dating from
1814, it has been remodelled and refurbished in
contemporary style, yet retains its old-world charm
and character – typically find roaring log fires fronted
by swish leather and cow hide seating. At the Whisky
Bar you have over 200 malts and real ales like
Deuchars IPA to choose from and in Mr C's, the
relaxed and informal dining room, you can tuck into
fresh, sustainable fish caught off Scottish shores.
Start with steamed mussels, Loch Fyne oysters or
chilli-coated squid with garlic mayonnaise, move on
to fishcakes with spinach and lemon hollandaise or
simply grilled cod or haddock served with chips,
or Buccleuch sirloin steak with herb butter.
Comfortable, individually styled rooms are split
between the inn and a sumptuous beach house
beside the loch, the latter featuring wooden floors,
hand-crafted furniture, crisp linen, and a hot tub.

LOCH NESS LODGE

ABRIACHAN, HIGHLAND (p116)

Loch Ness Lodge is an elegant and intimate
exclusive-use retreat in the heart of the Scottish
Highlands overlooking the mysterious and beautiful
Loch Ness. A small family-run business, Loch Ness
Lodge brings together the very best of traditional
Scottish architecture and contemporary design,
boasting elegant reception rooms, a spa and therapy
area, and fine dining in its two Rosette-awarded
restaurant. The lodge's seven bedrooms have been
individually styled and are inspired by the natural
beauty of the surrounding Highlands, each named
after a well-loved Highland loch or glen.

Loch Achray and Ben Venue

Doubletree by Hilton Aberdeen

★★★★ 78% HOTEL

☎ 01224 633339 & 380000 📠 01224 638833
Beach Boulevard AB24 5EF
e-mail: sales.doubletreeaberdeen@hilton.com
web: www.hilton.co.uk/aberdeencity
dir: From A90 follow signs for city centre, then for beach. On Beach Blvd, left at lights, hotel on right

This modern, purpose-built hotel lies close to the seafront. Bedrooms come in two different styles - the retro-style Classics and spacious Premiers. In addition the Platinum Club offers a unique experience of 44 superb high-spec bedrooms that have their own reception bar, lounge and dinner and breakfast room. The restaurant and striking Atrium bar are housed In the main building.

Rooms 168 (44 annexe) (8 fmly) (22 GF) (41 smoking) **S** £65-£200; **D** £65-£200 **Facilities** Spa STV 🏊 Gym Steam room Treatment room Sauna Solarium Fitness Studio New Year Wi-fi **Conf** Class 80 Board 50 Thtr 150 Del from £130 to £185 **Services** Lift **Parking** 172

Norwood Hall

★★★★ 76% HOTEL

🏵 British, European

Fine dining in a grand Victorian mansion

☎ 01224 868951 📠 01224 869868
Garthdee Rd, Cults AB15 9FX
e-mail: info@norwood-hall.co.uk
web: www.norwood-hall.co.uk
dir: off A90, at 1st rdbt cross Bridge of Dee, left at rdbt onto Garthdee Rd (B&Q & Sainsburys on left) continue to hotel sign

This imposing Victorian mansion has retained many of its features, most notably the fine oak staircase, stained glass and ornately decorated walls and ceilings. Accommodation comes in three different styles - individually designed bedrooms in the main house, a wing of spacious superior rooms and an older wing of modern but less spacious rooms. The extensive grounds ensure the hotel is popular as a wedding venue. As you settle in to dinner in the opulent oak-panelled Tapestry restaurant, it becomes clear where the restaurant gets its name, as the walls are indeed clad with lovely tapestries framing widely-spaced candlelit tables laid with classy crockery and glassware. Top-class seasonal Scottish produce, with an emphasis on game and seafood, drives the kitchen's repertoire of classic and more inventive dishes. Simple, well-balanced flavours are what it's all about here, and a starter of pan-fried wood pigeon with wild mushrooms and creamed cabbage sums up the style. Mains could be straight-up grills of beef, lamb or trout.

Rooms 36 (6 GF) **S** £185-£225; **D** £205-£245 (incl. bkfst)*
Facilities STV Xmas New Year Wi-fi **Conf** Class 100 Board 70 Thtr 200 **Services** Lift **Parking** 100 **Notes** LB ⊗ Civ Wed 150

Owner Monument Leisure **Restaurant Times** 12-2.30/6.30-9.45 Closed L Mon-Fri **Prices** Food prices not confirmed for 2010. Please telephone for details. **Wines** 43 bottles over £20, 23 bottles under £20, 9 by glass **Notes** Vegetarian available, Dress restrictions, Smart casual 180 **Seats** 28, Pr/dining room 180 **Children** Portions, Menu

Copthorne Hotel Aberdeen

★★★★ 75% HOTEL

☎ 01224 630404 📠 01224 640573
122 Huntly St AB10 1SU
e-mail: reservations.aberdeen@millenniumhotels.co.uk
web: www.millenniumhotels.co.uk/aberdeen
dir: West end of city centre, off Union St, up Rose St, hotel 0.25m on right on corner with Huntly St

Situated just outside of the city centre, this hotel offers friendly, attentive service. The smart bedrooms are well proportioned and guests will appreciate the added quality of the Connoisseur rooms. Mac's bar provides a relaxed atmosphere in which to enjoy a drink or to dine informally, whilst Poachers Restaurant offers a slightly more formal dining experience.

Rooms 89 (15 fmly) **S** £57-£208; **D** £65-£216 **Facilities** STV New Year Wi-fi **Conf** Class 100 Board 70 Thtr 200 Del from £150 to £250 **Services** Lift **Parking** 15 **Notes** LB RS 24-26 Dec Civ Wed 180

Holiday Inn Aberdeen West

★★★★ 74% HOTEL

☎ 01224 270300 📠 01224 270323
Westhill Dr, Westhill AB32 6TT
e-mail: info@hiaberdeenwest.co.uk
web: www.holidayinn.co.uk
dir: On A944 in Westhill

In a good location at the west side of the city, this modern hotel caters well for the needs of both business and leisure guests. The nicely appointed bedrooms and bathrooms have a contemporary feel. Luigi's restaurant serves modern Italian food, and the popular lounge offers more informal dining. There is a separate pub operation with wide-screen TVs showing a range of sporting events.

Rooms 86 (30 fmly) (6 smoking) **Facilities** STV Gym Beautician services Wi-fi **Conf** Class 150 Board 80 Thtr 300 **Services** Lift Air con **Parking** 90 **Notes** LB Civ Wed 250

Mercure Ardoe House Hotel & Spa

★★★★ 74% HOTEL

☎ 01224 860600 📠 01224 861283
South Deeside Rd, Blairs AB12 5YP
e-mail: h6626@accor.com
web: www.mercure-uk.com
dir: 4m W of city off B9077

From its elevated position on the banks of the River Dee, this 19th-century baronial-style mansion commands excellent countryside views. Beautifully decorated, thoughtfully equipped bedrooms are located in the main house, and in the more modern extension. Public

continued

rooms include a spa and leisure club, a cosy lounge and cocktail bar and impressive function facilities.

Rooms 109 **D** £80-£225 (incl. bkfst)* **Facilities** Spa STV 🕐 ♨ Gym Aerobics studio Xmas New Year Wi-fi **Conf** Class 200 Board 150 Thtr 600 Del from £155 to £280 **Services** Lift **Parking** 220 **Notes** LB ⊗ Civ Wed 250

Maryculter House Hotel

★★★★ 73% HOTEL

⊛ Scottish

Historic old mansion with modern Scottish cooking

☎ 01224 732124 📠 01224 733510
South Deeside Rd, Maryculter AB12 5GB
e-mail: info@maryculterhousehotel.com
web: www.maryculterhousehotel.com
dir: Off A90 on S side of Aberdeen, onto B9077. Hotel 8m on right, 0.5m beyond Lower Deeside Caravan Park

Set in grounds on the banks of the River Dee, this charming Scottish mansion dates back to medieval times and is now a popular wedding and conference venue; bedrooms are equipped with business travellers in mind. The comfortingly traditional Priory restaurant is in the oldest part of the building, where exposed stone walls, an open fire and candlelight work together in a romantic setting. The kitchen thinks local with its sourcing and turns out good honest cooking in a classic Scottish style with some modern flourishes. You're never far from fantastic fresh fish and seafood here, so start with brandade of smoked haddock and watercress with cauliflower cream, and move on to the likes of pan-roasted Scottish hake with trompette de mort mushrooms, olive crushed potatoes, baby fennel and vanilla broth.

Rooms 40 (1 fmly) (16 GF) **S** £90-£155; **D** £135-£165 (incl. bkfst) **Facilities** STV FTV Fishing Clay pigeon shooting Archery Xmas New Year **Conf** Class 100 Board 50 Thtr 220 Del from £140 to £150 **Parking** 150 **Notes** LB ⊗ Civ Wed 150

Chef David Bell **Owner** James Gilbert **Restaurant Times** 7-9 Closed L all week **Prices** Starter £5.95-£7.95, Main £16.95-£25.95, Dessert £5.95-£7.95, Service optional **Wines** 23 bottles over £20, 18 bottles under £20, 2 by glass **Notes** 8 course gourmet menu available Fri & Sat, Vegetarian available, Dress restrictions, Smart casual, no jeans or T-shirts **Seats** 40, Pr/dining room 18 **Children** Portions

The Caledonian by Thistle

★★★★ 71% HOTEL

☎ 0870 333 9151 📠 0870 333 9251
10-14 Union Ter AB10 1WE
e-mail: aberdeencaledonian@thistle.co.uk
web: www.thistlehotels.com/thecaledonian
dir: Follow signs to city centre & Union St. Turn into Union Terrace. Hotel on left

Centrally located just off Union Street and overlooking Union Terrace Gardens this traditional hotel offers comfortable and well-appointed bedrooms, and public areas in keeping with the age of the building. The upbeat Café Bar Caley serves informal food, but for a more

formal dining experience there's the Restaurant on the Terrace. A small car park is available to the rear.

Rooms 80 (1 fmly) **Facilities** STV Wi-fi **Conf** Class 50 Board 30 Thtr 80 Del from £100 to £195* **Services** Lift **Parking** 22 **Notes** ⊗ Civ Wed 40

Malmaison Aberdeen

★★★ 86% HOTEL

⊛⊛ Modern British ☙

Stylish brasserie with theatre kitchen serving modern Scottish cuisine

☎ 01224 327370 📠 01224 327371
49-53 Queens Rd AB15 4YP
e-mail: info.aberdeen@malmaison.com
dir: A90, 3rd exit onto Queens Rd at 3rd rdbt, hotel on right

Popular with business travellers and as a function venue, this well-established hotel lies east of the city centre. Public areas include a reception lounge and an intimate restaurant; the extensive bar menu remains a preferred choice for many regulars. There are two styles of accommodation, with the superior rooms being particularly comfortable and well equipped. A glass tunnel leads to the Brasserie restaurant and houses the wine cellar - look down and there's more beneath a glass floor. Sexy modern tartans clothe the seating, or you could grab a bar stool at the grill next to the chefs toiling over the coals of the centrepiece Josper oven. Modern Scottish cuisine founded on cracking materials is the order of the day - say hand-dived Orkney scallops with cauliflower purée, lime segments and crispy pancetta to start, followed by seared loin of venison with dauphinoise potato, sautéed foie gras and raspberry tea syrup.

Rooms 80 (8 fmly) (10 GF) **D** £95-£180 **Facilities** Spa STV FTV Gym Steam room Xmas New Year Wi-fi **Conf** Board 12 **Services** Lift **Parking** 50

Chef Mark Pollock **Owner** Malmaison **Restaurant Times** 12-2.30/5.30-10.30 Closed D 25 Dec **Prices** Fixed L 2 course £14.50, Fixed D 3 course £17.50, Starter £4.95-£11.50, Main £10.50-£35, Dessert £4.95-£8.50, Service added but optional 10% **Wines** 161 bottles over £20, 7 bottles under £20, 13 by glass **Notes** Sunday L, Vegetarian available, Air con **Seats** 90, Pr/dining room 12 **Children** Portions, Menu

Atholl Hotel

★★★ 81% HOTEL

☎ 01224 323505 📄 01224 321555
54 Kings Gate AB15 4YN
e-mail: info@atholl-aberdeen.co.uk
web: www.atholl-aberdeen.com
dir: In West End 400yds from Anderson Drive (A90)

High levels of hospitality and guest care are found at this hotel which is set in the suburbs within easy reach of central amenities and the ring road. The modern bedrooms include free broadband. Guests can choose between the restaurant and bar to enjoy the great value lunch and dinner menus.

Rooms 34 (1 fmly) **S** £60-£105; **D** £80-£150 (incl. bkfst)*
Conf Class 25 Board 25 Thtr 60 **Parking** 60 **Notes** LB ⊗ Closed 1 Jan

The Mariner Hotel

★★★ 79% HOTEL

Atlantis at the Mariner Hotel

⊛ Modern British, Seafood **V**

Family-run hotel dining with focus on local seafood and meats

☎ 01224 588901 📄 01224 571621
349 Great Western Rd AB10 6NW
e-mail: info@themarinerhotel.co.uk
web: www.themarinerhotel.co.uk
dir: E off Anderson Drive (A90) at Great Western Rd. Hotel on right on corner of Gray St

This well maintained, family operated hotel is located west of the city centre. The smart, spacious bedrooms are well equipped and particularly comfortable, with executive suites available. The public rooms are restricted to the lounge bar, which is food driven, and the Atlantis Restaurant. Fresh local seafood is the mainstay of the extensive menu in the restaurant, with its wood floors, panelled walls and conservatory extension. In addition to oysters, Cove lobsters and the cold seafood platter (for two), you can sample mussels with herb and chilli crust, teriyaki seafood brochette, and baked calamari. Carnivores are not forgotten - try the excellent Aberdeen Angus steaks or roast venison with redcurrant jus - and finish with sticky toffee pudding.

Rooms 25 (8 annexe) (4 GF) **S** £55-£100; **D** £85-£130 (incl. bkfst)*
Facilities STV New Year Wi-fi **Parking** 50 **Notes** ⊗

Chef George Bennett **Restaurant Times** 12-2.30/6-10 Closed 26 Dec, 1-2 Jan, L Sat **Prices** Fixed L 2 course £17, Fixed D 3 course £21, Starter £4-£8.50, Main £11.50-£28, Dessert £4.50 £5.50, Service optional **Wines** 31 bottles over £20, 12 bottles under £20, 9 by glass **Notes** Sunday L, Vegetarian menu **Seats** 50 **Children** Portions, Menu

Thistle Aberdeen Altens

★★★ 78% HOTEL

☎ 0871 376 9002 📄 0871 376 9102
Souter Head Rd, Altens AB12 3LF
e-mail: aberdeenaltens@thistle.co.uk
web: www.thistle.com/aberdeenaltens
dir: A90 onto A956 signed Aberdeen Harbour. Hotel just off rdbt

Popular with oil industry personnel, this large purpose-built hotel lies in the Altens area, south east of the city. It's worth asking for one of the executive bedrooms that provide excellent space. Guests can eat in the restaurant, brasserie or the bar.

Rooms 216 (7 fmly) (39 GF) (2 smoking) **S** £50-£195; **D** £50-£195*
Facilities STV ⊕ Gym Sauna Steam room Solarium Aerobic studio New Year Wi-fi **Conf** Class 144 Board 30 Thtr 400 **Services** Lift **Parking** 300 **Notes** LB Civ Wed 150

The Craighaar

★★★ 77% HOTEL

☎ 01224 712275 📄 01224 716362
Waterton Rd, Bucksburn AB21 9HS
e-mail: info@craighaar.co.uk
dir: From A96 (Airport/Inverness) onto A947, hotel signed

Conveniently located for the airport, this welcoming hotel is a popular base for business people and tourists alike. Guests can make use of a quiet library lounge, and enjoy meals in the bar or restaurant. All bedrooms are well equipped, plus there is a wing of duplex suites that provide additional comfort.

Rooms 55 (6 fmly) (18 GF) (6 smoking) **S** £109; **D** £129 (incl. bkfst)
Facilities STV FTV Wi-fi **Conf** Class 33 Board 30 Thtr 90 **Parking** 80 **Notes** LB ⊗ Closed 26 Dec Civ Wed 40

Express by Holiday Inn Aberdeen City Centre

BUDGET HOTEL

☎ 01224 623500 📄 01224 623523
Chapel St AB10 1SQ
e-mail: info@hieaberdeen.co.uk
web: www.hiexpress.com/exaberdeencc
dir: In west end of city, just off Union Street

A modern hotel ideal for families and business travellers. Fresh and uncomplicated, the spacious rooms include Sky TV, power shower and tea and coffee-making facilities. Continental buffet breakfast is included in the room rate; other meals may be taken at the nearby family pub or restaurant. See also the Hotel Groups pages on theAA.com.

Rooms 155 (102 fmly) (30 smoking) **S** £49-£149; **D** £49-£149 (incl. bkfst)* **Conf** Class 18 Board 16 Thtr 35

Express by Holiday Inn Aberdeen-Exhibition Centre

BUDGET HOTEL

☎ 0871 423 4876
Parkway East, Bridge of Don AB23 8AJ
e-mail: info@hieaberdeenexhibitioncentre.co.uk

Rooms 155 **Conf** Board 18 Thtr 35

Travelodge Aberdeen Bucksburn

BUDGET HOTEL

☎ 0871 984 6118 📠 01224 715609
Inverurie Rd, Bucksburn AB21 9BB
web: www.travelodge.co.uk
dir: West of A96 & A947 junct, towards Inverurie

Travelodge offers good quality, good value, modern accommodation. Ideal for families, the spacious en suite bedrooms include remote-control TV, tea and coffee-making facilities and comfortable beds. Meals can be taken at the nearby family restaurant. See also the Hotel Groups pages on theAA.com.

Rooms 48 **S** fr £29; **D** fr £29

Travelodge Aberdeen Central

BUDGET HOTEL

☎ 0871 984 6117 📠 01224 584587
9 Bridge St AB11 6JL
web: www.travelodge.co.uk
dir: Into city on A90. Lodge at junct of Union St & Bridge St

Rooms 97 **S** fr £29; **D** fr £29

The Jays Guest House

★★★★ GUEST HOUSE

☎ 01224 638295 📠 01224 638360
422 King St AB24 3BR
e-mail: alice@jaysguesthouse.co.uk
web: www.jaysguesthouse.co.uk
dir: A90 from S onto Main St & Union St & A92 to King St N

Guests are warmly welcomed to this attractive granite house on the north side of the city. Maintained in first-class order throughout, it offers attractive bedrooms, smartly furnished to appeal to business guests and tourists. Freshly prepared breakfasts are enjoyed in the carefully appointed dining room.

Rooms 10 rms (8 en suite) (2 pri facs) (1 GF) S £50-£60; D £90-£120* **Facilities** STV FTV tea/coffee Cen ht Wi-fi **Parking** 9
Notes ⊗ No Children 12yrs Closed mid Dec-mid Jan

Arkaig

★★★ GUEST HOUSE

☎ 01224 638872 📠 01224 622189
43 Powis Ter AB25 3PP
e-mail: info@arkaig.co.uk
dir: On A96 at junct with Bedford Rd

A friendly welcome and relaxed atmosphere is assured at this well-presented guest house, situated on the north side of the city close to the university and city centre. Bedrooms vary in size, are attractively decorated and are all thoughtfully equipped to appeal to business and leisure guests. There is a cosy sun lounge with magazines, and an attractive breakfast room where delicious freshly cooked breakfasts are served. Parking is also available.

Rooms 8 rms (6 en suite) (1 fmly) (5 GF) **Facilities** TVL tea/coffee Direct Dial Cen ht **Parking** 10

The Silver Darling

◉◉ French, Seafood

Locally landed seafood prepared with a French touch

☎ 01224 576229 📠 01224 588119
Pocra Quay, North Pier AB11 5DQ
dir: At Aberdeen Harbour entrance

The one-time customs house turned conservatory restaurant is located at the entrance to Aberdeen harbour, meaning diners can enjoy stunning views of passing ships and, if you're lucky, dolphins. Tables all have panoramic views with linen tablecloths and sparkling glasses and service from the experienced front-of-house team is attentive without being cloying. The intimate setting makes for romantic dining with lunch trade particularly busy. The name - silver darling - is a reference to a colloquial term for herring and the focus of the French influenced menu is firmly on the locally landed fruits de mer. Lunch dishes may include perfectly cooked seared king scallops served with Parma ham, an aubergine and new potato caviar and Parma ham and chervil cappuccino, or an excellent steamed halibut with caramelised fennel and baby vine tomatoes, tapenade, frisée salad and Riviera sauce.

Restaurant Times 12-1.45/6.30-9.30 Closed Xmas-New Year, Sun, L Sat

Old Blackfriars ☏

☎ 01224 581922   📄 01224 582153
52 Castle St AB11 5BB
dir: From train station down Deeside to Union St. Turn right. Pub at end on right

Stunning stained glass and a warm, welcoming atmosphere are features of this traditional city centre pub, situated in Aberdeen's historic Castlegate. It is built on the site of property owned by Blackfriars Dominican monks, hence the name. The menu runs from sandwiches and filled potatoes through to hearty dishes such as bangers and mash; chicken tikka masala; and beef au poivre. Finish with sticky toffee pudding or pancakes in maple syrup.

Open all wk Closed: 25 Dec, 1 Jan ⊕ BELHAVEN ◀ Abbot Ale, Deuchars IPA, Caledonian 80/-, Inveralmond, Ossian, Guest ales. ☕ 12

ABERDEEN AIRPORT   Map 5 NJ81

Thistle Aberdeen Airport

★★★★ 79% HOTEL

☎ 0871 376 9001   📄 0871 376 9101
Aberdeen Airport, Argyll Rd AB21 0AF
e-mail: aberdeenairport@thistle.co.uk
web: www.thistle.com/aberdeenairport
dir: Adjacent to Aberdeen Airport

Ideally located at the entrance to the airport this hotel offers ample parking plus a courtesy bus service to the terminal. This is a well presented establishment that benefits from good-sized bedrooms and comfortable public areas. Just Gym offers a good variety of exercise equipment.

Rooms 147 (3 fmly) (74 GF) (18 smoking) **S** £65-£195; **D** £75-£205 (incl. bkfst)* **Facilities** STV Gym Wi-fi **Conf** Class 350 Board 100 Thtr 600 Del from £135 to £165* **Parking** 300 **Notes** LB ⊗

Aberdeen Marriott Hotel

★★★★ 74% HOTEL

☎ 01224 770011   📄 01224 722347
Overton Circle, Dyce AB21 7AZ
e-mail: reservations.scotland@marriotthotels.com
web: www.aberdeenmarriott.co.uk
dir: Follow A96 to Bucksburn, right at rdbt onto A947. Hotel in 2m at 2nd rdbt

Close to the airport and conveniently located for the business district, this purpose-built hotel is a popular conference venue. The well-proportioned bedrooms come with many thoughtful extras. Public areas include an informal bar and lounge, a split-level restaurant and a leisure centre that can be accessed directly from a number of bedrooms.

Rooms 155 (81 fmly) (61 GF) (10 smoking) **Facilities** STV ⊗ supervised Gym Saunas (male & female) Solarium New Year Wi-fi **Conf** Class 200 Board 60 Thtr 400 Del from £190 to £240* **Services** Air con **Parking** 180 **Notes** ⊗ Civ Wed 90

Menzies Dyce Aberdeen Airport

★★★ 74% HOTEL

☎ 01224 723101   📄 01224 773883
Farburn Ter, Dyce AB21 7DW
e-mail: dyce@menzieshotels.co.uk
dir: A96/A947 airport E after 1m turn left at lights. Hotel in 250yds

Benefiting from a refurbishment throughout this hotel is transformed. Spacious, well-equipped bedrooms cater well for the needs of the modern traveller. Public areas are welcoming and comfortable. Secure parking and Wi-fi are also provided.

Rooms 198 (198 annexe) (3 fmly) (107 GF) (54 smoking) **S** £60-£180; **D** £60-£180* **Facilities** STV Xmas New Year Wi-fi **Conf** Class 160 Board 120 Thtr 400 Del from £120 to £165* **Parking** 150 **Notes** Civ Wed 220

Travelodge Aberdeen Airport

BUDGET HOTEL

☎ 0871 984 6309   📄 01224 772968
Burnside Dr, off Riverside Dr, Dyce AB21 0HW
web: www.travelodge.co.uk
dir: From Aberdeen A96 towards Inverness, right at rdbt onto A947, at 2nd rdbt right then 2nd right

Travelodge offers good quality, good value, modern accommodation. Ideal for families, the spacious en suite bedrooms include remote-control TV, tea and coffee-making facilities and comfortable beds. Meals can be taken at the nearby family restaurant. See also the Hotel Groups pages on theAA.com.

Rooms 40 **S** fr £29; **D** fr £29

PETERCULTER   Map 5 NJ80

Furain

★★★ 🅰 GUEST HOUSE

☎ 01224 732189   📄 01224 739070
92 North Deeside Rd AB14 0QN
e-mail: furain@btinternet.com
dir: 7m W of city centre on A93

Rooms 8 en suite (2 fmly) (3 GF) **S** £45-£50; **D** £56-£65* **Facilities** FTV tea/coffee Cen ht Wi-fi **Parking** 7 **Notes** Closed Xmas & New Year

ABERDEENSHIRE

ABOYNE
Map 5 NO59

Huntly Arms

★★★ 68% HOTEL

☎ 01339 886101 📠 01339 886804
Charlestown Rd AB34 5HS
e-mail: generalmanager.huntlyarms@ohiml.com
web: www.oxfordhotelsandinns.com
dir: On A93 from Ballater to Aberdeen

This popular hotel, originally built in 1432, is among the oldest coaching inns in Scotland and enjoys a prominent position in the charming village of Aboyne. The bedrooms are thoughtfully equipped and brightly decorated, and the day rooms extend to a traditionally-styled dining room and a cosy bar. A warm welcome is assured from the friendly staff.

Rooms 49 (4 fmly) **Facilities** ♫ Xmas New Year **Conf** Class 70 Board 70 Thtr 120 **Parking** 10 **Notes** LB ⊗

BALLATER
Map 5 NO39

Darroch Learg

★★★ SMALL HOTEL

⊛⊛⊛ Modern Scottish ⚑

Country-house splendour in the Highlands

☎ 013397 55443 📠 013397 55252
Braemar Rd AB35 5UX
e-mail: enquiries@darrochlearg.co.uk
web: www.darrochlearg.co.uk
dir: on A93, W of Ballater

Set high above the road in extensive wooded grounds, this long-established hotel offers superb views over the hills and countryside of Royal Deeside. Nigel and Fiona Franks are caring and attentive hosts who improve their hotel every year. Bedrooms, some with four-poster beds, are individually styled, bright and spacious. Food is a highlight of any visit, whether it is a freshly prepared breakfast or the fine cuisine served in the delightful conservatory restaurant, where a fairly traditional culinary philosophy nonetheless draws on some modern technique and makes the most of the provender of north-east Scotland, from the legendary Arbroath smokies to incomparable Highland raspberries in the season. Dinner might begin with wood pigeon en croûte, dressed with spiced pear chutney, or perhaps smoked haddock in a raviolo with its own velouté. Aberdeen Angus beef fillet is treated with fitting dignity as one main course, with accompaniments of ox tongue, potato gratin and a relish of beetroot and horseradish. The finale may be sticky toffee pudding with caramel sauce, banana, and rum and raisin ice cream. A six-course tasting menu offers the option of avoiding having to make choices.

Rooms 17 (5 annexe) (1 GF) **S** £130-£190; **D** £210-£310 (incl. bkfst & dinner) **Facilities** New Year **Conf** Board 12 Thtr 25 Del from £155 to £220 **Parking** 25 **Notes** LB Closed Xmas & Jan (ex New Year)

Chef David Mutter **Owner** The Franks family **Restaurant**

Times 12.30-2/7-9 Closed Xmas, last 3wks Jan, L Mon-Sat
Prices Fixed L course £25, Fixed D 3 course £45-£52, Tasting menu £56, Service included **Wines** 186 bottles over £20, 4 by glass
Notes Sunday L, Vegetarian available, Dress restrictions, Smart casual **Seats** 48 **Children** Portions, Menu

Loch Kinord

★★★ 80% HOTEL

⊛ Modern British

Victorian hotel with imaginative cooking

☎ 013398 85229 📠 013398 87007
Ballater Rd, Dinnet AB34 5JY
e-mail: stay@kinord.com
dir: Between Aboyne & Ballater, on A93, in village of Dinnet

Family-run, this roadside hotel is well located for leisure and sporting pursuits. It has lots of character and a friendly atmosphere, and bedrooms are stylish, withsmart bathrooms. There are two bars, one outside and a cosy one inside, plus a dining room with a bold colour scheme, serving a regionally based menu of imaginative Scottish food. Spring pea soup with dry-cured bacon and crème fraîche is a straightforward enough opener, and could be followed by a beautifully timed piece of sea-fresh cod on crushed potatoes, with wild garlic purée and aubergine caviar. To finish, a lustrously smooth crème brûlée is revved up with the flavour of espresso coffee.

Rooms 20 (3 fmly) (4 GF) **Facilities** Pool table Xmas Child facilities **Conf** Class 30 Board 30 Thtr 40 **Parking** 20 **Notes** LB Civ Wed 50

Restaurant Times 6.30-9 Closed L all week

Cambus O'May

★★★ ⚑ COUNTRY HOUSE HOTEL

☎ 013397 55428 📠 013397 55428
AB35 5SE
e-mail: mckechnie@cambusomay.freeserve.co.uk
web: www.cambusomayhotel.co.uk
dir: A93 from Ballater, 4m towards Aberdeen, hotel on left

Rooms 12 (1 fmly) **S** £45-£48; **D** £90-£106 (incl. bkfst) **Parking** 12 **Notes** LB

The Green Inn

★★★★ RESTAURANT WITH ROOMS

⊛⊛ Modern British **V**

Intimate, family-run conservatory-style restaurant

☎ 013397 55701
9 Victoria Rd AB35 5QQ
e-mail: info@green-inn.com
web: www.green-inn.com
dir: In village centre

A former temperance hotel, the Green Inn enjoys a central location in the pretty village of Ballater. Bedrooms are of a high standard and attractively presented. Breakfast is not to be missed, and the genuine hospitality of the enthusiastic proprietors is a real feature of any stay. The addition of a conservatory has boosted seating capacity, but dinners are still an intimate affair, and everything unfolds at a relaxed pace. Chef Chris O'Halloran - ably assisted by mum, Evelyn - directs the action at the stoves, while dad Trevor takes care of front-of-house duties. Chris trained with Raymond Blanc, so expect modern cooking founded on solid French classical technique. His eye-catching dishes are based on top-drawer local produce, home-grown when available. Roasted local wood pigeon wrapped in Parma ham with creamed wild mushrooms and date sauce shows the style, then perhaps navarin of Scottish lamb with confit shoulder served with buttered vegetables, pesto, turnip purée and thyme jus.

Rooms 3 en suite S £50-£60; D £70-£90 **Facilities** FTV TVL tea/coffee Dinner available Cen ht Wi-fi **Parking** On street & car park nearby **Notes** Closed 1st 2 wks Nov, last 2 wks Jan No coaches.

Chef Chris & Evelyn O'Halloran **Owner** Trevor & Evelyn O'Halloran **Restaurant Times** 7-9 Closed 2 wks Nov, 2 wks Jan, Sun, Mon, L all week **Prices** Fixed D 3 course £32.50, Service optional **Wines** 59 bottles over £20, 5 bottles under £20, 7 by glass **Notes** Vegetarian menu, Dress restrictions, Smart casual **Seats** 30, Pr/dining room 24

The Auld Kirk

★★★★ RESTAURANT WITH ROOMS

⊛ Modern Scottish ❦

Fine Scottish cuisine in former church

☎ 01339 755762 & 07918 698000 📄 0700 6037 559
Braemar Rd AB35 5RQ
e-mail: info@theauldkirk.com
dir: From A93 Braemar, on right just before town centre

A Victorian Scottish Free Church building that is now a contemporary restaurant with rooms boasting newly refurbished and well-appointed bedrooms and bathrooms. Many original features of this kirk have been restored and incorporated in the design. The Spirit Restaurant has the expected high-vaulted ceilings and ecclesiastic windows, while wood-panelled walls, chandeliers and centrepiece Spirit Statue catch the eye, too. Canvas-style artwork and white leather seating give the space a contemporary feel, while the accomplished Scottish cooking takes its cue from fresh, prime local produce and proudly advertises its suppliers. Generous portions, accuracy and seasonality prevail in dishes like fillet of pork with a potato, apple and haggis pie with apple and cider jus, or warm tart of plums and hazelnut frangipane served with wild blackberry ice cream.

Rooms 7 en suite (1 fmly) S £67.50-£85; D £100-£130* **Facilities** tea/coffee Dinner available Direct Dial Cen ht Wi-fi **Conf** Max 25 Thtr 25 Class 18 Board 16 **Parking** 7 **Notes** RS Sun closed No coaches

Chef Tony Fuell **Owner** Tony Fuell & Peter Graydon **Restaurant Times** 6.30-9 Closed Xmas, 1st 2 wks Jan, Tue & Wed (winter), D Sun (summer) **Prices** Fixed D 3 course £33.50-£35.50, Service optional **Wines** 15 bottles over £20, 22 bottles under £20, 4 by glass **Notes** Vegetarian available **Seats** 26, Pr/dining room 20 **Children** Portions

Cock & Bull

⊛ Modern Scottish

Atmospheric inn with local flavour

☎ 01358 743249 📄 01358 742466
Ellon Rd, Blairton AB23 8XY
e-mail: info@thecockandbull.co.uk
dir: 6m N of Aberdeen on A90

Located north of Aberdeen, close to the famous sand dunes of Balmedie, this former coaching inn has broad appeal, whether you're looking for a light lunch in the bar or dinner in the atmospheric restaurant with its bare-stone walls, beams and smart table settings (there's a more informal conservatory, too). The work of local artists is displayed throughout, adding a bit of local flavour. The modern Scottish cooking sees squash soup enlivened with a touch of chilli, and crisp, golden crab cakes are also given the chilli treatment (a sweet, spicy sauce), while dark chocolate cheesecake is a delightful ending.

Chef Ryan Paterson **Owner** Rodger Morrison **Restaurant Times** 12-5.30/5.30-late Closed 25-26 Dec, 1-2 Jan, **Prices** Starter £3.95-£6.25, Main £9.75-£22.95, Dessert £5.25-£6.95, Service optional **Wines** 13 bottles over £20, 15 bottles under £20, 7 by glass **Notes** Sunday L, Vegetarian available **Seats** 80 **Children** Portions, Menu

Banchory Lodge Hotel

★★★ 81% COUNTRY HOUSE HOTEL

⊛ Traditional British ❦

Great Scottish produce in a tranquil setting

☎ 01330 822625 & 822681 📄 01330 825019
AB31 5HS
e-mail: enquiries@banchorylodge.co.uk
web: www.banchorylodge.co.uk
dir: off A93, 13m W of Aberdeen, hotel off Dee St

This hotel enjoys a scenic setting in grounds by the River Dee. Inviting public areas include a choice of lounges, a cosy bar and a restaurant with views of the river. Bedrooms come in two distinct styles; those in the original part of the house contrasting with the newer wing rooms, which are particularly spacious. Game, salmon and Aberdeen Angus beef regularly feature on the dinner menu. The traditional, Victorian-style dining room makes the most of the river view and the classic Scottish menu uses local seasonal produce to great effect. Well-executed dishes display a passion for traditional Scottish flavours as seen in oak-smoked haddock with Cullen skink, roast venison with bacon and winter cabbage and red wine jus, and creamed rice with pears poached in mulled wine.

Rooms 22 (10 fmly) (3 smoking) S £90-£120; D £130-£150 (incl. bkfst)* **Facilities** Fishing Children's play area Xmas New Year Child facilities **Conf** Class 30 Board 28 Thtr 90 Del from £140* **Parking** 50 **Notes** LB Civ Wed 150

continued

Chef Jeff Purvis Owner Mrs M Jaffray Restaurant
Times 12-2.30/6.30-9 Prices Food prices not confirmed for 2010.
Please telephone for details. Wines 43 bottles over £20, 31 bottles
under £20, 10 by glass Notes Vegetarian available, Dress
restrictions, Smart casual Seats 90, Pr/dining room 20
Children Portions, Menu

Best Western Burnett Arms Hotel

★★★ 64% SMALL HOTEL

☎ 01330 824944 📠 01330 825553
25 High St AB31 5TD
e-mail: theburnett@btconnect.com
dir: Town centre on N side of A93

This popular hotel is located in the heart of the town centre and gives
easy access to the many attractions of Royal Deeside. Public areas
include a choice of eating and drinking options, with food served in
the restaurant, bar and foyer lounge. Bedrooms are thoughtfully
equipped and comfortably modern.

Rooms 18 (1 fmly) S £69-£79; D £94-£98 (incl. bkfst) Facilities STV
FTV Xmas New Year Wi-fi Conf Class 50 Board 50 Thtr 100
Del from £96 to £106 Parking 23 Notes Civ Wed 100

BANFF   Map 5 NJ66

The Banff Springs Hotel

Ⓤ

☎ 01261 812881 📠 01261 815546
Golden Knowes Road AB45 2JE
e-mail: info.banffsprings@mckeverhotels.co.uk
web: www.mckeverhotels.co.uk
dir: Western outskirts of town on A98 (Banff to Inverness Road)

Currently the rating for this establishment is not confirmed. This
may be due to a change of ownership or because it has only recently
joined the AA rating scheme.

Rooms 35 (2 fmly) (4 GF) S £69-£110; D £89-£120 (incl. bkfst)
Facilities Wi-fi Parking 60 Conf Thtr 300 Class 100 Board 40

BRAEMAR   Map 5 NO19

Callater Lodge Guest House

★★★★ GUEST HOUSE

☎ 013397 41275
9 Glenshee Rd AB35 5YQ
e-mail: info@hotel-braemar.co.uk
web: www.callaterlodge.co.uk
dir: Next to A93, 300yds S of Braemar centre

Located in the picturesque village of Braemar, a very well presented
property under the new ownership of the Shores. Bedrooms are
comfortable with many thoughtful extras provided as standard.
Public areas are welcoming with a home- away-from-home feel.
Breakfast is served on individual tables with local quality ingredients

used. The gardens are a very pleasant feature.

Rooms 6 en suite (1 fmly) S £38-£40; D £72-£74* Facilities tea/
coffee Cen ht Licensed Parking 6 Notes ⊗ Closed Xmas

CRATHES   Map 5 NO79

The Milton Restaurant

◉ Modern Scottish

Contemporary Scottish dining at the gateway to Royal Deeside

☎ 01330 844566 📠 01330 844474
Banchory AB31 5QH
web: www.themilton.co.uk
dir: Please telephone for directions

With the gateway to Royal Deeside and the Whisky and Castle Trails
starting at its doorstep, the Milton is in a top spot for exploring this
special part of Scotland. You could lose yourself for hours browsing
the art galleries and craft shops clustered all around, and when
hunger strikes, the restaurant makes a smart rustic venue, with yet
more artworks on its whitewashed walls, or there's an airy, light-
flooded conservatory extension. The kitchen serves up a thoughtful
menu of modern international cuisine utilising great Scottish
ingredients, as in a terrine of free-range duck, chicken and wild
rabbit with pickled wild mushrooms and morello cherry chutney to
start. Halibut with a macadamia nut crust is served with bok choi
and a lemongrass and coconut emulsion among main courses.

Chef David Littlewood Owner Neil Rae Restaurant Times 9.30am-
9.30pm Prices Starter £3.95-£6.45, Main £9.95-£23, Dessert £5.50
Notes Early D available 5-6.30pm 2/3 course £13.25-£17.50,
Vegetarian available

HUNTLY   Map 5 NJ53

Gordon Arms Hotel

★★ 64% SMALL HOTEL

☎ 01466 792288 📠 01466 794556
The Square AB54 8AF
e-mail: reception@gordonarms.demon.co.uk
dir: Off A96 (Aberdeen to Inverness road) at Huntly. Hotel
immediately on left after entering town square

This friendly, family-run hotel is located in the town square and
offers a good selection of tasty, well-portioned dishes served in the
bar, and also in the restaurant at weekends or midweek by
appointment. Bedrooms come in a variety of sizes, but all have a
good range of accessories.

Rooms 13 (3 fmly) S £45-£55; D £58.50-£68.50 (incl. bkfst)*
Facilities FTV ♪ Wi-fi Conf Class 80 Board 60 Thtr 160

Macdonald Pittodrie House

★★★★ 74% HOTEL

☎ 0870 1942111 & 01467 681744 📠 01467 681648
Chapel of Garioch, Pitcaple AB51 5HS
e-mail: pittodrie@macdonald-hotels.co.uk
web: www.macdonald-hotels.com/pittodrie
dir: From A96 towards Inverness, pass Inverurie under bridge with
lights. Turn left & follow signs

Set in extensive grounds this house dates from the 15th century and
retains many of its historic features. Public rooms include a gracious
drawing room, restaurant, and a cosy bar boasting an impressive
selection of whiskies. The well-proportioned bedrooms are found in
both the original house and in the extension that was designed to
match the existing building.

Rooms 27 (3 fmly) **Facilities** STV Clay pigeon shooting Quad biking
Outdoor activities Xmas New Year Wi-fi **Conf** Class 75 Board 50
Thtr 150 **Parking** 200 **Notes** Civ Wed 120

Kintore Arms

★★★★ INN

☎ 01467 621367 📠 01467 625620
83 High St AB51 3QJ
e-mail: manager.kintore@ohiml.com
web: www.oxfordhotelsandinns.com
dir: From A96 at rdbt turn signed Inverurie, onto main High St, on left

Well situated within easy walking distance from the town centre,
benefiting from off-road parking this traditional inn is currently
undergoing a programme of refurbishment. Good-sized bedrooms are
thoughtfully equipped for the modern traveller. Regular evening
entertainment is provided.

Rooms 28 en suite (1 fmly) S £65; D £75-£85* **Facilities** FTV TVL
tea/coffee Dinner available Cen ht Wi-fi **Conf** Max 150 Thtr 150 Class
75 Board 75 **Parking** 30 **Notes** Civ Wed 150

Kildrummy Castle Hotel

★★★★ Ⓐ COUNTRY HOUSE HOTEL

☎ 019755 71288 📠 019755 71345
AB33 8RA
e-mail: kildrummy@btconnect.com
web: www.kildrummycastlehotel.co.uk
dir: Off A97 (Huntly to Ballater road)

Rooms 16 (2 fmly) **Facilities** Fishing Xmas New Year Wi-fi
Conf Board 18 **Parking** 25 **Notes** LB Closed 3-24 Jan

Old Mill Inn

☎ 01224 733212 📠 01224 732884
South Deeside Rd AB12 5FX
e-mail: Info@oldmillinn.co.uk
dir: 5m W of Aberdeen on B9077

This delightful family-run 200-year-old country inn stands on the
edge of the River Dee, five miles from Aberdeen city centre. A former
mill house, the 18th-century granite building has been tastefully
modernised to include a restaurant where the finest Scottish
ingredients feature on the menu: venison stovies, peppered carpaccio
of beef, cullen skink, and chicken and venison terrine are typical.

Open all wk **Bar Meals** L served all wk 12-2 D served all wk 5.30-9
Restaurant L served all wk 12-2 D served all wk 5.30-9 ⊕ FREE
HOUSE ◄ Interbrew Bass, Caledonian Deuchars IPA, Timothy Taylor
Landlord. **Facilities** Children's menu Garden Parking

The Lairhillock Inn ♥

☎ 01569 730001 📠 01569 731175
AB39 3QS
e-mail: info@lairhillock.co.uk
dir: From Aberdeen take A90. Right towards Durris on B9077 then left
onto B979 to Netherley

Set in beautiful rural Deeside yet only 15 minutes drive from
Aberdeen, this award-winning 200-year-old former coaching inn
offers real ales in the bar and real fires in the lounge to keep out the
winter chill. Dishes are robust and use a bounty of fresh, quality,
local and regional produce such as langoustines from Gourdon,
mussels from Shetland, scallops from Orkney, wild boar and venison
from the Highlands and salmon from the Dee and Don, not forgetting
certified Aberdeen Angus beef. For lunch, try the Lairhillock lasagne
which layers pasta with minced venison, beef and pork topped with
wild mushroom sauce. For a more formal dining option, the
atmospheric Crynoch restaurant menu might feature shredded confit
duck leg and beetroot timbale, followed by chicken supreme filled
with sage and sausagemeat. Quality abounds on the children's menu
too, where spicy spare ribs and Finnan haddock fishcakes can be
found.

Open all wk 11am-mdnt Closed: 25-26 Dec, 1-2 Jan **Bar Meals** L
served all wk 12-2 booking required D served all wk 6-9.30 booking
required Av main course £9.95 **Restaurant** D served Tue-Sat 7-9.30
booking required Av 3 course à la carte fr £27.50 ⊕ FREE
HOUSE ◄ Timothy Taylor Landlord, Courage Directors, Cairngorm,
Tradewinds, Greene King IPA. ♥ 7 **Facilities** Children's menu Dogs
allowed Garden Parking

Balmedie Beach

NEWBURGH
Map 5 NJ92

Udny Arms

★★★ 70% HOTEL

☎ 01358 789444 📠 01358 789012
Main St AB41 6BL
e-mail: generalmanager.udnyarms@ohiml.com
web: www.oxfordhotelsandinns.com
dir: A90 N, 8m N of Aberdeen turn right to Newburgh (A975), hotel in village centre

Overlooking the picture postcard scenery of the Ythan Estuary and the Newburgh links golf course this hotel offers friendly service in relaxed and comfortable surroundings. The well equipped and nicely presented bedrooms have flat screen TVs. The split-level restaurant looks out onto the golf course.

Rooms 30 (1 fmly) **Facilities** Xmas New Year Wi-fi **Conf** Class 100 Board 60 Thtr 60 Del from £115 to £185 **Parking** 70 **Notes** Civ Wed 115

OLDMELDRUM
Map 5 NJ82

Meldrum House Hotel Golf & Country Estate

★★★ 85% COUNTRY HOUSE HOTEL

⑧ Modern British

Elegant dining in a splendid country mansion

☎ 01651 872294 📠 01651 872464
AB51 0AE
e-mail: enquiries@meldrumhouse.co.uk
dir: 11m N of Aberdeen (from Aberdeen to Dyce), A947 towards Banff, through Newmachen along outskirts of Oldmeldrum, main entrance large white archway

Set in 350 acres of wooded parkland this imposing baronial country mansion has a golf course as its centrepiece. Tastefully restored to highlight its original character it provides a peaceful retreat. Bedrooms are massive, and like the public rooms, transport guests back to a bygone era, but at the same time provide stylish modern amenities including smart bathrooms. The kitchen thinks local with its approach to sourcing produce for its European-accented Scottish country-house cooking. Tortellini of smoked haddock with lemon and chive sauce might serve as a curtain raiser to a main course of roast loin of venison with braised red cabbage, roasted root vegetables, gratin potato and sage sauce. To finish, there's the likes of blood orange bavarois with sablé biscuits, aniseed sauce and chocolate ice cream.

Rooms 22 (13 annexe) (1 fmly) (1 GF) **S** £65-£140; **D** £80-£180 (incl. bkfst)* **Facilities** FTV ♨ 18 Putt green ⛳ Xmas New Year Wi-fi **Conf** Class 20 Board 30 Thtr 80 Del from £125 to £145* **Parking** 45 **Notes** LB Civ Wed 70

Restaurant Times 12-2.30/6.30-9

Cromlet Hill

★★★★ Ⓐ BED AND BREAKFAST

☎ 01651 872315 📠 01651 872164
South Rd AB51 0AB
e-mail: johnpage@cromlethill.co.uk
dir: In town centre

Rooms 3 en suite (1 fmly) S £36-£45; D £56-£70* **Facilities** FTV TVL tea/coffee Cen ht **Parking** 4 **Notes** ⊗ ☺

The Redgarth

☎ 01651 872353 📠 01651 873763
Kirk Brae AB51 0DJ
e-mail: redgarth1@aol.com
dir: On A947 (bypass) Oldmeldrum located east side. Follow signs to golf club/pleasure park

A family-run inn, The Redgarth was built as a house in 1928 and has an attractive garden offering magnificent views of Bennachie and the surrounding countryside. Cask-conditioned ales, such as Orkney Scapa and Isle of Skye Red Cullin, and fine wines are served along with dishes prepared on the premises using fresh local produce. A typical selection might start with duo of hot and cold salmon with horseradish mayonnaise, or game terrine; continue with pork fillet stuffed with black pudding served with red cabbage in pear cider gravy, or pan-fried Barbary duck breast with Grand Marnier and orange glaze; and finish with apple pie or chocolate fudge cake.

Open all wk 11-3 5-11 (Fri-Sat 11-3 5-11.45) Closed: 25-26 Dec, 1-3 Jan **Bar Meals** L served all wk 12-2 D served Sun-Thu 5-9, Fri-Sat 5-9.30 **Restaurant** L served all wk 12-2 booking required D served Sun-Thu 5-9, Fri-Sat 5-9.30 booking required ⊕ FREE HOUSE ◀ Inveralmond Thrappledouser, Caledonian Deuchars IPA, Timothy Taylor Landlord, Isle of Skye Red Cullin, Orkney Scapa. **Facilities** Garden Parking

PETERHEAD
Map 5 NK14

Buchan Braes Hotel

★★★★ 75% HOTEL

The Grill Room at Buchan Braes Hotel

⑧ Modern Scottish ☺

Stylish modern hotel serving seriously good food

☎ 01779 871471 📠 01779 871472
Boddam AB42 3AR
e-mail: info@buchanbraes.co.uk
dir: From Aberdeen take A90 , follow Fraserburgh/Peterhead signs. Right at Toll of Birness. 1st right in Stirling signed Boddam. 50mtrs, 1st right

A contemporary hotel located in Boddam that is an excellent base for exploring the attractions of this wonderful part of Scotland. All the bedrooms, including three suites, have 32" flat-screen TVs with satellite channels, king-sized beds and free Wi-fi. Originally the officers' mess at RAF Buchan, the building has been smartly made over in a bold modern style with jazzy colours in the open-plan lounge and grill room, where an open kitchen lets diners watch the chefs at the stoves. Local produce is showcased with pride on a broad-based modern Scottish menu that reads enticingly. Ravioli of Amity langoustine with fennel and cucumber relish might start, then garlic-scented roast best end of lamb with herb crust comes with dauphinoise potatoes and rosemary jus. Finish with the intense flavours of hot chocolate fondant with lemon curd ice cream and kumquat compôte.

Rooms 47 (1 fmly) (27 GF) **S** £75-£110; **D** £105-£120 (incl. bkfst)* **Facilities** FTV Xmas New Year Wi-fi **Conf** Class 100 Board 80 Thtr 250 **Services** Lift **Parking** 40 **Notes** ⊗ Civ Wed 220

Chef Gary Christie, Paul McLean **Owner** Kenneth Watt **Restaurant Times** 11.45-2.30/6-9.30 **Prices** Food prices not confirmed for 2010. Please telephone for details. **Wines** 16 bottles over £20, 16 bottles under £20, 7 by glass **Notes** Sunday L, Vegetarian available, Air con **Seats** 70 **Children** Portions, Menu

Palace

★★★ 80% HOTEL

☎ 01779 474821 📄 01779 476119
Prince St AB42 1PL
e-mail: info@palacehotel.co.uk
web: www.palacehotel.co.uk
dir: A90 from Aberdeen, follow signs to Peterhead, on entering town turn into Prince St, then right into main car park

This town centre hotel is popular with business travellers and for social events. Bedrooms come in two styles, with the executive rooms being particularly smart and spacious. Public areas include a themed bar, an informal diner reached via a spiral staircase, and a brasserie restaurant and cocktail bar.

Rooms 64 (2 fmly) (14 GF) **S** £70-£80; **D** £80-£90 (incl. bkfst)* **Facilities** Pool table Snooker room ♫ Xmas New Year Wi-fi **Conf** Class 120 Board 50 Thtr 250 Del from £130 to £150* **Services** Lift **Parking** 50 **Notes** Civ Wed 280

STONEHAVEN   **Map 5 NO88**

Woodside Of Glasslaw

★★★★ GUEST ACCOMMODATION

☎ 01569 763799 📄 01569 763799
AB39 3XQ
e-mail: aileenpaton@hotmail.com
dir: A90 N, 1st sign for Stonehaven, at end turn right, next left

A warm welcome is assured at this charming guest house, which has a rural setting, yet close to major road network. The stylish bedrooms are all spacious and attractively presented. Freshly prepared breakfasts are served at individual tables and the new conservatory lounge is spacious and most comfortable. Wi-fi is available.

Rooms 6 en suite (1 fmly) (4 GF) S fr £40; D £60-£65 **Facilities** TVL tea/coffee Cen ht Wi-fi Small fitness room **Parking** 6 **Notes** Closed Xmas

Carron Art Deco Restaurant

⊛ Modern British

Eye-catching temple of art deco with modern Scottish cooking

☎ 01569 760460
20 Cameron St AB39 2HS
e-mail: jacki@cleaverhotels.eclipse.co.uk
dir: From Aberdeen, right at town centre lights, 2nd left onto Ann St, right at road end, 3rd building on right

Lovers of the eponymous design movement will relish the place. Accessed via a sunken garden, and boasting a nine-foot mirror adorned with a naked female form in Picasso style, the restaurant first opened in the 1930s. Brilliantly renovated, it now offers a menu in tune with the times that moves from the signature crab soup, deepened with sherry and cream, or deep-fried battered beetroot in chilli mango mayonnaise, to parmesan-crusted sea bass served on sweetly rich bean cassoulet. To finish, there may be pears poached in mulled wine, or well-made raspberry crème brûlée with a shortbread biscuit.

Chef Robert Cleaver **Owner** Robert Cleaver **Times** 12-2/6-9.30 Closed 24 Dec-10 Jan, Sun-Mon **Prices** Starter £3.45-£5.95, Main £11.50-£16.95, Dessert £5.10-£6.25, Service optional **Wines** 12 bottles over £20, 15 bottles under £20, 5 by glass **Notes** Vegetarian available **Seats** 80, Pr/dining room 30 **Children** Portions, Menu **Parking** Town Square

Tolbooth Restaurant

⊛ Modern British, Seafood ⊕

Quayside restaurant serving seafood straight off the boats

☎ 01569 762287
Old Pier, Stonehaven Harbour AB39 2JU
e-mail: enquiries@tolbooth-restaurant.co.uk
dir: 15m S of Aberdeen on A90, located in Stonehaven harbour

The aim of this restaurant is to transfer the freshest local fish and seafood from the quayside onto the plate in the shortest possible time. And it is in the right spot to pull it off: Stonehaven's oldest building - four centuries and counting - is right on the quayside. Steady legs are a help for the steep stairs ascending to the upstairs restaurant - a fresh, well-lit place with whitewashed and panelled walls, wooden floors and classy table settings. Light aromatic sauces and dressings complement the piscine produce without bullying it into submission, in offerings such as crab and lobster cakes with red pepper and ginger coulis, and turbot poached in red wine with mussel risotto, asparagus spears and vanilla sauce.

Chef Craig Somers **Owner** J Edward Abbott **Times** 12-4/6-12 Closed 2 wks Xmas & Jan, Sun (Oct-Apr) & Mon **Prices** Fixed L 2 course £12.95, Starter £3.95-£7.25, Main £13.95-£19.95, Dessert £5.95-£6.95, Service optional, Groups min 10 service 10% **Wines** 24 bottles over £20, 8 bottles under £20, 3 by glass **Notes** Vegetarian available **Seats** 46 **Children** Portions **Parking** Public car park, 100 spaces

Map 5 NJ31

The Glenkindie Arms

★★★ INN

French, Scottish ⚘

☎ 01975 641288
Glenkindie AB33 8SX
e-mail: iansimpson1873@live.co.uk
web: www.theglenkindiearmshotel.com
dir: On the A97 between Alford & Strathdon

A 400 year old traditional Scottish inn, the Glenkindie Arms enjoys a peaceful rural location and has an excellent reputation (and a loyal following) for its modern Scottish food. Ingredients are locally sourced for the daily changing dinner menu, which might feature perfectly executed hand-dived West coast scallops with cauliflower and pea puree and a smoked bacon crisp, followed, perhaps, by seafresh turbot, served with samphire and lemon velouté. End with hazelnut and howdie crowdie tort, served with Cointreau baked apricots. Accommodation is provided in brightly decorated and airy rooms, and the bathrooms are thoughtfully equipped. The Inn enjoys a peaceful rural location and has a built up a good reputation and a loyal following. Breakfast is not to be missed and lunches feature traditional dishes and the best of local produce.

Rooms 3 en suite (1 fmly) S £25-£45; D £40-£80 **Facilities** tea/coffee Dinner available Cen ht Wi-fi Fishing **Conf** Max 40 Thtr 20 Class 20 Board 30 **Parking** 25 **Notes** LB ⊗ Closed 3wks Nov RS Jan wknds only

Owners Ian Simpson & Aneta Olechno **Chef** Ian Simpson **Restaurant Times** 12-10pm Closed 3 wks Nov **Prices** Fixed L 3 course fr £14 Fixed D fr £14 Starter £3.75-£7.25, Main £7.50-£21.50, Dessert £3.50-£6.50, Service optional **Wines** 12 bottles under £20, 4 by glass **Notes** Sunday L, Vegetarian available **Seats** 40 Pr/dining room 20 **Children** Portions, Menu

---

Map 3 NO53

Carnoustie Golf Hotel & Spa

★★★★ 76% HOTEL

Dalhousie Restaurant

⚘ Traditional British

Fine dining in a championship location

☎ 01241 411999 & 411978 🖷 01241 411998
The Links DD7 7JE
e-mail: reservations.carnoustie@ohiml.com
web: www.oxfordhotelsandinns.com
dir: Adjacent to Carnoustie Golf Links

This fine hotel enjoys an enviable location and is adjacent to the 1st and 18th green of the famous Championship Course of Carnoustie. All bedrooms are spacious and attractively presented; most overlook the magnificent course and enjoy breathtaking coastal views. The Dalhousie Restaurant is certainly a prime spot for golf buffs; the restaurant also overlooks the course and is bright and airy, contemporary but elegant, and has well appointed tables set off with quality silver and sparkling glassware. Service is attentive and friendly, and the cooking style is modern Scottish with an emphasis on seasonal ingredients. A typical starter might be oak-roasted smoked salmon with potato salad, Arran mustard and dill crème fraîche. Main-course roasted loin of venison with Savoy cabbage, game and thyme jus could precede a dessert of raspberry shortcake with fresh whipped cream.

Rooms 85 (11 fmly) S £63.50-£389.50; D £69-£395 (incl. bkfst)*
Facilities Spa FTV ✇ Putt green Gym Xmas New Year Wi-fi
Conf Class 200 Board 100 Thtr 350 Del from £89 to £189*
Services Lift Air con **Parking** 100 **Notes** LB ⊗ Civ Wed 325

Restaurant Times 7-9.30 Closed L all week

Map 3 NO34

Castleton House

★★★ COUNTRY HOUSE HOTEL

⚘⚘ Modern & Traditional British

Victorian country house with culinary flair

☎ 01307 840340 🖷 01307 840506
Castleton of Eassie DD8 1SJ
e-mail: hotel@castletonglamis.co.uk
web: www.castletonglamis.co.uk
dir: On A94 midway between Forfar & Coupar Angus, 3m W of Glamis

This impressive Victorian house has a relaxed and friendly atmosphere. Accommodation is provided in individually designed, spacious bedrooms. Personal service from the enthusiastic proprietors is noteworthy and many guests return time and again. Beautiful moated grounds include a croquet lawn and a menagerie of ducks, chickens and pigs. Vases of seasonal flowers adorn the conservatory dining room, overlooking the garden that also supplies the kitchen with fresh vegetables and herbs. Prime-quality ingredients drive the menu, and there is a strong emphasis on local, seasonal produce from the abundant Scottish larder. Take seared hand-dived scallops from Orkney served on cauliflower purée with a fennel and apple salad, and to follow, perhaps a loin of Glen Prosen venison, delivered with pearl barley risotto, port-braised shallots and parsnip crisps.

Rooms 6 (2 fmly) **Facilities** FTV Putt green ⛳ Xmas Wi-fi
Conf Class 20 Board 20 Thtr 30 **Parking** 50 **Notes** Civ Wed 50

Restaurant Times 12-2/6.30-9 Closed 25 Dec, New Year

Gordon's

★★★★ ≣ RESTAURANT WITH ROOMS

@@ Modern British

Creative Scottish cooking from a friendly family team

☎ 01241 830364
Main St DD11 5RN
e-mail: gordonsrest@aol.com
dir: From A92 exit at signs for Inverkeilor (between Arbroath & Montrose)

It's well worth a detour into the tiny village of Inverkeilor to this welcoming family-run restaurant with rooms. Inside, there's a real sense of Scotland in the cosy dining room with its beams, huge open fire and rugs on wooden floors. Mum Maria is the front-of-house star, while the eponymous Gordon and his son Garry make a talented team in the kitchen, turning out sharp modern cooking with a definite wow factor. A sound grasp of classical technique and what works with what, and why, underpins the tersely-worded menus. Quail boudin with black pudding, spinach, apple and Puy lentils may start off proceedings, before an intermediate course - perhaps an artichoke velouté with scallop brunoise, pancetta and truffle crème fraîche. Scotch beef might appear as a main course, as slow-cooked

featherblade and seared fillet cassoulet with confit shallot, vanilla parsnip and Pinot Noir jus. If there's room left, try pear soufflé with marzipan ice cream, tonka bean anglaise and pear tuile. The excellent breakfasts are equally memorable. A huge fire dominates the restaurant on cooler evenings and there is a small lounge with limited seating. The attractive bedrooms are tastefully decorated and thoughtfully equipped, the larger two being furnished in pine.

Rooms 4 en suite 1 annexe en suite (1 GF) S £75; D £90-£120
Facilities FTV Dinner available Cen ht **Parking** 6 **Notes** ⊗ No Children 12yrs Closed 2wks Jan No coaches

Chef Gordon Watson, Garry Watson **Owner** Gordon & Maria Watson
Restaurant Times 12-1.45/7-9 Closed 1st 2 wks Jan, Mon, L Sat, D Sun (in Winter) **Prices** Fixed L course £27, Fixed D 4 course £44, Service optional **Wines** 19 bottles over £20, 25 bottles under £20, 3 by glass **Notes** Sunday L, Vegetarian available, Dress restrictions, Smart casual **Seats** 24, Pr/dining room 8

Oaklands

★★★ GUEST HOUSE

☎ 01674 672018 🖷 01674 672018
10 Rossie Island Rd DD10 9NN
e-mail: oaklands1@btopenworld.com
dir: On A92 at S end of town

A genuine welcome and attentive service are assured at this smart detached house situated on the south side of the town. Bedrooms come in a variety of sizes and are neatly presented. There is a lounge on the ground floor next to the attractive dining room, where hearty breakfasts are served. Motorcycle guided tours can be arranged with tourists travelling with their own motorbikes.

Rooms 7 en suite (1 fmly) (1 GF) S £30-£40; D £60-£75*
Facilities FTV TVL tea/coffee Cen ht Wi-fi **Parking** 8 **Notes** ⊗

ARGYLL & BUTE

APPIN
Map 2 NM94

Pineapple House

★★★★ 🏠 GUEST HOUSE

☎ 01631 740557 📠 01631 740557
Duror PA38 4BP
e-mail: info@pineapplehouse.co.uk
web: www.pineapplehouse.co.uk
dir: In Duror, off A828. 5m S of A82

Ideally located just south of Glencoe and just north of Appin. This period farmhouse has been lovingly restored and is extremely well presented using a great mix of modern and traditional. Dinners are available on request and use the best local quality produce. Service is friendly and genuine making for a wonderful base to tour this area of Scotland.

Rooms 6 en suite (1 fmly) S £35-£40; D £70-£95 **Facilities** FTV tea/coffee Dinner available Cen ht Wi-fi **Parking** 10 **Notes** ⊗ No Children 7yrs

ARDUAINE
Map 2 NM71

Loch Melfort

★★★ 81% HOTEL

◉◉ Modern British 🍷

Great local seafood in restaurant with stunning views

☎ 01852 200233 📠 01852 200214
PA34 4XG
e-mail: reception@lochmelfort.co.uk
web: www.lochmelfort.co.uk
dir: on A816, midway between Oban & Lochgilphead

Enjoying one of the finest locations on the West Coast, this popular, family-run hotel has outstanding views across Asknish Bay towards the Islands of Jura, Scarba and Shuna. Accommodation is provided in either the balconied rooms of the Cedar wing or the more traditional rooms in the main hotel. The setting is the perfect complement to the wonderful local fish and seafood on offer in the attractive dining room with its stunning views. Skilful cooking makes excellent use of an abundance of local produce. Start with langoustines from Luing served in the shell with mayonnaise or hot garlic butter and follow with roast rack of Barbreck lamb, creamed Savoy cabbage and cranberry sauce. Finish with a selection of Scottish cheeses.

Rooms 25 (20 annexe) (2 fmly) (10 GF) D £180-£250 (incl. bkfst & dinner)* **Facilities** 4 moorings Beauty treatments 🎵 Xmas New Year Wi-fi Child facilities **Conf** Class 40 Board 20 Thtr 50 Del from £100 to £200* **Parking** 50 **Notes** Closed 12 Jan-2 Feb Civ Wed 100

Chef Matt Mitchell **Owner** Calum & Rachel Ross **Restaurant Times** 7-9 Closed L all week **Prices** Fixed D 4 course £31, Starter £4.95-£9.95, Main £8.95-£18.95, Dessert £4.95-£7.95, Service optional **Wines** 25 bottles over £20, 40 bottles under £20, 8 by glass **Notes** Vegetarian available, Dress restrictions, Smart casual, no jeans **Seats** 75, Pr/dining room 14 **Children** Portions, Menu

CAIRNDOW
Map 2 NN11

Cairndow Stagecoach Inn

★★★ INN

☎ 01499 600286 & 600252 📠 01499 600252
PA26 8BN
e-mail: enq@cairndowinn.com
dir: From N, take either A82 to Tarbet, A83 to Cairndow, or A85 to Palmally, A819 to Inverary & A83 to Cairndow

A relaxed, friendly atmosphere prevails at this 18th-century inn, overlooking the beautiful Loch Fyne. Bedrooms offer individual decor and thoughtful extras.Traditional public areas include a comfortable beamed lounge, a well-stocked bar where food is served throughout the day, and a spacious restaurant with conservatory extension. New deluxe bedrooms are currently being built to offer more space and luxury.

Rooms 13 en suite 5 annexe en suite (2 fmly) (5 GF) S £35-£85; D £65-£140* **Facilities** STV FTV tea/coffee Dinner available Direct Dial Cen ht Wi-fi Sauna Solarium **Conf** Max 30 Thtr 30 Class 30 Board 30 **Notes** LB

CARDROSS
Map 2 NS37

Kirkton House

★★★★★ GUEST ACCOMMODATION

☎ 01389 841951 📠 01389 841868
Darleith Rd G82 5EZ
e-mail: aa@kirktonhouse.co.uk
web: www.kirktonhouse.co.uk
dir: 0.5m N of village. Turn N off A814 onto Darleith Rd at W end of village. Kirkton House 0.5m on right

Dating from the 18th century, this converted farmstead around an attractive courtyard has stunning views over the Clyde estuary from its elevated location. The individually styled bedrooms are well equipped and generally spacious, with two on the ground floor. Stone walls and large fireplaces feature in public areas, and home-cooked wide choice breakfasts using fresh produce are served in the delightful dining room.

Rooms 6 en suite (4 fmly) (2 GF) S £30-£45; D £60-£70 **Facilities** FTV TVL tea/coffee Direct Dial Cen ht Wi-fi Riding **Parking** 10 **Notes** LB Closed Dec-Jan

Dunvalanree

★★★★ GUEST ACCOMMODATION

⊕ Modern British **V** ☺

Superb seafood (and more) in stunning coastal location

☎ 01583 431226   🖷 01583 431339
Port Righ Bay PA28 6SE
e-mail: stay@dunvalanree.com
web: www.dunvalanree.com
dir: On B879. In Carradale turn right at x-rds, restaurant at end of road

Set in stunning scenery on the Mull of Kintyre, Dunvalanree has been welcoming guests for over 70 years. Standing in delightful gardens on the edge of Port Righ Bay, the house enjoys splendid views over Kilbrannan Sound, to the Isle of Arran. Robert the Bruce landed here in 1306 while he was fleeing the English army, and it's an ideal place to explore this lovely area. This is a genuine family-run operation with mum in the kitchen and father and daughter welcoming guests in the traditional restaurant. There is one sitting, which adds to the dinner party feel. Skilful Scottish cuisine is conjured from the very best local ingredients in a daily-changing menu that might include Kilbrannon scallops with coriander and lime, followed by Kintyre venison with celeriac mash and red wine jus.

Rooms 5 en suite (1 GF); D £142-£172ᴬ (incl.dinner) **Facilities** tea/coffee Dinner available Cen ht Licensed Wi-fi Golf 9 ♨ Fishing **Parking** 8 **Notes** LB ⊗

Chef Alyson Milstead **Owner** Alan & Alyson Milstead **Restaurant Times** 7 Closed Jan-Feb, L all week **Prices** Fixed D 3 course £26, Service optional **Wines** 12 bottles under £20, 4 by glass **Notes** Vegetarian menu **Seats** 20 **Children** Portions

Tigh an Truish Inn

☎ 01852 300242
PA34 4QZ
dir: 14m S of Oban take A816. 12m, onto B844 towards Atlantic Bridge

Following the Battle of Culloden in 1746, kilts were outlawed on pain of death. In defiance of this edict the islanders wore their kilts at home; but, on excursions to the mainland, they would stop at the Tigh an Truish – the 'house of trousers' – to change into the hated

trews. Now popular with tourists and members of the yachting fraternity, the inn is handy for good walks and lovely gardens. Ales from local brewers stock the bar, along with a range of single malts, while an appetising menu based on the best local produce is particularly well endowed with fresh seafood: moules marinière, locally caught prawns served with garlic mayonnaise and salad, and smoked salmon of course. Look out for venison, perhaps prepared in a pepper cream and Drambuie sauce. If this all sounds rather sophisticated, families need not worry; a separate lounge off the main bar is furnished with children's books – another indication of the pub's genuinely warm welcome.

Open all wk 11-11 (Mon-Fri 11-2.30 5-11 Oct-Mar) Closed: 25 Dec & 1 Jan **Bar Meals** L served all wk 12-2 D served all wk 6-8.30 (Apr-Oct) Av main course £7.50 ⊕ FREE HOUSE ◀ Local guest ales changing regularly. **Facilities** Family room Dogs allowed Garden Parking

Falls of Lora

★★★ 77% HOTEL

☎ 01631 710483   🖷 01631 710694
PA37 1PB
e-mail: enquiries@fallsoflora.com
web: www.fallsoflora.com
dir: From Glasgow take A82, A85. Hotel 0.5m past Connel sign

Personally run and welcoming, this long-established and thriving holiday hotel enjoys inspiring views over Loch Etive. The spacious ground floor takes in a comfortable, traditional lounge and a cocktail bar with over a hundred whiskies and an open log fire. Guests can eat in the popular, informal bistro, which is open all day. Bedrooms come in a variety of styles, ranging from the cosy standard rooms to high quality luxury rooms.

Rooms 30 (4 fmly) (4 GF) (30 smoking) **S** £47.50-£59.50; **D** £55-£139 (incl. bkfst)* **Facilities** Wi-fi Child facilities **Conf** Class 20 Board 15 Thtr 45 **Parking** 40 **Notes** LB Closed mid Dec & Jan

CONNEL CONTINUED

Ards House

★★★★★ ⌂ GUEST HOUSE

☎ 01631 710255 📠 01631 710857
PA37 1PT
e-mail: info@ardshouse.com
web: www.ardshouse.com
dir: On A85, 4m N of Oban

This delightful Victorian villa on the approaches to Loch Etive has stunning views over the Firth of Lorne and the Morven Hills beyond. The stylish bedrooms come with added touches such as home-made shortbread and mineral water. There is an inviting drawing room complete with piano, games and books, plus a fire on cooler evenings. The attractive dining room is the setting for delicious breakfasts.

Rooms 4 en suite **Facilities** FTV TVL tea/coffee Cen ht **Parking** 12 **Notes** LB ⊗ No Children 10yrs Closed mid Dec-mid Jan

---

Ronebhal Guest House

★★★★ GUEST HOUSE

☎ 01631 710310 📠 01631 710310
PA37 1PJ
e-mail: info@ronebhal.co.uk
dir: A85, W from village centre, 4th house after turn for Fort William

The Strachan family extends a friendly welcome to their lovely detached home, which has stunning views of Loch Etive. The bedrooms are well equipped and comfortably furnished in modern styles. There is a sitting room, and an attractive dining room where hearty traditional breakfasts are served at individual tables. Gardens are pleasing on the eye.

Rooms 5 rms (4 en suite) (1 pri facs) (1 fmly) (1 GF) S £25-£35; D £54-£90 **Facilities** FTV TVL tea/coffee Cen ht Wi-fi **Parking** 6 **Notes** LB ⊗ No Children 7yrs Closed Nov-Feb

---

The Oyster Inn

☎ 01631 710666 📠 01631 710042
PA37 1PJ
e-mail: stay@oysterinn.co.uk
dir: Please telephone for directions

A comfortable, informal hotel overlooking the tidal whirlpools and white water of the Falls of Lora, and enjoying glorious views of the mountains of Mull. It was built in the 18th century to serve ferry passengers, but the ferry is no more, superseded by the modern road bridge. Years ago it was known as The Glue Pot, because canny locals knew they could be 'stuck' here between ferries, and thus get round complicated Sunday licensing laws. Food is served all day, using locally-sourced, quality produce, particularly from the sea and lochs, such as West Coast mussels marinière; Ferryman's ocean pie; and seafood pancakes. Other dishes include steak and ale pie; bangers and mash; local lamb shank; and tempura battered vegetables. There's a log fire in the bar, where regular live music is performed, and where your companions are reasonably certain to be walkers, divers, canoeists, fishermen or yachting enthusiasts.

Open all wk noon-mdnt **Bar Meals** L served all wk 12.30-2.30 D served all wk 5.30-8.30 Av main course £9.95 **Restaurant** D served all wk 6-8.30 booking required ⊕ FREE HOUSE ◀ Guinness. **Facilities** Children's menu Dogs allowed Garden Parking

Crinan Hotel

☎ 01546 830261 📠 01546 830292
PA31 8SR
e-mail: reservations@crinanhotel.com
dir: From M8, at end of bridge take A82, at Tarbert left onto A83. At Inverary follow Campbeltown signs to Lochgilphead, follow signs for A816 to Oban. 2m, left to Crinan on B841

At the north end of the Crinan Canal which connects Loch Fyne to the Atlantic Ocean, the Crinan is a romantic retreat enjoying fabulous views across the sound of Jura. It's a long-standing place of welcome at the heart of community life in this tiny fishing village. The hotel dates back some 200 years and has been run by owners Nick and Frances Ryan for nearly 40 of them. The Panther Arms is the hotel's public bar, where you can sample Scottish beers or whiskies while chatting to the locals. You can eat here too, or in the Mainbrace Bar which has a menu served both at lunchtime and in the evening. The award-winning cuisine is firmly based on the freshest of seafood – it's landed daily just 50 metres from the hotel. Some bar meals can be served in either starter or main course quantities: warm tart of Loch Crinan scallops and smoked bacon is served with organic leaves and a goats' cheese cream; Loch Etive mussels are classically steamed in lemon, thyme and garlic; and oak-smoked salmon from Rothesay are three examples. If in the evening a full à la carte dinner is required, head for the Westward restaurant on the ground floor with its views over Loch Crinan to Jura, Scarba and the mountains of Mull. If you've eaten enough seafood, a typical choice could start with Pithiviers of free range chicken and wood pigeon, with winter truffles and salsify; continue with roasted saddle of Argyll venison with slow-cooked haunch, Savoy cabbage and confit potatoes; and finish with hot chocolate fondant, poached mandarins and vanilla ice cream. Boat trips can be arranged to the islands, and there is a classic boats regatta in the summer.

Open all wk Closed: Xmas ⊕ FREE HOUSE ◀ Belhaven, Interbrew, Worthington Bitter, Tennents Velvet, Guinness, Loch Fyne Ales. **Facilities** Dogs allowed Garden Parking

Selborne

★★ 76% HOTEL

☎ 01369 702761 📠 01369 704032
Clyde St, West Bay PA23 7HU
e-mail: selborne.dunoon@alfatravel.co.uk
dir: From Caledonian MacBrayne pier. Past castle, left into Jane St, right into Clyde St

This holiday hotel is situated overlooking the West Bay and provides unrestricted views of the Clyde Estuary towards the Isles of Cumbrae. Tour groups are especially well catered for in this good-value establishment, which offers entertainment most nights. Bedrooms are comfortable and many have sea views.

Rooms 98 (6 fmly) (14 GF) S £34-£45; D £54-£76 (incl. bkfst)
Facilities FTV Pool table Table tennis ♫ Xmas New Year
Services Lift Parking 30 Notes LB ⊗ Closed Dec-Feb (ex Xmas)
RS Nov & Mar

Coylet Inn

☎ 01369 840426
Loch Eck PA23 8SG
e-mail: reservations@coylet-locheck.co.uk
dir: 9m N of Dunoon on A815

Overlooking the shores of Loch Eck, this beautifully refurbished 17th-century coaching inn is a blissful hideaway with no television or games machines to disturb the peace. The inn is famous for its ghost, the Blue Boy; a film was even made of the story, starring Emma Thompson. Unwind by one of three log fires or plunder the impressive menus, where choices range from venison burger and chips to grilled sole with mussel cream.

Closed: 25 Dec, Mon & Tue (Oct-Mar) ⊕ FREE HOUSE ◄ Caledonian Deuchars IPA, Highlander. **Facilities** Garden Parking

Isle of Eriska

★★★★★ COUNTRY HOUSE HOTEL

⊛⊛⊛ Traditional British ♨ 🐾

Luxurious island retreat with first-class team in the kitchen

☎ 01631 720371 📠 01631 720531
Eriska PA37 1SD
e-mail: office@eriska-hotel.co.uk
dir: Exit A85 at Connel, onto A828, follow for 4m, then follow hotel signs from N of Benderloch

Situated on its own private island with delightful beaches and walking trails, this hotel offers a tranquil, personal setting for total relaxation. Spacious bedrooms are comfortable and boast some fine antique pieces. Leisure facilities include an indoor swimming pool, gym, spa treatment rooms and a small golf course. Once you've crossed from the mainland over the iron bridge you are on the 300-acre island estate, with the Victorian baronial-style house (doing a fine impression of a castle) at its heart. The newly refurbished restaurant is headed up by the talented Robert MacPherson. The new-look dining areas - now open to non-residents, too - make the best of the proportions of the rooms and their period details, with wood-panelling and ornate plasterwork alongside modishly lit shelves, richly coloured fabrics and tables traditionally set with crisp linen cloths. It looks Scottish but with no hint of a cliché. The kitchen's daily-changing dinner menu is based around top-notch Scottish produce - some from the hotel's garden - and offers refined, intelligently constructed dishes which are based on classical techniques and seek to maximise flavour. Pithivier of ham hough with a quince purée, pickled shiitake and mustard velouté is an impressive first course; next up, perhaps local Dover sole filled with a scallop and dill mousseline and served with a surf clam essence and Swiss chard. The creativity and attention to detail continues with desserts such as orange chiboust with a black olive cake and citrus sorbet. The wine list does justice to the excellent food.

Rooms 23 (2 GF) Facilities Spa FTV ⊗ supervised ♨ 9 ⌣ Putt green Fishing ⚘ Gym Sauna Steam room Skeet shooting Nature trails Xmas New Year Wi-fi Conf Class 30 Board 30 Thtr 30 Del from £200 to £400* Parking 40 Notes Closed Jan Civ Wed 50

Chef Robert MacPherson Owner Mr Buchanan-Smith Restaurant Times -8-9 Closed Jan, Prices Fixed D 4 course £40, Service optional Wines 236 bottles over £20, 43 bottles under £20, 10 by glass Notes Vegetarian available, Air con Seats 50, Pr/dining room 20 Children Portions, Menu

Innkeeper's Lodge Helensburgh

BUDGET HOTEL

☎ 0845 112 6005 📠 0845 112 6295
112-17 West Clyde St G84 8ES
web: www.innkeeperslodge.com/helensburgh
dir: M8 junct 30, M898. Over Erskine Bridge take exit for Crianlarich onto A82 to Dumbarton. At junct with A814, left, at rdbt follow Helensburgh signs. 10m, Lodge on right near pier

Innkeeper's Lodge represents an exciting, high value concept within the budget hotel market. Comfortable bedrooms provide excellent facilities that include satellite TV and modem points. Options include family rooms; and for the corporate guest, cutting edge IT includes Wi-fi access. Food is served all day in the adjacent Country Pub. The extensive continental breakfast is complimentary. See also the Hotel Groups pages on theAA.com.

Rooms 44 Conf Thtr 200

Lethamhill

★★★★★ GUEST ACCOMMODATION

☎ 01436 676016 & 07974 798593 📠 01436 676016
West Dhuhill Dr G84 9AW
e-mail: lethamhill@talk21.com
web: www.lethamhill.co.uk
dir: 1m N of pier/town centre. Off A818 onto West Dhuhill Dr. Cross Upper Colcough St, then 3rd entrance on right

From the red phone box in the garden to the old typewriters and slot machines inside, this fine house is an Aladdin's cave of unusual collectibles and memorabilia. The house itself offers spacious and comfortable bedrooms with superb bathrooms. The home-cooked breakfasts and delicious baking earn much praise.

Rooms 3 en suite S £65-£85; D fr £85* Facilities TVL tea/coffee Cen ht Wi-fi Parking 6 Notes LB ⊗

Rest and Be Thankful Pass near Arrochar

KILCHRENAN
Map 2 NN02

The Ardanaiseig

★★★ 86% COUNTRY HOUSE HOTEL

◎◎ Modern Scottish V

Excellent food in peaceful hotel with stunning views

☎ 01866 833333 ▤ 01866 833222
by Loch Awe PA35 1HE
e-mail: ardanaiseig@clara.net
dir: From A85 at Taynuilt onto B845 to Kilchrenan. Left in front of pub (road very narrow) signed 'Ardanaiseig Hotel' & 'No Through Road'. Continue for 3m

Accessed via a long and winding single-track road, and set amid lovely gardens and breathtaking scenery beside the shore of Loch Awe, this peaceful country-house hotel was built in a Scottish baronial style in 1834. Many fine pieces of furniture are evident in the bedrooms and charming day rooms, which include a drawing room and a library bar.The interiors are very much in keeping with the early Victorian period, with gorgeous antiques and fine art, all very understated and uncluttered. The kitchen produces innovative food, skilfully and faultlessly cooked with good use made of local produce. Dinner is a complete five-course experience, with dishes such as seared scallops with Chantenay carrots and Sauternes sauce and fillet of line-caught sea bass with ratatouille, sautéed langoustines, tortellini of clam and shellfish essence.

Rooms 18 (4 fmly) (5 GF) **S** £64-£137; **D** £128-£274 (incl. bkfst) **Facilities** FTV Fishing ◆ Boating Clay pigeon shooting Bikes for hire Xmas New Year Wi-fi **Parking** 20 **Notes** Closed 2 Jan-1 Feb Civ Wed 50

Chef Gary Goldie **Owner** Bennie Gray **Restaurant Times** 12-2/7-9 Closed 2 Jan- 10 Feb, **Prices** Fixed D 4 course £48, Service optional **Wines** 94 bottles over £20, 4 bottles under £20, 16 by glass **Notes** Vegetarian menu, Dress restrictions, Smart casual, no jeans or trainers **Seats** 36 Children Portions, Menu

Taychreggan

★★★ 86% COUNTRY HOUSE HOTEL

◎◎ Traditional British V

Highland hospitality by the shores of the loch

☎ 01866 833211 & 833366 ▤ 01866 833244
PA35 1HQ
e-mail: info@taychregganhotel.co.uk
dir: W from Crianlarich on A85 to Taynuilt, S for 7m on B845 (single track) to Kilchrenan

Surrounded by stunning Highland scenery, this stylish and superbly presented hotel, once a drover's cottage, enjoys an idyllic setting in 40 acres of wooded grounds on the shores of Loch Awe. Now refurbished the hotel has a smart bar with adjacent courtyard Orangerie and a choice of quiet lounges with deep, luxurious sofas. Families, and also dogs and their owners, are welcome. The beautiful views can be taken in from the arched windows of the stylish dining room, where the imaginative menus make full use of fine Scottish produce to create a range of British dishes that are both rustic and

contemporary. A starter partridge sits on celeriac and potato rösti and is surrounded by a Puy lentil and chanterelle broth, and main-course herb-crusted halibut comes with a warm potato and fine bean salad and an egg, onion and parsley sauce.

Rooms 18 **S** £85-£167; **D** £110-£274 (incl. bkfst)* **Facilities** FTV Fishing ◆ Clay pigeon shooting Falconry Archery Air rifle range Mock deer stalk New Year Wi-fi **Conf** Class 15 Board 20 **Parking** 40 **Notes** Closed 25-26 Dec & 3 Jan-10 Feb Civ Wed 60

Chef Alan Hunter **Owner** North American Country Inns **Restaurant Times** 7.30-8.45 Closed 24-26 Dec, **Prices** Food prices not confirmed for 2010. Please telephone for details, Service added but optional 10% **Wines** 23 bottles over £20, 16 bottles under £20, 2 by glass **Notes** Fixed D 5 course £44, Vegetarian menu, Dress restrictions, Smart casual **Seats** 45, Pr/dining room 18 **Children** Portions, Menu

KILFINAN
Map 2 NR97

Kilfinan Hotel Bar

☎ 01700 821201 ▤ 01700 821205
PA21 2EP
e-mail: kilfinanhotel@btconnect.com
dir: 8m N of Tighnabruaich on B8000

The hotel, on the eastern shore of Loch Fyne set amid spectacular Highland scenery on a working estate, has been welcoming travellers since the 1760s. The bars are cosy with log fires in winter, and offer a fine selection of malts. There are two intimate dining rooms, with the Lamont room for larger parties. Menus change daily and offer the best of local produce: Loch Fyne oysters, of course, and langoustine grilled in garlic butter; cullen skink soup; and moules marinière, plus game, Aberdeen Angus beef and a variety of Scottish sweets and cheeses. Enjoy the views from the garden on warmer days.

Open all wk **Bar Meals** L served all wk 12.30-4 D served all wk 6.30-9.30 Av main course £7.95 **Restaurant** L served all wk 12.30-4 booking required D served all wk 6.30-9.30 booking required Av 3 course à la carte fr £22 ⊕ FREE HOUSE ◀ McEwens 70/-, McEwens 80/-. **Facilities** Children's menu Family room Dogs allowed Garden Parking

KILMARTIN
Map 2 NR89

Ford House

★★★ ⚑ GUEST ACCOMMODATION

PA31 8RH

☎ 01546 810273
e-mail: info@ford-house.com

Rooms 6 rms (5 en suite) (1 pri facs) (1 fmly) S £30-£37; D £56-£60* **Facilities** STV TVL tea/coffee Cen ht Licensed **Parking** 7 **Notes** LB ⊗ ◉

Cairnbaan

★★★ 78% HOTEL

◉ British, European

Traditional fish cookery by the canal

☎ 01546 603668   🖷 01546 606045
Crinan Canal, Cairnbaan PA31 8SJ
e-mail: info@cairnbaan.com
web: www.cairnbaan.com
dir: 2m N, A816 from Lochgilphead, hotel off B841

Next to the Crinan canal, this small hotel offers relaxed hospitality in a delightful setting. Bedrooms are thoughtfully equipped, generally spacious and benefit from stylish decor. With alfresco dining available in the summer, the hotel restaurant is a split-level space with fine watery views. Colourful artworks abound, and the tone is one of unforced informality. A menu of simple classics majors on fish, with satisfying langoustine chowder to begin, then maybe Parma-wrapped monkfish to follow, or the traditional house fish pie. Meat-eaters might go for a chargrilled rib-eye steak with chips and a choice of sauces. Poppyseed cheesecake with blueberry coulis is an unusual and enjoyable dessert, or there is a range of Mövenpick ice creams.

Rooms 12 **Facilities** Xmas **Conf** Class 100 Board 80 Thtr 160
Parking 53 **Notes** Civ Wed 120

Restaurant Times 12-2.30/6-9.30

The Lodge on Loch Lomond

★★★★ 75% HOTEL

Colquhoun's

◉◉ Modern British ◔

Idyllic Loch Lomond location for fine dining

☎ 01436 860201   🖷 01436 860203
G83 8PA
e-mail: res@loch-lomond.co.uk
web: www.loch-lomond.co.uk
dir: off A82, follow sign for hotel

Idyllically set on the edge of Loch Lomond, The Lodge on Loch Lomond boasts a delightful location with magnificent views across the water. Public areas consist of an open-plan, split-level bar and fine dining restaurant overlooking the loch. The pine-finished bedrooms also enjoy the views and are comfortable, spacious and well equipped; all have saunas and some have DVDs and internet access. There is also a stunning state-of-the-art leisure suite. Colquhoun's restaurant blends traditional Scottish décor with Scandinavian-style touches of pinewood walls and pillars, as well as has glass-topped tables, good table appointments and an open-plan kitchen. There's a balconied terrace where guests can dine outside in the summer. The brasserie-style modern menu has strong Scottish flair and features good quality, locally-sourced produce, while service is friendly and

efficient. To start, try Isle of Mull Old Smokehouse fish tian with cucumber and dill salad, lemon and baby caper dressing, followed by oven-roasted loin of Blairatholl Estate venison with fondant potato, spiced red cabbage, maple-glazed butternut squash, redcurrant and bramble jus.

Rooms 47 (17 annexe) (20 fmly) (13 GF) **Facilities** Spa STV FTV ◔
Fishing Boating Xmas New Year Wi-fi **Conf** Class 80 Board 60
Thtr 150 **Parking** 120 **Notes** Civ Wed 100

Chef Donn Eadie **Owner** Niall Colquhoun **Restaurant**
Times 12-5/6-9.45 **Prices** Fixed L 2 course £7.90-£16.90, Fixed D 3
course £29.95, Starter £6.50, Main £16.95, Dessert £6.50, Service
optional **Wines** 29 bottles over £20, 20 bottles under £20, 7 by glass
Notes ALC 3 course, Sunday L, Vegetarian available **Seats** 100, Pr/
dining room 40 **Children** Portions, Menu

The Inn at Inverbeg

★★★★ ⇌ INN ♟

☎ 01436 860678   🖷 01436 860203
Inverbeg G83 8PD
e-mail: inverbeg.reception@loch-lomond.co.uk
dir: A82 N of Balloch

Dating back to the 1814 and commanding stunning views across Loch Lomond and its surrounding hills, the Inn is Scotland's first boutique inn. Remodelled and refurbished in contemporary style, it retains its old-world charm and character – roaring log fires fronted by swish leather and cow hide seating. Offering very stylish, comfortable bedrooms, bathrooms and public areas. The Beach House accommodation is a real treat for that special occasion.

At the Whisky Bar you have over 200 malts and real ales like Deuchars IPA to choose from. In Mr C's, the relaxed and informal dining room, you can tuck into fresh, sustainable fish caught off Scottish shores. Start with steamed mussels, Loch Fyne oysters or chilli-coated squid with garlic mayonnaise, move on to fishcakes with spinach and lemon hollandaise or simply grilled cod or haddock served with chips, or Buccleuch sirloin steak with herb butter. Comfortable, individually styled rooms are split between the inn and a sumptuous beach house beside loch, the latter featuring wooden floors, hand-crafted furniture, crisp linen, and a hot tub. The Inn at Inverbeg is AA Pub of the Year for Scotland 2009-2010.

Rooms 12 en suite 8 annexe en suite (1 fmly) (5 GF) S £89-£149; D
£99-£159* **Facilities** STV FTV TVL tea/coffee Dinner available Cen ht
Wi-fi **Parking** 60 **Notes** LB ⊗ Civ Wed 60

Open all day all wk 11-11 **Bar Meals** Av main course £9.95 food
served all day **Restaurant** food served all day ◄ Killellan,
Highlander, Deuchars IPA. ♟ 30 **Facilities** Children's menu

OBAN
Map 2 NM82

Manor House

★★★ 83% HOTEL

◉ Traditional European

Elegant Georgian dower house with quality local produce

☎ 01631 562087   🖶 01631 563053
Gallanach Rd PA34 4LS
e-mail: info@manorhouseoban.com
web: www.manorhouseoban.com
dir: Follow MacBrayne Ferries signs, pass ferry entrance for hotel on right

Handy for the ferry terminal and with views of the bay and harbour, this elegant Georgian residence was built in 1780 as the dower house for the family of the Duke of Argyll. Comfortable and attractive public rooms invite relaxation, whilst most of the well-equipped bedrooms are furnished with period pieces. The hotel has been spared a modern makeover and revels in its authentic feel. Watch the Calmac ferries come and go from the harbour below over pre-dinner drinks in the bar and classy drawing room, then settle in to the traditional dining room, with its deep green walls, tartan carpet and white linen. Five-course dinners work around a repertoire of European-influenced cuisine; kick off with a twice-baked goat's cheese soufflé with poached pear and walnuts, and progress via soup and sorbet to grilled fillet of turbot with Oban Bay prawns, scallop and asparagus tagliatelle.

Rooms 11 (1 GF) **S** £95-£160; **D** £108-£193 (incl. bkfst) **Facilities** New Year Wi-fi **Parking** 20 **Notes** No children 12yrs Closed 25-26 Dec Civ Wed 30

Chef Patrick Freytag, Shaun Squire **Owner** Mr P L Crane **Restaurant Times** 12-2.30/6.45-8.45 Closed 25-26 Dec, **Prices** Starter £3-£8, Main £15-£25, Dessert £7, Service optional **Wines** 27 bottles over £20, 24 bottles under £20, 7 by glass **Notes** Fixed D 5 course £36, Vegetarian available, Dress restrictions, Smart casual **Seats** 34 **Children** Portions

The Oban Caledonian Hotel

★★★ 74% HOTEL

☎ 0844 855 9135   🖶 01631 562998
Station Square PA34 5RT
e-mail: gm.caledonian@foliohotels.com
web: www.foliohotels.com/caledonian
dir: At head of main pier, close to rail terminal

This Victorian hotel, overlooking the bay, has an enviable location close to the ferry terminal and parking, as well as Oban's many attractions. Public areas are modern and stylish and include a smart restaurant, spacious lounges and an informal dining option in Café Caledonian. Attractive bedrooms come in a number of different styles and grades, some with comfortable seating areas, feature bathrooms and fine sea views.

Rooms 59 (6 fmly) **Facilities** Xmas New Year Wi-fi **Conf** Class 90 Board 50 Thtr 100 **Services** Lift **Notes** Civ Wed 100

Royal

★★★ 73% HOTEL

☎ 01631 563021   🖶 01631 562811
Argyll Sqaure PA34 4BE
e-mail: salesroyaloban@strathmorehotels.com
dir: A82 from Glasgow towards Loch Lomond & Crianlarich then A85 (pass Loch Awe) to Oban

Well situated in the heart of Oban, just minutes from the ferry terminal and with all the shops on its doorstep, this hotel really is central. The comfortable and well presented bedrooms differ in size, and all public areas are smart

Rooms 91 (5 fmly) **Facilities** ♫ Xmas New Year Wi-fi **Conf** Class 60 Board 30 Thtr 140 **Services** Lift **Parking** 25

The Columba Hotel
Ⓤ

☎ 01631 562183   🖶 01631 564683
The Esplanade PA34 5QD
e-mail: columba@mckeverhotels.co.uk
web: www.mckeverhotels.co.uk
dir: A85 to Oban, 1st set of lights in town and turn right

Currently the rating for this establishment is not confirmed. This may be due to a change of ownership or because it has only recently joined the AA rating scheme.

Rooms 49 (5 fmly) **Facilities** Wi-fi FTV Passenger lift Night porter **Parking** 6

Blarcreen House

★★★★★ 🍽 GUEST HOUSE

☎ 01631 750272
Ardchattan, Connel PA37 1RG
e-mail: info@blarcreenhouse.com
web: www.blarcreenhouse.com
dir: 9.5m NE of Oban. N over Connel Bridge, 1st right, 7m, pass
church & Ardchattan Priory Gardens. Blarcreen House 2m

Built in 1886 this elegant Victorian farmhouse stands on the shores
of Loch Etive and has lovely views of the surrounding mountains.
Bedrooms are beautifully furnished and very well equipped. There is
a comfortable drawing room with deep sofas, a plentiful supply of
books and videos, and a log-burning fire. Delicious home-cooked fare
featuring the very best of local produce is served in the dining room.
Hospitality is strong and the atmosphere relaxed in this charming
house.

Rooms 3 en suite S £66-£75; D £92-£110* **Facilities** STV TVL tea/
coffee Dinner available Cen ht Licensed Wi-fi **Parking** 5 **Notes** LB ⊗
No Children 16yrs

Alltavona House

★★★★ GUEST HOUSE

☎ 01631 565067 & 07771 708301 📠 01631 565067
Corran Esplanade PA34 5AQ
e-mail: carol@alltavona.co.uk
dir: From Oban centre along seafront past cathedral, 5th house from
end of Esplanade

Alltavona is an elegant Victorian villa with a delightful location on
the Corran Esplanade with stunning views over Oban Bay to the
islands of Lismore and Kererra. The attractive bedrooms are
individually styled and feature quality furnishings. Delicious
breakfasts featuring the best of local produce are served in the
charming dining room.

Rooms 6 en suite (3 fmly) **Facilities** tea/coffee Cen ht **Parking** 6
Notes ⊗ No Children 12yrs Closed 12-30 Dec

Glenburnie House

★★★★ GUEST HOUSE

☎ 01631 562089 📠 01631 562089
The Esplanade PA34 5AQ
e-mail: graeme.strachan@btinternet.com
dir: On Oban seafront. Follow signs for Ganavan

This impressive seafront Victorian house has been lovingly restored
to a high standard. Bedrooms (including a four-poster room and a
mini-suite) are beautifully decorated and very well equipped. There is
a cosy ground-floor lounge and an elegant dining room, where hearty
traditional breakfasts are served at individual tables.

Rooms 12 en suite (2 GF) S £45-£50; D £80-£100* **Facilities** FTV
tea/coffee Cen ht Wi-fi **Parking** 12 **Notes** LB ⊗ No Children 12yrs
Closed Nov-Mar

Braeside

★★★★ GUEST HOUSE

☎ 01631 770243 📠 01631 770343
Kilmore PA34 4QR
e-mail: braeside.guesthouse@virgin.net
web: www.braesideguesthouse.net
dir: On A816 5m from Oban

The family-run bungalow stands in gardens overlooking the
spectacular Loch Feochan. Bedrooms, all en suite, are bright and
airy, well equipped and have easy access. The lounge-dining room
has a loch view, a bar with a range of single malts and wines, and
offers a varied choice of tasty home-cooked evening meals and
breakfasts.

Rooms 5 en suite (1 fmly) (5 GF) S £30-£35; D £60-£70*
Facilities tea/coffee Dinner available Cen ht Licensed Wi-fi **Parking** 6
Notes LB ⊗ No Children 8yrs

Corriemar House

★★★★ GUEST HOUSE

☎ 01631 562476 📠 01631 564339
Corran Esplanade PA34 5AQ
e-mail: info@corriemarhouse.co.uk
web: www.corriemarhouse.co.uk
dir: A85 to Oban. Down hill in right lane & follow sign for Gamavan
at mini rdbt onto Esplanade

Billy and Sandra Russell have created a stylish haven of tranquillity
at this detached Victorian house close to the town centre. Bedrooms
are furnished with panache, range from massive to cosy, and even
include a suite. Those to the front of the house have stunning views
across Oban Bay to the Isle of Mull. Expect a substantial breakfast
and friendly attentive service.

Rooms 9 en suite 4 annexe en suite (3 fmly) (1 GF) **Facilities** tea/
coffee Cen ht **Parking** 9 **Notes** ⊗

Greencourt

★★★★ GUEST HOUSE

☎ 01631 563987
Benvoullin Rd PA34 5EF
e-mail: relax@greencourt-oban.co.uk
dir: At Oban, left at Kings Knoll Hotel, over x-rds & follow Dalriach
Rd. Pass leisure centre & bowling green on left, then left. Left again,
sharp left onto lane, Greencourt 2nd house on left

This welcoming family home stands on an elevated location
overlooking the bowling green and leisure centre. The delightful
detached house has attractive, comfortable bedrooms of varying
sizes, and all are well equipped. Freshly prepared breakfasts are
served in the bright airy dining room, which has lovely views.

Rooms 6 rms (5 en suite) (1 pri facs) (6 GF) S £35-£38; D £70-£76
Facilities tea/coffee Cen ht Wi-fi **Parking** 6 **Notes** LB ⊗ Closed Dec-
Jan

Lancaster

★★ GUEST ACCOMMODATION

☎ 01631 562587 📄 01631 562587
Corran Esplanade PA34 5AD
e-mail: lancasteroban@btconnect.com
dir: On seafront next to Columba's Cathedral

A family-run establishment on the esplanade that offers budget accommodation; many bedrooms boast lovely views out over the bay towards the Isle of Mull. Public areas include a choice of lounges and bars that also benefit from the panoramic views. A swimming pool, sauna and jacuzzi are added benefits.

Rooms 27 rms (24 en suite) (3 fmly) (27 smoking) **Facilities** TVL tea/coffee Cen ht Licensed ⓢ Sauna Pool Table jacuzzi, steam room **Conf** Max 30 Thtr 30 Class 20 Board 12 **Parking** 20 **Notes** LB

Coast

⊚⊚ Modern

Contemporary design and fabulously fresh local seafood

☎ 01631 569900
104 George St PA34 5NT
e-mail: coastoban@yahoo.co.uk
web: www.coastoban.co.uk
dir: On main street in town centre

Within the granite façade of a former bank, this impeccably-styled Oban restaurant has created a soothing interior of trendy cream and cocoa hues, pale wood, classy fabrics, metal and modern art. It's all rather a quantum leap from the neighbouring chippies, as is the food: the kitchen takes a modern Scottish line to deliver imaginative but uncomplicated dishes that rely on the zinging fresh quality of local raw materials - wriggling-fresh fish and seafood, for example, only has to cross the road after it is landed on Oban's quayside. Among starters, might be crab with crème fraîche, avocado, tomato mousse and pesto, followed by pan-seared scallops with chive gnocchi, buttered leeks and roast Stornoway black pudding; round it off with chocolate mousse with peanut brittle and tonka bean ice cream.

Chef Richard Fowler **Owner** Richard & Nicola Fowler
Times 12-2/5.30-9.30 Closed 25 Dec, Sun (Nov-Mar), L Sun
Prices Fixed L 2 course £12, Starter £4.50-£8.95, Main £12.50-£22.50, Dessert £5.95, Service optional, Groups min 8 service 10%
Wines 19 bottles over £20, 22 bottles under £20, 6 by glass
Notes Early eve menu 2-3 course £12-£15, Vegetarian available
Seats 46 **Parking** On street

Airds

★★★★ SMALL HOTEL

⊚⊚⊚ Modern British V 🍷NOTABLE WINE LIST

Memorable surroundings and high-quality seasonal food

☎ 01631 730236 📄 01631 730535
PA38 4DF
e-mail: airds@airds-hotel.com
web: www.airds-hotel.com
dir: From A828 (Oban to Fort William road), turn at Appin signed Port Appin. Hotel 2.5m on left

The views are stunning from this luxurious small hotel on the shores of Loch Linnhe where the staff are delightful and nothing is too much trouble. The well-equipped bedrooms provide style and luxury whilst many bathrooms are furnished in marble and have power showers. Comfortable lounges with deep sofas and roaring fires provide the ideal retreat for relaxation, this is a real get-away-from-it-all experience. Low ceilings, rich fabrics and candlelit tables coupled with large windows to drink in the surroundings make for a relaxed and romantic atmosphere in the dining room. The very short menu is modern British with Scottish and French influences. Fish and seafood comes fresh from the Oban fishing boats and the small kitchen team sets great store by seasonality. Combinations are uncomplicated allowing the clean, clear flavours of the superior local ingredients to shine through. Hand-dived local scallops with Stornoway black pudding and grape chutney might start, followed by local turbot and salmon wrapped in pastry with mushroom, served with a beurre blanc, while desserts include marbled chocolate cake with orange sauce. Service is formal but not stuffy, and the wine list has something for the most erudite of wine drinkers.

Rooms 11 (3 fmly) (2 GF) **S** £180-£370; **D** £245-£435 (incl. bkfst & dinner)* **Facilities** FTV Putt green ⚑ Xmas New Year Wi-fi **Conf** Class 16 Board 16 Thtr 16 **Parking** 20 **Notes** RS Nov-Jan Civ Wed 40

Chef J Paul Burns **Owner** Mr & Mrs S McKivragan **Restaurant Times** 12-1.45/7.30-9.30 **Prices** Fixed L 2 course fr £21.95, Fixed D 4 course £49.50, Service optional **Wines** 151 bottles over £20, 13 bottles under £20, 6 by glass **Notes** Sunday L, Vegetarian menu, Dress restrictions, Smart casual at D, no jeans/trainers/T-shirts **Seats** 32, Pr/dining room 8 **Children** Portions, Menu

The Pierhouse Hotel & Seafood Restaurant

★★★ SMALL HOTEL

◉ Modern International ✪

☎ 01631 730302 & 730622 📄 01631 730400
PA38 4DE
e-mail: reservations@pierhousehotel.co.uk
web: www.pierhousehotel.co.uk
dir: A828 from Ballachulish to Oban. In Appin right at Port Appin & Lismore ferry sign. After 2.5m left after post office, hotel at end of road by pier

Originally the residence of the Pier Master, with parts of the building dating back to the 19th century, this hotel is on the shores of Loch Linnhe with picture-postcard views to the islands of Lismore and Mull. The beautifully appointed, individually designed bedrooms have Wi-fi access and include Arran Aromatics toiletries. The hotel has a Finnish sauna, and also offers a range of treatments. You arrive along a narrow road from Appin, or by boat, tying up to one of the hotel's ten moorings near the pier. It prides itself on the freshness and quality of its seafood, game and meats, and sources virtually all such produce locally. On offer are a selection of menus featuring oysters hand-picked from the Lismore beds; mussels and langoustines harvested from Loch Linnhe and Loch Etive; and lobsters and crab kept fresh in creels at the end of the pier. As well as fish, there are several seafood platters – the Pierhouse, for example, consists of those local langoustines and mussels, as well as plump grilled Mull scallops, oysters, fresh and smoked salmon and a roll mop. There are alternatives to seafood, such as Highland fillet steak served on creamy herb mash with a whisky and peppercorn sauce; and pappardelle with fresh mushrooms, herbs, white wine, garlic and cream topped with Gruyère cheese. Bedrooms include two with four-poster beds and loch views, and three family rooms. Country sports enthusiasts will love the deer-stalking and fly-fishing, both of which the hotel can arrange.

Rooms 12 (3 fmly) (6 GF) **S** £70-£100; **D** £100-£160 (incl. bkfst)
Facilities FTV ⚑ Aromatherapy Massage Sauna New Year Wi-fi **Conf** Class 20 Board 20 Thtr 20 Del from £125 to £150 **Parking** 20 **Notes** Closed 25-26 Dec Civ Wed 70

Chef Stuart McMillan **Owners** Nicholas & Nicolette Horne **Restaurant Times** 12-2.30/6.30-9.30 Closed 25-26 Dec **Prices** Starter £4.95-£9.95 Main £13.50-£32.50 Dessert £4.50-£6.95 **Wines** 8 bottles over £20, 23 bottles under £20, 5 by glass **Notes** Sunday L, Vegetarian available Groups min 8 service 15% **Seats** 45 Pr/dining 20 **Children** Portions, Menu

Rosslea Hall Hotel

Ⓤ

☎ 01436 439955 📄 01436 820897
Ferry Road G84 8NF
web: www.mckeverhotels.co.uk
dir: On A814, opposite church

Currently the rating for this establishment is not confirmed. This may be due to a change of ownership or because it has only recently

joined the AA rating scheme.

Rooms 30 (3 fmly) (2 GF) **S** £69-£109; **D** £89-£169 (incl. bkfst)
Facilities FTV Direct dial tea/coffee Wi-fi **Parking** 30 **Conf** Thtr 150 Class 60 Board 80

Creggans Inn

★★★ 82% HOTEL

◉◉ Modern British ✪

Fine food in breathtaking location

☎ 01369 860279 📄 01369 860637
PA27 8BX
e-mail: info@creggans-inn.co.uk
web: www.creggans-inn.co.uk
dir: A82 from Glasgow, at Tarbet take A83 towards Cairndow, left onto A815 to Strachur

This charming, family-run country hotel occupies a stunning spot overlooking Loch Fyne, set against a breathtaking backdrop of rugged, unspoilt countryside. Many of the bedrooms are generous in size and are enhanced with picture postcard views onto the loch. During the cooler months open log fires are lit in the bar lounge and restaurant. Wi-fi is available throughout. Sit with a glass of whisky from a large selection and take in the fabulous vista as you peruse the menus in the elegant, terracotta-painted restaurant. Five picture windows overlook the hotel garden and loch beyond. In summertime, posies of home-grown flowers decorate the tables. In winter, the real log fire and candlelit tables create an intimate atmosphere, and the baby grand piano stands open, inviting guests to play. Scottish dishes star on a menu that makes the most of local produce; sautéed salmon fillet on a fine vegetable and vermouth sauce could be followed by seared loin of Balagowan venison with celeriac purée, Lyonnaise potatoes, red onion and thyme jus.

Rooms 14 (2 fmly) **S** £75-£115; **D** £100-£180 (incl. bkfst) **Facilities** New Year Wi-fi **Conf** Del from £120 to £160 **Parking** 16 **Notes** LB Civ Wed 80

Chef Gordon Smilie Owner The MacLellan Family Restaurant Times -7-9 Closed 25-26 Dec, L all week Prices Fixed D 4 course fr £37, Service optional Wines 32 bottles over £20, 33 bottles under £20, 6 by glass Notes Vegetarian available, Dress restrictions, Smart casual Seats 35 Children Portions, Menu

---

TARBERT LOCH FYNE   **Map 2 NR86**

Stonefield Castle

★★★★ 73% HOTEL

◉ Modern British

Plenty of local flavours in an old baronial keep

☎ 01880 820836   📠 01880 820929
PA29 6YJ
e-mail: reservations.stonefieldcastle.@ohiml.com
web: www.oxfordhotelsandinns.com
dir: From Glasgow take M8 towards Erskine Bridge, follow signs for Loch Lomond on A82. From Arrochar follow signs for A83 through Inveraray & Lochgilphead, hotel on left 2m before Tarbert

This fine castle commands a superb lochside setting amidst beautiful woodland gardens renowned for their rhododendrons - visit in late spring to see them at their best. Bedrooms are split between the main house and a purpose-built wing. Elegant public rooms are a feature, and the restaurant is rich in baronial elegance, with picture windows commanding stunning views over Loch Fyne. Food offers a good balance of classical and modern cooking, with an emphasis on quality produce, including seafood landed at Tarbert and local estate game, accurate cooking and good flavours. Take crisp, well-balanced lobster and halibut fishcakes to start, treacle-glazed pork belly with black pudding, white bean and apple mash for main course, and a light, fluffy orange syrup sponge with cardamom syrup for pudding.

Rooms 32 (2 fmly) (10 GF) **S** £55-£140; **D** £65-£180 (incl. bkfst)* **Facilities** Xmas New Year Wi-fi **Conf** Class 40 Board 50 Thtr 120 Del from £135 to £195 **Services** Lift **Parking** 50 **Notes** LB Civ Wed 100

Chef Oscar Sinjorgo Owner Oxford Hotels & Inns Restaurant Times 12-9 Prices Starter £5-£15, Main £9-£30, Dessert £5-£15, Service optional Wines 23 bottles over £20, 38 bottles under £20, 6 by glass Notes Sunday L, Vegetarian available, Dress restrictions, Smart casual Seats 120, Pr/dining room 40 Children Portions, Menu

---

TAYVALLICH   **Map 2 NR78**

Tayvallich Inn

☎ 01546 870282
PA31 8PL
dir: From Lochgilphead take A816 then B841/B8025

Following a change of hands in recent times, the Tayvallich Inn is now run by Glen and Lynne Hyde. The property was converted from an old bus garage in 1976. The name translates as 'house in the pass' and it has the most spectacular setting. The inn stands by a natural harbour at the head of Loch Sween with stunning views over the anchorage, particularly from the decking, where food and drinks can be enjoyed. Those seated inside can gaze out over the village and Tayvallich Bay from the large picture windows. A selection of fine wines and single malts are served as well as Loch Fyne Ales. Not

surprisingly given the location, fresh seasonal seafood is the house speciality, available along with good quality pub food. Those interested in the works of 19th century engineer Thomas Telford will find plenty of bridges and piers in the area.

Open Closed: 25-26 Dec, Mon (Nov-Mar) **Bar Meals** L served all wk 12-2.15 D served all wk 6-8.45 **Restaurant** L served all wk 12-2.15 booking required D served all wk 6-8.45 booking required ⊕ FREE HOUSE ◀ Tennents, Guinness, Loch Fyne Ales. **Facilities** Children's menu Dogs allowed Garden Parking

---

TIGHNABRUAICH   **Map 2 NR97**

An Lochan

★★★ SMALL HOTEL

◉◉ Modern Scottish ♨

Complex modern cooking with wonderful sea views

☎ 01700 811239   📠 01700 811300
Shore Rd PA21 2BE
e-mail: info@anlochan.co.uk
web: www.anlochan.co.uk
dir: From Strachur on A886 right onto A8003 to Tighnabruaich. Hotel on right at bottom of hill

This outstanding family-run hotel provides high levels of personal care from the proprietors and their locally recruited staff. Set just yards from the loch shore, stunning views are guaranteed from many rooms. Guests can expect to find Egyptian cotton sheets, fluffy towels and locally produced toiletries in the individually-styled, luxuriously appointed bedrooms. A choice of dining options is available, either the wood-floored Deck, or the more formal Crustacean room, with its enclosed terrace making the most of those marine views. The modern Scottish cooking features some vibrant ideas, as in a pairing of pork cheek and foie gras in a terrine, accompanied by red onion jam and a 'sour apple explosion'. Mains introduce a gentler note in the form of infusions and foams, in multi-faceted dishes such as venison loin cooked sous-vide, with braised red cabbage, blackcurrant jelly, roast parsnip and a potato infusion. Even desserts keep things interesting, with combinations such as carrot and orange fondant, with beetroot tartare and lavender ice cream.

Rooms 11 **Facilities** Sailing Fishing Windsurfing Riding New Year Wi-fi **Conf** Class 20 Board 10 **Parking** 20 **Notes** Closed 4 days Xmas Civ Wed 40

Chef Paul Scott Owner The McKie family Restaurant Times 12-2.30/6.30-9 Closed Xmas, Prices Starter £7-£10, Main £11-£25, Dessert £5-£8, Service optional Wines 50 bottles over £20, 14 bottles under £20, 6 by glass Notes Tasting menu available, Sunday L, Vegetarian available Seats 35, Pr/dining room 20 Children Portions

Kilmarnock Water in Dean Park.

EAST AYRSHIRE

DALRYMPLE — Map 2 NS31

The Kirkton Inn

☎ 01292 560241 📄 01292 560835
1 Main St KA6 6DF
e-mail: kirkton@cqm.co.uk
dir: 6m SE from centre of Ayr just off A77

This inn's motto is, 'There are no strangers here, only friends who have never met', and the welcoming atmosphere makes it easy to feel at home. It's a stoutly traditional setting, with open fires and polished brasses, set in the village of Dalrymple. As we went to press we understand there was a change of hands.

Open all wk ⊕ FREE HOUSE ◀ Belhaven Best, Tennents.
Facilities Dogs allowed Garden Parking

GATEHEAD — Map 2 NS33

The Cochrane Inn

☎ 01563 570122
45 Main Rd KA2 0AP
dir: From Glasgow A77 to Kilmarnock, then A759 to Gatehead

There's a friendly, bustling atmosphere inside this traditional village centre pub, which sits just a short drive from the Ayrshire coast. The menus combine British and international flavours. At lunch this might translate as cullen skink with crayfish tails followed by penne Arrabiata or spicy lamb curry. In the evening, maybe crispy bacon and houmous on toast ahead of a hearty steak pie with carrots and mash.

Open all wk noon-2.30 5.30 onwards (Sun noon 9) **Bar Meals** food served all day **Restaurant** food served all day ⊕ FREE HOUSE ◀ John Smiths. **Facilities** Children's menu Garden Parking

KILMARNOCK — Map 2 NS43

Fenwick Hotel

★★★ 77% HOTEL

☎ 01560 600478 📄 01560 600334
Fenwick KA3 6AU
e-mail: fenwick@bestwestern.co.uk
web: www.thefenwickhotel.co.uk
dir: B7038 right signed Fenwick. Through 1st rdbt, left at next. Hotel 1st on left

Benefiting from a great location alongside the M77 and offering easy links to Ayr, Kilmarnock and Glasgow. The spacious bedrooms are thoughtfully equipped; complimentary Wi-fi is available throughout the hotel. The bright restaurant offers both formal and informal dining and there are two bars to choose from.

Rooms 30 (1 fmly) (9 GF) **Facilities** STV Xmas New Year Wi-fi
Conf Class 70 Thtr 160 **Notes** LB Civ Wed 110

Travelodge Kilmarnock

BUDGET HOTEL

☎ 0871 984 6149 📄 01563 573810
Bellfield Interchange KA1 5LQ
web: www.travelodge.co.uk
dir: On Bellfield Interchange, just off A77

Travelodge offers good quality, good value, modern accommodation. Ideal for families, the spacious en suite bedrooms include remote-control TV, tea and coffee-making facilities and comfortable beds. Meals can be taken at the nearby family restaurant. See also the Hotel Groups pages on theAA.com.

Rooms 40 **S** fr £29; **D** fr £29

SORN — Map 2 NS52

The Sorn Inn

★★★★ RESTAURANT WITH ROOMS

⊛⊛ Modern British ❁

Contemporary-styled coaching inn with modern cuisine

☎ 01290 551305 📄 01290 553470
35 Main St KA5 6HU
e-mail: craig@sorninn.com
dir: From A77 take A76 to Mauchline. Take B743, 4m to Sorn

Centrally situated in the village, which is convenient for many of Ayrshire's attractions, The Sorn Inn sets out its manifesto clearly as a 'gastro-pub with rooms'. And it does exactly what it says on the tin with great flair. Inside, the whitewashed 18th century coaching inn puts on modern clothes in a glowing, rustic-posh décor. The freshly decorated bedrooms have comfortable beds and good facilities. The restaurant has restyled its menu to offer a medley of fine dining and brasserie-style dishes, whether you choose to eat in the cosier pub-style Chop House or the rather more chic fine-dining restaurant. Well-established favourites from the modern British arsenal are raised to a higher level by judicious tweaks and twists on a wide-ranging, seasonally-changing menu. Kick off with a salad of smoked wild mallard breast with pickled walnut vinaigrette, before chump of lamb with chorizo crushed potatoes, balsamic braised shallots, sun-dried tomatoes and rosemary jus.

Rooms 4 en suite (1 fmly) S £40-£50; D £70-£95* **Facilities** tea/coffee Dinner available Direct Dial Cen ht Wi-fi Fishing **Parking** 9 **Notes** Closed 2wks Jan RS Mon Closed

Chef Craig Grant **Owner** The Grant Partnership **Restaurant Times** 12-2.30/6-9 Closed 2 wks Jan, Mon, D Sun **Prices** Fixed L 2 course £14.95-£15.95, Fixed D 3 course £23.95-£24.95, Starter £4-£5.50, Main £9-£23.50, Dessert £4.50-£5.50, Service optional, Groups min 8 service 10% **Wines** 42 bottles over £20, 17 bottles under £20, 13 by glass **Notes** Sunday L, Vegetarian available **Seats** 42 **Children** Portions, Menu

45

DALRY
Map 2 NS24

Braidwoods

@@ Modern Scottish

Creative flair from a talented husband-and-wife-team

☎ 01294 833544 ▤ 01294 833553
Drumastle Mill Cottage KA24 4LN
e-mail: keithbraidwood@btconnect.com
dir: 1m from Dalry on Saltcoats road

With two very talented and passionate chef-patrons in the kitchen, Braidwoods delivers a level of culinary expertise way beyond what you might expect from its rustic whitewashed cottage exterior. The two dining areas within are a natty mix of dark beams and exposed stone with a modern décor of jaunty stripes, hues of blue and white and stylish high-backed metal chairs. Husband-and-wife-team Keith and Nicola Braidwood both have impressive CVs, and know that any good kitchen has to start by getting the basics right, so their approach to local sourcing is of the highest order. This painstaking preparation pays off in delivering top-quality modern Scottish dishes of intense flavour and clarity. Four course dinners might start with seared hand-dived Wester Ross scallops, perfectly timed and served on a bed of cardamom, coriander and lentil dhal, then procede via a creamy soup of local carrots and cumin to honey-glazed breast of Gressingham duck with a wee cottage pie of duck confit.

Times 12-1.45/7-9 Closed 25-26 Dec, 1st 3 wks Jan, 1st 2 wks Sep, Mon, L Tue (Sun Etr-Sep), D Sun

IRVINE
Map 2 NS33

Menzies Irvine

★★★★ 74% HOTEL

☎ 01294 274272 ▤ 01294 277287
46 Annick Rd KA11 4LD
e-mail: irvine@menzieshotels.co.uk
web: www.menzieshotels.co.uk
dir: From A78 at Warrix Interchange follow Irvine Central signs. At rdbt 2nd exit (town centre). At next rdbt right onto A71/Kilmarnock. Hotel 100mtrs on left

Situated on the edge of Irvine with good transportation links (including Prestwick Airport just seven miles away), this is a well-presented hotel that has an extremely friendly team with good customer care awareness. After major refurbishment the decor is contemporary throughout, and there is a brasserie-style restaurant, cocktail bar and spacious lounge.

Rooms 128 (14 fmly) (64 GF) **S** £59-£160; **D** £59-£160*
Facilities STV ⊕ ♪ 9 Putt green Fishing Xmas New Year Wi-fi
Conf Class 140 Board 100 Thtr 280 Del from £95 to £135*
Parking 220 **Notes** Civ Wed 200

LARGS
Map 2 NS25

Willowbank

★★★ 74% HOTEL

☎ 01475 672311 & 675435 ▤ 01475 689027
96 Greenock Rd KA30 8PG
e-mail: iaincsmith@btconnect.com
dir: On A78

A relaxed, friendly atmosphere prevails at this well maintained hotel where hanging baskets are a feature in summer months. The nicely decorated bedrooms are, in general, spacious and offer comfortable modern appointments. The public areas include a large, well-stocked bar, a lounge and a dining room.

Rooms 30 (4 fmly) **S** £60-£100; **D** £80-£140 (incl. bkfst)* **Facilities** ♪ Xmas **Conf** Class 100 Board 40 Thtr 200 Del from £90 to £120*
Parking 40 **Notes** LB

South Whittlieburn Farm

★★★★ ⌂ BED AND BREAKFAST

☎ 01475 675881 ▤ 01475 675080
Brisbane Glen KA30 8SN
e-mail: largsbandb@southwhittlieburnfarm.freeserve.co.uk
dir: 2m NE of Largs off A78 signed Brisbane Glen, after Vikingar centre

This comfortable and welcoming farmhouse is on a working sheep farm surrounded by gently rolling countryside. The attractive bedrooms are well equipped with all having DVD and video players. There is a spacious ground-floor lounge and a bright airy dining room where delicious breakfasts are served.

Rooms 3 en suite (1 fmly) **S** £35-£37.50; **D** £59-£65* **Facilities** STV FTV TVL tea/coffee Cen ht Golf 18 **Parking** 10 **Notes** LB ⊗ RS Xmas ⊕

AYR   Map 2 NS32

The Western House Hotel

★★★★ 84% HOTEL

@@ Traditional British

Modern and traditional cuisine within sight of the racing at Ayr

☎ 0870 055 5510   📠 0870 055 5515
2 Whitletts Rd KA8 0HA
e-mail: pdavies@westernhousehotel.co.uk
dir: From Glasgow M77 then A77 towards Ayr. At Whitletts rdbt take A719 towards town centre

This impressive hotel is located in its own attractive gardens on the edge of Ayr racecourse. Bedrooms in the main house are superbly appointed, and the courtyard rooms offer much comfort too. The staff are attentive and welcoming. Nicely appointed day rooms include the light and airy Jockey Club restaurant, adorned with old monochrome racing photos against a relaxing cappuccino-hued decorative scheme. A mix of modern and traditional Scottish cooking is on offer, running from well-timed langoustine risotto, followed by herb-crusted rack of lamb with sugar snaps and onion confit, to more complex dishes such as lemon sole fillets filled with crab and salmon mousseline, with fennel and leek 'spaghetti' and lemon butter. Super-rich Scots tablet might be the basis for an ice cream to accompany textbook tarte Tatin, or there could be ginger-based lemon and champagne cheesecake with citrus syrup. Home-made breads are of real quality.

Rooms 49 (39 annexe) (39 fmly) (16 GF) **Facilities** STV Xmas New Year **Conf** Class 300 Board 36 Thtr 1200 **Services** Lift **Parking** 250 **Notes** ⊗ Civ Wed 200

Restaurant Times 12-2/7-9.30

Fairfield House

★★★★ 78% HOTEL

@@ Traditional British

Modern Scottish cooking in hotel with sea views

☎ 01292 267461   📠 01292 261456
12 Fairfield Rd KA7 2AR
e-mail: reservations@fairfieldhotel.co.uk
dir: From A77 towards Ayr South (A30). Follow town centre signs, down Miller Rd, left, then right into Fairfield Rd

Situated in a leafy cul-de-sac close to the esplanade, this magnificent Victorian mansion enjoys stunning seascapes towards to the Isle of Arran. Bedrooms are in either modern or classical styles, the latter featuring impressive bathrooms. Public areas provide stylish, modern rooms in which to relax. Once the home of a Glasgow tea merchant, the seafront hotel is full of original features with the Martin's Bar and Grill boasting Grecian-style pillars as well as feature plants and original artwork. An outside terrace makes the most of the views and is spot-on for pre-meal drinks. The cooking is unpretentious and simple with a focus on local ingredients in the Scottish dishes. Try roast loin of Scotch venison with braised red

cabbage, fondant potatoes, honey-roast root vegetables and berry vinegar reduction, finishing with pineapple tarte Tatin and vanilla ice cream. There is a wide selection of fine wines, plus a good collection of single malts.

Rooms 44 (4 annexe) (3 fmly) (9 GF) **S** £75-£105; **D** £89-£169 (incl. bkfst)* **Facilities** STV FTV ♨ supervised Gym Fitness room Sauna Steam room Xmas New Year Wi-fi **Conf** Class 50 Board 40 Thtr 80 Del from £125 to £145 **Services** Lift **Parking** 50 **Notes** LB ⊗ Civ Wed 150

Owner G Martin **Restaurant Times** 11am-9.30pm **Prices** Food prices not confirmed for 2010. Please telephone for details. **Wines** 34 bottles over £20, 16 bottles under £20, 6 by glass **Notes** Air con **Seats** 80, Pr/dining room 12 **Children** Portions, Menu

Enterkine Country House

★★★★ 77% COUNTRY HOUSE HOTEL

@@ Traditional V

The best of Scottish produce in an art deco country house

☎ 01292 520580   📠 01292 521582
Annbank KA6 5AL
e-mail: mail@enterkine.com
dir: 5m east of Ayr on B743

This luxurious art deco country mansion dates from the 1930s and retains many original features, notably some splendid bathroom suites. The focus is very much on dining, and in country house tradition there is no bar, drinks being served in the elegant lounge and library. The well-proportioned bedrooms are furnished and equipped to high standards, many with lovely countryside views.

Inside, there's something of the feel of an Agatha Christie novel set in a posh private house, with food served in an expansive restaurant with low ceilings, a log fire in winter and Shaker-style panelling. The kitchen deals in French-influenced Scottish country house-style cooking using materials such as the estate's own pork, local berries and Buccleuch organic beef. Straightforward, modern-style dishes might include Arbroath smokie and goat's cheese soufflé with spinach, red pepper and Meaux mustard, followed by Blackface Castle Douglas lamb three ways - roast loin, caramelised sweetbreads and seared kidneys. Meals end with lush desserts such as dark Valrhona chocolate fondant with chocolate ice cream and griottine cherries.

Rooms 13 (7 annexe) (6 fmly) (5 GF) **Facilities** FTV Beauty treatments Clay pigeon shooting Quad biking Archery ♫ Xmas New Year Wi-fi **Conf** Class 140 Board 140 Thtr 200 **Parking** 40 **Notes** Civ Wed 70

Chef Paul Moffat **Owner** Mr Browne **Restaurant Times** 12-2/7-9 **Prices** Fixed L 3 course £18.50-£25, Fixed D 4 course £30-£45, Service optional **Wines** 36 bottles over £20, 14 bottles under £20, 4 by glass **Notes** Tasting menu available, Sunday L, Vegetarian menu, Dress restrictions, Jackets required **Seats** 40, Pr/dining room 14 **Children** Portions, Menu

Savoy Park

★★★ 80% HOTEL

☎ 01292 266112 🗐 01292 611488
16 Racecourse Rd KA7 2UT
e-mail: mail@savoypark.com
dir: From A77 follow A70 for 2m, through Parkhouse Str, left into Beresford Terr, 1st right into Bellevue Rd

This well-established hotel retains many of its traditional values including friendly, attentive service. Public rooms feature impressive panelled walls, ornate ceilings and open fires. The restaurant is reminiscent of a Highland shooting lodge and offers a wide ranging, good-value menu to suit all tastes. The large superior bedrooms retain a classical elegance while others are smart and modern; all have well equipped modern bathrooms.

Rooms 15 (3 fmly) **S** £50-£80; **D** £60-£120 (incl. bkfst)*
Facilities FTV Xmas New Year Wi-fi Child facilities **Conf** Class 40 Board 30 Thtr 50 Del from £80 to £120 **Parking** 60 **Notes** LB Civ Wed 100

Express by Holiday Inn Ayr

BUDGET HOTEL

☎ 0870 890 5100 🗐 0870 890 5200
Wheatpark Place KA8 9RT
web: www.hiexpress.co.uk

A modern hotel ideal for families and business travellers. Fresh and uncomplicated, the spacious rooms include Sky TV, power shower and tea and coffee-making facilities. Continental buffet breakfast is included in the room rate; other meals may be taken at the nearby family pub or restaurant. See also the Hotel Groups pages on theAA.com.

Rooms 84

Travelodge Ayr

BUDGET HOTEL

☎ 08719 846 321 🗐 01292 880357
Highfield Dr KA8 9SH
web: www.travelodge.co.uk
dir: A719, next rdbt 3rd exit onto B743

Travelodge offers good quality, good value, modern accommodation. Ideal for families, the spacious en suite bedrooms include remote-control TV, tea and coffee-making facilities and comfortable beds. Meals can be taken at the nearby family restaurant. See also the Hotel Groups pages on theAA.com.

Rooms 56 **S** fr £29; **D** fr £29

The Crescent

★★★★★ GUEST HOUSE

☎ 01292 287329
26 Bellevue Crescent KA7 2DR
e-mail: joyce&mike@26crescent.co.uk
web: www.26crescent.co.uk
dir: Leave A79 onto rdbt, 3rd exit onto King St. Left onto Bellevue Crescent

Located in a quiet residential area of Ayr, close to the seafront, town centre and race course, this guest house offers a traditional warm welcome with well appointed and comfortable bedrooms. Bathrooms are of a high standard, as is the hearty breakfast served on individual tables in the charming dining room.

Rooms 5 en suite S £50; D £70-£80* **Facilities** FTV tea/coffee Cen ht Wi-fi **Notes** LB ⊗

Daviot House

★★★★ GUEST HOUSE

☎ 01292 269678
12 Queens Ter KA7 1DU
e-mail: daviothouse@hotmail.com
web: www.daviothouse.com
dir: Off A719 onto Wellington Sq & Bath Place, turn right

This well-maintained Victorian house stands in a peaceful location close to the beach and town centre. Bedrooms are modern in style and well equipped. Hearty breakfasts are served in the dining room. Daviot House is a member of Golf South Ayrshire - golf booking service for local municipal courses, so let your hosts know if you'd like a round booked.

Rooms 5 rms (4 en suite) (1 pri facs) (1 fmly) S £35-£45; D £60-£85* **Facilities** FTV tea/coffee Cen ht Wi-fi **Notes** LB ⊗ No Children

Greenan Lodge

★★★★ BED AND BREAKFAST

☎ 01292 443939
39 Dunure, Doonfoot KA7 4HR
e-mail: helen@greenanlodge.com
dir: 2m S of town centre on A719 (coast road)

Guests are made to feel truly welcome at this modern bungalow in a quiet residential area, convenient for the coast and attractions around Ayr. The bright, well-furnished bedrooms offer numerous extras and there is a spacious lounge. Expect a generous Scottish breakfast.

Rooms 3 en suite (3 GF) S fr £45; D fr £60* **Facilities** TVL tea/coffee Cen ht **Parking** 10 **Notes** No Children 7yrs ☺

Fouters

☺☺ French, Scottish

Intimate basement restaurant with ambitious cooking

☎ 01292 261391 ▤ 01292 619323
2A Academy St KA7 1HS
e-mail: chef@fouters.co.uk
dir: Town centre, opposite Town Hall

An old bank vault, dating from 1772, provides the setting for this small basement restaurant, located down a narrow, cobbled lane in the seaside town of Ayr. The vaulted ceiling and flagstone floor provide atmosphere, while linen-clothed tables and modern artworks add a touch of warmth and comfort. The imaginative menus are based on great ingredients, including plenty of local seafood and game. Main-course duck, pink and tender, is set on a bed of red cabbage and sultanas with chocolate and Grand Marnier sauce - a fine combination. Choux beignets, covered in cinnamon, filled with Chantilly cream and served with apple purée and Calvados ice cream is an indulgent end to proceedings.

Chef Adele Wylie, Victoria Semple **Owner** Barry Rooney
Times 12-2/6-9 Closed 2 wks Feb, 2 wks Nov, 1 Jan, Sun-Mon
Prices Starter £3.95-£6.50, Main £12.95-£24.95, Dessert £3.95-£6.50, Service optional **Wines** 22 bottles over £20, 10 bottles under £20, 3 by glass **Notes** Pre-theatre D Tue-Sat 6-7pm 2/3 course £14.95-16.95, Vegetarian available, Air con **Seats** 36, Pr/dining room 22 **Children** Portions **Parking** On street

Glenapp Castle

★★★★★ HOTEL

☺☺☺ Modern British V ☺

Elegant castle hideaway with accomplished, innovative cuisine

☎ 01465 831212 ▤ 01465 831000
KA26 0NZ
e-mail: enquiries@glenappcastle.com
web: www.glenappcastle.com
dir: 1m from A77 near Ballantrae

Glenapp Castle is a romantic Victorian confection of towers and turrets in 36 acres of heavenly grounds that are an oasis of mature woodland and exotic colour amid the native bracken and gorse. Impeccably furnished bedrooms are graced with antiques and period pieces. Breathtaking views of Arran and Ailsa Craig can be enjoyed from the delightful, sumptuous day rooms and from many of the bedrooms. Guests should make a point of walking round the wonderful grounds, to include the azalea lake and walled vegetable gardens with their fine restored greenhouses. The stately interior is all opulence - endless expanses of oak panels, chandeliers, antiques, oil paintings - and the kitchen team rises to the occasion. Dishes here are designed to wow at every stage; cooking is sharp, innovative, accurate and, when necessary, highly technical. The very finest from Scotland's larder, including fruit, veg and herbs from the castle's gardens, underpins the menus, which run from three courses at lunch, to well-balanced six-course dinner menus. An amuse-bouche of carrot and vanilla velouté with liquorice cream precedes a terrine of rabbit and Morteau sausage with home-made piccalilli and hazelnuts. The pace continues with a fish course - pan-fried red mullet with langoustine and minestrone consommé, then a choice appears at the main course - perhaps roasted grey leg partridge with salsify, red cabbage and a cannelloni of confit leg. Perfectly-ripened Scottish cheeses come before dessert: Scottish cranachan soufflé with raspberries and raspberry sorbet. Formal service is correct without being intimidating.

Rooms 17 (2 fmly) (7 GF) **S** £255-£455; **D** £375-£575 (incl. bkfst & dinner)* **Facilities** STV FTV ☺ ☺ New Year Wi-fi **Conf** Class 12 Board 17 Thtr 17 Del from £295 to £495* **Services** Lift **Parking** 20 **Notes** LB Closed Jan-mid Mar Civ Wed 40

Chef Adam Stokes **Owner** Graham & Fay Cowan **Restaurant**
Times 12.30-2/7-10 Closed 2 Jan-14 Mar, Xmas, **Prices** Fixed L 3 course fr £35, Service optional **Wines** 200 bottles over £20, 8 by glass **Notes** Fixed D 6 course £55, Sunday L, Vegetarian menu **Seats** 34, Pr/dining room 20 **Children** Portions, Menu

Balkissock Lodge

★★★★ 🛏️ 🍽️ GUEST ACCOMMODATION

☎ 01465 831537
Balkissock KA26 0LP
e-mail: howard.balkissock@btinternet.com
dir: S through Ballantrae (A77) over river, 1st left at campsite sign.
Right at T-junct, 1.5m

A warm and genuine welcome awaits after a scenic drive. Set in the
rolling South Ayrshire countryside, surrounded by wonderful gardens,
Balkissock Lodge is a perfect getaway. New owners show great
hospitality and customer care in a very comfortable and well-
appointed property.

Rooms 3 en suite (1 fmly) (2 GF) **Facilities** TVL tea/coffee Cen ht
Parking 3 **Notes** ⊗ No Children 🍽️

Map 2 NS21

Dunduff (NS265160)

★★★★ FARMHOUSE

☎ 01292 500225 📠 01292 500222
Dunure KA7 4LH
Mrs A Gemmell
e-mail: gemmelldunduff@aol.com
dir: On A719, 400yds past village school

Parts of this working farm date from the 15th and 17th centuries. It
stands on an elevated position with stunning views across the Firth
of the Clyde towards Arran and the Mull of Kintyre. Bedrooms are
comfortable and well-equipped, with a comfortable lounge enhancing
the "home away from home" feel. Expect genuine Scottish hospitality,
and breakfast specialities including locally smoked kippers.

Rooms 3 rms (2 en suite) (1 pri facs) (2 fmly) **Facilities** TVL tea/
coffee Cen ht Fishing **Parking** 10 **Notes** LB ⊗ No Children 11yrs
Closed Nov-Feb 600 acres beef sheep

Map 2 NS20

Ladyburn

★★★★★ 🛏️ 🍽️ GUEST ACCOMMODATION

☎ 01655 740585 📠 01655 740580
KA19 7SG
e-mail: jh@ladyburn.co.uk
dir: A77 (Glasgow/Stranraer) at Maybole turn to B7023 to Crosshill
and right at War Memorial. In 2m turn left for approx 1m on right

This charming country house is the home of the Hepburn family, who
take great pride in the warmth of their welcome. Sitting in open
countryside with attractive gardens, it's a great place to come to
relax. Classically styled bedrooms, two with four-poster beds, offer
every comfort and are complemented by the library and the drawing
room. Dinner comprises a carefully cooked three course set menu,
and is served in a gracious candlelit setting.

Rooms 5 en suite S £60-£70; D £110-£120 **Facilities** tea/coffee
Direct Dial Cen ht Licensed Wi-fi 🍽️ **Parking** 12 **Notes** ⊗ No Children
16yrs Civ Wed 60

Map 2 NS32

Parkstone

★★★ 77% HOTEL

☎ 01292 477286 📠 01292 477671
Esplanade KA9 1QN
e-mail: info@parkstonehotel.co.uk
web: www.parkstonehotel.co.uk
dir: From Main St (A79) W to seafront, hotel 600yds

Situated on the seafront in a quiet residential area only one mile
from Prestwick Airport, this family-run hotel caters for business
visitors as well as golfers. Bedrooms come in a variety of sizes; all
are furnished in a smart, contemporary style. The attractive, modern
look of the bar and restaurant is matched by an equally up-to-date
menu.

Rooms 30 (2 fmly) (7 GF) **S** £59-£79; **D** £98-£109 (incl. bkfst)*
Facilities FTV Xmas New Year Wi-fi **Conf** Thtr 100 **Parking** 34
Notes LB ⊗ Civ Wed 100

Map 2 NS33

Wheatsheaf Inn

☎ 01563 830307 📠 01563 830307
Main St KA1 5QB
dir: Telephone for directions

This 17th-century inn lies in a lovely village setting close to the Royal
Troon Golf Course, and there has been a hostelry here since the
1500s. Log fires burn in every room and the work of local artists
adorns the walls. Seafood dominates the menu - maybe pan-fried
scallops in lemon and chives - and alternatives include honey
roasted lamb shank; haggis, tatties and neeps in Drambuie and
onion cream, and the renowned steak pie.

Open all day all wk 11-11 (Fri-Sat 11am-mdnt) Closed: 25 Dec, 1 Jan
Bar Meals food served all day **Restaurant** food served all
day ⊕ BELHAVEN ◀ Belhaven Best, Old Speckled Hen, Guinness.
Facilities Garden Parking

TROON
Map 2 NS33

Lochgreen House Hotel

★★★★ COUNTRY HOUSE HOTEL

🏵🏵🏵 Modern British

Grand restaurant in grand golf hotel

☎ 01292 313343 📠 01292 318661
Monktonhill Rd, Southwood KA10 7EN
e-mail: lochgreen@costley-hotels.co.uk
web: www.costley-hotels.co.uk
dir: From A77 follow Prestwick Airport signs. 0.5m before airport take B749 to Troon. Hotel 1m on left

Set in 30 acres of immaculately maintained grounds, Lochgreen House is graced by tasteful extensions which have created stunning public rooms and spacious, comfortable and elegantly furnished bedrooms. Extra facilities include a coffee shop, gift shop and beauty treatments in The Retreat. The Tapestry restaurant is the culinary draw, with its large, grand atrium-style room, chandeliers cascading from the vaulted ceiling, high-backed chairs and well-spaced tables. Head chef Andrew Costley takes great pride in his Scottish heritage and it shows through on the menu with the use of high quality, seasonal ingredients. Highly original canapés kick things off with aplomb while the excellent texture and strong flavours in a terrine of Ayrshire ham hough and foie gras with sauce gribiche and a herb salad hit the mark. Main course wild sea bass with hand-dived scallops, langoustines, Provençale vegetable tart and langoustine vinaigrette might precede rhubarb crème brûlée with ginger parfait and pain d'épice. Formal service comes from an impeccably presented team.

Rooms 38 (7 annexe) (17 GF) **Facilities** Beauty treatments Xmas **Conf** Class 50 Board 50 Thtr 70 **Services** Lift **Parking** 50 **Notes** ❸ Civ Wed 100

Chef Andrew Costley **Owner** Mr W Costley **Restaurant Times** 12-2/7-9 **Prices** Fixed L 2 course £19.95 **Wines** 82 bottles over £20, 27 bottles under £20, 9 by glass **Notes** Fixed D 5 course £42.50, Dress restrictions, Smart casual, Air con **Seats** 80, Pr/dining room 30 **Children** Portions, Menu

Barceló Troon Marine Hotel

★★★★ 74% HOTEL

☎ 01292 314444 📠 01292 316922
Crosbie Rd KA10 6HE
e-mail: marine@barcelo-hotels.co.uk
web: www.barcelo-hotels.co.uk
dir: A77, A78, A79 onto B749. Hotel on left after golf course

A favourite with conference and leisure guests, this hotel overlooks Royal Troon's 18th fairway. The cocktail lounge and split-level restaurant enjoy panoramic views of the Firth of Clyde across to the Isle of Arran. Bedrooms and public areas are attractively appointed.

Rooms 89 **Facilities** Spa STV ❸ supervised Gym Squash Steam room Beauty room Xmas New Year Wi-fi **Conf** Class 100 Board 40 Thtr 200 Del from £95* **Services** Lift **Parking** 200 **Notes** ❸ Civ Wed 100

MacCallums of Troon

🏵 British

Simple seafood cookery by the harbour

☎ 01292 319339
The Harbour KA10 6DH
dir: Please telephone for directions

Wander down Memory Lane via the Americas Cup yachting depicted in sketches and paraphernalia on the walls of this harbourside restaurant. It was once the hydraulic pump station, and still commands views of trawlers landing their catch. Informal, friendly service provides a welcome for the European-influenced seafood cookery. Lobster and langoustine cocktail is fresh and flavourful, or there may be gravad lax or oysters to start. Mains keep things reasonably simple, with the likes of a parmesan-glazed seafood crêpe bursting with goodies, served with wild mushrooms and a rocket salad, and finish with strawberry Pavlova, served with top-notch white chocolate and Amaretto ice cream.

Chef Philip Burgess, Neil Marriot **Owner** John & James MacCallums **Times** 12-2.30/6.30-9.30 Closed Xmas, New Year, Mon, D Sun **Prices** Starter £4.95-£8.95, Main £9.50-£27.50, Dessert £4.85-£5.85, Service optional, Groups min 12 service 10% **Wines** 9 bottles over £20, 17 bottles under £20, 4 by glass **Notes** Sunday L **Seats** 43 **Children** Portions **Parking** 12

TURNBERRY
Map 2 NS20

Turnberry Resort, Scotland

★★★★★ HOTEL

🏵🏵 Traditional

Fine dining with views to match at luxury golf resort

☎ 01655 331000 📠 01655 331706
KA26 9LT
e-mail: turnberry@luxurycollection.com
web: www.luxurycollection.com/turnberry
dir: From Glasgow take A77/M77 S towards Stranraer, 2m past Kirkoswald, follow signs for A719/Turnberry. Hotel 500mtrs on right

This famous hotel enjoys magnificent views over to Arran, Ailsa Craig and the Mull of Kintyre. Facilities include a world-renowned golf course, the excellent Colin Montgomerie Golf Academy, a luxurious spa and a host of outdoor and country pursuits. Elegant bedrooms and suites are located in the main hotel, while adjacent lodges provide spacious, well-equipped accommodation. The Ailsa lounge is very welcoming, and in addition there is the Mediterranean Terrace Brasserie and the relaxed Clubhouse. The main restaurant has been renamed 1906 after the year Turnberry opened, and it makes the most of those sweeping views over the golf links to the Ailsa Craig through its picture windows. The menu hadn't been finalised as we went to print, but expect classic dishes inspired by the surrounding landscape and using the best local ingredients. The hotel's Grand Tea Lounge has been resurrected as part of the revamp, plus there are two new bars and a more informal restaurant - the Tappie Toorie - within the golf clubhouse.

Rooms 207 (89 annexe) (2 fmly) (12 GF) **S** £377-£792; **D** £397-£812

continued

TURNBERRY CONTINUED

(incl. bkfst)* **Facilities** Spa STV ⓧ supervised ♨ 36 Putt green
Fishing Gym Leisure club Outdoor activity centre Colin Montgomerie
Golf Academy New Year Wi-fi **Conf** Class 145 Board 80 Thtr 300
Services Lift **Parking** 200 **Notes** LB Closed 25 Dec Civ Wed 220

Restaurant Times 7-10 Closed Xmas, L Mon-Sun

Malin Court

★★★ 83% HOTEL

🍴 Scottish

Bistro cooking in a golfing hotel with great coastal views

☎ 01655 331457 📠 01655 331072
KA26 9PB
e-mail: info@malincourt.co.uk
web: www.malincourt.co.uk
dir: On A74 to Ayr then A719 to Turnberry & Maidens

Forming part of the Malin Court Residential and Nursing Home
Complex, this friendly and comfortable hotel enjoys delightful views
over the Firth of Clyde and Turnberry golf courses. Standard and
executive rooms are available; all are well equipped. Public areas are
plentiful, with the restaurant serving high teas, dinners and light
lunches. The tone in Cotters restaurant is fairly formal, though staff
are friendly, and the menu offers a balance of traditional and modern
bistro dishes. Smoked duck with pineapple and peppery chutney is
one way to begin, or you might opt for textbook prawn cocktail.
Salmon rolled in couscous, served on buttered cabbage with (faintly)
cumin-spiked crème fraîche, is a neat idea, while meat dishes might
include mushroom-stuffed pork fillet with toasted cashews in white
wine sauce.

Rooms 18 (9 fmly) **S** £84-£94; **D** £128-£148 (incl. bkfst)
Facilities STV Putt green Wi-fi **Conf** Class 60 Board 30 Thtr 200
Del from £105 to £160 **Services** Lift **Parking** 110 **Notes** LB ⊗
RS Oct-Mar Civ Wed 80

Restaurant Times 12.30-2/7-9

DOLLAR   Map 3 NS99

Castle Campbell Hotel

★★★ 77% SMALL HOTEL

☎ 01259 742519 📠 01259 743742
11 Bridge St FK14 7DE
e-mail: bookings@castle-campbell.co.uk
web: www.castle-campbell.co.uk
dir: On A91 (Stirling to St Andrews road), in centre of Dollar, by
bridge overlooking Dollar Burn & Clock Tower

Built in 1822 as a coaching inn this small hotel offers comfortable
and welcoming public areas. Bedrooms are comfortable with many
thoughtful extras provided as standard. Easy striking distance for
Edinburgh, Glasgow, Perth and Gleneagles is just a few miles away.
Food is served in both the stylish restaurant or the relaxed bar.
Recognised as a Whisky Ambassador, the hotel has over 50 malts;
local ale is always on tap and the wine list runs to several pages.
Prime Scottish produce features on both bar and restaurant menus,
with options ranging from lunchtime sandwiches to Arbroath
haddock fillet in crisp beer batter, or lamb with minted mash.

Rooms 9 (1 fmly) **S** £67.50; **D** £105 (incl. bkfst)* **Facilities** Wi-fi
Conf Class 40 Board 30 Thtr 80 **Notes** LB Civ Wed 80

Pub Open all wk ⊕ FREE HOUSE ◀ Harviestoun Bitter & Twisted,
Deuchars IPA (guest), McEwans 70'. ♟ 7 **Facilities** Dogs allowed
Parking

TILLICOULTRY   Map 3 NS99

Westbourne House

★★★★ BED AND BREAKFAST

☎ 01259 750314
10 Dollar Rd FK13 6PA
e-mail: info@westbournehouse.co.uk
dir: A91 to St Andrews. Establishment on left just past mini rdbt

This former mill-owner's home, set in wooded gardens on the edge of
the village, is adorned with memorabilia gathered by the owners
during their travels abroad. They offer a friendly welcome and an
excellent choice is offered at breakfast.

Rooms 3 rms (2 en suite) (1 pri facs) (1 fmly) (1 GF) **S** £35-£40; **D**
£56-£60* **Facilities** STV TVL tea/coffee Cen ht Wi-fi ⊌ **Parking** 3
Notes Closed Xmas-New Year

DUMFRIES & GALLOWAY

AUCHENCAIRN   Map 3 NX75

Balcary Bay

★★★ 86% HOTEL

◉◉ Modern French **V**

Top-notch food on the glorious Solway coastline

☎ 01556 640217 & 640311 📠 01556 640272
DG7 1QZ
e-mail: reservations@balcary-bay-hotel.co.uk
web: www.balcary-bay-hotel.co.uk
dir: On A711 between Dalbeattie & Kirkcudbright, hotel 2m from
village

Taking its name from the bay on which it lies, this hotel has lawns
running down to the shore. The larger bedrooms enjoy stunning views
over the bay, whilst others overlook the gardens. Comfortable public
areas invite relaxation. The day starts and finishes with the sound of
waves lapping the sandy beach, and superb views soar beyond the
Solway coast to the peaks of Cumbria. It's the perfect location to
work up a healthy appetite on a beachcombing ramble, or visiting the
art galleries of nearby Kircudbright. And it's an equally ideal spot for
the hotel's kitchen to source seasonal local produce - Galloway beef,
lamb, seafood, and Balcary Bay salmon. Sound technical skills are
evident here, establishing a refined but unpretentious tone with
clever combinations and sharp, clear flavours. Seared king scallops
with pea and lettuce purée, crisp pancetta and shiitake vinaigrette
might start, followed by poached saddle of rabbit, Jerusalem
artichoke risotto, wild mushrooms and liquorice foam. And if it's a
hard call between desserts and exciting Scottish cheeses - Mull
Cheddar, Dunsyre Blue and ewe's milk Cairnsmore or an iced Glayva
parfait with rhubarb compôte - why not do both?

Rooms 20 (1 fmly) (3 GF) **S** £71; **D** £126-£156 (incl. bkfst)
Facilities FTV **Parking** 50 **Notes** LB Closed 1st Sun Dec-1st Fri Feb

Chef Stewart Taylor **Owner** Graeme A Lamb & family **Restaurant
Times** 12-2/7-8.30 Closed early Dec-early Feb, L prior booking only
Mon-Sat **Prices** Fixed L course £19.75, Fixed D 4 course £36.75,
Starter £5.25-£9.95, Main £11.95-£23.95, Dessert £7.95-£8.25,
Service optional **Wines** 60 bottles over £20, 25 bottles under £20, 12
by glass **Notes** Sunday L, Vegetarian menu, Dress restrictions, Smart
casual **Seats** 55 **Children** Portions, Menu

CASTLE DOUGLAS   Map 3 NX76

Craigadam

★★★★ 🏠 🍴 GUEST HOUSE

☎ 01556 650233 & 650100 📠 01556 650233
Craigadam DG7 3HU
e-mail: inquiry@craigadam.com
web: www.craigadam.com
dir: From Castle Douglas E on A75 to Crocketford. In Crocketford turn
left on A712 for 2m. House on hill

Set on a farm, this elegant country house offers gracious living in a
relaxed environment. The large bedrooms, most set around a
courtyard, are strikingly individual in style. Public areas include a

billiard room with comprehensive honesty bar, and the panelled
dining room which features a magnificent 15-seater table, the
setting for Celia Pickup's delightful meals.

Rooms 10 en suite (2 fmly) (7 GF) S £45-£80; D £90-£100*
Facilities FTV tea/coffee Dinner available Cen ht Licensed Wi-fi 🍴
Fishing Snooker Private fishing & shooting **Conf** Max 22 **Parking** 12
Notes LB Closed Xmas & New Year Civ Wed 150

DUMFRIES   Map 3 NX97

Best Western Station Hotel

★★★ 79% HOTEL

☎ 01387 254316 📠 01387 250388
49 Lovers Walk DG1 1LT
e-mail: info@stationhotel.co.uk
web: www.stationhoteldumfries.co.uk
dir: A75, follow signs to Dumfries town centre, hotel opp railway
station

This friendly hotel, sympathetically modernised in harmony with its
fine Victorian features, offers well-equipped bedrooms. The Courtyard
Bistro offers a popular menu in an informal atmosphere during the
evening. In addition good value meals are also served in the lounge
bar and conservatory.

Rooms 32 (2 fmly) **Facilities** Wi-fi Use of local gym **Conf** Class 35
Board 30 Thtr 60 **Services** Lift **Parking** 34 **Notes** LB Civ Wed 60

Cairndale Hotel & Leisure Club

★★★ 79% HOTEL

☎ 01387 254111 📠 01387 240288
English St DG1 2DF
e-mail: sales@cairndalehotel.co.uk
web: www.cairndale.co.uk
dir: From S on M6 take A75 to Dumfries, left at 1st rdbt, cross rail
bridge to lights, hotel 1st building on left

Within walking distance of the town centre, this hotel provides a wide
range of amenities, including leisure facilities and an impressive
conference and entertainment centre. Bedrooms range from stylish
suites to cosy singles. There's a choice of eating options in the
evening. The Reivers Restaurant is smartly modern with food to
match.

Rooms 91 (22 fmly) (5 GF) **Facilities** ⓣ supervised Gym Steam room
Sauna 🎵 Xmas New Year Wi-fi **Conf** Class 150 Board 50 Thtr 300
Services Lift **Parking** 100 **Notes** Civ Wed 200

Travelodge Dumfries

BUDGET HOTEL

☎ 0871 984 6134 📠 01387 750658
Annan Rd, Collin DG1 3SE
web: www.travelodge.co.uk
dir: 2m E of Dumfries, on A75

Travelodge offers good quality, good value, modern accommodation.
Ideal for families, the spacious en suite bedrooms include remote-
control TV, tea and coffee-making facilities and comfortable beds.
Meals can be taken at the nearby family restaurant. See also the
Hotel Groups pages on theAA.com.

Rooms 40 **S** fr £29; **D** fr £29

Wallamhill House

★★★★★ BED AND BREAKFAST

☎ 01387 248249
Kirkton DG1 1SL
e-mail: wallamhill@aol.com
dir: 3m N of Dumfries. Off A701 signed Kirkton, 1.5m on right

Wallamhill House is set in well-tended gardens, in a delightful rural
area three miles from Dumfries. Bedrooms are spacious and
extremely well equipped. There is a peaceful drawing room, and a
mini health club with sauna, steam shower and gym equipment.

Rooms 3 en suite (1 fmly) **S** £38; **D** £60 **Facilities** FTV TVL tea/coffee
Cen ht Wi-fi 🏊 Sauna Gymnasium Steam room **Parking** 6 **Notes** LB
⊗

Rivendell

★★★★ GUEST HOUSE

☎ 01387 252251 📠 01387 263084
105 Edinburgh Rd DG1 1JX
e-mail: info@rivendellbnb.co.uk
web: www.rivendellbnb.co.uk
dir: On A701 Edinburgh Rd, 400yds S of A75 junct

Situated just north of the town and close to the bypass, this lovely
1920s house, standing in extensive landscaped gardens, has been
restored to reflect the period style of the property. Bedrooms are
thoughtfully equipped, many are spacious and all offer modern
facilities. Traditional breakfasts are served in the elegant dining
room.

Rooms 5 en suite (2 fmly) **S** £35-£50; **D** £60 **Facilities** FTV tea/coffee
Cen ht Wi-fi **Parking** 12 **Notes** LB ⊗

Southpark House

★★★★ GUEST ACCOMMODATION

☎ 01387 711188 & 0800 970 1588 📠 01387 711155
Quarry Rd, Locharbriggs DG1 1QG
e-mail: info@southparkhouse.co.uk
web: www.southparkhouse.co.uk
dir: 3.5m NE of Dumfries. Off A701 in Locharbriggs onto Quarry Rd,
last house on left

With a peaceful location commanding stunning views, this well-
maintained property offers comfortable, attractive and well-equipped
bedrooms. The peaceful lounge has a log fire on colder evenings, and
fax and e-mail facilities are available. Friendly proprietor Ewan
Maxwell personally oversees the hearty Scottish breakfasts served in
the conservatory breakfast room.

Rooms 4 en suite (1 fmly) **S** £30-£50; **D** £50-£70 **Facilities** STV FTV
TVL tea/coffee Cen ht Wi-fi 2 acres of garden **Parking** 13 **Notes** LB ⊗

GATEHOUSE OF FLEET Map 2 NX55

Cally Palace

★★★★ 74% COUNTRY HOUSE HOTEL

⊛ Traditional V

Scottish cooking in a stately setting

☎ 01557 814341 📠 01557 814522
DG7 2DL
e-mail: info@callypalace.co.uk
web: www.callypalace.co.uk
dir: M6 & A74, signed A75 Dumfries then Stranraer. At Gatehouse-of-
Fleet turn right onto B727, left at Cally

Situated in 150 acres of grounds on the Solway coast, the Cally
Palace is an opulent country mansion with the ambience of a bygone
age. Built in 1763 in a superb setting overlooking the Galloway hills
and bordered by the Fleet Oak Woods, the hotel has its own 18-hole
golf course sculpted into the natural contours of the parkland.
Bedrooms are spacious and well equipped, whilst public rooms retain

a quiet elegance. The dining room is in keeping with its grand past; a pianist plays most evenings and a jacket and tie are obligatory for men. The chef and his team use the local Galloway produce, including wild Solway salmon, for their Scottish menu. Expect pan-fried Galloway venison with parsnip purée, fondant potato, green beans and rosemary jus, or steamed sea bass, wilted greens, moules marinière and saffron potatoes.

Rooms 55 (7 fmly) **S** £101-£107; **D** £96-£114 (incl. bkfst & dinner)* **Facilities** ⓣ ⚖ 18 ⚲ Putt green Fishing ⚒ Gym Table tennis Practice fairway Xmas New Year Wi-fi **Conf** Class 40 Board 25 Thtr 40 **Services** Lift **Parking** 100 **Notes** LB ⊗ Closed Jan-early Feb

Chef Jamie Muirhead **Owner** McMillan Hotels **Restaurant Times** 12-1/6.45-9 Closed 3 Jan-early Feb, **Prices** Fixed D 4 course £29.50-£39.50, Starter £2.90-£4.25, Main £12.95-£15, Dessert £3.75-£4.75, Service optional **Wines** 34 bottles over £20, 48 bottles under £20, 11 by glass **Notes** Sunday L, Vegetarian menu, Dress restrictions, Jacket and tie, Air con **Seats** 110 **Children** Portions, Menu

---

GRETNA (WITH GRETNA GREEN)   Map 3 NY36

Smiths at Gretna Green

★★★★ 74% HOTEL

◉ Modern Scottish, International

Contemporary hotel with modern, globally-inspired food

☎ 01461 337007 🖹 01461 336000
Gretna Green DG16 5EA
e-mail: info@smithsgretnagreen.com
web: www.smithsgretnagreen.com
dir: From M74 junct 22 follow signs to Old Blacksmith's Shop. Hotel opposite

Smiths injects a note of contemporary gloss to the capital of runaway weddings, so any couples getting hitched here nowadays can expect modishly minimal décor with modern art, sumptuous fabrics and tastefully muted colours. The bedrooms offer a spacious environment, complete with flat-screen TVs, DVD players and broadband. Family rooms feature a separate children's area with bunk beds, each with its own TV. Three suites and a penthouse apartment are also available. Contemporary day rooms are open-plan; impressive conference and banqueting facilities are provided. Suitably polished service in the bar and brasserie-style dining room sets the right tone for a menu of well-balanced dishes. Scottish produce from the nearby coast and farmland is pepped up with international global influences. Chicken liver parfait comes with baked plums, toasted brioche and kumquat compôte, while a main course of roast Goosnargh duck breast is served with sweet potato gratin, spiced pear and Madeira jus. Try a Valrhona dark chocolate mousse with light coconut cream and rosé champagne sorbet to finish.

Rooms 50 (8 fmly) **S** £110-£252; **D** £156-£480 (incl. bkfst) **Facilities** STV FTV New Year Wi-fi **Conf** Class 100 Board 40 Thtr 250 Del from £125 to £175 **Services** Lift Air con **Parking** 115 **Notes** LB Civ Wed 150

Restaurant Times 12-9.30

Gretna Chase

★★★ 78% HOTEL

☎ 01461 337517 🖹 01461 337766
DG16 5JB
e-mail: enquiries@gretnachase.co.uk
dir: Off M74 onto B7076, left at top of slip road, hotel 400yds on right

With its colourful landscaped gardens, this hotel is a favourite venue for wedding parties. Bedrooms range from the comfortable, traditional, standard rooms to the impressively spacious superior and honeymoon rooms; all are well equipped. There is a foyer lounge, a spacious dining room that can accommodate functions, and a popular lounge bar serving food.

Rooms 19 (9 fmly) **S** £64.95-£150; **D** £99-£250 (incl. bkfst)* **Conf** Class 30 Board 20 Thtr 50 Del from £125 to £175* **Parking** 40 **Notes** LB ⊗

Garden House

★★★ 74% HOTEL

☎ 01461 337621 🖹 01461 337692
Sarkfoot Rd DG16 5EP
e-mail: info@gardenhouse.co.uk
web: www.gardenhouse.co.uk
dir: Just off M6 junct 45

This purpose-built modern hotel lies on the edge of the village. With a focus on weddings its landscaped gardens provide an ideal setting, while inside corridor walls are adorned with photographs portraying that 'special day'. Accommodation is well presented including bedrooms that overlook the Japanese water gardens.

Rooms 38 (11 fmly) (14 GF) **Facilities** ⓣ supervised 🎶 Xmas New Year **Conf** Class 80 Board 40 Thtr 150 **Services** Lift **Parking** 105 **Notes** ⊗ Civ Wed 150

The Gables Hotel

Ⓤ

☎ 01461 338300 🖹 01461 338626
1 Annan Road DG16 5DQ
e-mail: info.gables@mckeverhotels.co.uk
web: www.mckeverhotels.co.uk
dir: M74 S or M6/M74 N follow signs for Gretna. At rdbt at Gretna Gateway take exit onto Annan Rd, hotel 200yds on right

Currently the rating for this establishment is not confirmed. This may be due to a change of ownership or because it has only recently joined the AA rating scheme.

Rooms 31 (5 fmly) (10 GF) **S** £69-£130 **D** £89-£250 (incl. bkfst) **Facilities** FTV tea/coffee direct dial Xmas New Year **Parking** 60 **Notes** Civ Wed

Barrasgate

★★★ GUEST ACCOMMODATION

☎ 01461 337577 & 07711 661938 📄 01461 337577
Millhill DG16 5HU
e-mail: info@barrasgate.co.uk
web: www.barrasgate.co.uk
dir: From N, A74(M) junct 24, 1m E take 2nd left signed Gretna
Green, Longtown on right; From S, M6 junct 45, A6071 towards
Longtown 1m on left

This detached house lies in attractive gardens in a rural setting near
the Blacksmith Centre and motorway links. Bedrooms are equipped
with thoughtful extras and have fine country views. Hearty
breakfasts, featuring local produce, are taken in an attractive dining
room, overlooking the gardens.

Rooms 5 en suite (2 fmly) (1 GF) S £25-£45; D £56-£65*
Facilities FTV TVL tea/coffee Cen ht Wi-fi **Parking** 9 **Notes** LB

Surrone House

★★★ GUEST ACCOMMODATION

☎ 01461 338341 📄 01461 338341
Annan Rd DG16 5DL
e-mail: enquiries@surronehouse.co.uk
web: www.surronehouse.co.uk
dir: In town centre on B721

You are assured of a warm welcome at this well-maintained guest
house set in attractive gardens well back from the road. Bedrooms
are sensibly furnished and including a delightful honeymoon suite.
Dinner, drinks and light refreshments are available.

Rooms 7 rms (6 en suite) (1 pri facs) (3 fmly) (2 GF) S £50; D £70*
Facilities FTV TVL tea/coffee Dinner available Cen ht Licensed Wi-fi
Parking 10 **Notes** ⊗

Kirkcroft Guest House

★★★ 🅰 BED AND BREAKFAST

☎ 01461 337403 📄 01461 337403
Glasgow Rd DG16 5DU
e-mail: info@kirkcroft.co.uk
dir: On B7076 next to rail station, at bottom of drive to Gretna Hall

Rooms 3 en suite S £40; D £54* **Facilities** FTV tea/coffee Cen ht
Parking 5 **Notes** LB ⊗

Days Inn Gretna Green

BUDGET HOTEL

☎ 01461 337566 📄 01461 337823
Welcome Break Service Area DG16 5HQ
e-mail: gretna.hotel@welcomebreak.co.uk
web: www.welcomebreak.co.uk
dir: Between junct 21/22 on M74 - accessible from both N'bound &
S'bound carriageway

This modern building offers accommodation in smart, spacious and
well-equipped bedrooms suitable for families and business
travellers, and all with en suite bathrooms. Continental breakfast is
available and other refreshments may be taken at the nearby family
restaurant. See also the Hotel Groups pages on theAA.com.

Rooms 64 (54 fmly) (64 GF) (20 smoking) **S** £39-£69; **D** £39-£79*

The Steam Packet Inn ☮

☎ 01988 500334 📄 01988 500627
Harbour Row DG8 8LL
e-mail: steampacketinn@btconnect.com
dir: From Newton Stewart take A714, then A746 to Whithorn, then Isle
of Whithorn

This lively quayside pub stands in a picturesque village at the tip of
the Machars peninsula. Sit by the picture windows and watch the
fishermen at work, then look to the menu for a chance to sample the
fruits of their labours. Extensive seafood choices - perhaps local
lobster thermidor or a kettle of fish with vermouth crème fraîche - are
supported by the likes of steak and baby onion suet pudding or Thai
pork ciabatta.

Open all wk 11-11 (Sun noon-11) Closed: 25 Dec, winter Tue-Thu
2.30-6 **Bar Meals** L served all wk 12-2 D served all wk 6.30-9
⊕ FREE HOUSE ◀ Timothy Taylor Landlord, Caledonian Deuchars IPA,
Black Sheep Best Bitter, Houston Killellan. ☮ 9 **Facilities** Dogs
allowed Garden Parking

Cavens

★★ COUNTRY HOUSE HOTEL

◉ British, French ☾

Sound cooking in peaceful country house

☎ 01387 880234 📄 01387 880467
DG2 8AA
e-mail: enquiries@cavens.com
web: www.cavens.com
dir: on entering Kirkbean on A710, hotel signed

Situated on the Solway coast, close to the stunning Galloway Forest
Park, Britain's largest forest park, Cavens is one of the most popular
country-house hotels in Dumfries & Galloway. Set in 6 acres of
peaceful, beautifully landscaped gardens, it was once a private

family manor house and is now owned by the Fordyce family who spared no effort in completing a fine renovation of the house and provide warm hospitality, welcoming guests like old friends. Bedrooms are delightfully individual and very comfortably equipped, and a choice of lounges invites peaceful relaxation. The intimate dining room has a limited number of well-spaced tables, and a daily set menu at dinner offers a choice of two dishes at each course, plus alternatives on request. Main courses could be sea bass on a bed of leeks with lemon butter sauce or rack of Galloway lamb with thyme crust and roasted baby tomato sauce.

Rooms 5 (1 GF) **S** £80-£150; **D** £80-£240 (incl. bkfst)* **Facilities** ⊌ Shooting Fishing Horse riding New Year **Conf** Class 20 Board 20 Thtr 20 **Parking** 12 **Notes** LB No children 12yrs Closed Jan Civ Wed 100

Chef A Fordyce **Owner** A Fordyce **Restaurant Times** 7-8.30 Closed Dec-1 Mar, L all week **Prices** Fixed D 3 course £35, Service included **Wines** 20 bottles over £20, 7 bottles under £20, 2 by glass **Notes** Vegetarian available, Dress restrictions, Smart casual **Seats** 16, Pr/dining room 20

KIRKCUDBRIGHT   Map 2 NX65

Best Western Selkirk Arms ♥

★★★ 77% HOTEL

☎ 01557 330402 ▤ 01557 331639
Old High St DG6 4JG
e-mail: reception@selkirkarmshotel.co.uk
web: www.selkirkarmshotel.co.uk
dir: On A71, 5m S of A75

A smart and stylish building set in secluded gardens just off the town centre; Robert Burns is reputed to have written the Selkirk Grace at this privately owned hotel, and the proprietors have created their own real ale, The Selkirk Grace, in conjunction with Sulwath Brewers. There are two bars, and a great choice of dishes is offered in The Bistro or more intimate Artistas Restaurant, including pan-seared Kirkcudbright king scallops; slow roast lamb shank; and Eccelfechan butter tart. Accommodation is provided in 17 en suite bedrooms.

Rooms 17 (3 annexe) (2 fmly) (1 GF) **S** £79; **D** £98-£110 (incl. bkfst)* **Facilities** STV FTV New Year Wi-fi **Conf** Class 30 Board 30 Thtr 50 **Parking** 10 **Notes** LB Closed 24-26 Dec

Pub Open all wk **Bar Meals** L served all wk 12-2 D served all wk 6-9 Av main course £9.95 **Restaurant** L served Sun 12-2 booking required D served all wk 7-9 booking required Fixed menu price fr £19 Av 3 course à la carte fr £30 ⊕ FREE HOUSE ◀ Youngers Tartan, John Smiths Bitter, Criffel, Timothy Taylor Landlord, The Selkirk Grace. ♥ 8 **Facilities** Children's menu Dogs allowed Garden

Arden House Hotel

★★ 72% HOTEL

☎ 01557 330544 ▤ 01557 330742
Tongland Rd DG6 4UU
dir: Off A57, 4m W of Castle Douglas onto A711. Follow Kirkcudbright, over Telford Bridge. Hotel 400mtrs on left

Set well back from the main road in extensive grounds on the northeast side of town, this spotlessly maintained hotel offers attractive bedrooms, a lounge bar and adjoining conservatory serving a range of popular dishes, which are also available in the dining room. It boasts an impressive function suite in its grounds.

Rooms 9 (7 fmly) (5 smoking) **S** fr £55; **D** £75-£80 (incl. bkfst)* **Conf** Class 175 Thtr 175 **Parking** 70 **Notes** LB

LOCKERBIE   Map 3 NY18

Dryfesdale Country House

★★★★ 71% HOTEL

☎ 01576 202427 ▤ 01576 204187
Dryfebridge DG11 2SF
e-mail: reception@dryfesdalehotel.co.uk
web: www.dryfesdalehotel.co.uk
dir: From M74 junct 17 follow Lockerbie North signs, 3rd left at 1st rdbt, 1st exit left at 2nd rdbt, hotel 200yds on left

Conveniently situated for the M74, yet discreetly screened from it, this friendly hotel provides attentive service. Bedrooms, some with access to patio areas, vary in size and style; all offer good levels of comfort and are well equipped. Creative, good value dinners make use of local produce and are served in the airy restaurant that overlooks the manicured gardens and rolling countryside.

Rooms 28 (5 fmly) (19 GF) **Facilities** STV FTV Putt green ⊌ Clay pigeon shooting Fishing ♫ Xmas New Year Wi-fi **Conf** Class 100 Board 100 Thtr 150 Del from £100 to £125 **Parking** 60 **Notes** Civ Wed 150

Kings Arms Hotel

★★ 78% HOTEL

☎ 01576 202410 ▤ 01576 202410
High St DG11 2JL
e-mail: reception@kingsarmshotel.co.uk
web: www.kingsarmshotel.co.uk
dir: A74(M), 0.5m into town centre, hotel opposite town hall

Dating from the 17th century this former inn lies in the town centre. Now a family-run hotel, it provides attractive well-equipped bedrooms with Wi-fi access. At lunch a menu ranging from snacks to full meals is served in both the two cosy bars and the restaurant at dinner.

Rooms 13 (2 fmly) **S** £47.50; **D** £80 (incl. bkfst)* **Facilities** FTV Xmas New Year Wi-fi **Conf** Class 40 Board 30 Thtr 80 **Parking** 8

Ravenshill House

★★ 71% HOTEL

☎ 01576 202882
12 Dumfries Rd DG11 2EF
e-mail: aaenquiries@ravenshillhotellockerbie.co.uk
web: www.ravenshillhotellockerbie.co.uk
dir: From A74(M) Lockerbie junct onto A709. Hotel 0.5m on right

A traditional hotel located within the heart of Ascot, grounds are well kept and offer ample guest parking for car users. Public areas include a comfortable guest lounge and bar, whilst the restaurant offers a selection of home made dishes. Bedrooms and bathrooms are well appointed and very much in keeping with the traditional feel of the house. Located close to a number of local attractions and major transport networks.

Rooms 8 (2 fmly) **S** £50-£65; **D** £75-£85 (incl. bkfst)* **Facilities** FTV **Conf** Class 20 Board 12 Thtr 30 **Parking** 35 **Notes** LB Closed 1-3 Jan

MOFFAT   Map 3 NT00

Best Western Moffat House

★★★ 73% HOTEL

☎ 01683 220039   📠 01683 221288
High St DG10 9HL
e-mail: reception@moffathouse.co.uk
dir: M74 junct 15 into town centre

This fine Adam mansion, in its own neatly tended gardens, is set back from the main road in the centre of this popular country town. Inviting public areas include a quiet sun lounge to the rear, a comfortable lounge bar serving tasty meals and an attractive restaurant for the more formal occasion. Bedrooms present a mix of classical and modern styles.

Rooms 21 (4 fmly) (4 GF) **S** £49-£79; **D** £69-£99 (incl. bkfst) **Facilities** STV Xmas New Year Wi-fi **Conf** Class 80 Board 50 Thtr 100 Del from £99 to £119 **Parking** 30 **Notes** Civ Wed 150

Well View

★★★★★ GUEST ACCOMMODATION

◉◉ Modern European V

Fine food and views in a homely setting

☎ 01683 220184
Ballplay Rd DG10 9JU
e-mail: johnwellview@aol.com
dir: M74 junct 15, into Moffat. Exit Moffat on A708 for 0.5m, left into Ballplay Rd. 300yds on right

Sitting in pretty gardens high up above the town, this small hotel enjoys fine views across historic Moffat to the hills beyond, and over the wild open fells. The house is traditionally decorated, and proprietors Janet and John Schuckardt pride themselves on their personal service and attention to detail. Janet is in charge of the kitchen and her cooking follows a classical route, making the most of

top quality local produce. A set six-course menu is served at dinner, with wines personally chosen by wine buff John. Canapés kick things off, next up, perhaps, Mull of Kintyre cheese and chive soufflé, followed by seared duck breast on a julienne of seasonal vegetables with pak choi in a red wine jus. A selection of cheeses precedes dessert - think chocolate chip steamed pudding with a vanilla crème anglaise, or Eton mess.

Rooms 3 en suite **Facilities** tea/coffee Dinner available Cen ht **Parking** 4

Chef Janet & Lina Schuckardt **Owner** Janet & John Schuckardt **Restaurant Times** 12.30-7.30 Closed L Mon-Sat **Prices** Fixed L 3 course £19-£22, Fixed D 4 course £40, Service included **Notes** Sunday L, Vegetarian menu, Dress restrictions, Smart dress **Seats** 10, Pr/dining room 10

Bridge House

★★★★ 🛏 GUEST HOUSE

☎ 01683 220558   📠 01683 220558
Well Rd DG10 9JT
e-mail: info@bridgehousemoffat.co.uk
dir: Off A708 The Holm onto Burnside & Well Rd, house 0.5m on left

A fine Victorian property, Bridge House lies in attractive gardens in a quiet residential area on the outskirts of the town. The atmosphere is very friendly and relaxed. The chef-proprietor provides interesting dinners (by arrangement) featuring local produce. The cosy guest lounge is the ideal venue for pre-dinner drinks.

Rooms 7 en suite (1 fmly) **S** £45-£50; **D** £70-£105* **Facilities** FTV tea/coffee Dinner available Cen ht Licensed **Parking** 7 **Notes** LB ⊗ No Children 2yrs Closed 23 Dec-13 Feb

Hartfell House & The Limetree Restaurant

★★★★ GUEST HOUSE

◉ Modern British 🍴

Modern cooking in Victorian house with views

☎ 01683 220153
Hartfell Crescent DG10 9AL
e-mail: enquiries@hartfellhouse.co.uk
web: www.hartfellhouse.co.uk
dir: Off High St at war memorial onto Well St & Old Well Rd. Hartfell Crescent on right

Built in 1850, this impressive Victorian house is in a peaceful terrace high above the town, has lovely countryside views. Beautifully maintained, the bedrooms offer high quality and comfort. The attractive dining room is transformed in the evening into The Limetree Restaurant, which was previously in the high street. The traditionally-styled dining room has an ornate ceiling with crystal chandeliers and local art on the walls. There is a simple, intuitive approach to the traditional and modern cooking here, big on taste and flavour with great combinations. Fillets of sea bream are pan-fried with fennel seeds, smoked paprika and lemon, and comes with fresh herb risotto and dressed baby spinach leaves; finish with steamed ginger pudding and orange curd ice cream.

Rooms 7 en suite (2 fmly) (1 GF) **S** £35-£40; **D** £60-£70*

Facilities tea/coffee Dinner available Cen ht Licensed Wi-fi **Parking** 6 **Notes** LB ⊗ Closed Xmas

Chef Matt Seddon **Owner** Robert & Mhairi Ash **Restaurant Times** 12.30-2.30/6.30-9 Closed Xmas, Mon, L Tue-Sat, D Sun **Prices** Fixed L 2 course £18, Fixed D 3 course £26.50, Service optional, Groups min 6 service 10% **Wines** 8 bottles over £20, 16 bottles under £20, 4 by glass **Notes** Sunday L **Seats** 26 **Children** Portions

Limetree House

★★★★ GUEST ACCOMMODATION

☎ 01683 220001
Eastgate DG10 9AE
e-mail: info@limetreehouse.co.uk
web: www.limetreehouse.co.uk
dir: Off High St onto Well St, left onto Eastgate, house 100yds on left

A warm welcome is assured at this well-maintained guest house, quietly situated behind the main high street. Recognisable by its colourful flower baskets in season, it provides an inviting lounge and bright cheerful breakfast room. Bedrooms are smartly furnished and include a large family room.

Rooms 6 en suite (1 fmly) (1 GF) S £42.50; D £65-£75* **Facilities** FTV tea/coffee Cen ht Wi-fi **Parking** 3 **Notes** LB No Children 5yrs RS Xmas & New Year

The Balmoral

★★★ INN

☎ 01683 220288   📠 01683 220451
High St DG10 9DL
web: www.thebalmoralhotel-moffat.co.uk
dir: 0.5m from A/M74 junct 15, halfway up High St on right

The Balmoral is situated in the centre of the town with free parking in the town square, a friendly welcome is guaranteed. Bar meals are available all day until 9.30pm. Bedrooms are very comfortably equipped with thoughtful extras. Moffat is a former spa town and is within easy reach of many major tourist attractions.

Rooms 16 en suite (2 fmly) S £32.50-£45; D £53* **Facilities** tea/coffee Dinner available Cen ht **Notes** ⊗

Barnhill Springs Country Guest House

★★ GUEST ACCOMMODATION

☎ 01683 220580
DG10 9QS
dir: A74(M) junct 15, A701 towards Moffat, Barnhill Rd 50yds on right

This former farmhouse has a quiet, rural location south of the town and within easy reach of the M74. Bedrooms are well proportioned; and have either en suite or private bathrooms. There is a comfortable lounge and separate dining room.

Rooms 5 rms (1 en suite) (2 pri facs) (1 fmly) (1 GF) S £30-£32; D £60-£64* **Facilities** TVL tea/coffee Dinner available Cen ht **Parking** 10 **Notes** ☺

Black Bull Hotel ♥

☎ 01683 220206   📄 01683 220483
Churchgate DG10 9EG
e-mail: hotel@blackbullmoffat.co.uk
dir: Telephone for directions

This historic pub was the headquarters of Graham of Claverhouse during the 17th-century Scottish rebellion, and was frequented by Robert Burns around 1790. The Railway Bar, in former stables across the courtyard, houses a collection of railway memorabilia and traditional pub games. Food is served in the lounge, Burns Room or restaurant. Dishes include Black Bull sizzlers (steak, chicken fillets, gammon) served on a cast iron platter; the daily roast, and deep-fried breaded haddock fillet.

Open all wk ⊕ FREE HOUSE ◀ McEwans, Theakston. ♥ 10 **Facilities** Garden Parking

NEW ABBEY   **Map 3 NX96**

Criffel Inn

☎ 01387 850305 & 850244   📄 01387 850305
2 The Square DG2 8BX
e-mail: criffelinn@btconnect.com
dir: A74/A74(M) exit at Gretna, A75 to Dumfries, A710 to New Abbey

A former 18th-century coaching inn set on the Solway Coast in the historic conservation village of New Abbey close to the ruins of the 13th-century Sweetheart Abbey. Expect a warm welcome and excellent home-cooked food using local produce. There's a lawned beer garden overlooking the corn-mill and square; ideal for touring Dumfries and Galloway.

Open all wk noon-2.30 5-11 (Mon-Tue 5-11 Fri-Sat noon-2.30 5-mdnt) **Bar Meals** L served Wed-Sun 12-2 D served Wed-Sun 5-8 Av main course £7.95 **Restaurant** L served Wed-Sun 12-2 D served Wed-Sun 5-8 ⊕ FREE HOUSE ◀ Belhaven Best, McEwans 60-, Guinness. **Facilities** Children's menu Family room Dogs allowed Garden Parking

NEW GALLOWAY   Map 2 NX67

Cross Keys Hotel ♈

☎ 01644 420494   🗎 01644 701071
High St DG7 3RN
e-mail: enquiries@thecrosskeys-newgalloway.co.uk
dir: At N end of Loch Ken, 10m from Castle Douglas on A712

A 17th-century coaching inn with a beamed period bar, where food is served in restored, stone-walled cells (part of the hotel was once the police station). The à la carte restaurant offers hearty food with a Scottish accent, chicken stuffed with haggis and served with whisky sauce being a prime example. Real ales are a speciality, and there's a good choice of malts in the whisky bar.

Open all wk **Bar Meals** L served Thu-Sun D served Wed-Sat 6-9 Av main course £6 **Restaurant** L served Thu-Sun D served Wed-Sat 6-9 Av 3 course à la carte fr £20 ◀ Houston, guest real ales. ♈ 9 **Facilities** Dogs allowed Garden

NEWTON STEWART   Map 2 NX46

Kirroughtree House

★★★ COUNTRY HOUSE HOTEL

◉◉ Modern European

Formal dining in Scottish mansion

☎ 01671 402141   🗎 01671 402425
Minnigaff DG8 6AN
e-mail: info@kirroughtreehouse.co.uk
web: www.kirroughtreehouse.co.uk
dir: From A75 take A712, entrance to hotel 300yds on left

Built in 1719 on the edge of Galloway Forest Park, Kirroughtree is a handsome country house in the Scottish baronial style, with various add-ons courtesy of a Victorian Major Armitage. The mansion's rich history has seen visits by poet Robert Burns, who sat on the grand staircase to recite his poetry. The inviting day rooms comprise a choice of lounges, and two elegant dining rooms. Well-proportioned, individually styled bedrooms include some suites and mini-suites and many rooms enjoy fine views. Service is very friendly and attentive, and dinner is a refined affair taken at tables set with good-quality china, linen and glassware. The chef makes good use of Galloway's bountiful larder, using local lobster, salmon, Kirroughtree venison and Cairnsmore cheeses in his modern British output. Expect starters such as breast of quail on barley, pancetta and celery risotto to precede supreme of guinea fowl filled with truffle mousse, served with carrot and potato rösti, Jerusalem artichoke and Madeira sauce.

Rooms 17 **S** £105-£115; **D** £180-£250 (incl. bkfst)* **Facilities** ☺ ⤴ 9 hole pitch and putt Xmas New Year Wi-fi **Conf** Class 20 Board 20 Thtr 30 Del from £160 to £170* **Services** Lift **Parking** 50 **Notes** LB No children 10yrs Closed 2 Jan-mid Feb

Chef Rolf Mueller **Owner** Mr D McMillan **Restaurant Times** 12-1.30/7-9 Closed 2 Jan-mid Feb, **Prices** Fixed D 3 course £35, Starter £3.50-£6.50, Main £12.75-£18.75, Dessert £3.50-£5.50, Service optional **Wines** 73 bottles over £20, 21 bottles under £20, 5 by glass **Notes** ALC available L only, Sunday L, Vegetarian available, Dress restrictions, Jacket must be worn after 6.30pm **Seats** 45

Bruce Hotel

★★★ 73% HOTEL

☎ 01671 402294   🗎 01671 402294
88 Queen St DG8 6JL
e-mail: mail@the-bruce-hotel.com
web: www.the-bruce-hotel.com
dir: Off A75 Newton Stewart rdbt towards town. Hotel 800mtrs on right

Named after the Scottish patriot Robert the Bruce, this welcoming hotel is just a short distance from the A75. One of the well-appointed bedrooms features a four-poster bed, and popular family suites contain separate bedrooms for children. Public areas include a traditional lounge, a formal restaurant and a lounge bar, both offering a good choice of dishes.

Rooms 20 (3 fmly) **S** £45-£49; **D** £80-£90 (incl. bkfst)* **Facilities** New Year Wi-fi **Conf** Class 50 Board 14 Thtr 100 Del from £75 to £95* **Parking** 14 **Notes** LB

Galloway Arms Inn

★★★ INN ♈

☎ 01671 402653   🗎 01671 401202
54-58 Victoria St DG8 6DB
e-mail: info@gallowayarmshotel.com
dir: In town centre, opp town clock

Built in 1750 by an Earl of Galloway, this inn has provided accommodation for the past 250 years and is older than the town of Newton Stewart, which was built around it. It is well positioned on the high street and benefits from off-road parking. The newly refurbished Earls Room lounge offers an unrivalled range of over 100 malt whiskies, as well as real ale and traditional Scottish beers. Local produce from a 20-mile radius is the foundation of most dishes, which might feature fresh Kirkcudbright scallops, beef sourced from only five local farms or Galloway venison. There are 17 en suite bedrooms if you would like to stay over, and breakfast is also noteworthy.

Rooms 17 en suite (3 GF) S £29.50-£39.50; D £70* **Facilities** STV FTV TVL Dinner available Cen ht Wi-fi **Conf** Max 150 Thtr 100 Class 50 Board 50 **Parking Notes** LB

Pub Open all day all wk 11am-mdnt (Fri-Sat 11am-1am) **Bar Meals** L served all wk 12-2 D served all wk 6-9 Av main course £8 **Restaurant** D served all wk 6-9 Av 3 course à la carte fr £17.95 ⊕ FREE HOUSE ◀ Belhaven Best, Guinness, Caledonian Deuchars IPA. ♈ 11 **Facilities** Children's menu Dogs allowed Garden

Knockinaam Lodge

★★★ HOTEL

◉◉◉ Modern Scottish V ♦

Classical Scottish cooking in an unbeatable coastal location

☎ 01776 810471   📠 01776 810435
DG9 9AD
e-mail: reservations@knockinaamlodge.com
web: www.knockinaamlodge.com
dir: From A77 or A75 follow signs to Portpatrick. Through Lochans. After 2m left at signs for hotel

Any tour of Dumfries & Galloway would not be complete without a night or two at this haven of tranquillity and relaxation. Knockinaam Lodge is an extended Victorian house, set in an idyllic cove and sheltered by majestic cliffs and woodlands. So secluded is it that Sir Winston Churchill met General Eisenhower here in the dark days of war. A warm welcome is assured from the proprietors and their committed team, and much emphasis is placed on providing a sophisticated but intimate home-from-home experience. The cooking is a real treat and showcases superb local produce - when the Knockinaam brochure mentions 'rock and roll' as one of the hotel's attractions, rest assured that musical evenings with AC/DC are not on the agenda. The reference is to the rolling of the surf against the rocks of the Galloway coastline beneath the lodge. There are 30 acres of gardens and woodland, a private strip of shore from which to gaze over towards Ireland, and a dining room done in restful pastels of orange and peach. When it comes to dinner, you won't even be subjected to the rigour of choosing (other than between cheese or dessert), as the drill is a daily-changing set menu. Tony Pierce has perfected an understated style of classical Scottish cooking, with one or two modern flourishes along the way. It's the kind of approach that knows when to leave well alone, so you might begin with a simply grilled fillet of salmon, served with nothing other than a relish of coriander pesto. A soup follows, perhaps butterbean and parsley with a topping of white truffle oil, and then the main meaty business, where stops are pulled out. Roast cannon of local lamb might appear with pomme purée, root veg and a little 'bonbon' of haggis, richly sauced with port and rosemary. If you're not in the market for the excellent British and French cheeses with walnut and sultana bread, the sweet alternative could be pear and almond tart with praline ice cream, Amaretto sabayon and vanilla custard.

Rooms 10 (1 fmly) **S** £145-£285; **D** £180-£400 (incl. bkfst & dinner)*
Facilities FTV Fishing ⚓ Shooting Walking Sea fishing Clay pigeon shooting Xmas New Year Wi-fi Child facilities **Conf** Class 10 Board 16 Thtr 30 **Parking** 20 **Notes** Civ Wed 40

Chef Antony Pierce **Owner** David & Sian Ibbotson **Restaurant Times** 12.30-2/7-9 **Prices** Food prices not confirmed for 2010. Please telephone for details, Service optional **Wines** 335 bottles over £20, 18 bottles under £20, 10 by glass **Notes** Fixed L 4 course £37.50, Fixed D 5 course £50, Sunday L, Vegetarian menu, Dress restrictions, No jeans **Seats** 32, Pr/dining room 18 **Children** Menu

Fernhill

★★★ 79% HOTEL

☎ 01776 810220   📠 01776 810596
Heugh Rd DG9 8TD
e-mail: info@fernhillhotel.co.uk
web: www.fernhillhotel.co.uk
dir: From Stranraer A77 to Portpatrick, 100yds past Portpatrick village sign, turn right before war memorial. Hotel 1st on left

Set high above the village, this hotel looks out over the harbour and Irish Sea; many of the bedrooms take advantage of the views. A modern wing offers particularly spacious and well-appointed rooms; some have balconies. The smart conservatory restaurant offers interesting, freshly prepared dishes.

Rooms 36 (9 annexe) (3 fmly) (8 GF) **S** £63-£83; **D** fr £116 (incl. bkfst & dinner)* **Facilities** Leisure facilities available at sister hotel in Stranraer Xmas New Year Wi-fi **Conf** Class 12 Board 12 Thtr 24 **Parking** 45 **Notes** LB Closed mid Jan-mid Feb Civ Wed 45

Crown Hotel ♟

☎ 01776 810261
9 North Crescent DG9 8SX
e-mail: info@crownportpatrick.com
dir: Take A77 from ferry port at Stranraer

Just a few yards from the water's edge in one of the region's most picturesque villages, the Crown has striking views across the Irish Sea. The rambling old bar has seafaring displays and a warming winter fire. Naturally seafood is a speciality: starters range from crab and scallop fish soup, to fresh local crab claws in dill sauce; main courses continue the briny celebration with a hot seafood platter, or whole fresh pan-fried sea bass.

Open all wk ⊕ FREE HOUSE ◀ John Smiths, McEwans 80/-, McEwans 70/-, Guinness. ♟ 8 **Facilities** Family room Garden Parking

Powfoot Golf Hotel

★★★ 78% HOTEL

☎ 01461 700254   📠 01461 700288
Links Av DG12 5PN
e-mail: reception@thepowfootgolfhotel.co.uk
dir: A75 onto B721, through Annan. B724, approx 3m, left onto unclassified road

This hotel has well presented and comfortable modern bedrooms, many of which overlook the championship golf course. Public areas have panoramic views onto the Solway Firth and the Lakeland hills beyond. The service is friendly and relaxed, and quality food is served in a choice of locations.

Rooms 24 (9 fmly) (5 GF) (2 smoking) **S** fr £60; **D** fr £90 (incl. bkfst) **Facilities** STV FTV ⚘ 18 Putt green Xmas New Year Wi-fi **Conf** Class 80 Board 80 Thtr 80 Del from £100 **Parking** 30 **Notes** LB ⊗ Civ Wed 100

Blackaddie House Hotel

★★★ 78% COUNTRY HOUSE HOTEL

◉◉ Modern Scottish

☎ 01659 50270
Blackaddie Rd DG4 6JJ
e-mail: ian@blackaddiehotel.co.uk
dir: Off A76 just N of Sanquhar at Burnside Service Station. Private road to hotel 300mtrs on right

Overlooking the River Nith, this family run country house hotel offers friendly and attentive hands-on service, . Accommodation is well presented and comfortable with many useful extras provided as standard. Award-winning food features, with imaginative dishes showing flair and demonstrating the passion of the kitchen team. With the sound of the river in the background and pleasant views of the gardens, this is a lovely setting for dishes where attention to detail and presentation are key. Produce is locally sourced, with producers listed with pride on the menu. Start with roasted quail with tomato fondou and parma ham scrambled eggs, maybe, followed by lamb with scallops, served with a warm terrine of lamb with asparagus, dauphinoise potato and tomato jus. For dessert try the apple assiette – apple crumble, apple sorbet and apple cake, with a puree of apple and ginger cream.

Rooms 14 (5 annexe) (2 fmly) (2 GF) **S** £50-£60; **D** £80-£120 (incl. bkfst)* **Facilities** Xmas New Year Wi-fi **Conf** Class 12 Board 16 Thtr 20 Del from £97 to £120* **Parking** 20 **Notes** LB Civ Wed 24

Restaurant times Please telephone for details

North West Castle

★★★★ 75% HOTEL

☎ 01776 704413 ▤ 01776 702646
DG9 8EH
e-mail: info@northwestcastle.co.uk
web: www.northwestcastle.co.uk
dir: on seafront, close to Stena ferry terminal

This long-established hotel overlooks the bay and the ferry terminal. The public areas include a lounge with large leather armchairs and blazing fire in season and a classically styled dining room where a pianist plays in the evening. There is a shop, leisure centre, and a curling rink that becomes the focus in winter. Bedrooms are comfortable and spacious.

Rooms 72 (2 annexe) (22 fmly) **S** £59.50-£83; **D** £99-£136 (incl. bkfst & dinner)* **Facilities** ⓢ Gym Curling (Oct-Apr) Games room Xmas New Year Wi-fi **Conf** Class 60 Board 40 Thtr 150 Del from £75 to £90* **Services** Lift **Parking** 100 **Notes** LB Civ Wed 130

Corsewall Lighthouse Hotel

★★★ 78% HOTEL

☎ 01776 853220 ▤ 01776 854231
Corsewall Point, Kirkcolm DG9 0QG
e-mail: lighthousehotel@btinternet.com
web: www.lighthousehotel.co.uk
dir: A718 from Stranraer to Kirkcolm (approx 8m). Follow hotel signs for 4m

Looking for something completely different? A unique hotel converted from buildings that adjoin a listed 19th-century lighthouse set on a rocky coastline. Bedrooms come in a variety of sizes, some reached by a spiral staircase, and like the public areas, are cosy and atmospheric. Cottage suites in the grounds offer greater space.

Rooms 10 (4 annexe) (4 fmly) (2 GF) (2 smoking) **S** £130-£150; **D** £150-£250 (incl. bkfst & dinner)* **Facilities** FTV Xmas New Year **Conf** Thtr 20 Del from £100 to £140* **Parking** 20 **Notes** LB Civ Wed 28

Balyett Bed & Breakfast

★★★ ⒶBED AND BREAKFAST

☎ 01776 703395
Cairnryan Rd DG9 8QL
e-mail: balyett@btconnect.com
dir: 0.5m N of Stranraer on A77 overlooking Loch Ryan

Rooms 3 en suite S £45-£55; D £55-£75*

THORNHILL   Map 3 NX89

Gillbank House

★★★★★ GUEST ACCOMMODATION

☎ 01848 330597 📠 01848 331713
8 East Morton St DG3 5LZ
e-mail: hanne@gillbank.co.uk
web: www.gillbank.co.uk
dir: In town centre off A76

Gillbank House was originally built for a wealthy Edinburgh
merchant. Convenient for the many outdoor pursuits in this area,
such as fishing and golfing, this delightful house offers comfortable
and spacious bedrooms and smart shower rooms en suite. Breakfast
is served at individual tables in the bright, airy dining room, which is
next to the comfortable lounge.

Rooms 6 en suite (2 GF) S £45-£55; D £65-£70 **Facilities** tea/coffee
Cen ht **Parking** 8 **Notes** ⊗ No Children 8yrs

Robert Burns, Dumfries

Cameron House on Loch Lomond

★★★★★ 84% HOTEL

Cameron Grill

◉ British

Scottish through and through on the shores of Loch Lomond

☎ 01389 755565   📠 01389 759522
G83 8QZ
e-mail: reservations@cameronhouse.co.uk
web: www.devere.co.uk
dir: M8 (W) junct 30 for Erskine Bridge. A82 for Crainlarich. 14m, at rdbt signed Luss, hotel on right

Enjoying an idyllic location on the banks of Loch Lomond in over 100 acres of wooded parkland, this stylish hotel offers an excellent range of leisure facilities. These include two golf courses, a world-class spa and a host of indoor and outdoor sporting activities. A choice of restaurants and bars cater for all tastes and include a fine dining operation run by acclaimed chef, Martin Wishart (see entry below). Bedrooms are stylish, well equipped and many boast wonderful loch views. The Cameron Grill offers something a little different. It's a fabulous space full of dark wood and leather chairs and banquettes, and a large mural depicting a raucous looking banquet being enjoyed by traditionally attired gents. The lively menu is full of Scottish favourites, brasserie classics and steaks. Start with cream of broccoli soup, moving on to roasted rack of lamb served with a mini shepherd's pie, and finish with Granny Smith tarte fine with vanilla ice cream.

Rooms 96 (9 fmly) **Facilities** ⊗ ⚃ 9 ⚄ Fishing ⚇ Gym Squash Outdoor sports Motor boat on Loch Lomond Hairdresser Xmas **Conf** Class 80 Board 80 Thtr 300 **Services** Lift **Parking** 200 **Notes** LB ⊗ Civ Wed 200

Owner De Vere Hotels **Restaurant Times** 5.30-9.30 Closed L all week **Prices** Food prices not confirmed for 2010. Please telephone for details. **Children** Menu

Martin Wishart at Loch Lomond

◉◉◉ Modern French V

Top chef's new venture in old baronial mansion hotel

☎ 01389 722504
Cameron House on Loch Lomond G83 8QZ
e-mail: info@mwlochlomond.co.uk
web: www.innkeeperslodge.com/lochlomond
dir: M8 (W) junct 30 for Erskine Bridge. A82 for Crainlarich. 14m, at rdbt signed Luss, hotel on right

Martin Wishart's Leith restaurant (see entry) has been flying the cross of St Andrew for Scottish fine dining since 1999 and it is only now that he has ventured to open a satellite restaurant. He's chosen Cameron House on Loch Lomond (where he once worked) and moved over some of his team from Leith, headed-up by Stewart Boyles, creating in so doing another key address on Scotland's culinary tour. The room, decorated in natural tones of browns and creams and designed around high quality fixtures and fittings, is in keeping with the refined and classy French-influenced Scottish cuisine. The fixed-price menus (set lunch, evening carte and tasting menus) are based on first-class produce, while individual flavours never seem to get lost in the mix. Presse of foie gras and confit Gressingham duck is a superb dish, with pickled beetroot and white radish salad, duck bonbon and praline toast providing well-judged and perfectly balanced flavours. Main-course braised shin of Ross-shire beef is allowed to take centre stage and a dessert of lemon mousseline has just the right amount of sharpness. The charming and professional service fits the bill.

Chef Stewart Boyles **Owner** Martin Wishart **Times** 12-2.30/6.30-10 Closed Mon-Tue, L Wed-Sat **Prices** Tasting menu £50, Service optional, Groups min 6 service 10% **Wines** 190 bottles over £20, 12 by glass **Notes** Fixed L £25, Fixed D ALC £45, Tasting menu 5 course, Sunday L, Vegetarian menu, Dress restrictions, Smart casual, Air con **Seats** 40 **Children** Portions

Innkeeper's Lodge Loch Lomond

BUDGET HOTEL

☎ 0845 112 6006 📠 0845 112 6294
Balloch Rd G83 8LQ
web: www.innkeeperslodge.com/lochlomond
dir: M8 junct 30 onto M898. Over Erskine Bridge onto A82 for Crainlarich towards Dumbarton/Loch Lomond. Follow National Park signs, right onto A811, left into Davait Rd, left into Balloch Rd. Lodge opposite

Innkeeper's Lodge represents an exciting, high value concept within the budget hotel market. Comfortable bedrooms provide excellent facilities that include satellite TV and modem points. This carefully restored lodge is in a picturesque setting and has its own unique style and quirky character. Food is served all day, and an extensive, complimentary continental breakfast is offered. See also the Hotel Groups pages on theAA.com.

Rooms 12 (4 fmly)

Sunnyside

★★★ BED AND BREAKFAST

☎ 01389 750282 & 07717 397548
35 Main St G83 9JX
e-mail: enquiries@sunnysidebb.co.uk>aa
dir: From A82 take A811 then A813 for 1m, over mini-rdbt 150mtrs on left

Set in its own grounds well back from the road by Loch Lomond, Sunnyside is an attractive, traditional detached house, parts of which date back to the 1830s. Bedrooms are attractively decorated and provide comfortable modern accommodation. Free wireless internet access is also available. The dining room is located on the ground floor, and is an appropriate setting for hearty Scottish breakfasts.

Rooms 6 en suite (2 fmly) (1 GF) S £30-£45; D £46-£56*
Facilities tea/coffee Dinner available Cen ht Wi-fi **Parking** 8

Beardmore Hotel

★★★★ 77% HOTEL

☎ 0141 951 6000 📠 0141 951 6018
Beardmore St G81 4SA
e-mail: info@beardmore.scot.nhs.uk
dir: M8 junct 19, follow signs for Clydeside Expressway to Glasgow road, then A814 (Dumbarton road), then follow Clydebank Business Park signs. Hotel on left

Attracting much business and conference custom, this stylish modern hotel lies beside the River Clyde and shares an impressive site with a hospital (although the latter does not intrude). Spacious and imposing public areas include the stylish Arcoona Restaurant providing innovative contemporary cooking. The café bar offers a more extensive choice of informal lighter dishes.

Rooms 166 **Facilities** STV ⊗ supervised Gym Sauna Steam room Whirlpool Xmas New Year Wi-fi **Conf** Class 84 Board 27 Thtr 240 Del from £115 to £165* **Services** Lift Air con **Parking** 300 **Notes** ⊗ Civ Wed 170

Travelodge Dumbarton

BUDGET HOTEL

☎ 0871 984 6133 📠 01389 765202
Milton G82 2TZ
web: www.travelodge.co.uk
dir: 2m E of Dumbarton, on A82 W'bound

Travelodge offers good quality, good value, modern accommodation. Ideal for families, the spacious en suite bedrooms include remote-control TV, tea and coffee-making facilities and comfortable beds. Meals can be taken at the nearby family restaurant. See also the Hotel Groups pages on theAA.com.

Rooms 32 **S** fr £29 **D** fr £29

BROUGHTY FERRY   Map 3 NO43

The Royal Arch Bar ☕

☎ 01382 779741 📠 01382 739174
285 Brook St DD5 2DS
dir: 3m from Dundee. 0.5 min from Broughty Ferry rail station

In Victorian times, the jute industry made Broughty Ferry the 'richest square mile in Europe'. Named after a Masonic lodge which was demolished to make way for the Tay road bridge, the pub dates from 1869. The deep, dry cellars are ideal for conditioning ale so look forward to a nice pint in the bar with its original hand-carved oak bar, sideboard and counter. An extensive selection of meals range from light snacks to three-course meals.

Open all wk Closed: 1 Jan **Bar Meals** L served Mon-Fri 12-2.15, Sat-Sun 12-5 booking required D served All wk 5-7.30 booking required Av main course £8 ⊕ FREE HOUSE ◀ McEwans 80/-, Belhaven Best, Guinness, Caledonian, Deuchars IPA. ☕ 12 **Facilities** Children's menu Family room Dogs allowed Garden

DUNDEE   Map 3 NO43

Apex City Quay Hotel & Spa

★★★★ 81% HOTEL

⊛⊛ French, Scottish V

Enterprising cooking in a modern riverside hotel

☎ 0845 365 0000 📠 01382 201401
1 West Victoria Dock Rd DD1 3JP
e-mail: dundee.reservations@apexhotels.co.uk
web: www.apexhotels.co.uk
dir: A85/Riverside Drive to Discovery Quay. Exit rdbt for City Quay

This stylish, purpose-built hotel occupies an enviable position at the heart of Dundee's regenerated quayside area. Bedrooms, including a number of smart suites, feature the very latest in design. Among the various eating options, Alchemy is where the fine dining goes on, with a thoroughly contemporary menu of enterprising Scottish cooking. Dishes are headlined by their main ingredient, so if 'Asparagus' catches your eye on a spring menu, expect a velouté of the spears with smoked salmon foam and brown bread ice cream. Among mains, 'Trout' turns out to involve a crisp-skinned fillet, with dill gnocchi and a mussel emulsion infused with saffron, while 'Lamb' delivers the rack pinkly roasted, with spiced aubergine, baby spinach and a Niçoise jus.

Rooms 152 (16 fmly) (32 smoking) **Facilities** Spa FTV ❄ Gym Steam room Sauna Xmas New Year Wi-fi **Conf** Class 180 Board 120 Thtr 400 **Services** Lift Air con **Parking** 150 **Notes** LB ⊗ Civ Wed 300

Chef Michael Robinson, Nigel Liston **Owner** Mr Norman Springford **Restaurant Times** 7-9 Closed Various dates throughout the year, Sun-Wed, L all week **Prices** Fixed D 3 course fr £34, Tasting menu £34-£38, Service optional **Wines** 12 bottles over £20, 8 bottles under £20, 2 by glass **Notes** Tasting menu 5 course, Vegetarian available, Vegetarian menu, Dress restrictions, Smart dress, Air con **Seats** 30, Pr/dining room 10

The Landmark Hotel

★★★★ 76% HOTEL

☎ 01382 641122 📠 01382 631201
Kingsway West DD2 5JT
e-mail: sales@thelandmarkdundee.co.uk
web: www.thelandmarkdundee.co.uk
dir: On A90 Dundee Kingsway at junct with A85

Benefitting from a total refurbishment in 2009, the Landmark offers modern contemporary bedrooms, and bathrooms equipped with many thoughtful extras for the modern guest. The restaurant overlooks the pleasant gardens. A good sized leisure club is an added benefit.

Rooms 95 (11 fmly) (45 GF) **Facilities** STV FTV ❄ supervised Gym Sauna Steam room Xmas New Year Wi-fi **Conf** Class 50 Board 45 Thtr 100 Del from £95 to £145* **Parking** 140 **Notes** ⊗ Civ Wed 100

Travelodge Dundee

BUDGET HOTEL

☎ 0871 984 6135 📠 01382 610488
A90 Kingsway DD2 4TD
web: www.travelodge.co.uk
dir: On A90

Travelodge offers good quality, good value, modern accommodation. Ideal for families, the spacious en suite bedrooms include remote-control TV, tea and coffee-making facilities and comfortable beds. Meals can be taken at the nearby family restaurant. See also the Hotel Groups pages on theAA.com.

Rooms 32 **S** fr £29; **D** fr £29

Travelodge Dundee Central

BUDGET HOTEL

☎ 0871 984 6301
152-158 West Marketgait DD1 1NL
web: www.travelodge.co.uk
dir: From Airport right towards city centre. At 3rd rbt take 1st exit. At next rbt take 2nd exit

Rooms 48 **S** fr £29; **D** fr £29

Speedwell Bar ☕

☎ 01382 667783
165-167 Perth Rd DD2 1AS
e-mail: jonathan_stewart@fsmail.net
dir: From city centre along Perth Rd, pass university, last bar on right

Popularly known as Mennies, this surviving Edwardian pub is listed for an interior full of period character. The same family owned it for 90 years, until the present landlord's father bought it in 1995. The bar offers 157 whiskies. A kitchen would be good, but since the pub is listed this is impossible, so signs encourage customers to bring in pies from next door.

Open all wk ⊕ FREE HOUSE ◀ McEwans, Belhaven Best. ☕ 10 **Facilities** Dogs allowed

EDINBURGH   Map 3 NT27

Prestonfield

★★★★★ TOWN HOUSE HOTEL

◉◉ Modern European 🍷NOTABLE WINE LIST

Opulent setting for impressive food

☎ 0131 225 7800   📠 0131 220 4392
Priestfield Rd EH16 5UT
e-mail: reservations@prestonfield.com   **web:** www.prestonfield.com
dir: A7 towards Cameron Toll. 200mtrs beyond Royal Commonwealth
Pool, into Priestfield Rd

Unapologetically opulent, Prestonfield Hotel is a stunning, lavishly
restored and richly refurbished Regency house set in 20 acres of
parkland on the outskirts of the city. This centuries-old landmark has
been lovingly restored and enhanced to provide deeply comfortable
and dramatically furnished bedrooms. Facilities and services are up-
to-the-minute, and the building demands to be explored: from the
tapestry lounge and the whisky room to the award-winning Rhubarb
restaurant, which occupies two richly appointed oval rooms. Portraits
of former owners, including Sir Alexander Dick, who first introduced
rhubarb to Scotland, adorn the walls, and there are fine views from
the crisp, linen-clothed tables. Top-notch seasonal Scottish produce
is found on the ambitious, modern European menu. Expect classic
dishes like lamb cutlets with mint hollandaise or beef sirloin with
peppercorn jus, alongside turbot with confit lemon, razor clams and
caper butter, or braised haunch and roast loin of venison with
smoked garlic cream. Desserts are a strength, such as bitter
chocolate tart with lime ice cream, mango and Thai basil.

Rooms 23 (6 GF) **Facilities** STV FTV ♨ 18 Putt green 🚲 Free bike hire
Xmas New Year Wi-fi **Conf** Class 500 Board 40 Thtr 700 **Services** Lift
Parking 250 **Notes** LB Civ Wed 350

Chef John McMahon **Owner** James Thomson OBE **Restaurant**
Times 12-2/6-11 **Prices** Fixed L 2 course £16.95, Fixed D 3 course
£30, Starter £7.50-£14, Main £10-£28, Dessert £6.95-£8.95, Service
optional, Groups min 8 service 10% **Wines** 500+ bottles over £20, 12
by glass **Notes** Theatre D 2 course £16.95, Afternoon tea £16.95,
Sunday L, Vegetarian available **Seats** 90, Pr/dining room 500
Children Portions

The Balmoral Hotel

★★★★★ 88% HOTEL

Hadrian's

◉ Modern European

Buzzy, stylish brasserie with a cosmopolitan menu

☎ 0131 556 2414   📠 0131 557 3747
1 Princes St EH2 2EQ
e-mail: reservations.balmoral@roccofortecollection.com
web: www.roccofortecollection.com
dir: Follow city centre signs. Hotel at E end of Princes St, adjacent to
Waverley Station

Edinburgh locations don't come much better than the landmark
Balmoral Hotel's pitch on Princes Street, from where this elegant
hotel enjoys fine views over the city and the castle. Bedrooms and
suites are stylishly furnished and decorated, all boasting a
thoughtful range of extras and impressive marble bathrooms. Hotel
amenities include a Roman-style health spa, extensive function
facilities, a choice of bars and two very different dining options;
Number One offers inspired fine dining (see entry below) while the
fashionable Hadrian's is every inch the slick contemporary brasserie,
from its staff in black waistcoats and long white aprons to the art
deco-influenced interior, with walnut floors and walls in hues of lime
and violet. The menu takes quality Scottish ingredients on a soothing
roam around Europe's classics. Comforting familiarity appears in a
warm tart of Dunsyre blue cheese and creamed leeks, main courses
like roast saddle of venison with braised cabbage and fondant potato
or, sizzling from the grill, a fillet of Shetland salmon with spiced
couscous and lemon butter. Old favourites such as tarte Tatin, or
lemon tart with thyme ice cream round things off nicely.

Rooms 188 (22 fmly) (15 smoking) **S** £305-£2000; **D** £360-£2000*
Facilities Spa STV 🏊 Gym 🎵 Xmas New Year Wi-fi **Conf** Class 180
Board 60 Thtr 350 Del from £245 to £430* **Services** Lift Air con
Parking 100 **Notes** LB ⊗ Civ Wed 120

Chef Jeff Bland **Owner** Rocco Forte Hotels **Restaurant**
Times 12-2.30/6.30-10.30 **Prices** Fixed L 2 course £14-£20, Fixed D
3 course £19-£25, Starter £7.50-£9.50, Main £10-£24, Dessert £5,
Service optional, Groups min 8 service 10% **Wines** 42 bottles over
£20, 8 by glass **Notes** Sunday L, Vegetarian available, Dress
restrictions, Smart casual, Air con **Seats** 100, Pr/dining room 26
Children Portions, Menu

Number One, The Balmoral Hotel

◉◉◉ Modern Scottish, French

First-class fine dining at prestigious Edinburgh hotel

☎ 0131 557 6727   📠 0131 557 8740
1 Princes St EH2 2EQ
e-mail: numberone@roccofortecollection.com

With a prestigious address at the top of Princes Street, and fine
views over the city and castle, this elegant hotel presides grandly
over the heart of the city. Fine-dining restaurant Number One is set
on the lower-ground floor, but is none the worse for that; designed by
Olga Polizzi, the space is opulent, luxurious and multi-textured. Walls
are rich, dark-red lacquered and adorned with modern artworks, the

carpet is a deep pile job, tables are well-spaced and the service is suitably formal; jackets are expected for gentlemen and other traditional touches such as the cheese, bread and liqueur trolleys all add to the sense of occasion. Classical preparations meet modern interpretations in dishes based on excellent Scottish produce and showing high technical skills. Start, perhaps, with crab millefeuille with brown crab pannacotta and wasabi mayo, then maybe a main course of fillet of Borders beef with oxtail ravioli, squash purée and braised leeks. Finish with a chocolate chiboust with blood oranges and Manjari chocolate sorbet. For less formal dining, there's the hotel's Hadrian's brasserie (see entry above).

Chef Jeff Bland, Craig Sandle **Owner** Rocco Forte Hotels
Times 6.30-10 Closed 1st 2 wks Jan, L all week **Prices** Fixed D 3 course £57.50, Tasting menu £65-£110, Service optional, Groups min 6 service 12.5% **Wines** 350 bottles over £20, 8 by glass **Notes** Tasting menu 6 course, Vegetarian available, Dress restrictions, Smart casual preferred, Air con **Seats** 50, Pr/dining room 50 **Children** Portions

The Howard

★★★★★ 84%   TOWN HOUSE HOTEL

Modern Scottish

Stylish Georgian townhouse with intimate dining room

☎ 0131 274 7402 & 557 3500   ▤ 0131 274 7405
34 Great King St EH3 6QH
e-mail: reserve@thehoward.com
web: www.thehoward.com
dir: E on Queen St, 2nd left, Dundas St. Through 3 lights, right, hotel on left

The five-star Howard is made up of three grand Georgian townhouses in the heart of the city, just a short walk from Princes Street. Quietly elegant and splendidly luxurious, The Howard provides an intimate and high quality experience for the discerning traveller. The sumptuous bedrooms, in a variety of styles, include spacious suites, well-equipped bathrooms and a host of thoughtful touches. Sip a cocktail in the elegant drawing room with its ornate chandeliers, lavish drapes and views of the wide cobbled streets, before moving onto the Georgian splendour of The Atholl, the small dining room with smartly laid tables and hand-painted murals on the walls dating back to the 1820s. The menu deals in classical dishes with flashes of innovation and plenty of Scottish touches; langoustine ravioli comes with pieces of lobster and a sharp citrus emulsion, followed by highland venison - pink and tender - with spiced red cabbage and roasted garlic and parsley mash.

Rooms 18 (1 fmly) (1 GF) **S** £90-£155; **D** £180-£415 (incl. bkfst)*
Facilities FTV Xmas New Year Wi-fi **Conf** Class 15 Board 20 Thtr 30 Del from £240 to £340* **Services** Lift **Parking** 10 **Notes** LB Civ Wed 40

Chef William Poncelet **Owner** Peter Taylor **Restaurant Times** 12-2/6-9.30 **Prices** Starter £6-£11, Main £14-£28, Dessert £7-£9, Service optional **Wines** 40 bottles over £20, 6 bottles under £20, 10 by glass **Notes** Pre-theatre menu available, Sunday L, Vegetarian available, Civ Wed 40 **Seats** 18, Pr/dining room 40 **Children** Portions

The Scotsman

★★★★★ 78% TOWN HOUSE HOTEL

North Bridge Brasserie

Modern British, Scottish

Stylish setting for relaxed, modern fine dining

☎ 0131 556 5565   ▤ 0131 652 3652
20 North Bridge EH1 1YT
e-mail: reservations@thescotsmanhotelgroup.co.uk
web: www.thescotsmanhotel.co.uk
dir: A8 to city centre, left onto Charlotte St. Right into Queen St, right at rdbt onto Leith St. Straight on, left onto North Bridge, hotel on right

Once the head office of The Scotsman newspaper, this stunning Victorian building, now an opulent hotel, combines the best of the grand original features with cutting-edge design. The classical elegance of the public areas, complete with a marble staircase, blends seamlessly with the contemporary bedrooms and their state-of-the-art technology. The superbly equipped leisure club includes a stainless steel swimming pool and large gym. Dining arrangements can be made in the funky North Bridge Brasserie or in the opulent, intimate Vermilion Restaurant, complete with pillars and baronial wood panelling. Housed in former offices, the brasserie offers technically accomplished and creative dishes, which make good use of quality Scottish produce, on sensibly compact menus. Take sea bream with smoked salmon risotto and braised onions, haunch of venison with braised red cabbage, and warm chocolate pudding.

Rooms 79 (4 GF) **Facilities** Spa STV supervised Gym Beauty treatments New Year Wi-fi **Conf** Class 50 Board 40 Thtr 100 **Services** Lift **Notes** Civ Wed 70

Chef Spencer Wilson **Owner** The Eton Collection/The Scotsman Hotel Group **Restaurant Times** 12-2.30/6-10.30 **Prices** Fixed L 2 course fr £12, Starter £5.50-£9.50, Main £9-£18.50, Dessert £5.50-£6, Service added but optional 10% **Wines** 80 bottles over £20, 12 bottles under £20, 14 by glass **Notes** Sunday L, Vegetarian available, Dress restrictions, Smart casual, Air con **Seats** 80, Pr/dining room 80 **Children** Portions, Menu

Sheraton Grand Hotel & Spa

★★★★★ 78% HOTEL

☎ 0131 229 9131   ▤ 0131 228 4510
1 Festival Square EH3 9SR
e-mail: grandedinburgh.sheraton@sheraton.com
dir: Follow City Centre signs (A8). Through Shandwick Place, right at lights into Lothian Rd. Right at next lights. Hotel on left at next lights

This modern hotel boasts one of the best spas in Scotland - the external top floor hydro pool is definitely worth a look whilst the thermal suite provides a unique venue for serious relaxation. The spacious bedrooms are available in a variety of styles, and the suites prove very popular. There is a wide range of eating options including The Terrace and Santini's - both have a loyal local following.

continued

EDINBURGH CONTINUED

Rooms 260 (21 fmly) **S** £105-£210; **D** £120-£240* **Facilities** Spa STV ⊕ ⊰ Gym Indoor/Outdoor Hydropool Kinesis studioThermal suite Fitness studio ♫ Xmas New Year Wi-fi **Conf** Class 350 Board 120 Thtr 485 Del from £199 to £400* **Services** Lift Air con **Parking** 122 **Notes** LB ⊗ Civ Wed 485

Channings

★★★★ TOWN HOUSE HOTEL

⊛ Modern British ⊜

Well-judged modern food in a bright basement

☎ 0131 332 3232 & 315 2226 ▤ 0131 332 9631
15 South Learmonth Gardens EH4 1EZ
e-mail: reserve@channings.co.uk
web: www.channings.co.uk
dir: From A90 & Forth Road Bridge, follow signs for city centre

Channings comes from the same boutique townhouse stable as the stylish Bonham (see entry), so you can expect a polished experience on all fronts. One of the houses in this quintet of converted Edwardian properties, just minutes from the centre of the city, was once home to the Antarctic explorer Sir Ernest Shackleton. The attractive and individually designed bedrooms have a hi-tech spec for business guests, while the public areas include sumptuous, inviting lounges and a choice of dining options. The Ochre Vita wine bar and Mediterranean restaurant offer the popular choice, but for a special-occasion dinner try the seven-course tasting menu with wines in Channings Restaurant. An intimate, modern basement room, it provides a fuss-free foodie bolt-hole here in the trendy urban village of Stockbridge. The kitchen has an intelligent approach and turns out a well-crafted repertoire of exciting modern dishes with clear focus on seasonality and top-quality organic produce. Pan-fried wood pigeon is teamed with pearl barley risotto, vegetable rösti and pigeon jus; next up, a pan-fried fillet of sea bream sits well with plum tomato and parmesan tart and sautéed potatoes.

Rooms 41 (4 GF) **S** £85-£200; **D** £125-£250 (incl. bkfst)*
Facilities STV FTV ♫ Xmas New Year Wi-fi **Conf** Class 40 Board 28 Thtr 60 **Services** Lift **Notes** LB ⊗

Chef Karen MacKay **Owner** Mr P Taylor **Restaurant Times** 12-2.30/6-10 **Prices** Fixed L 2 course £13, Starter £5.50-£8, Main £15-£25, Dessert £6-£7, Service optional, Groups min 10 service 10% **Wines** 26 bottles over £20, 16 bottles under £20, 6 by glass **Notes** Sunday L, Vegetarian available **Seats** 40, Pr/dining room 30 **Children** Portions

Norton House

★★★★ 88% HOTEL

⊛⊛⊛ Modern British, French

Sophisticated fine-dining restaurant in elegant hotel

☎ 0131 333 1275 ▤ 0131 333 5305
Ingliston EH28 8LX
e-mail: nortonhouse@handpicked.co.uk
web: www.handpicked.co.uk
dir: off A8, 5m W of city centre

Norton House was always intended as a refuge from the hurly-burly of Edinburgh; the Usher family of Scottish brewing wealth once tucked themselves away here amid 55 acres of parkland and woods, peacefully situated just outside the city and convenient for the airport. Both the contemporary bedrooms and the very spacious traditional ones have an impressive range of accessories including plasma screen TVs with DVD recorders. In addition to all that, you can be pampered in the top-drawer spa and tuck into seriously good food. A chic new black leather and dark-wood brasserie offers a relaxed way in to sample the kitchen's talents, but if you really want to see what the team is capable of, Ushers is the sophisticated fine-dining option. It's a soothingly stylish, low-lit space rather like stepping into an upmarket Parisian chocolatier with its luscious colours of café crème, caramel and milk chocolate brown. With just 8 well-spaced tables to care for, the staff deliver impeccable service, always attentive, arriving with first-class breads and clever canapés. The kitchen takes a modern tack with classic French cuisine; as with all top-level cooking, prime ingredients are the key here, impeccably sourced and put into the talented hands of a team that has the technical skills and confidence to let the materials talk for themselves. Dishes are composed with deceptive simplicity and precise, balanced flavours, as with torchon of duck foie gras married with a tangy rhubarb chutney and toasted gingerbread preceding pan-fried sea bass fillet with olive gnocchi and a cassoulet-style confection of butterbeans, tomato fondant, chorizo and caper berries. Unmissable desserts include a textbook prune and Armagnac soufflé with white chocolate cappuccino and bitter chocolate spring roll.

Rooms 83 (10 fmly) (20 GF) **S** £99-£495; **D** £109-£505 (incl. bkfst)
Facilities Spa ⊕ Gym Archery Laser Clay shooting Quad biking Xmas New Year Wi-fi **Conf** Class 100 Board 60 Thtr 300 Del from £135 to £205 **Services** Lift **Parking** 200 **Notes** LB ⊗ Civ Wed 140

Chef Graeme Shaw, Glen Bilins **Owner** Hand Picked Hotels **Restaurant Times** 7-9.30 Closed 26 Dec, 1 Jan, Sun-Mon, L all week **Prices** Starter £8.50-£12.95, Main £23.95-£26.95, Dessert £8.50-£8.95, Service optional **Wines** 168 bottles over £20, 12 by glass **Notes** Vegetarian available, Air con **Seats** 22, Pr/dining room 40 **Children** Portions

Marriott Dalmahoy Hotel & Country Club

★★★★ 81% HOTEL

◎◎ Modern, Traditional

Stylish Scots cooking in Georgian splendour

☎ 0131 333 1845 📄 0131 333 1433
Kirknewton EH27 8EB
e-mail: mhrs.edigs.frontdesk@marriotthotels.com
web: www.marriottdalmahoy.co.uk
dir: Edinburgh City Bypass (A720) turn onto A71 towards Livingston, hotel on left in 2m

The handsome Georgian mansion was built in the 1720s to a design by William Adam; the modern history of the place began in 1976, when it became a country club. Sheltered at the foot of the Pentland hills, it sits in 1,000 acres of wooded parkland, but is not so distant from Edinburgh that you can't see the castle. With two championship golf courses and a health and beauty club, there is plenty here to occupy guests. Bedrooms are spacious and most have fine views, while public rooms offer a choice of formal and informal drinking and dining options. Fine Scottish produce is shown off to great effect in the main dining room, with smoked salmon, oatmeal-crumbed haggis and Arbroath smokies turning up among the starters alone. Main courses might offer slow-cooked pork belly with red cabbage and creamed haricots, but see also the catch of the day. Then finish with regional cheeses and oatcakes, or perhaps rum savarin with poached sultanas and cream.

Rooms 215 (172 annexe) (59 fmly) (6 smoking) **S** £95-£175;
D £95-£175* **Facilities** Spa STV ⊗ ♨ 18 ♨ Putt green Gym Health & beauty treatments Steam room Dance studio Driving range Golf lessons Xmas New Year Wi-fi **Conf** Class 200 Board 120 Thtr 300 Del from £150 to £195* **Services** Lift Air con **Parking** 350 **Notes** LB ⊗ Civ Wed 250

Chef Alan Matthew **Owner** Marriott Hotels Ltd **Restaurant Times** 7-10 **Prices** Starter £5.50-£8.50, Main £16.50-£24, Dessert £5.50-£6.50, Service optional **Wines** 18 bottles over £20, 8 bottles under £20, 8 by glass **Notes** Vegetarian available, Dress restrictions, Smart casual, Air con **Seats** 120, Pr/dining room 16 **Children** Portions, Menu

Hotel du Vin Edinburgh

★★★★ 80% TOWN HOUSE HOTEL

◎ European

Modern Scottish brasserie cooking in a fashionable small chain hotel

☎ 0131 247 4900 📄 0131 247 4901
11 Bristo Place EH1 1EZ

In its Edinburgh outpost, the Hotel du Vin brand has sprinkled its magic on a former lunatic asylum in a prime location in the Old Town. All bedrooms display the Hotel du Vin trademark facilities - air conditioning, free Wi-fi, plasma TVs, monsoon showers and Egyptian cotton linen to name but a few. The interior goes for a timeless clubby look - there are scuffed leather armchairs and tartans to suit a Highland laird in the whisky snug, while a bustling mezzanine bar overlooks the brasserie with the chain's trademark wooden floors, unclothed tables and wine-related memorabilia on its walls. Waiting

staff know their stuff, and the kitchen injects a sense of place into its Scottish-inflected brasserie menus, kicking off with an Isle of Mull cheddar soufflé and moving on to pan-seared salmon with lentils and chorizo. As with all branches of HdV, you can be sure of a cracking wine list. For the real connoisseur there's La Roche tasting room where wines from around the world can be appreciated.

Rooms 47 **Restaurant Times** 12-2.30/5.30-10.30

Edinburgh Marriott Hotel

★★★★ 80% HOTEL

☎ 0131 334 9191 📄 0131 316 4507
111 Glasgow Rd EH12 8NF
e-mail: edinburgh@marriotthotels.com
web: www.EdinburghMarriott.co.uk
dir: M8 junct 1 for Gogar, at rdbt turn right for city centre, hotel on right

This smart, modern hotel is located on the city's western edge which is convenient for the bypass, airport, showground and business park. Public areas include an attractive marbled foyer, extensive conference facilities and a restaurant serving a range of international dishes. The air-conditioned bedrooms are spacious and equipped with a range of extras.

Rooms 245 (76 fmly) (64 GF) (6 smoking) **Facilities** Spa STV ⊗ Gym Steam room Sauna Massage & beauty treatment room Hairdresser Xmas New Year Wi-fi **Conf** Class 120 Board 50 Thtr 250 **Services** Lift Air con **Parking** 300 **Notes** LB ⊗ Civ Wed 80

George Hotel Edinburgh

★★★★ 80% HOTEL

☎ 0131 225 1251 📄 0131 226 5644
19-21 George St EH2 2PB
e-mail: Inquires.campbell@principal-hayley.com
web: www.principal-hayley.com/thegeorge
dir: In city centre

A long-established hotel, the George enjoys a city centre location. The splendid public areas have many original features such as intricate plasterwork, a marble-floored foyer and chandeliers. The Tempus Bar offers menus that feature a wide range of dishes to suit most tastes. The elegant, modern bedrooms come in a mix of sizes and styles; the upper ones having fine city views.

Rooms 249 (20 fmly) (4 GF) **S** £79-£229; **D** £79-£399* **Facilities** STV Xmas New Year Wi-fi **Conf** Class 120 Board 50 Thtr 300 Del from £129 to £299* **Services** Lift **Notes** LB ⊗ Civ Wed 300

Apex International Hotel

★★★★ 79% HOTEL

◉◉ Modern Scottish

Accomplished cooking and magnificent castle views

☎ 0845 365 0000 & 0131 300 3456 🖷 0131 220 5345
31/35 Grassmarket EH1 2HS
e-mail: edinburgh.reservations@apexhotels.co.uk
web: www.apexhotels.co.uk
dir: Into Lothian Rd at west end of Princes St, then 1st left into King Stables Rd, leads into Grassmarket

A sister to the Apex City Hotel close by, the International lies in a historic and very fashionable square in the shadow of Edinburgh Castle. It has a versatile business and conference centre, and also Yu Time leisure and fitness facility with a stainless steel ozone pool. Bedrooms are contemporary in style and very well equipped. The dramatic and appropriately-named Heights Restaurant boasts stunning views of the city. Occupying the 5th floor of this contemporary, stylish boutique hotel, the modern décor combines floor-to-ceiling windows with glass and chrome, wood and marble and subdued minimalist lighting. The menu is short but to the point, with a focus on the best seasonal Scottish ingredients, with plentiful seafood and game. Expect well-tuned, intelligent and defined flavours in dishes like carpaccio of venison, roasted pear, sloe gin tartare and roasted walnuts. A main course of fillet of sea bream, saffron potato, pancetta and mint pea broth could be followed by espresso sabayon and lemon biscotti.

Rooms 171 (99 fmly) (12 smoking) **Facilities** ⊙ Gym Tropicarium Xmas New Year Wi-fi **Conf** Class 80 Board 40 Thtr 200 **Services** Lift **Parking** 60 **Notes** LB ⊗ Civ Wed 200

Chef John Newton **Owner** Norman Springford **Restaurant Times** 7-9.30 Closed Sun-Wed, L all week **Prices** Fixed D 3 course £23.50-£25, Starter £5.50-£8.95, Main £14-£17.95, Dessert £5.50-£9.95, Service optional **Wines** 11 bottles over £20, 9 bottles under £20, 6 by glass **Notes** Vegetarian available **Seats** 85, Pr/dining room 120

Apex Waterloo Place Hotel

★★★★ 78% HOTEL

☎ 0131 523 1819
23 - 27 Waterloo Place EH1 3BH

This stunning, newly converted hotel provides a state-of-the-art experience with slick interior design. Bedrooms, many with city views, are well appointed for both the business and leisure guest; stunning duplex suites provide extra space, surround-sound TV systems and luxurious feature bathrooms. The restaurant provides an appealing menu both at dinner and breakfast. There is also a well-equipped fitness centre and indoor pool. The hotel has direct, pedestrian access to Edinburgh's Waverley Station.

Novotel Edinburgh Park

★★★★ 78% HOTEL

☎ 0131 446 5600 🖷 0131 446 5610
15 Lochside Av EH12 9DJ
e-mail: h6515@accor.com
dir: Near Hermiston Gate shopping area

Located just off the city by-pass and within minutes of the airport, this new concept hotel brings a modern and fresh approach to the Novotel brand. Bedrooms are spacious and comfortable as is the open-plan lobby, bar and restaurant with some tables that boast their own TVs.

Rooms 170 (130 fmly) **S** £89-£160; **D** £89-£160* **Facilities** ⊙ Gym Wi-fi **Conf** Class 60 Board 40 Thtr 150 Del from £120 to £160 **Services** Lift **Parking** 96 **Notes** LB

The Bonham

★★★★ 77% TOWN HOUSE HOTEL

◉◉ Modern Scottish ◔

Stylish urban setting for lively, modern cooking

☎ 0131 274 7400 🖷 0131 274 7405
35 Drumsheugh Gardens EH3 7RN
e-mail: reserve@thebonham.com
web: www.thebonham.com
dir: Close to West End & Princes St

Overlooking tree-lined gardens, this Victorian town house combines classical elegance with very modish contemporary style. Inviting day rooms include a reception lounge and bedrooms, in a variety of sizes, are smart and stylish with good internet access and an interactive TV system. And instead of buying glossy magazines for interior décor inspiration, come for dinner in the very swish restaurant. The Bonham ticks all the boxes: oodles of period charm - wooden floors, oak panelling and intricate plasterwork in abundance - blended with a permanent modern art exhibition to form a palette of exuberantly tasteful colour. The restaurant set-up oozes class with its dark-wood tables set with fine glassware, cutlery, linen napkins and candles, and the slick service and imaginative cuisine both rise to the challenge. The French chef marries classical influences with modern Scottish flair and faultless raw materials in his well-judged dishes. A starter of roasted hand-dived scallops with gutsy pig's trotter croquettes and langoustine ravioli sets the bar high, and the momentum is kept up through roast loin of venison with gnocchi, braised red cabbage cracker and bitter chocolate sauce.

Rooms 48 (1 GF) **S** £110-£250; **D** £135-£280 (incl. bkfst)* **Facilities** STV FTV Xmas New Year Wi-fi **Conf** Board 26 Thtr 50 **Services** Lift **Parking** 20 **Notes** LB ⊗

Chef Michel Bouyer **Owner** Peter Taylor, The Town House Company **Restaurant Times** 12-2.30/6.30-10 **Prices** Fixed L 2 course £13.50, Starter £6-£12, Main £15-£23, Dessert £6-£8.50, Service added but optional 10%, Groups min 6 service 10% **Wines** 22 bottles over £20, 12 bottles under £20 **Notes** Sunday L, Vegetarian available **Seats** 60, Pr/dining room 26 **Children** Portions

The Royal Terrace

★★★★ 77% HOTEL

🏵 Modern British

Creative brasserie food in handsome Georgian Edinburgh

☎ 0131 557 3222   📠 0131 557 5334
18 Royal Ter EH7 5AQ
e-mail: sales@royalterracehotel.co.uk
web: www.royalterracehotel.co.uk
dir: A8 to city centre, follow one-way system, left into Charlotte Sq. At end right into Queens St. Left at rdbt. At next island right into London Rd, right into Blenheim Place leading to Royal Terrace

Part of an immaculately restored Georgian terrace not far from the city centre, the hotel is in as handsome a location as Edinburgh affords. Bedrooms successfully blend the historic architecture of the building with state-of-the-art facilities, and although most rooms afford lovely views, the top floor rooms provide excellent panoramas of the city, and two of the 13 Ambassador Suites have glass bathrooms. High ceilings and lovely cornices inside set the tone for the ground-floor restaurant, which extends into a conservatory area that overlooks the impeccably maintained sloping gardens. Danish chef Morten Rengtved is something of an old Scottish hand by now, and brings a natural brasserie sensibility to conscientiously sourced materials. It all looks good too, as witnessed by a croquette of smoked haddock bedded on vivid pea purée, with mustard-dressed leaves, on a slate slab. Continue to finely judged pork, served two ways in the modern style: Parma ham-wrapped fillet and slow-cooked belly.

Rooms 107 (13 fmly) (7 GF) **Facilities** ⊗ Gym Steam room Sauna Aromatherapy shower Xmas New Year Wi-fi **Conf** Class 40 Board 40 Thtr 100 **Services** Lift **Notes** ⊗ Civ Wed 80

Prices Food prices not confirmed for 2010. Please telephone for details.

Best Western Bruntsfield Hotel

★★★★ 77% HOTEL

☎ 0131 229 1393   📠 0131 229 5634
69 Bruntsfield Place EH10 4HH
e-mail: sales@thebruntsfield.co.uk
web: www.thebruntsfield.co.uk
dir: From S into Edinburgh on A702. Hotel 1m S of west end of Princes Street

Overlooking Bruntsfield Links and only minutes from the city centre, this smart hotel has stylish public rooms including a spacious lounge and a new contemporary bar and brasserie with an outside terrace. The individually styled bedrooms come in a variety of sizes but all are well appointed. Smart staff provide good levels of service and attention.

Rooms 67 (5 fmly) (10 GF) **Facilities** STV FTV New Year Wi-fi **Conf** Class 70 Board 45 Thtr 120 **Services** Lift **Parking** 25 **Notes** ⊗ Closed 25 Dec Civ Wed 100

Macdonald Holyrood

★★★★ 75% HOTEL

🏵 Modern Scottish

Relaxed dining in the shadow of Holyrood Palace

☎ 0870 1942106   📠 0131 550 4545
Holyrood Rd EH8 8AU
e-mail: general.holyrood@macdonald-hotels.co.uk
web: www.macdonaldhotels.co.uk/holyrood
dir: Parallel to Royal Mile, near Holyrood Palace & Dynamic Earth

You'd be pushed to find a better base for exploring Edinburgh than this sizeable modern hotel in the heart of the Old Town, a short stroll from the Scottish Parliament and Holyrood Palace. Air-conditioned bedrooms are comfortably furnished, whilst the Club floor boasts a private lounge. Full business services complement the extensive conference suites. The Opus 504 restaurant fits the surroundings neatly with its clean-cut contemporary décor and unfussy modern Scottish cuisine with cosmopolitan twists. This is just the spot to show off Scotland's superb produce, thus a starter pairs pan-seared Loch Fyne scallops with caper and cauliflower purée, and a whole Arbroath smokie comes with creamed mash and spinach in a simple, hearty main course. Finish with a luscious chocolate and hazelnut terrine with strawberry coulis.

Rooms 156 (16 fmly) (13 GF) **Facilities** Spa STV ⊗ Gym Beauty treatment rooms Sun bed ♫ Xmas New Year Wi-fi **Conf** Class 100 Board 80 Thtr 200 Del from £160 to £290 **Services** Lift Air con **Parking** 35 **Notes** ⊗ Civ Wed 100

Restaurant Times 12-2/6.30-10 Closed D 25 Dec

The King James by Thistle

★★★★ 75% HOTEL

☎ 0871 376 9016   📠 0871 376 9116
107 Leith St EH1 3SW
e-mail: edinburgh@thistle.co.uk
web: www.thistlehotels.com/edinburgh
dir: M8/M9 onto A8 signed city centre. Hotel at end of Princes St adjacent to St James shopping centre

This purpose-built hotel adjoins one of Edinburgh's premier shopping malls at the east end of Princes Street. A friendly team of staff are keen to please whilst stylish, well-equipped bedrooms provide excellent levels of comfort and facilities. Public areas include a spacious restaurant, popular bar, and an elegant lobby lounge.

Rooms 143 (12 fmly) **S** £60-£180; **Facilities** STV FTV Xmas New Year Wi-fi **Conf** Class 160 Board 50 Thtr 250 Del from £140 to £300* **Services** Lift **Parking** 18 **Notes** LB ⊗ Civ Wed 250

Edinburgh Castle, Edinburgh

The Roxburghe Hotel

★★★★ 74% HOTEL

☎ 0844 879 9063 & 0131 240 5500 ▤ 0131 240 5555
38 Charlotte Square EH2 4HQ
e-mail: general.roxburghe@macdonaldhotels.co.uk
web: www.macdonaldhotels.co.uk/roxburghe
dir: on corner of Charlotte Sq & George St

This long-established hotel lies in the heart of the city overlooking Charlotte Square Gardens. Public areas are inviting and include relaxing lounges, a choice of bars (in the evening) and an inner concourse that looks onto a small lawned area. Smart bedrooms come in both classic and contemporary styles. There is a secure underground car park.

Rooms 196 (3 fmly) **S** £85-£260; **D** £95-£270 **Facilities** Spa FTV ☜ Gym Dance studio Sauna Steam room Xmas New Year Wi-fi **Conf** Class 160 Board 50 Thtr 300 Del from £150 to £260 **Services** Lift Air con **Parking** 20 **Notes** LB ⊗ Civ Wed 280

Holiday Inn Edinburgh

★★★★ 73% HOTEL

☎ 0870 400 9026 ▤ 0131 334 9237
Corstorphine Rd EH12 6UA
e-mail: edinburghhi@ihg.com
web: www.holidayinn.co.uk
dir: On A8, adjacent to Edinburgh Zoo

A modern hotel situated three miles west of Edinburgh and near Edinburgh Business Park. The hotel enjoys panoramic views of the Pentland Hills and makes a good base for visiting the attractions of the city. Bedrooms include family and executive rooms. The eating options are Traders Restaurant or Sampans Oriental Restaurant, as well as a café and bar. The Spirit Health and Fitness Club has a gym, swimming pool, sauna, spa and beauty treatments. There is also a conference centre.

Rooms 303 (76 fmly) (41 smoking) **Facilities** Spa STV ☜ supervised Gym New Year Wi-fi **Conf** Class 60 Board 45 Thtr 120 Del from £135 to £185* **Services** Lift Air con **Parking** 105 **Notes** ⊗

Novotel Edinburgh Centre

★★★★ 73% HOTEL

☎ 0131 656 3500 ▤ 0131 656 3510
Lauriston Place, Lady Lawson St EH3 9DE
e-mail: H3271@accor.com
web: www.novotel.com
dir: From Edinburgh Castle right onto George IV Bridge from Royal Mile. Follow to junct, then right onto Lauriston Place. Hotel 700mtrs on right

One of the new generations of Novotels, this modern hotel is located in the centre of the city, close to Edinburgh Castle. Smart and stylish public areas include a cosmopolitan bar, brasserie-style restaurant and indoor leisure facilities. The air-conditioned bedrooms feature a

comprehensive range of extras and bathrooms with baths and separate shower cabinets.

Rooms 180 (146 fmly) (17 smoking) **Facilities** STV ☜ Gym Sauna Steam room Xmas Wi-fi **Conf** Class 50 Board 32 Thtr 80 **Services** Lift Air con **Parking** 15

Barceló Carlton Hotel

★★★★ 72% HOTEL

☎ 0131 472 3000 ▤ 0131 556 2691
North Bridge EH1 1SD
e-mail: carlton@barcelo-hotels.co.uk
web: www.barcelo-hotels.co.uk
dir: On North Bridge which links Princes St to The Royal Mile

The Carlton occupies a city centre location just off the Royal Mile. Inside, it is modern and stylish in design, with an impressive open-plan reception/lobby, spacious first-floor lounge, bar and restaurant, plus a basement leisure club. Bedrooms, many air-conditioned, are generally spacious, with an excellent range of accessories.

Rooms 189 (20 fmly) **Facilities** STV ☜ supervised Gym Squash Table tennis Dance studio Creche Exercise classes Treatment rooms ♫ Xmas New Year Wi-fi **Conf** Class 110 Board 60 Thtr 220 Del from £115* **Services** Lift **Notes** Civ Wed 160

Apex City Hotel

★★★★ Ⓐ HOTEL

☎ 0845 365 0000 & 0131 243 3456 ▤ 0131 225 6346
61 Grassmarket EH1 2JF
e-mail: edinburgh.reservations@apexhotels.co.uk
web: www.apexhotels.co.uk
dir: Into Lothian Rd at west end of Princes St, 1st left into King Stables Rd. Leads into Grassmarket

Rooms 119 (10 smoking) **Facilities** Complimentary use of leisure facilities at nearby hotel Xmas New Year Wi-fi **Conf** Class 30 Board 34 Thtr 70 **Services** Lift Air con **Parking** 10 **Notes** LB ⊗ Civ Wed 60

Malmaison Edinburgh

★★★ 86% HOTEL

◉ British, French ☜

Unpretentious, well cooked food in brasserie with waterfront views

☎ 0131 468 5000 ▤ 0131 468 5002
One Tower Place EH6 7DB
e-mail: edinburgh@malmaison.com
web: www.malmaison.com
dir: A900 from city centre towards Leith, at end of Leith Walk , & through 3 sets of lights, left into Tower St. Hotel on right at end of road

Perched on the banks of the Forth in Leith, and only minutes from the hubbub of the city centre, the Edinburgh hotel in this chic chain was originally built as a seaman's mission. The hotel has a castle-like appearance and inside there's a decidedly French vibe. Inside, bold contemporary designs make for a striking effect. Bedrooms are comprehensively equipped with CD players, mini-bars and loads of individual touches. Ask for one of the stunning superior room for a really memorable stay. The brasserie has recently been restored to its original atmospheric glory, and is dressed with leather banquettes and an abundance of candlelight and wrought ironwork. Look out across the cobbled concourse to the quayside as you enjoy unfussy, classic dishes using plenty of local produce (there is a separate 'Homegrown and Local' menu). Try Scotch egg with curried mayonnaise and move on to confit pork belly, rösti potato, apple and prune compôte. Finish with Bakewell tart and pear sorbet.

Rooms 100 (18 fmly) **Facilities** STV Gym Xmas New Year Wi-fi **Conf** Class 30 Board 40 Thtr 55 **Services** Lift **Parking** 50 **Notes** LB

Chef Colin Manson **Owner** Malmaison Hotels Ltd **Restaurant Times** 12-2.30/6-10.30 Closed D 25 Dec **Prices** Fixed L 2 course £13.50, Fixed D 3 course £15.50, Starter £5.50-£8.95, Main £11.50-£19.95, Dessert £5.95-£8.50, Service added but optional 10% **Wines** 132 bottles over £20, 18 bottles under £20, 24 by glass **Notes** Sunday L, Vegetarian available, Civ Wed 60, Air con **Seats** 72, Pr/dining room 60 **Children** Portions, Menu

Dalhousie Castle and Aqueous Spa

★★★ 82% HOTEL

◉◉ Modern European

Creative cuisine in a truly unique setting

☎ 01875 820153 ▤ 01875 821936
Bonnyrigg EH19 3JB
e-mail: info@dalhousiecastle.co.uk
web: www.dalhousiecastle.co.uk
dir: A7 S from Edinburgh through Lasswade/Newtongrange, right at Shell Garage (B704), hotel 0.5m from junct

A popular wedding venue, this imposing medieval castle sits amid lawns and parkland and even has a falconry. Bedrooms offer a mix of styles and sizes, including richly decorated rooms named after historical figures. The Orangery serves food all day, while the spa offers many relaxing and therapeutic treatments and hydro facilities. It's not often you have the chance to eat in a vaulted dungeon beneath a castle. Descend to the Dungeon restaurant, and you're in an arsenal of medieval weaponry and armour hung from stone walls beneath vaulted ceilings, all candlelit for romance. With so much to bring in the customers, some kitchens might rest on their laurels. Not so here: there's a vibrant creativity going on in the French-influenced menus, giving modern twists to classic dishes; take smoked duck with a thyme and bitter chocolate mousse, dandelion salad and nettle coulis, followed by lamb loin and casserole with lavender jus, pea purée, cocotte potatoes and smoked aubergine.

Rooms 36 (7 annexe) (3 fmly) **S** £125-£245; **D** £140-£345 (incl. bkfst)* **Facilities** Spa FTV Fishing Falconry Clay pigeon shooting Archery Laserday Xmas New Year Wi-fi **Conf** Class 60 Board 45 Thtr 120 Del from £188 to £208* **Parking** 110 **Notes** LB Civ Wed 100

Chef Francois Graud **Owner** von Essen Hotels **Restaurant Times** 7-10 Closed L all week **Prices** Starter £5.10-£7.75, Main £13-£19.10, Dessert £6.30-£6.90, Service optional **Wines** 100 bottles over £20, 23 bottles under £20, 15 by glass **Notes** Fixed D 5 course £47, Sunday L **Seats** 45, Pr/dining room 100 **Children** Portions

Best Western Braid Hills Hotel

★★★ 81% HOTEL

☎ 0131 447 8888 ▤ 0131 452 8477
134 Braid Rd EH10 6JD
e-mail: bookings@braidhillshotel.co.uk
web: www.braidhillshotel.co.uk
dir: 2.5m S A702, opposite Braid Burn Park

From its elevated position on the south side, this long-established hotel enjoys splendid panoramic views of the city and castle. Bedrooms are smart, stylish and well equipped. The public areas are comfortable and inviting, and guests can dine in either the restaurant or popular bistro/bar.

Rooms 67 (14 fmly) (14 GF) **S** £60-£140; **D** £80-£195 (incl. bkfst)* **Facilities** STV Xmas New Year Wi-fi **Conf** Class 50 Board 30 Thtr 100 **Parking** 38 **Notes** LB ❽ Civ Wed 100

Best Western Edinburgh Capital

★★★ 80% HOTEL

☎ 0131 535 9988 ▤ 0131 334 9712
187 Clermiston Rd EH12 6UG
e-mail: manager@edinburghcapitalhotel.co.uk
dir: From A8 into Clermiston Rd at National Tyre Garage. Hotel at top of hill

Attracting business, conference and leisure guests alike, this purpose-built hotel lies on the west side of the city and is convenient for the airport and the north. Modern in style throughout, the hotel offers a wide range of well-appointed bedrooms including family rooms. The West View restaurant and lounge bar is the setting for a good choice of dishes and snacks.

Rooms 111 (6 fmly) (14 GF) **Facilities** FTV ❽ Gym Sunbed room New Year Wi-fi **Conf** Class 130 Board 80 Thtr 320 **Services** Lift **Parking** 106 **Notes** Civ Wed 200

Old Waverley

★★★ 79% HOTEL

☎ 0131 556 4648 ▤ 0131 557 6316
43 Princes St EH2 2BY
e-mail: reservations@oldwaverley.co.uk
web: www.oldwaverley.co.uk
dir: In city centre, opposite Scott Monument, Waverley Station & Jenners

Occupying a commanding position opposite Sir Walter Scott's famous monument on Princes Street, this hotel lies right in the heart of the city close to the station. The comfortable public rooms are all on first-floor level and along with front-facing bedrooms enjoy the fine views. All bedrooms have now been refurbished.

Rooms 85 (5 fmly) **S** £60-£209; **D** £80-£299* **Facilities** Leisure facilities at sister hotel Wi-fi **Services** Lift **Notes** ❽

Best Western Edinburgh City

★★★ 78% HOTEL

☎ 0131 622 7979 ▤ 0131 622 7900
79 Laurieston Place EH3 9HZ
e-mail: reservations@bestwesternedinburghcity.co.uk
dir: Follow signs for city centre A8. Onto A702, 3rd exit on left, hotel on right

Occupying a site where there was once a memorial hospital, this stylish conversion is located close to the city centre. Spacious bedrooms are smartly modern and well equipped. Meals can be enjoyed in the bright contemporary restaurant and guests can relax in the cosy, bar and reception lounge. Staff are friendly and obliging.

Rooms 52 (12 fmly) (5 GF) **Facilities** FTV New Year Wi-fi **Services** Lift **Parking** 4 **Notes** ✖

Best Western Kings Manor

★★★ 78% HOTEL

☎ 0131 669 0444 & 468 8003 ▤ 0131 669 6650
100 Milton Road East EH15 2NP
e-mail: reservations@kingsmanor.com
web: www.kingsmanor.com
dir: A720 E to Old Craighall junct, left into city, right at A1/A199 junct, hotel 400mtrs on right

Lying on the eastern side of the city and convenient for the by-pass, this hotel is popular with business guests, tour groups and for conferences. It boasts a fine leisure complex and a bright modern bistro, which complements the quality, creative cooking in the main restaurant.

Rooms 95 (8 fmly) (13 GF) **S** £50-£95; **D** £60-£180* **Facilities** Spa STV FTV ③ ⌂ Gym Health & beauty salon Steam room Sauna Xmas New Year Wi-fi **Conf** Class 70 Board 50 Thtr 140 **Services** Lift **Parking** 120 **Notes** LB Civ Wed 100

Mercure Point Hotel Edinburgh

★★★ 78% HOTEL

☎ 0131 221 5555 & 221 5554 ▤ 0131 221 9929
34 Bread St EH3 9AF
e-mail: H6989@accor.com
dir: A71 to Haymarket Station. Straight on at jct & right on Torphichen St, left to Morrison St, straight to Bread St, hotel on right

Built in 1892 as a Co-op which once employed Sean Connery as a milkman, the hotel has won many awards for its design and presentation. Bedrooms are spacious and cater well for the needs of the modern guest. Open-plan public areas are enhanced with coloured lighting and an array of artwork. The Point Restaurant offers imaginative dishes. The Glass Box Penthouse conference room affords fantastic views of the city.

Rooms 139 **S** £75-£145; **D** £80-£175 (incl. bkfst) **Facilities** FTV New Year Wi-fi **Conf** Class 60 Board 40 Thtr 120 Del from £135 to £160* **Services** Lift **Parking** 8 **Notes** LB ✖ Civ Wed 80

Quality Hotel Edinburgh Airport

★★★ 77% HOTEL

☎ 0131 333 4331 ▤ 0131 333 4124
Ingliston EH28 8AU
e-mail: info@qualityhoteledinburgh.com
dir: From M8, M9 & Forth Road Bridge follow signs for airport then follow brown tourist signs to hotel

Just 20 minutes from the city centre, this modern hotel is convenient for Edinburgh International Airport, which is only two minutes away by courtesy minibus. The spacious executive bedrooms are the pick of the accommodation, and there is a bright restaurant offering a range of contemporary dishes.

Rooms 95 (15 fmly) (35 GF) **S** £60-£200; **D** £60-£200 **Facilities** STV FTV Wi-fi **Conf** Class 24 Board 24 Thtr 70 **Services** Lift **Parking** 100 **Notes** LB Civ Wed 80

Holiday Inn Edinburgh North

★★★ 74% HOTEL

☎ 0870 400 9025 ▤ 0131 332 3408
107 Queensferry Rd EH4 3HL
e-mail: reservations-edinburgh@ihg.com
web: www.holidayinn.co.uk
dir: on A90 approx 1m from city centre

Situated on the north-west side of the city, close to Murrayfield Stadium and just five miles from the airport, this purpose-built hotel has a bright contemporary look. The colourful, modern bedrooms are well equipped and three specifications are available - with two double beds; with a double bed and sofa; or with a double bed and separate lounge. Some have great views of the city too. There is limited free parking.

Rooms 101 (17 smoking) **Facilities** STV New Year Wi-fi **Conf** Class 60 Board 50 Thtr 140 **Services** Lift Air con **Parking** 80 **Notes** LB ✖ Civ Wed 120

Apex European Hotel

★★★ A HOTEL

☎ 0845 365 0000 & 0131 474 3456 ▤ 0131 474 3400
90 Haymarket Ter EH12 5LQ
e-mail: edinburgh.reservations@apexhotels.co.uk
web: www.apexhotels.co.uk
dir: A8 to city centre

Rooms 66 (3 GF) (8 smoking) **Facilities** FTV Xmas New Year Wi-fi **Conf** Class 30 Board 36 Thtr 80 **Services** Lift **Parking** 10 **Notes** LB ✖ Closed 24-27 Dec

Express by Holiday Inn Edinburgh Waterfront

BUDGET HOTEL

☎ 0131 555 4422   📠 0131 555 4646
Britannia Way, Ocean Dr, Leith EH6 6JJ
e-mail: info@hiex-edinburgh.com
web: www.hiexpress.com/exedinburghwat
dir: Follow signs for Royal Yacht Britannia. Hotel just before Britannia on right

A modern hotel ideal for families and business travellers. Fresh and uncomplicated, the spacious rooms include Sky TV, power shower and tea and coffee-making facilities. Continental buffet breakfast is included in the room rate; other meals may be taken at the nearby family pub or restaurant. See also the Hotel Groups pages on theAA.com.

Rooms 145 (36 fmly) **Conf** Class 15 Board 18 Thtr 35

Holiday Inn Express Edinburgh City Centre

BUDGET HOTEL

☎ 0131 558 2300   📠 0131 558 2323
Picardy Place EH1 3JT
e-mail: info@hieedinburgh.co.uk
web: www.hiexpress.com/edinburghctyct
dir: Follow signs to city centre & Greenside NCP. Hotel near east end of Princes St off Picardy Place rdbt

A modern hotel ideal for families and business travellers. Fresh and uncomplicated, the spacious rooms include Sky TV, power shower and tea and coffee-making facilities. Continental buffet breakfast is included in the room rate; other meals may be taken at the nearby family pub or restaurant. See also the Hotel Groups pages on theAA.com.

Rooms 161 (53 fmly) (27 GF) (13 smoking) **S** £79-£229; **D** £79-£229 (incl. bkfst)* **Conf** Class 8 Board 18 Thtr 20 Del from £90 to £180^

Holiday Inn Express Edinburgh Royal Mile

BUDGET HOTEL

☎ 0131 524 8400   📠 0131 524 8401
South Grays Close, Cowgate EH1 1NA
e-mail: info@hiexpressedinburgh.co.uk
web: www.hiexpressedinburgh.co.uk

Rooms 78 (50 fmly) (10 GF) **S** £59-£229; **D** £59-£229 (incl. bkfst)* **Conf** Class 20 Board 20 Thtr 40

Ibis Edinburgh Centre

BUDGET HOTEL

☎ 0131 240 7000   📠 0131 240 7007
6 Hunter Square, (off The Royal Mile) EH1 1QW
e-mail: H2039@accor.com **web:** www.ibishotel.com
dir: M8/M9/A1 over North Bridge (A7) & High St, take 1st right off South Bridge, into Hunter Sq

Modern, budget hotel offering comfortable accommodation in bright and practical bedrooms. Breakfast is self-service and dinner is available in the restaurant. See also Hotel Groups pages on theAA.com.

Rooms 99 (2 GF)

Innkeeper's Lodge Edinburgh West

BUDGET HOTEL

☎ 0845 112 6002   📠 0845 112 6298
114-116 St John's Rd, Corstophine EH12 8AX
web: www.innkeeperslodge.com/edinburghwest
dir: M8 junct 1, N on A720. At Gogar rdbt, right onto A8 towards Edinburgh, over next rdbt, lodge on left past church at St John's Rd

Innkeeper's Lodge represents an exciting, high value concept within the budget hotel market. Comfortable bedrooms provide excellent facilities that include satellite TV and modem points. Options include family rooms; and for the corporate guest, cutting edge IT which includes Wi-fi access. A popular Carvery provides all-day food, including an extensive, complimentary continental breakfast. See also the Hotel Groups pages on theAA.com.

Rooms 28 (4 fmly)

Travelodge Edinburgh Central

BUDGET HOTEL

☎ 0871 984 6137   📠 0131 557 3681
33 Saint Marys St EH1 1TA
web: www.travelodge.co.uk
dir: From A1 follow signs to city centre, after Meadow Bank Stadium left at lights, follow signs to Earth Museum. Lodge opposite

Travelodge offers good quality, good value, modern accommodation. Ideal for families, the spacious en suite bedrooms include remote-control TV, tea and coffee-making facilities and comfortable beds. See also the Hotel Groups pages on theAA.com.

Rooms 193 **S** fr £29; **D** fr £29

Travelodge Edinburgh Dreghorn

BUDGET HOTEL

☎ 0871 984 6139   📠 0131 441 4296
46 Dreghorn Link EH13 9QR
web: www.travelodge.co.uk
dir: On eastbound carriageway of A720 (Edinburgh city bypass) at Dreghorn/Colinton exit. One exit W of junct with A702 (Biggar Rd)

Rooms 72 **S** fr £29; **D** fr £29

Travelodge Edinburgh Haymarket

BUDGET HOTEL

☎ 0871 984 6365   📠 0131 347 2808
24 Eglinton Crescent, Haymarket EH12 5BY
e-mail: edinburghhaymkt@travelodge.co.uk
web: www.travelodge.co.uk
dir: From W: enter city centre, pass zoo, 1st left into Coates Grdns.
Eglinton Cres ahead. From all other directions: towards West End,
Haymarket & airport. Pass Haymarket rail station, 2nd right

Rooms 73 **S** fr £29; **D** fr £29

Travelodge Edinburgh Learmonth

BUDGET HOTEL

☎ 0871 984 6415   📠 01844 358681
18-20 Learmonth Ter EH4 1PW
web: www.travelodge.co.uk
dir: Please see Travelodge website for detailed directions

Rooms 64 **S** fr £29; **D** fr £29

Travelodge Edinburgh Mussleburgh

BUDGET HOTEL

☎ 0871 984 6138   📠 0131 653 6106
Moto Service Area, A1, Old Craighall EH21 8RE
web: www.travelodge.co.uk
dir: At Services just off rdbt of A1 & A720 city bypass

Rooms 45 **S** fr £29; **D** fr £29

Travelodge Edinburgh West End

BUDGET HOTEL

☎ 0871 984 6418   📠 0131 315 4632
69 Belford Rd EH4 3DG
web: www.travelodge.co.uk
dir: From city centre take A90 towards W, left at 2nd rdbt into
Queensferry Terrace, straight ahead into Belford Rd. Lodge on right

Rooms 146 **S** fr £29; **D** fr £29 **Conf** Class 50 Board 45 Thtr 120

Radisson Blu Hotel Edinburgh

Ⓤ

☎ 0131 557 9797   📠 0131 557 8789
80 High Street The Royal Mile EH1 1TH
e-mail: sales.edinburgh@radissonblu.com
dir: On Royal Mile

Currently the rating for this establishment is not confirmed. This may
be due to a change of ownership or because it has only recently
joined the AA rating scheme.

Rooms 238 (5 fmly) S £85-£270; D£95-£280 **Facilities** Spa STV FTV

indoor heated pool Wifi **Conf** 52 Class 105 Board Thtr 240 Del daily
rate fr £165 **Parking** 131 sauna **Services** Lift **Notes** ⊗ Civ wed 180

21212

★★★★★ RESTAURANT WITH ROOMS

🍵🍵🍵

☎ 0131 523 1030   📠 0131 553 1038
3 Royal Ter EH7 5AB
e-mail: reservations@21212restaurant.co.uk

Manchester's loss is Edinburgh's gain: after leaving Altrincham in
the suburbs of the north-western English city, chef Paul Kitching and
front-of-house Katie O'Brien are now based in a splendid townhouse
in a smart part of Edinburgh. Those in the know will expect the
unexpected, starting perhaps with the name of the restaurant (not
the rhythms of a military march, but rather the number of dishes to
choose from at each course); the four coolly modern rooms are in on
the joke, too, numbered, 1, 2, 12 and 21. Paul's cooking has long
defied classification: modern French is a good starting point, with a
personal stamp that pretty much makes his cooking unique. The
open-plan design of the dining room gives a view of the kitchen
alchemy from which emerges dishes bursting with creative ideas and
tantalising combinations of flavours; at lunch the choice is 2, 3, 4, or
5 courses, but for dinner it is in for a penny in for pound with the full
5-courses. A soup in the hands of Paul Kitching could be expected to
contain a surprise or two, and so it is with yellow-split pea with
confit and caramelised onion, roasted garlic and chestnut, the dish a
thrilling combination of textures and flavours. Both an impressive
talent for maintaining balance on the plate and a ready playfulness
are evident in chicken and cheesy chips, haggis, bacon, prunes,
walnuts, girolles, mustard and blue cheese flapjack. The cheese
course is first-rate and desserts such as baked lemon curd with
cumin wild cherries and sticky rice are impressive.

Rooms 4 en suite **Notes** RS Sun & Mon closed

Chef Paul Kitching **Restaurant Times** Please telephone for details

The Witchery by the Castle

★★★★★ RESTAURANT WITH ROOMS

⊛ Traditional Scottish ⚑NOTABLE WINE LIST

A one-off destination restaurant in historic location

☎ 0131 225 5613 📠 0131 220 4392
352 Castlehill, The Royal Mile EH1 2NF
e-mail: mail@thewitchery.com
web: www.thewitchery.com
dir: Top of Royal Mile at gates of Edinburgh Castle

Originally built in 1595, The Witchery by the Castle is situated in a historic building at the gates of Edinburgh Castle. The two luxurious and theatrically decorated suites, known as the Inner Sanctum and the Old Rectory, are located above the restaurant and are reached via a winding stone staircase. Filled with antiques, opulently draped beds, large roll-top baths and a plethora of memorabilia, this ancient and exciting establishment is often described as one of the country's most romantic destinations - and it is something of a celeb-magnet to boot. It takes its name from the benighted period of history when hundreds of people were burnt at the stake as witches on Castlehill. The décor in the dining rooms is darkly opulent: tapestry-hung walls, 17th-century oak panelling, flagged floors and magnificent candelabra conjure a moody setting in the Witchery, while the Secret Garden, reached via a stone staircase from the courtyard has lovely painted ceiling panels. Well-sourced Scottish materials provide a rock-solid base for a menu of straightforward contemporary classics. Fish bisque comes with garlic croûtons, gruyère and rouille, while braised rump, seared liver and grilled cutlet of Borders lamb is served with broad bean purée and aubergine relish.

Rooms 2 en suite 5 annexe en suite (1 GF) S £295; D £295*
Facilities STV FTV tea/coffee Dinner available Direct Dial Cen ht
Notes ⊗ No Children 12yrs Closed 25-26 Dec No coaches Civ Wed 60

Chef Douglas Roberts **Owner** James Thomson OBE **Restaurant Times** 12-4/5-11.30 Closed 25-26 Dec, **Prices** Fixed L 2 course £12.95, Fixed D 3 course £30, Starter £6.95-£12.95, Main £14.95-£30, Dessert £6.95-£7.50, Service optional, Groups min 8 service 10% **Wines** 700+ bottles over £20, 20 bottles under £20, 14 by glass **Notes** Theatre supper 2 course £12.95, Sunday L, Vegetarian available, Air con **Seats** 120, Pr/dining room 70

Elmview

★★★★★ GUEST ACCOMMODATION

☎ 0131 228 1973
15 Glengyle Ter EH3 9LN
e-mail: nici@elmview.co.uk
web: www.elmview.co.uk
dir: 0.5m S of city centre. Off A702 Leven St onto Valleyfield St, one-way to Glengyle Ter

Elmview offers stylish accommodation on the lower ground level of a fine Victorian terrace house. The bedrooms and smart bathrooms are comfortable and extremely well equipped, with thoughtful extras such as safes, and fridges with fresh milk and water. Breakfasts are excellent and are served at a large, elegantly appointed table in the charming dining room.

Rooms 3 en suite (3 GF) S £60-£100; D £80-£120* **Facilities** FTV tea/coffee Direct Dial Cen ht Wi-fi **Notes** ⊗ No Children 15yrs Closed Dec-Feb

Kew House

★★★★★ GUEST ACCOMMODATION

☎ 0131 313 0700 📠 0131 313 0747
1 Kew Ter, Murrayfield EH12 5JE
e-mail: info@kewhouse.com
web: www.kewhouse.com
dir: 1m W of city centre A8

Forming part of a listed Victorian terrace, Kew House lies within walking distance of the city centre, and is convenient for Murrayfield rugby stadium and tourist attractions. Meticulously maintained throughout, it offers attractive bedrooms in a variety of sizes, all thoughtfully equipped to suit business and leisure guests. There is a comfortable lounge offering a supper and snack menu. Internet access is also available.

Rooms 6 en suite (1 fmly) (2 GF) S £75-£95; D £85-£180*
Facilities FTV tea/coffee Direct Dial Cen ht Wi-fi **Parking** 6 **Notes** LB

Bonnington Guest House

★★★★ GUEST HOUSE

☎ 0131 554 7610   📄 0131 554 7610
202 Ferry Rd EH6 4NW
e-mail: booking@thebonningtonguesthouse.com
web: www.thebonningtonguesthouse.com
dir: On A902, near corner of Ferry Rd & Newhaven Rd

This delightful Georgian house offers individually furnished bedrooms on two floors, that retain many of their original features. Family rooms are also available. A substantial freshly prepared breakfast is served in the newly refurbished dining room. Off-street parking is an added bonus.

Rooms 7 rms (5 en suite) (2 pri facs) (4 fmly) (1 GF) **Facilities** FTV tea/coffee Cen ht Wi-fi **Parking** 9 **Notes** ⊛

Ellesmere House

★★★★ GUEST HOUSE

☎ 0131 229 4823
11 Glengyle Ter EH3 9LN
e-mail: ruth@edinburghbandb.co.uk
web: www.edinburghbandb.co.uk
dir: S of city centre off A702

This delightful terrace house overlooks Bruntsfield Links and is convenient for the city centre. Benefiting from investment from the new proprietors, the attractive bedrooms vary in size and have many thoughtful touches. Breakfast, featuring the best of local produce, is enjoyed in the elegant dining room.

Rooms 4 en suite **Facilities** FTV TVL tea/coffee Cen ht Wi-fi **Notes** ⊛ 🐾

Fraoch House

★★★★ 🛏 GUEST ACCOMMODATION

☎ 0131 554 1353
66 Pilrig St EH6 5AS
e-mail: info@fraochhouse.com
dir: 1m from Princes St

Situated within walking distance of the city centre and convenient for many attractions, Fraoch House, which dates from the 1900s, has been appointed to offer well-equipped and thoughtfully furnished bedrooms. Delicious, freshly cooked breakfasts are served in the charming dining room on the ground floor.

Rooms 9 rms (7 en suite) (2 pri facs) (1 fmly) (1 GF) S £30-£70; D £55-£105* **Facilities** FTV tea/coffee Cen ht Wi-fi Free use of DVDs and CDs, & internet access **Notes** ⊛

Millers64

★★★★ BED AND BREAKFAST

☎ 0131 454 3666   📄 0131 454 3666
64 Pilrig St EH6 5AS
e-mail: millers64@hotmail.com
web: www.millers64.com
dir: At E end of Princes St onto Leith Walk. Pilrig St, 3rd main street on left

Situated in the heart of Edinburgh, Millers64 offers unique bed and breakfast accommodation in an extensively upgraded beautiful Victorian house. Millers64 is a small, very personal establishment, modern in style and offering a warm traditional welcome. Breakfasts are served around one table in the morning room which overlooks the garden, an interesting range of traditional Scottish and modern dishes are available.

Rooms 2 en suite (1 fmly) S £60-£100; D £80-£140* **Facilities** FTV tea/coffee Cen ht Wi-fi **Notes** ⊛ No Children 5yrs 🐾

Southside

★★★★ 🛏 GUEST HOUSE

☎ 0131 668 4422   📄 0131 667 7771
8 Newington Rd EH9 1QS
e-mail: info@southsideguesthouse.co.uk
web: www.southsideguesthouse.co.uk
dir: E end of Princes St onto North Bridge to Royal Mile, continue S, 0.5m, house on right

Situated within easy reach of the city centre and convenient for the major attractions, Southside is an elegant sandstone house. Bedrooms are individually styled, comfortable and thoughtfully equipped. Traditional, freshly cooked Scottish breakfasts are served at individual tables in the smart ground-floor dining room.

Rooms 8 en suite (2 fmly) (1 GF) S £60-£80; D £80-£140 **Facilities** FTV tea/coffee Direct Dial Cen ht Licensed Wi-fi **Notes** LB ⊛ No Children 10yrs

New Town, Edinburgh

23 Mayfield

★★★★ ≜ GUEST ACCOMMODATION

☎ 0131 667 5806 📠 0131 667 6833
23 Mayfield Gardens EH9 2BX
e-mail: info@23mayfield.co.uk
web: www.23mayfield.co.uk
dir: A720 bypass S, follow city centre signs. Left at Craigmillar Park,
0.5m on right

Well located en route into Edinburgh with the added benefit of off-road parking. The spacious accommodation has many of the original period features retained. Breakfast is a real delight with the very best local produce used to give the guest a great start to their day. Many thoughtful extras are provided in accord with the needs of the modern traveller.

Rooms 9 en suite (2 fmly) (2 GF) S £55-£65; D £65-£130*
Facilities FTV tea/coffee Cen ht Wi-fi **Parking** 10 **Notes** LB ⊗

Allison House

★★★★ GUEST ACCOMMODATION

☎ 0131 667 8049 📠 0131 667 5001
17 Mayfield Gardens EH9 2AX
e-mail: info@allisonhousehotel.com
web: www.allisonhousehotel.com

Part of a Victorian terrace, Allison House offers modern comforts in a splendid building. It's convenient for the city centre, theatres, tourist attractions and is on the main bus route. The attractive bedrooms are generally spacious and very well equipped. Breakfast is served at individual tables in the ground-floor dining room. Off-road parking is available.

Rooms 11 rms (10 en suite) (1 pri facs) (1 fmly) (2 GF) (2 smoking)
Facilities tea/coffee Direct Dial Cen ht Wi-fi **Parking** 6 **Notes** ⊗

Aonach Mor Guest House

★★★★ GUEST HOUSE

☎ 0131 667 8694
14 Kilmaurs Ter EH16 5DR
e-mail: info@aonachmor.com
dir: A7 to Cameron Toll rdbt, follow city centre signs, Dalkeith Rd 5th on right

Situated in the residential area, within easy reach of the city and major tourist attractions. Aonach Mor offers well equipped accommodation including a stylish four-poster feature bedroom which boasts its own steam room. The combined lounge dining room is available to relax in and internet access is available.

Rooms 7 rms (5 en suite) (2 fmly) **Facilities** FTV tea/coffee Cen ht Wi-fi Steam room **Notes** ⊗ No Children 3yrs

Ashlyn Guest House

★★★★ GUEST HOUSE

☎ 0131 552 2954
42 Inverleith Row EH3 5PY
e-mail: info@ashlynguesthouse.com
web: www.ashlyn-edinburgh.co.uk
dir: Adjacent to Edinburgh Botanic Gardens, then follow signs for North Edinburgh & Botanics

The Ashlyn Guest House is a warm and friendly Georgian home, ideally located to take advantage of Edinburgh's attractions. The city centre is within walking distance and the Royal Botanical Gardens are minutes away. Bedrooms are all individually decorated and furnished to a high standard. A generous and hearty breakfast gives a great start to the day.

Rooms 8 rms (4 en suite) (2 pri facs) (1 fmly) (1 GF) S £30-£40; D £65-£90* **Facilities** TVL tea/coffee Cen ht **Notes** ⊗ No Children 7yrs Closed 23-28 Dec

The Edinburgh Lodge

★★★★ GUEST HOUSE

☎ 0131 337 3682 📠 0131 313 1700
6 Hampton Ter, West Coates EH12 5JD
e-mail: info@thelodgehotel.co.uk
dir: On A8, 0.75m W of Princes St

Situated at the west end of Edinburgh, benefiting from off-road parking this well presented property offers comfortable bedrooms with many thoughtful extras which are provided as standard including complimentary Wi-fi. A well cooked breakfast is served on individual tables which over look the well maintained gardens.

Rooms 12 en suite (2 fmly) (4 GF) S £65-£80; D £75-£140*
Facilities STV TVL tea/coffee Direct Dial Cen ht Licensed Wi-fi
Conf Max 16 **Parking** 8 **Notes** ⊗

Heriott Park

★★★★ GUEST HOUSE

☎ 0131 552 3456
256 Ferry Rd, Goldenacre EH5 3AN
e-mail: reservations@heriottpark.co.uk
web: www.heriottpark.co.uk
dir: 1.5m N of city centre on A902

A conversion of two adjoining properties, which retain many original features. The guest house is on the north side of the city and has lovely panoramic views of the Edinburgh skyline including the castle and Arthur's Seat. The attractive bedrooms are well equipped and have excellent en suite bathrooms.

Rooms 15 rms (14 en suite) (1 pri facs) (7 fmly) (1 GF) S £40-£80; D £60-£110 **Facilities** FTV tea/coffee Cen ht Wi-fi **Notes** ⊗

International Guest House

★★★★ GUEST HOUSE

☎ 0131 667 2511 & 0845 241 7551 📠 0131 667 1112
37 Mayfield Gardens EH9 2BX
e-mail: intergh1@yahoo.co.uk
web: www.accommodation-edinburgh.com
dir: On A701 1.5m S of Princes St

Guests are assured of a warm and friendly welcome at this attractive Victorian terraced house situated to the south of the city centre. The smartly presented bedrooms are thoughtfully decorated, comfortably furnished and well equipped. Hearty Scottish breakfasts are served at individual tables in the traditionally styled dining room, which boasts a beautiful ornate ceiling.

Rooms 9 en suite (3 fmly) (1 GF) S £35-£75; D £65-£130 **Facilities** STV tea/coffee Direct Dial Cen ht Wi-fi **Parking** 3 **Notes** LB ⊗

Sherwood

★★★★ GUEST HOUSE

☎ 0131 667 1200 📠 0131 667 2344
42 Minto St EH9 2BR
e-mail: enquiries@sherwood-edinburgh.com
web: www.sherwood-edinburgh.com
dir: On A701, S of city centre

Lying on the south side of the city, this guest house is immaculately maintained and attractively presented throughout. Bedrooms vary in size, the smaller ones being thoughtfully appointed to make the best use of space. All include iron/board and several come with a fridge and microwave. Continental breakfast is served in the elegant dining room.

Rooms 6 rms (5 en suite) (1 pri facs) (2 fmly) (1 GF) S £40-£65; D £55-£100* **Facilities** FTV tea/coffee Cen ht Wi-fi **Parking** 3 **Notes** LB ⊗ Closed 20-29 Dec & 5 Jan-2 Mar

Gildun

★★★★ Ⓐ GUEST HOUSE

☎ 0131 667 1368 📠 0131 668 4989
9 Spence St EH16 5AG
e-mail: gildun.edin@btinternet.com
dir: A720 city bypass to Sheriffhall rdbt onto A7 for 4m to Cameron Toll rdbt. Under rail bridge follow A7 sign onto Dalkeith Rd. Spence St 4th left opp church

Rooms 8 rms (6 en suite) (2 pri facs) (5 fmly) (2 GF) **Facilities** FTV tea/coffee Cen ht Wi-fi **Parking** 4 **Notes** LB

Abbotsford

★★★ GUEST HOUSE

☎ 0131 554 2706 📠 0131 555 4550
36 Pilrig St EH6 5AL
e-mail: info@abbotsfordguesthouse.co.uk
web: www.abbotsfordguesthouse.co.uk

Situated just off Leith Walk and within easy walking distance of the city centre, this charming and friendly guest house offers individually decorated, pleasantly furnished and thoughtfully equipped bedrooms. There is an elegant ground-floor dining room where hearty breakfasts are served at individual tables.

Rooms 8 rms (5 en suite) S £35-£55; D £70-£130* **Facilities** STV tea/coffee Cen ht **Notes** ⊗

Arden Guest House

★★★ GUEST HOUSE

☎ 0131 664 3985 📠 0131 621 0866
126 Old Dalkeith Rd EH16 4SD
e-mail: ardenguesthouse@btinternet.com
dir: 2m SE of city centre nr Craigmillar Castle. On A7 200yds W of hospital

Well situated on the south side of the city, close to the hospital. Benefiting from off road parking and refurbishment in a number of areas. Many thoughtful extras are provided as standard including Wi-fi. Attentive and friendly service enhances the guest experience.

Rooms 8 en suite (2 fmly) (3 GF) S £35-£65; D £55-£99* **Facilities** STV tea/coffee Cen ht Wi-fi **Parking** 8 **Notes** Closed 22-27 Dec

Corstorphine Lodge

★★★ GUEST HOUSE

☎ 0131 539 4237 & 476 7116   📠 0131 539 4945
186-188 St Johns Rd, Corstorphine EH12 8SG
e-mail: corsthouse@aol.com
web: www.corstorphinehotels.co.uk
dir: From M8 take city bypass N towards city centre for 1m on A8.
Lodge on left before zoo

Occupying two large detached Victorian villas, Corstorphine is
convenient for the airport and the city centre. Bedrooms, which vary
in size, are carefully decorated and well equipped. There is a
spacious conservatory-dining room where traditional, continental or
vegetarian breakfasts can be enjoyed at individual tables. Ample off-
road parking is available.

Rooms 12 en suite 5 annexe en suite (8 fmly) (5 GF) S £35-£59; D
£55-£109 **Facilities** STV FTV TVL tea/coffee Cen ht Wi-fi **Parking** 14
Notes LB ⊗

Ecosse International

★★★ GUEST HOUSE

☎ 0131 556 4967   📠 0131 556 7394
15 McDonald Rd EH7 4LX
e-mail: erlinda@ecosseguesthouse.fsnet.co.uk
dir: Off A900 NE of city centre

Situated just off Leith Walk to the north, and within easy walking
distance of the city centre, this well-maintained guest house offers
comfortable and cheerful accommodation. The cosy lounge area and
the adjacent dining room, where hearty breakfasts are served at
individual tables, are situated on the lower-ground floor.

Rooms 5 en suite (3 fmly) **Facilities** TVL tea/coffee Cen ht **Notes** ⊗

Elder York Guest House

★★★ GUEST HOUSE

☎ 0131 556 1926   📠 0131 624 7140
38 Elder St EH1 3DX
e-mail: reception@elderyork.co.uk
web: www.elderyork.co.uk
dir: Close to Princes St, next to bus station

Centrally located just minutes from the bus station, Harvey Nichols
and the St. James Shopping centre. Accommodation is situated up
flights of stairs but all bedrooms are well appointed with many
thoughtful extras including Wi-fi. Quality breakfast is served on
individual tables overlooking Queen Street.

Rooms 13 rms (10 en suite) (1 fmly) S £40-£70; D £80-£140*
Facilities FTV tea/coffee Cen ht Wi-fi **Notes** ⊗

The Lairg

★★★ GUEST HOUSE

☎ 0131 337 1050   📠 0131 346 2167
11 Coates Gardens EH12 5LG
e-mail: lairgmarie@aol.com
dir: From A8 under rail bridge, stately home 150yds on left, Coates
Gardens next 2nd left

Situated in a residential area close to the Haymarket at the west end
of the city, The Lairg is well located for the train station, Murrayfield,
the city centre and tourist attractions. It offers attractive, generally
spacious, well-equipped accommodation in a friendly relaxed
environment. Breakfasts featuring the best of local produce are
served at individual tables in the elegant ground-floor dining room.

Rooms 9 en suite (2 fmly) (1 GF) **Facilities** tea/coffee Direct Dial
Cen ht **Notes** ⊗

Ardbrae House

★★★ 🅰 BED AND BREAKFAST

☎ 0131 467 5787
85 Drum Brae South, Corstorphine EH12 8TD
e-mail: info@ardbrae.com
dir: From W enter Edinburgh on A8. At PC World/Drum Brae rdbt turn
left, up hill, on left, adjacent to speed camera

Rooms 3 en suite (3 GF) S £35-£55; D £50-£80* **Facilities** FTV tea/
coffee Cen ht Wi-fi **Parking** 5 **Notes** LB ⊗ Closed 24-28 Dec

Charleston House

★★★ 🅰 GUEST HOUSE

☎ 0131 667 6589 & 07904 022205   📠 0131 668 3800
38 Minto St EH9 2BS
e-mail: joan_wightman@hotmail.com
web: www.charleston-guesthouse.co.uk
dir: 1.5m SE of city centre on A701 at corner Duncan St

Rooms 5 rms (2 en suite) (2 fmly) (1 GF) S £35-£80; D £55-£90*
Facilities FTV TVL tea/coffee Cen ht Wi-fi **Notes** LB Closed 24-27 Dec

Classic House

★★★ 🅰 GUEST HOUSE

☎ 0131 667 5847   📠 0131 662 1016
50 Mayfield Rd EH9 2NH
e-mail: info@classicguesthouse.co.uk
web: www.classichouse.demon.co.uk
dir: From bypass follow signs for A701 city centre. At Liberton Brae,
keep left, 0.5m on left

Rooms 7 rms (6 en suite) (1 pri facs) (2 fmly) S £30-£50; D
£50-£90* **Facilities** TVL Cen ht **Notes** LB ⊗

Ravensdown Guest House

★★★ A GUEST HOUSE

☎ 0131 552 5438
248 Ferry Rd EH5 3AN
e-mail: david@ravensdownhouse.com
web: www.ravensdownhouse.com
dir: N of city centre, close to Royal Botanic Gardens

Rooms 7 en suite (5 fmly) (1 GF) S £45-£105; D £75-£125
Facilities FTV tea/coffee Cen ht Wi-fi **Parking** 2 **Notes** LB ⊗

The St Valery

★★★ A GUEST HOUSE

☎ 0131 337 1893 📠 0131 346 8529
36 Coates Gardens, Haymarket EH12 5LE
e-mail: info@stvalery.co.uk
web: www.stvalery.com
dir: A8 towards city centre, pass Donaldson school on left, two streets before Haymarket station on left

Rooms 11 en suite (3 fmly) (1 GF) S £28-£66; D £50-£108*
Facilities STV FTV TVL tea/coffee Dinner available Direct Dial Cen ht Wi-fi **Notes** Closed 24-26 Dec

Averon City Centre Guest House

★★ GUEST HOUSE

☎ 0131 229 9932
44 Gilmore Place EH3 9NQ
e-mail: info@averon.co.uk
web: www.averon.co.uk
dir: From W end of Princes St onto A702, right at Kings Theatre

Situated within walking distance of the west end of the city and close to the Kings Theatre, this guest house offers comfortable good value accommodation, with a secure car park to the rear.

Rooms 10 rms (6 en suite) (1 pri facs) (3 fmly) **Facilities** tea/coffee Cen ht **Parking** 19 **Notes** ⊗

The Osbourne

★★ GUEST ACCOMMODATION

☎ 0131 556 5577 📠 0131 556 1012
51-59 York Place EH1 3JD
e-mail: reservations@osbournehotel.com
web: www.osbournehotel.com

The friendly Osbourne offers budget accommodation ideally located at the east end of the city centre, close to the bus station and Harvey Nichols. The bedrooms vary in size but all offer good overall ease of use, the property also benefits from a lounge on the ground floor. Traditional breakfasts are served at individual tables in the spacious dining room.

Rooms 57 rms (54 en suite) (10 fmly) **Facilities** TVL tea/coffee Direct Dial Cen ht Lift Wi-fi **Notes** ⊗

Atrium

◉◉ Modern Scottish ♨

Good, clear flavours from the best of Scottish produce

☎ 0131 228 8882 📠 0131 228 8808
10 Cambridge St EH1 2ED
e-mail: eat@atriumrestaurant.co.uk
web: www.atriumrestaurant.co.uk
dir: Restaurant to left of Usher Hall. Shares entrance with Blue Bar Café & Traverse Theatre

In the heart of the financial district, flanked on each side by period buildings, Atrium serves a daily-changing menu featuring the best of local Scottish produce simply prepared and presented. The modern, clean lines in the restaurant - an abundance of copper and rustic furnishings, dark-wood tables and soft lighting - make for a cool and stylish setting. Local artisan producers, growers and breeders take pride of place on a menu which delivers clear flavours by using 4 or less core ingredients per dish. Start with pigeon carpaccio with pickled vegetables and wild herbs, move on to pan-fried wild sea bass with clam and potato vinaigrette and wild garlic, and round things off with warm apricot and sultana bread-and-butter pudding.

Chef Neil Forbes **Owner** Andrew & Lisa Radford **Times** 12-2/6-10 Closed 25-26 Dec, 1-2 Jan, Sun (apart from Aug), L Sat (apart from Aug & international rugby matches) **Prices** Fixed L 2 course £14, Fixed D 3 course £20-£44, Starter £5.50-£12.50, Main £15.50-£23.50, Dessert £6-£9, Service optional, Groups min 5 service 10% **Wines** 250+ bottles over £20, 10 bottles under £20, 250 by glass **Notes** Vegetarian available, Civ Wed 100, Air con **Seats** 80, Pr/dining room 20 **Children** Portions **Parking** Castle Terrace Car Park and on Cambridge St

La Favorita

◉ Italian

☎ 0131 554 2430
325-331 Leith Walk EH6 8SA
e-mail: info@la-favorita.com

This cheerful and welcoming Italian restaurant prides itself on the use of fine produce as much as on its wood burning pizza ovens. Very contemporary in style, with vibrant art on white walls and a large glass frontage overlooking Leith Walk – there are even seats outside if the weather is warm – and a menu to match, modern Italian with some Sicilian favourites featuring throughout the well-balanced choice. You could start with bucatini alla norma – long pasta tubes in a rich tomato sauce with a hint of chilli, along with fresh basil, aubergine and smoked and fresh ricotta making a great combination of flavours. Follow with one of the excellent pizzas this place is famous for, and finish with the Sicilian Favorita – crisp tortellini filled with mascarpone, ricotta and cream rolled in dark chocolate and crushed pistachios.

Times 12-11

continued

La Garrigue

◎◎ Traditional French

Classic regional French cuisine in the heart of the city

☎ 0131 557 3032
31 Jeffrey St EH1 1DH
e-mail: lagarrigue@btconnect.com
web: www.lagarrigue.co.uk
dir: Halfway down Royal Mile towards Holyrood Palace, turn left at lights into Jeffrey St

This French neighbourhood restaurant, with its wooden floors and cool blue walls, brings a taste of Languedoc to Edinburgh. The woodcarver and artist Tim Stead made the chunky wooden tables and chairs, and the restaurant showcases the work of Scottish painter Andrew Walker. The authentic regional cooking style delivers homely rustic dishes with a great balance of flavours, using fine local produce as well as specialist ingredients sourced by the chef. To start there's traditional fish soup, or snails in walnut and parsley sauce with smoked bacon, followed by a classic cassoulet, which is a textbook version, and finish with the likes of lavender crème brûlée with almond tuile.

Chef Jean Michel Gauffre **Owner** Jean Michel Gauffre **Times** 12-3/6.30-10.30 Closed 25-26 Dec, 1-2 Jan, Sun **Prices** Fixed L 2 course £13.50, Fixed D 3 course £28, Service added but optional 10% **Wines** 24 bottles over £20, 10 bottles under £20, 11 by glass **Notes** Vegetarian available, Air con **Seats** 48, Pr/dining room 11 **Children** Portions **Parking** On street, NCP

Haldanes

◎◎ Modern

Clubby basement restaurant beneath an Edinburgh hotel

☎ 0131 556 8407 ▤ 0131 653 2240
The Albany, 39a Albany St EH1 3QY
e-mail: dinehaldanes@aol.com
web: www.haldanesrestaurant.com
dir: Please telephone for directions

After a brief sojourn in other premises, the restaurant has returned to its original home in a basement room beneath The Albany. Dark wood and leather chairs help to create a relaxed, clubby ambience, while the place is still a shrine to the work of Scotland's modern maestro, Jack Vettriano. A menu of modern European dishes, drawing quite heavily on French technique, furnishes the likes of green pea velouté with contrastive garnishes of coconut foam and mint oil, or haggis bonbons with turnip purée and whisky sauce, to start, succeeded by a fine pairing of baked halibut with pork cheek ravioli in tomato butter, where the counterpoints of flavour and texture are a triumph. Dessert may be chocolate fondant with candied oranges, or lemon tart with raspberry coulis and orange sorbet.

Times 12-2.15/5.30-10.15 Closed Mon, L Sat-Sun

Iggs

◎ Spanish

Convivial and welcoming taste of Spain near the Royal Mile

☎ 0131 557 8184 ▤ 0131 652 3774
15 Jeffrey St EH1 1DR
e-mail: info@iggs.co.uk
dir: In heart of Old Town, 0.5m from castle, just off Royal Mile

This modern glass-fronted restaurant is the more formal dining option to the next-door tapas bar (Barioja) under the same ownership. Situated just a stone's throw from the Royal Mile, the restaurant brings a touch of the Mediterranean to the city, with its warm shades of terracotta complemented by large cast-iron candlesticks and antique dressers, and oils and mirrors adorning the walls. The cooking also speaks with a Spanish accent, creating simple, well-constructed modern dishes that deliver quality ingredients and good flavours. Try a traditional dish from Northern Spain like white bean soup with chorizo and jamon, and for main course perhaps pan-fried fillet of sea bass with carrot and heather honey sauce. The wine list is equally patriotic.

Times 12-2.30/6-10.30 Closed Sun

The Indian Cavalry Club

◎ Indian

Quality Indian restaurant in West End of Edinburgh

☎ 0131 220 0138 & 343 1712
22 Coates Crescent EH3 7AF
e-mail: shahid@indiancavalryclub.co.uk
dir: 3 mins walk from Haymarket Railway Stn

Well and truly settled into its elegant new surroundings, this Edinburgh Indian restaurant continues to offer a fine-dining experience. It's all very understated inside with neutral décor and elegant table settings, including ICC branded vases. Well-sourced ingredients and spices are cooked in the traditional styles of both North and South India, the extensive menu featuring recommended side dishes and wine suggestions for each main course; various banquet options are also available. Start with South Indian baby dosa, or green herb pakora, before a main-course methi (flavoured with fenugreek leaves and ginger) and its recommended accompaniment, pineapple sambhar.

Chef Muktar Miah, Firoz Hossain **Owner** Shahid Choudhury **Times** 12-4/5.30-11.30 **Prices** Fixed L course £10, Fixed D 3 course £26.90-£33.90, Starter £4.85-£10.85, Main £13.95-£24.50, Dessert £3.85-£6.50, Service added but optional 10% **Wines** 15 bottles over £20, 16 bottles under £20, 2 by glass **Notes** Vegetarian available **Seats** 120, Pr/dining room 50 **Parking** On street

The Kitchin

@@@ Scottish, French ⒈🍴 🌱

Nature-to-plate cooking of a very high order in fashionable Leith

☎ 0131 555 1755 📠 0131 553 0608
78 Commercial Quay, Leith EH6 6LX
e-mail: info@thekitchin.com
dir: In Leith opposite Scottish Executive building

Part of the buzzy Leith waterfront scene, The Kitchin is an old whisky distillery fronting on to the piazza. The outer view may be serene enough, but inside is even more restful, a gently subdued atmosphere with soft lights and blinds, the better to coax your attention in the direction of the kitchen window, where you can see the team calmly working hard. Tom Kitchin lends his readily punning name to the place, and his culinary philosophy - 'From nature to plate' - is inscribed all over the menus. French-oriented technique of a very high order is applied to the best the Scots larder has to offer, with many out-of-the-ordinary ingredients showing up. Arisaig razorfish with chorizo and lemon confit is one starter, or there could be a duo of boned and rolled pig's cheek with roasted Anstruther langoustines, alongside a galette made from the crisply shredded pig's ear. The daily market menu is always worth a look, and might offer rump of Dornoch lamb with a brochette of the kidneys, served with peas à la française, braised lettuce hearts and tapenade. Memorable desserts include pear and Earl Grey crumble with Poire William ice cream.

Chef Tom Kitchin **Owner** Tom & Michaela Kitchin **Times** 12.30-1.45/6.45-10 Closed Xmas, New Year, 1st wk Jul, Sun, Mon **Prices** Fixed L course £24.50, Tasting menu £60-£100, Starter £12.50-£17, Main £24-£67, Dessert £8.50-£9.50, Service optional, Groups min 8 service 10% **Wines** 116 bottles over £20, 15 bottles under £20, 28 by glass **Notes** Tasting menu 7 course, Vegetarian available **Seats** 45 **Children** Portions **Parking** On site parking eve. Parking nearby daytime

---

Plumed Horse

@@@ Modern European

Imaginative cuisine served in Georgian grandeur

☎ 0131 554 5556 & 05601 123266
50-54 Henderson St, Leith EH6 6DE
e-mail: plumedhorse@aol.com
web: www.plumedhorse.co.uk
dir: From city centre N on Leith Walk, left into Great Junction St & 1st right into Henderson St. Restaurant 200mtrs on right

The AA's Restaurant of the Year for Scotland 2009-2010 is the brainchild of chef-proprietor Tony Borthwick, and makes the most of its relocation from Castle Douglas to Leith by using locally landed fish and seafood. With its rather sedate exterior, the Georgian building sits in the middle of a mainly residential area. Once inside though, the grandeur of its heritage comes to the fore with many features being sympathetically retained and formal table settings with matching chair covers and crisp linen adding to the grand atmosphere. Service is formal but delivered with genuine friendliness by a small team. Imaginative cooking is perfectly executed and plenty of local ingredients appear on the menus alongside that fine seafood. Start perhaps with a twice-baked Parmesan and truffle soufflé with tomato and cucumber salad and move onto a fillet of

monkfish roasted with curry spices, gratin of Jerusalem artichokes, green beans and orange and vermouth sauce before pushing the boat out with fudge and ginger parfait, ginger beer, vanilla, lime and 'Sailor Jerry' sorbet.

Chef Tony Borthwick **Owner** The Company of The Plumed Horse Ltd **Times** 12-3.30/7-11.30 Closed Xmas, New Year, 2 wks Summer, 1 wk Nov, Sun-Mon **Prices** Fixed L 2 course £23-£25, Fixed D 3 course £43, Service optional **Wines** 165 bottles over £20, 24 bottles under £20, 10 by glass **Notes** Air con **Seats** 36, Pr/dining room 10 **Parking** On street

---

Restaurant Martin Wishart

@@@@ Modern French **V** 🍷NOTABLE WINE LIST

Imaginative, memorable French cooking in intimate, fashionable waterfront venue

☎ 0131 553 3557 📠 0131 467 7091
54 The Shore, Leith EH6 6RA
e-mail: info@martin-wishart.co.uk
web: www.martin-wishart.co.uk
dir: Please telephone for directions/map on website

During his 10 years in Leith, Martin Wishart has created a restaurant with a reputation that spreads far beyond the city limits, county boundaries, and the national border. There is now a cookery school bearing his name just five minutes from the restaurant, and a new outpost - Martin Wishart at Loch Lomond - has opened in Cameron House on Loch Lomond, in West Dunbartonshire (see entry). But fear not, Mr Wishart is not spreading himself too thinly. His flagship restaurant remains a bastion of elegant simplicity, where classical French traditions and a lightness of touch, plus exciting combinations and first-class Scottish produce, equals a stunning dining experience. The room is chic and elegant, based around natural tones of brown and cream, with stylish fixtures-and-fittings, contemporary artworks and well-spaced, well-dressed tables. The fixed-price menus (set-lunch, carte, tasting, plus a bespoke vegetarian version) are full of excitingly creative combinations and it is clear from the canapés (gougére and many others) and excellent bread that you are in safe hands. Langoustine ravioli with endive braised with orange and a langoustine and olive oil jus displays well-judged flavours, while main-course grilled lemon sole with sautéed veal kidneys is a delicate and highly successful partnership, with caramelised cauliflower, capers and endive. Assiette of rhubarb and yogurt, ginger beer sorbet and lemongrass sauce come together in a divine dessert. Service is suitably slick and avoids pomposity, and the sommelier is on hand to guide the way through the seriously impressive wine list.

continued

EDINBURGH CONTINUED

Chef Martin Wishart **Owner** Martin Wishart **Times** 12-2/6.30-10 Closed 25-26 Dec, 1 Jan, 2 wks Jan, Sun-Mon **Prices** Fixed L 3 course £24.50-£60, Fixed D 3 course fr £60, Tasting menu £65, Service optional, Groups min 6 service 10% **Wines** 200+ bottles over £20, 2 bottles under £20, 12 by glass **Notes** Tasting menu 6 course, Vegetarian menu, Dress restrictions, Smart casual **Seats** 50, Pr/dining room 10 **Children** Portions **Parking** On street

Stac Polly

◉ Modern Scottish

Scottish cuisine in city centre

☎ 0131 229 5405 & 558 3083 🖺 0131 557 9779
8-10 Grindlay St EH3 9AS
e-mail: bookings@stacpolly.com
dir: In city centre beneath castle, near Lyceum Theatre

Situated in the lee of the castle and a few minutes' walk from the Princes Street shops, this popular restaurant is one of three in the city; the others are in Dublin Street (see next entry) and St Mary's Street. Lurking behind a plain exterior is a colourful basement restaurant of softly lit rooms, furnished with tartan chairs and curtains, and prints on the walls. The menu delivers Scottish food with some well-judged international flavours and preparations, so filo pastry parcels of haggis are served with red wine and sweet plum sauce, and main-course roast rack of lamb with cocotte potatoes, Stornoway black pudding and a game and Madeira reduction.

Chef Steven Harvey **Owner** Roger Coulthard **Times** 12-2/6-10 Closed Xmas, New Year, Sun, L Sat **Prices** Fixed L 2 course £12.95-£15.95, Starter £6.95-£8.25, Main £17.95-£19.95, Dessert £6.65-£8.55, Service added but optional 10% **Wines** 50 bottles over £20, 6 bottles under £20, 6 by glass **Notes** Pre-theatre menu 6-7pm, 2 course £15.95, 3 course £19.95 **Seats** 98, Pr/dining room 50 **Children** Portions **Parking** NCP - Castle Terrace

Stac Polly

◉ Modern Scottish

Modern Scottish cuisine in atmospheric surroundings

☎ 0131 556 2231
29-33 Dublin St EH3 6NL
e-mail: enquiry@stacpolly.com
dir: On corner of Albany St & Dublin St

The Dublin Street branch of the three Stac Polly restaurants in Edinburgh is located in the basement labyrinth of rough stone-walled cellars of a 200-year-old building. Named after Stac Pollaidh, a mountain on the North-West coast of Scotland, the restaurants serve modern Scottish cuisine with a flourish, putting a bit of zest into traditional fare while showing off the Scottish larder to best advantage. The cosily rustic restaurant serves up warm salad of honey-glazed duck breast and Puy lentils with a raspberry vinegar and ginger dressing, followed by baked fillet of halibut with prawn risotto, broccoli and sun-blush tomatoes and basil oil.

Chef Andre Stanislas **Owner** Roger Coulthard **Times** 12-2/6-10 Closed 25-26 Dec, 1 Jan, Sun, L Sat **Prices** Fixed L 2 course fr £12.95, Fixed D 3 course fr £20, Starter £6.95-£8.25, Main £17.95-£19.95, Dessert £6.65-£8.25, Service added but optional 10%

Wines 40+ bottles over £20, 7 bottles under £20, 8 by glass **Seats** 100, Pr/dining room 54 **Children** Portions **Parking** On street - after 6.30pm

The Stockbridge Restaurant

◉ Modern European

Dramatic basement restaurant focussing on well-sourced produce

☎ 0131 2266766
54 Saint Stephen St EH3 5AL
e-mail: jane@thestockbridgerestaurant.com
web: www.thestockbridgerestaurant.com
dir: From A90 towards city centre, left Craigleith Rd B900, 2nd exit at rdbt B900, straight on to Kerr St, turn left onto Saint Stephen St

Follow the fairy light trail down the steps into this charmingly quirky theatrical grotto in the heart of bohemian Stockbridge. You can't fail to fall under the spell of the decadent boudoir setting: Gothic black walls, gold satin drapes and bold Scottish colourist prints, all candlelit for maximum opulence and romance. Not to be upstaged, the kitchen's output also has oodles of flair and flourishes, wrought from a sound foundation of well-sourced produce and solid technique. Modern European dishes are conceived with imagination and kept sensibly uncomplicated. To start, there might be smoked haddock risotto with roasted butternut squash and parmesan crisp, then perhaps seared bream with ratatouille, parmesan crackling, sautéed ratte potatoes and pesto.

Chef Jason Gallagher **Owner** Jason Gallagher & Jane Walker **Times** 12.30-2.30/7-9.30 Closed 1st 2 wks Jan after New Year, Mon, L Tue-Fri **Prices** Fixed L 2 course £12.95-£13.95, Fixed D 3 course £22.95-£24.95, Starter £4.95-£12.95, Main £16.95-£22.95, Dessert £3.95-£6.95, Service optional, Groups min 6 service 10% **Wines** 34 bottles over £20, 19 bottles under £20, 5 by glass **Notes** Pre-theatre menu available in Aug, Sunday L, Vegetarian available **Seats** 40 **Parking** On street

Tower Restaurant & Terrace

◉ Modern British ⬥NOTABLE WINE LIST

Inventive cooking with fantastic rooftop city views

☎ 0131 225 3003 🖺 0131 220 4392
National Museum of Scotland, Chambers St EH1 1JF
e-mail: reservations@tower-restaurant.com
web: www.tower-restaurant.com
dir: Above Museum of Scotland building at corner of George IV Bridge & Chambers St, on level 5

The smartly uniformed doorman guides you to the express lift that takes you to the rooftop restaurant of the Museum of Scotland. The views from the terrace towards the castle and cathedral are not to be missed. Contemporary design has produced a chic, colourful interior with velvet hangings and sexily curvaceous tweed banquettes. Lighting is agreeably low, and the food offers an eclectic mix of styles, based on choice Scots produce. Start with soused red mullet with marinated endive and beetroot purée, before a good, thick, chunky fillet of cod with lentil 'kedgeree' and coriander gremolata, then ginger cake with confit apples and Granny Smith ice cream.

Chef Gavin Elden **Owner** James Thomson OBE **Times** 12-11.30 Closed 25-26 Dec, **Prices** Fixed L 2 course £12.95, Fixed D 3 course £30, Starter £6.50-£9, Main £14-£26, Dessert £6.50-£9, Service optional, Groups min 8 service 10% **Wines** 150 bottles over £20, 30 bottles under £20, 14 by glass **Notes** Theatre supper £12.95, Sunday L, Vegetarian available, Air con **Seats** 96, Pr/dining room 90 **Parking** On street

The Vintners Rooms

◉◉ French

Candlelit restaurant with vintage charm

☎ 0131 554 6767 📄 0131 555 5653
The Vaults, 87 Giles St, Leith EH6 6BZ
e-mail: enquiries@thevintnersrooms.com
dir: At end of Leith Walk, left into Great Junction St, right into Henderson St. Restaurant in old warehouse on right

Leith can stake a claim as the restaurant capital of Scotland and the Vintners Rooms has been helping put the area on the map for a long time now. The restaurant, lit only by flickering candles, is housed in the old wine merchants' auction room of a 16th-century former warehouse, set over the historic vaults, and is full of charm and character. The food is refined and imaginative, with modern French dishes created from quality Scottish produce, and the wine list runs to 200 bins. Perfectly cooked, sea-fresh scallops are set on sautéed girolles and gremolata, while main-course lamb (pink and tender) is full of flavour, with a herb crust and rosemary jus.

Chef Patrice Ginestière **Owner** Patrice Ginestière **Times** 12-7-10 Closed 1-16 Jan, Sun-Mon **Prices** Starter £6.50-£13.50, Main £14.50-£30, Dessert £6-£7.50, Service added but optional 10%, Groups min 5 service 10% **Wines** 160 bottles over £20, 12 bottles under £20, 6 by glass **Notes** Vegetarian available **Seats** 64, Pr/dining room 34 **Children** Portions **Parking** 4

Bennets Bar ♀

☎ 0131 229 5143
8 Leven St EH3 9LG
e-mail: kinight@hotmail.com
dir: Next to Kings Theatre. Please phone for more detailed directions

Bennets is a friendly pub, popular with performers from the adjacent Kings Theatre, serving real ales, over 120 malt whiskies and a decent selection of wines. It's a listed property dating from 1839 with hand-painted tiles and murals on the walls, original stained glass windows and brass beer taps. Reasonably priced home-made food ranges from toasties, burgers and salads to stovies, steak pie, and macaroni cheese. There's also a daily roast and traditional puddings.

Open all wk 11-11 (Sun noon-1am) Closed: 25 Dec **Bar Meals** L served Mon-Sat 12-2 D served Mon-Sat 5-8.30 Av main course £6.25

⊕ IONA PUB ◀ Caledonian Deuchars IPA, Guinness, Caledonian 80/-. ♀ 14 **Facilities** Children's menu Family room

The Bow Bar ♀

☎ 0131 226 7667
80 The West Bow EH1 2HH
dir: Telephone for directions

Located in the heart of Edinburgh's old town, the Bow Bar reflects the history and traditions of the area. Tables from decommissioned railway carriages and a gantry from an old church used for the huge selection of whiskies create interest in the bar, where 150 malts are on tap, and eight cask ales are dispensed from antique equipment. Bar snacks only are served, and there are no gaming machines or music to distract from conversation.

Open all wk Closed: 25-26 Dec, 1-2 Jan ⊕ FREE HOUSE ◀ Deuchars IPA, Belhaven 80/-, Timothy Taylor Landlord, Harviestown Bitter & Twisted, Atlas Lattitude, Trade Winds, Stewarts Pentland IPA. ♀ 6 **Facilities** Dogs allowed

Doric Tavern

☎ 0131 225 1084
15-16 Market St EH1 1DE
e-mail: info@the-doric.com
dir: In city centre opp Waverly Station & Edinburgh Dungeons

The property dates from 1710, when it was built as a private residence. It became a pub in the mid-1800s and takes its name from a language that used to be spoken in north-east Scotland, mainly in Aberdeenshire. It's conveniently located for Waverley Station, just a short walk from Princes Street and Edinburgh Castle. Public rooms include a ground-floor bar, and a wine bar and bistro upstairs. In these pleasantly informal surroundings a wide choice of fresh, locally sourced food is prepared by the chefs on site. While sipping a pint of Deuchars, you can nibble on home-made roasted red pepper houmous served with warm pitta bread. For those in need of something with chips, a home-made cheeseburger or chicken fillet burger will suffice. Starter options include steamed mussels; stuffed aubergines; and pan-seared king scallops. Main dishes range from herb-crusted sea bream to medallions of venison. Haggis, neeps and tatties covered with a whisky jus will certainly satisfy traditionalists. There is a pre-theatre menu available.

Open all wk 11.30am-mdnt (Thu-Sat 11.30am-1am) Closed: 25-26 Dec, 1 Jan **Bar Meals** Av main course £7.20 food served all day **Restaurant** Fixed menu price fr £9.95 Av 3 course à la carte fr £22 food served all day ⊕ FREE HOUSE ◀ Deuchars IPA, Tennents, Guinness. **Facilities** Family room

The Shore Bar & Restaurant ☂

☎ 0131 553 5080   📠 0131 553 5080
3 Shore, Leith EH6 6QW
e-mail: info@theshore.biz
dir: Please telephone for directions

Part of this historic pub was a 17th-century lighthouse and, befitting its location beside the Port of Leith, it has a fine reputation for fish and seafood. The carte changes at every sitting during the day to ensure the freshest produce is on offer. A typical meal could be roast rabbit with gnocchi and blue cheese sauce, followed by chargrilled tuna with roasted vegetables, Sardinian cous cous and black olive tapenade. Recent change of hands.

Open all wk noon-1am (Sun 12.30-1am) Closed: 25-26 Dec, 1 Jan **Bar Meals** L served all wk 12-2.30 booking required D served all wk 6-10.30 booking required Av main course £12 **Restaurant** L served all wk 12-2.30 booking required D served all wk 6-10.30 booking required Fixed menu price fr £8.95 Av 3 course à la carte fr £22 ⊕ FREE HOUSE ◀ Belhaven 80/-, Deuchars IPA, Guinness. ☂ 14 **Facilities** Dogs allowed

| RATHO | Map 3 NT17 |

The Bridge Inn ☂

☎ 0131 333 1320   📠 0131 333 3480
27 Baird Rd EH28 8RA
e-mail: info@bridgeinn.com
dir: From Newbridge at B7030 junct, follow signs for Ratho and Edinburgh Canal Centre

An 18th-century former farmhouse was converted to create this canal-side pub in 1820 with the opening of the Union Canal. It was once owned by the family of the last man to be hanged in public in Edinburgh, and his ghost is still reputed to haunt the building. In addition to the restaurant and two bars, The Bridge Inn also has a restaurant barge on the canal, providing the perfect venue for wedding parties, dinner dances, birthdays and other special events. Dishes range from bar snacks and light bites, such as mushrooms stuffed with haggis and black pudding, battered, deep-fried and served with red onion marmalade, to main courses of smoked

haddock fishcakes with lime and tarragon dressing, or pork and beef medallions with wholegrain mustard sauce and crushed potatoes. The canal's towpath is ideal for walkers and cyclists.

Open all day all wk 11-11 (Fri-Sat 11am-mdnt) Closed: 25-26 Dec, 1-2 Jan **Bar Meals** L served Mon-Sat 11-9, Sun 12-30-9 D served Mon-Sat 11-9, Sun 12-30-9 Av main course £9 food served all day **Restaurant** L served Mon-Sat 12-2.30, Sun 12.30-8.30 booking required D served Mon-Sat 6.30-9.30, Sun 12.30-8.30 booking required Fixed menu price fr £9.50 Av 3 course à la carte fr £16 ⊕ FREE HOUSE ◀ Belhaven, Deuchars IPA, Tennents, Stewarts Pentland. ☂ 6 **Facilities** Children's menu Family room Garden Parking

| SOUTH QUEENSFERRY | Map 3 NT17 |

Innkeeper's Lodge Edinburgh South Queensferry

BUDGET HOTEL

☎ 0845 112 6001   📠 0845 112 6299
7 Newhalls Rd EH30 9TA
web: www.innkeeperslodge.com/southqueensferry
dir: M8 junct 2 follow signs for Forth Road Bridge, onto M9/A8000. At rdbt take B907, to junct with B249. Turn right

Innkeeper's Lodge represents an exciting, high value concept within the budget hotel market. Comfortable bedrooms provide excellent facilities that include satellite TV and modem points. This carefully restored lodge is in a picturesque setting and has its own unique style and quirky character. Food is served all day, and an extensive, complimentary continental breakfast is offered. See also the Hotel Groups pages on theAA.com.

Rooms 14 (5 fmly) **Conf** Thtr 40

FALKIRK

Glenskirlie House & Castle

★★★★ 86% HOTEL

◉◉ Modern British

Fashionable Scottish castle with terrific food

☎ 01324 840201 ▤ 01324 841054
Kilsyth Rd FK4 1UF
e-mail: macaloneys@glenskirliehouse.com
dir: M80 junct 4 (East), at T-junct turn right. Hotel 1m on right

Forget the tartan-and-antlers school of Scottish castles: Glenskirlie gives a 21st-century kick in the pants to the old genre with boutique-style boudoirs to pamper yourself in and the food follows through with a genuine wow factor. The made-over Edwardian country house sits bang in the centre of Scotland in tranquil parkland. Bedrooms are beautifully designed and boast sumptuous beds, iPod stations and many accessories. Equally eye-catching bathrooms with under floor heating are equipped with high quality bespoke amenities. Guests can dine in the long-established, fine dining Glenskirlie House restaurant, or the new more informal Castle Grill. Two adjacent venues for meetings and special events are also available. Every aspect of the restaurant is finely tuned: knowledgeable staff deliver slick service, a sumptuous décor boosts the feel-good factor and the kitchen team deals in meticulously prepared food with razor-sharp technical execution. Modern takes on classic Scottish dishes might kick off with honey-roast pork belly with seared foie gras, Puy lentils and cider jus; hot-carved venison arrives with skirlie - a stuffing of oatmeal and onion - caramelised apple, red onion marmalade and a nicely gamey port and thyme jus. Desserts appear on the showpiece trolley.

Rooms 15 (3 fmly) **S** £185-£205; **D** £205-£255 (incl. bkfst)*
Facilities STV FTV Wi-fi **Conf** Class 100 Board 60 Thtr 150
Services Lift **Parking** 80 **Notes** LB ⊗ Civ Wed 150

Chef David Jordan **Owner** John Macaloney, Colin Macaloney
Restaurant Times 12-2/6-9.30 Closed 26-27 Dec, 1-3 Jan, D Mon
Prices Fixed L 2 course fr £18.75, Starter fr £6.25, Main fr £19.50, Dessert fr £8.25, Service optional **Wines** 40 bottles over £20, 20 bottles under £20, 8 by glass **Notes** Sunday L, Vegetarian available, Air con **Seats** 54, Pr/dining room 150 **Children** Portions, Menu

Travelodge Falkirk

BUDGET HOTEL

☎ 0871 984 6359 ▤ 01324 715742
West Beancross Farm, Junction 5 M9 FK2 0XS
web: www.travelodge.co.uk
dir: M9 junct 5, A9. 1st right. Lodge behind Beancross restaurant

Travelodge offers good quality, good value, budget accommodation. All offer family rooms sleeping up to four (two adults, two children) with en suite bathroom/shower-room, remote-control TV, tea- and coffee-making facilities and comfortable beds. Food options vary. Breakfast is at the on-site Bar Café restaurant (if available) or to take away. See also the Hotel Groups pages on theAA.com.
Rooms 52 **S** fr £29; **D** fr £29

The Grange Manor

★★★★ 77% HOTEL

☎ 01324 474836 ▤ 01324 665861
Glensburgh FK3 8XJ
e-mail: info@grangemanor.co.uk
web: www.grangemanor.co.uk
dir: E: off M9 junct 6, hotel 200mtrs to right. W: off M9 junct 5, A905 for 2m

Located south of town and close to the M9, this stylish hotel, popular with business and corporate clientele, benefits from hands-on family ownership. It offers spacious, high quality accommodation with superb bathrooms. Public areas include a comfortable foyer area, a lounge bar and a smart restaurant. Wallace's bar and restaurant is adjacent to the main house in the converted stables. Staff throughout are very friendly.

Rooms 36 (30 annexe) (6 fmly) (15 GF) **S** £80-£140; **D** £90-£160 (incl. bkfst) **Facilities** STV FTV Xmas New Year Wi-fi **Conf** Class 68 Board 40 Thtr 190 Del from £120 to £180 **Services** Lift **Parking** 154 **Notes** LB Civ Wed 160

Macdonald Inchyra Grange

★★★★ 72% HOTEL

☎ 01324 711911 ▤ 01324 716134
Grange Rd FK2 0YB
e-mail: inchyra@macdonald-hotels.co.uk
web: www.macdonaldhotels.co.uk
dir: Just beyond BP Social Club on Grange Rd

Ideally placed for the M9 and Grangemouth terminal, this former manor house has been tastefully extended. It provides extensive conference facilities and a choice of eating options: the relaxed atmosphere of the Café Crema or the Opus 504 Restaurant, which provides a more formal dining experience. Bedrooms are comfortable and mostly spacious.

Rooms 98 (6 annexe) (35 fmly) (33 GF) **Facilities** Spa STV ⓢ ⌁ Gym Steam room Sauna New Year **Conf** Class 300 Board 80 Thtr 750 **Services** Lift **Parking** 500 **Notes** LB Civ Wed

ABERDOUR   Map 3 NT18

Woodside

★★★ 🅰 HOTEL

☎ 01383 860328   📠 01383 860920
High St KY3 0SW
e-mail: reception@thewoodsidehotel.co.uk
web: www.thewoodsidehotel.co.uk
dir: M90 junct 1, E on A291 for 5m, hotel on left on entering village

Rooms 20 (4 fmly) **S** £57-£80; **D** £87.50-£97.50 (incl. bkfst)
Facilities FTV Wi-fi **Conf** Class 80 Board 10 Thtr 60 **Parking** 22
Notes LB ⊗ Civ Wed 80

The Cedar Inn

★★ 67% HOTEL

☎ 01383 860310
20 Shore Rd KY3 0TR
e-mail: cedarinn@btinternet.com
web: www.cedarinn.co.uk
dir: In Aberdour turn right off A921 into High St then right into Shore
Rd. Hotel 100yds on left

Lying between the village centre and the beach, this small hotel has
three character bars, one dedicated to malt whiskies, and impressive
bar and dinner menus. Bedrooms offer a mix of standards but all are
well equipped.

Rooms 9 (2 fmly) **S** £45-£55; **D** £65-£85 (incl. bkfst)* **Facilities** 🎵
Xmas New Year Wi-fi **Parking** 12 **Notes** LB ⊗

ANSTRUTHER   Map 3 NO50

The Waterfront

★★★★ 🖥 🍽 RESTAURANT WITH ROOMS

☎ 01333 312200   📠 01333 312288
18-20 Shore St KY10 3EA
e-mail: chris@anstruther-waterfront.co.uk
dir: Off A917 opposite marina

Situated overlooking the harbour, The Waterfront offers spacious,
stylish, contemporary accommodation with bedrooms located in
lovingly restored buildings in a courtyard behind the restaurant.
There is a comfortable lounge with a smartly fitted kitchen and
dining room, and laundry facilities are available in the granary.
Dinner and breakfast are served in the attractive restaurant that
offers a comprehensive menu featuring the best of local produce.

Rooms 8 annexe en suite (3 fmly) (1 GF) S £20-£40; D £40-£80*
Facilities STV TVL tea/coffee Dinner available Cen ht **Notes** LB ⊗

The Spindrift

★★★★ 🖥 🍽 GUEST HOUSE

☎ 01333 310573   📠 01333 310573
Pittenweem Rd KY10 3DT
e-mail: info@thespindrift.co.uk
web: www.thespindrift.co.uk
dir: Enter town from W on A917, 1st building on left

This immaculate Victorian villa stands on the western edge of the
village. The attractive bedrooms offer a wide range of extra touches;
the Captain's Room, a replica of a wood-panelled cabin, is a
particular feature. The inviting lounge has an honesty bar, while
imaginative breakfasts, and enjoyable home-cooked meals by
arrangement, are served in the cheerful dining room.

Rooms 8 rms (7 en suite) (1 pri facs) (2 fmly) S £45-£55; D
£64-£80* **Facilities** FTV TVL tea/coffee Dinner available Direct Dial
Cen ht Licensed Wi-fi **Parking** 12 **Notes** LB No Children 10yrs Closed
Xmas-late Jan

The Cellar

◉◉◉ Seafood

Excellent fish and seafood cooking in a former smokery

☎ 01333 310378 🖹 01333 312544
24 East Green KY10 3AA
web: www.cellaranstruther.co.uk
dir: Behind Scottish Fisheries Museum

Hiding behind the Scottish Fisheries Museum, a little way from Anstruther's harbour front, is this little gem. Housed in a 17th-century listed building, it has a charming cobbled courtyard, and original beams inside. On winter evenings, the fire crackles welcomingly, candles flicker on the tables, and the cooking is never less than a delight. Susan Jukes is a good advocate for husband Peter's food, knows her wines, and is full of useful advice when needed. The premises were once a cooperage and smokery in Scotland's herring industry, and something of that past is honoured in the starter of marinated herring with gravad lax that has been a tradition here for many years. Alternative, equally memorable dishes include crayfish bisque glazed with gruyère and cream, or an omelette stuffed with Finnan haddock. Mains continue to celebrate the harvest of the sea, perhaps with pesto-crusted cod with pak choi, basil mash and balsamic, or grilled halibut with smoked bacon, pine nuts and hollandaise. Meat-eaters might consider a piece of prime Scots beef, served with wild mushrooms, caramelised onions and stovies, in a grain mustard sauce. For dessert try Pavlova, filled with lemon curd ice cream, on rhubarb coulis.

Chef Peter Jukes **Owner** Peter Jukes **Times** 12.30-1.30/6.30-9.30 Closed Xmas, Sun (Sun & Mon Winter), L Mon-Tue **Prices** Fixed L course £23.50, Fixed D 3 course fr £37.50, Service optional **Wines** 5 by glass **Seats** 38 **Children** Portions **Parking** On street

The Dreel Tavern 🍷

☎ 01333 310727 🖹 01333 31057716
High Street West KY10 3DL
e-mail: dreeltavern@aol.com
dir: From Anstruther centre take A917 towards Pittenweem

Complete with a local legend concerning an amorous encounter between James V and a local gypsy woman, the welcoming 17th-century Dreel Tavern has plenty of atmosphere. Its oak beams, open fire and stone walls retain much of the distant past, while home-cooked food and cask-conditioned ales are served to hungry visitors of the present. Peaceful gardens overlook Dreel Burn.

Open all wk 11am-mdnt **Bar Meals** L served all wk 12-3 D served all wk 5.30-9.30 **Restaurant** L served all wk 12-3 D served all wk 5.30-9.30 🍴 FREE HOUSE 🍺 Deuchars IPA, 2 guest ales. 🍷 20 **Facilities** Children's menu Family room Dogs allowed Garden Parking

---

BURNTISLAND   **Map 3 NT28**

Kingswood

★★★ 75% HOTEL

☎ 01592 872329 🖹 01592 873123
Kinghorn Rd KY3 9LL
e-mail: rankin@kingswoodhotel.co.uk
web: www.kingswoodhotel.co.uk
dir: A921 (coast road) at Burntisland, right at rdbt, left at T-junct, at bottom of hill to Kinghorn road, hotel 0.5m on left

Lying east of the town, this hotel has views across the Firth of Forth to Edinburgh. Public rooms feature a range of cosy sitting areas, a spacious and attractive restaurant serving good value meals. There is also a good-size function room and multi-purpose conservatory. Bedrooms include two family suites and front-facing rooms with balconies.

Rooms 13 (3 fmly) (1 GF) **S** £59-£75; **D** £99-£120 (incl. bkfst) **Facilities** New Year Wi-fi **Conf** Class 20 Board 40 Thtr 150 Del from £90 to £110* **Parking** 50 **Notes** LB ⊗ Closed 26 Dec & 1 Jan Civ Wed 120

Inchview Hotel

★★★ 73% SMALL HOTEL

☎ 01592 872239
65-69 Kinghorn Rd KY3 9EB
e-mail: reception@inchview.co.uk
dir: M90 junct 1, follow Fife Coastal Route signed Burntisland

Looking out across the links to the Firth of Forth, this friendly hotel has been sympathetically restored. Bedrooms provide a variety of styles, with the superior rooms reflecting the Georgian character of the house; front-facing rooms have excellent views of the coastline. Both the restaurant and bar menus offer a wide and interesting choice.

Rooms 12 **Facilities** FTV Wi-fi **Conf** Class 64 Board 16 Thtr 64 **Parking** 12 **Notes** LB ⊗ No children 14yrs

Burntisland Sands Hotel

☎ 01592 872230 🖹 01592 872230
Lochies Rd KY3 9JX
e-mail: clarkelinton@hotmail.com
dir: Towards Kirkcaldy, Burntisland on A921. Hotel on right before Kinghorn

This small, family-run hotel, just 50 yards from an award-winning sandy beach, was once a highly regarded girls' boarding school. Reasonably priced breakfasts, snacks, lunches and evening meals are always available, with a good selection of specials. Try breaded haddock and tartare sauce; gammon steak Hawaii; or crispy shredded beef. Desserts include hot naughty fudge cake, and banana boat. There is also an excellent choice of hot and cold filled rolls, and a children's menu.

Open all wk 🍴 FREE HOUSE 🍺 Scottish Courage ales, Guinness, guest ales. **Facilities** Play area Garden Parking

Balcomie Links Hotel

★★ 71% SMALL HOTEL

☎ 01333 450237 🗐 01333 450540
Balcomie Rd KY10 3TN
e-mail: mikekadir@balcomie.fsnet.co.uk
web: www.balcomie.co.uk
dir: Follow road to village shops, at junct of High St & Market Gate turn right. This road becomes Balcomie Rd, hotel on left

Especially popular with visiting golfers, this family-run hotel on the east side of the village represents good value for money and has a relaxing atmosphere. Bedrooms come in a variety of sizes and styles and offer all the expected amenities. Food is served from midday in the attractive lounge bar, and also in the bright cheerful dining room in the evening.

Rooms 14 (2 fmly) **Facilities** Games room Xmas New Year Wi-fi **Parking** 20 **Notes** Civ Wed 45

The Golf Hotel ☙

☎ 01333 450206 🗐 01333 450795
4 High St KY10 3TD
e-mail: enquiries@thegolfhotelcrail.com
dir: At the end of High Street opposite Royal Bank

The present day Golf Hotel occupies a striking 18th-century Grade I listed building, but the first inn on the site opened its doors 400 years earlier. The characterful bars have an old world atmosphere. Well known for its traditional Scottish high tea with home-made pancakes and cakes, the inn is also popular for its home cooking. Choices range from fresh Crail crab salad and macaroni cheese through to steak and Deuchars ale pie or grilled fresh haddock in garlic butter from the carte menu.

Open all day all wk 11am-mdnt (Sun noon-mdnt) **Bar Meals** Av main course £6.50 food served all day **Restaurant** Av 3 course à la carte fr £15 food served all day ⊕ FREE HOUSE 🍺 McEwans 60/-, 80/-, 70/-, Belhaven Best, real ale. ☙ 6 **Facilities** Children's menu Dogs allowed Garden Parking

Ostlers Close Restaurant

◉◉ Modern British V ☙

Modern, elegant restaurant making good use of excellent local ingredients

☎ 01334 655574
Bonnygate KY15 4BU
dir: In small lane off main street, A91

This restaurant in a 17th-century dwelling and erstwhile temperance hotel is tucked up a skinny alley off Cupar main street and is easy to miss if you don't know where to look. The owners are so committed to sourcing fresh, local ingredients, that they have taken things into their own hands: their kitchen garden ensures fruit, veg and herbs appear in the kitchen half-an-hour after being picked. Wild mushrooms, picked from local woodland are a particular passion,

too. Handwritten menus see classic dishes brought up-to-date with clear unfussy flavours, and saucing driven more by punchy stocks and reductions than dairy produce. A roast fillet of Pittenweem hake with smoked haddock mash, parsley velouté and crispy Serrano ham makes a robust starter. Moving on, meaty main courses offer roast saddle of venison with wild mushrooms, roast root vegetables and red wine sauce. Desserts are a match for intensity with chocolate mocha tart with white chocolate ice cream and espresso sauce.

Chef James Graham **Owner** James & Amanda Graham **Times** 12.15-1.30/7-9.30 Closed 25-26 Dec, 1-2 Jan, 2 wks Oct, 2 wks Apr, Sun-Mon, L Tue-Fri **Prices** Starter £5.95-£12.50, Main £12.50-£21.50, Dessert £6.25-£7.25, Service optional **Wines** 60 bottles over £20, 31 bottles under £20, 6 by glass **Notes** Vegetarian menu **Seats** 26 **Children** Portions **Parking** On street, public car park

Best Western Keavil House Hotel

★★★★ 74% HOTEL

◉ Modern, Traditional

Contemporary cooking in relaxed conservatory restaurant

☎ 01383 736258 🗐 01383 621600
Crossford KY12 8QW
e-mail: reservations@keavilhouse.co.uk
web: www.keavilhouse.co.uk
dir: 2m W of Dunfermline on A994

Dating from the 16th century, this former manor house is set in gardens and parkland. With a modern health club and conference rooms it is suited to both business and leisure guests. Bedrooms come in a variety of sizes and occupy the original house and a modern wing. Expect modern, brasserie-style cooking in the stylish conservatory restaurant, Cardoon, overlooking the gardens of this 16th-century former manor house. Rich colours and a bright, airy, relaxed atmosphere set the tone, while the crowd-pleasing menu focuses on quality produce and some unusual combinations. Dishes are well balanced and accurately cooked, as witnessed in a full-flavoured smoked ham hock terrine with balsamic mayonnaise, perfectly-cooked scallops with cauliflower risotto, and a rich and visually pleasing chocolate parfait served with a griottine cherry jelly. Extras include an array of quality flavoured breads.

Rooms 73 (4 fmly) (29 GF) **S** £90-£120; **D** £110-£150 (incl. bkfst)* **Facilities** STV 🕒 supervised Gym Aerobics studio Beautician Xmas New Year Wi-fi **Conf** Class 80 Board 60 Thtr 300 Del from £135 to £155* **Parking** 250 **Notes** LB ◉ Civ Wed 200

Chef Phil Yates **Owner** Queensferry Hotels Ltd **Restaurant Times** 12-2/6.30-9.30 **Prices** Food prices not confirmed for 2010. Please telephone for details. **Wines** 12 bottles over £20, 22 bottles under £20, 9 by glass **Notes** Sunday L, Vegetarian available, Dress restrictions, No football colours **Seats** 80, Pr/dining room 22 **Children** Portions, Menu

Pitbauchlie House

★★★ 77% HOTEL

☎ 01383 722282 📠 01383 620738
Aberdour Rd KY11 4PB
e-mail: info@pitbauchlie.com
web: www.pitbauchlie.com
dir: M90 junct 2, onto A823, then B916. Hotel 0.5m on right

Situated in three acres of wooded grounds this hotel is just a mile south of the town and has a striking modern interior. The bedrooms are well equipped, and the deluxe rooms now have 32-inch LCD satellite TVs and CD micro systems; there is one bedroom designed for less able guests. The eating options include Harvey's Conservatory bistro and Restaurant 47 where Scottish and French influenced cuisine is offered.

Rooms 50 (3 fmly) (19 GF) **S** £63-£95; **D** £75-£110 (incl. bkfst)*
Facilities STV FTV Gym Wi-fi **Conf** Class 80 Board 60 Thtr 150
Parking 80 **Notes** LB Civ Wed 150

King Malcolm

★★★ 71% HOTEL

☎ 01383 722611 📠 01383 730865
Queensferry Rd KY11 8DS
e-mail: info@kingmalcolm-hotel-dunfermline.com
web: www.peelhotels.co.uk
dir: On A823, S of town

Located to the south of the city, this purpose-built hotel remains popular with business clientele and is convenient for access to both Edinburgh and Fife. Public rooms include a smart foyer lounge and a conservatory bar, as well as a restaurant. Bedrooms, although not large, are well laid out and well equipped.

Rooms 48 (2 fmly) (24 GF) **Facilities** 🎵 Xmas New Year Wi-fi
Conf Class 60 Board 50 Thtr 150 **Parking** 60 **Notes** LB Civ Wed 120

Express by Holiday Inn Dunfermline

BUDGET HOTEL

☎ 01383 748220 📠 01383 748221
Lauder College, Halbeath KY11 8DY
e-mail: info@hiexpressdunfermline.co.uk
web: www.hiexpress.com/dunfermline
dir: M9 junct 7 signed A994/A907, 3rd exit Lynebank rdbt or M90 junct 3, 2nd exit for A907, next rdbt 3rd exit, next rdbt 1st exit

A modern hotel ideal for families and business travellers. Fresh and uncomplicated, the spacious rooms include Sky TV, power shower and tea and coffee-making facilities. Continental buffet breakfast is included in the room rate; other meals may be taken at the nearby family pub or restaurant. See also the Hotel Groups pages on theAA.com.

Rooms 82 **Conf** Class 8 Board 16 Thtr 25 Del from £70 to £80

Travelodge Dunfermline

BUDGET HOTEL

☎ 0871 984 6287
Halbeath Junction KY11 8PG
web: www.travelodge.co.uk
dir: M90 junct 3, follow signs for Halbeath, 1st right. Lodge on right

Travelodge offers good quality, good value, modern accommodation. Ideal for families, the spacious en suite bedrooms include remote-control TV, tea and coffee-making facilities and comfortable beds. Meals can be taken at the nearby family restaurant. See also the Hotel Groups pages on theAA.com.

Rooms 50 **S** fr £29; **D** fr £29

ELIE	Map 3 NO40

Sangsters

◉◉ Modern British

Good Scottish cooking in relaxed surroundings

☎ 01333 331001
51 High St KY9 1BZ
e-mail: bruce@sangsters.co.uk
dir: From St Andrews on A917 take B9131 to Anstruther, right at rdbt onto A917 to Elie. (11m from St Andrews)

A small seaside village restaurant it may be, with a relaxed atmosphere and comfortable lounge, yet the place has pedigree. Chef-patron Bruce Sangster's cooking is skilful, precise and accomplished, his modern approach driven by fresh, quality seasonal ingredients from the Scottish larder. Take a twice-baked cheese soufflé starter using Isle of Mull Tobermoray cheddar, or to follow, Scotch beef fillet accompanied by a red cabbage compôte, onion marmalade and gratin potatoes. Heading-up desserts, a caramelised apple pastry with Calvados custard, caramel sauce and apple sorbet might catch the eye. The dining room comes in bright, clean and simple lines, the walls hung with local prints and watercolours.

Times 12.30-1.30/7-9.30 Closed 25-26 Dec, early Jan, mid Feb/Oct, mid Nov, Mon, L Tue & Sat, D Sun

The Ship Inn ♥

☎ 01333 330246 📠 01333 330864
The Toft KY9 1DT
e-mail: info@ship-elie.com
dir: Follow A915 & A917 to Elie. From High Street follow signs to Watersport Centre & The Toft

Standing right on the waterfront at Elie Bay, this lively free house has been a pub since 1838 and run by the enthusiastic Philip family for 20 years. The cricket team plays regular fixtures on the beach, live music is performed, and there is a regular programme of summer barbecues and other eagerly anticipated events throughout the year. Local bakers, butchers and fishmongers and their produce feature in the pub's colourful and concise menu.

Open all wk Closed: 25 Dec ⊕ FREE HOUSE ◀ Caledonian Deuchars IPA, Belhaven Best, Tetleys Xtra Cold, Caledonian 801, Tartan Special. ♥ 7 **Facilities** Play area Family room Dogs allowed Garden

GLENROTHES Map 3 NO20

Express by Holiday Inn Glenrothes

BUDGET HOTEL

☎ 01592 745509 🖷 01592 743377
Leslie Roundabout, Leslie Rd KY6 3EP
e-mail: ebhi-glenrothes@btconnect.com
web: www.hiexpress.com/glenrothes
dir: M90 junct 2A left onto A911 for Leslie. Through 4 rdbts, hotel on left

A modern hotel ideal for families and business travellers. Fresh and uncomplicated, the spacious rooms include Sky TV, power shower and tea and coffee-making facilities. Continental buffet breakfast is included in the room rate; other meals may be taken at the nearby family pub or restaurant. See also the Hotel Groups pages on theAA.com.

Rooms 49 (40 fmly) (21 GF) **S** £59.95-£69.95; **D** £59.95-£69.95 (incl. bkfst)* **Conf** Class 16 Board 16 Thtr 30

Travelodge Glenrothes

BUDGET HOTEL

☎ 0871 984 6278 🖷 01476 577500
Bankhead Park KY7 6GH
web: www.travelodge.co.uk
dir: M90/A92 to junct with A910/B981(signed Glenrothes), follow to Redhouse rdbt take 2nd exit (signed Glenrothes, Tay Bridge) follow to Bankhead rdbt junct with B921

Travelodge offers good quality, good value, modern accommodation. Ideal for families, the spacious en suite bedrooms include remote-control TV, tea and coffee-making facilities and comfortable beds. Meals can be taken at the nearby family restaurant. See also the Hotel Groups pages on theAA.com.

Rooms 50 **S** fr £29; **D** fr £29

INVERKEITHING Map 3 NT18

The Roods

★★★★★ BED AND BREAKFAST

☎ 01383 415049 🖷 01383 415049
16 Bannerman Av KY11 1NG
e-mail: isobelmarley@hotmail.com
web: www.the-roods.co.uk
dir: N of town centre off B981(Church St/Chapel Place)

This charming house stands in secluded, well-tended gardens close to the station. Bedrooms are individually styled and have state-of-the-art bathrooms. There is an inviting lounge, and breakfast is served at individual tables in an attractive conservatory.

Rooms 2 en suite (2 GF) **Facilities** TVL tea/coffee Dinner available Direct Dial Cen ht **Parking** 4 **Notes** ⊗ ⊜

KINCARDINE Map 3 NS98

The Unicorn 🍷

☎ 01259 739129
15 Excise St FK10 4LN
e-mail: info@theunicorn.co.uk
dir: Exit M9 junct 7 towards Kincardine Bridge. Cross bridge, bear left. 1st left, then sharp left at rdbt

This 17th-century pub-restaurant in the heart of the historic port of Kincardine used to be a coaching inn. And it was where, in 1842, Sir James Dewar, inventor of the vacuum flask, was born. Leather sofas and modern decor blend in well with the older parts of the building. There is a comfortable lounge bar, a grillroom, and a more formal dining room upstairs. In decent weather, have a drink by the old well in the walled garden.

Open noon-2.30 5.30-mdnt (Sun 12.30-mdnt) Closed: 3rd wk Jul, Mon **Bar Meals** L served Tue-Sat 12-2.30, Sun 12.30-8 D served Tue-Sat 5.30-9.30, Sun 12.30-8 ⊕ FREE HOUSE ◀ Bitter & Twisted. 🍷 8 **Facilities** Children's menu Parking

KIRKCALDY Map 3 NT29

Dean Park

★★★ 78% HOTEL

☎ 01592 261635 🖷 01592 261371
Chapel Level KY2 6QW
e-mail: reception@deanparkhotel.co.uk
dir: Signed from A92, Kirkcaldy West junct

Popular with both business and leisure guests, this hotel has extensive conference and meeting facilities. Executive bedrooms are spacious and comfortable, and all are well equipped with modern decor and amenities. Twelve direct access, chalet-style rooms are set in the grounds and equipped to the same specification as main bedrooms. Public areas include a choice of bars and a restaurant.

Rooms 46 (12 annexe) (2 fmly) (5 GF) **Facilities** STV FTV Wi-fi **Conf** Class 125 Board 54 Thtr 250 **Services** Lift **Parking** 250 **Notes** ⊗

Drinking fountain, Falkland, Fife

LEUCHARS Map 3 NO42

Hillpark House

★★★★ GUEST HOUSE

☎ 01334 839280 📠 01334 839051
96 Main St KY16 0HF
e-mail: enquiries@hillparkhouse.com
web: www.hillparkhouse.com
dir: Leaving Leuchars for St Michaels, house last on right

Lying peacefully on the edge of the village, Hillpark House is an impressive Edwardian home offering comfortable, well-appointed and equipped bedrooms. There is an inviting lounge, a conservatory and a peaceful dining room.

Rooms 5 rms (3 en suite) (1 pri facs) (1 fmly) S £38-£45; D £70-£110* **Facilities** TVL tea/coffee Cen ht Wi-fi Golf 0 **Parking** 6 **Notes** ⊗

LEVEN Map 3 NO30

Dunclutha Guest House

★★★★ GUEST HOUSE

☎ 01333 425515 📠 01333 422311
16 Victoria Rd KY8 4EX
e-mail: pam.leven@blueyonder.co.uk
web: www.dunclutha.myby.co.uk
dir: A915, B933 Glenlyon Rd into Leven, rdbt left onto Commercial Rd & Victoria Rd, Dunclutha opp church on right

Set in a quiet street close to the town centre, Dunclutha is an inviting Victorian property that was formerly the rectory for the nearby Episcopalian church. Lovingly restored and refurbished to its original splendour it offers comfortable, well-equipped accommodation. A splendid lounge adjoins the dining room where hearty breakfasts are served at individual tables.

Rooms 4 rms (3 en suite) (1 pri facs) (2 fmly) S £30-£40; D £60-£120 **Facilities** FTV TVL tea/coffee Cen ht Piano **Parking** 3 **Notes** ⊗ RS 2wks Jan annual holiday

LOWER LARGO Map 3 NO40

The Crusoe Hotel

☎ 01333 320759 📠 01333 320865
2 Main St KY8 6BT
e-mail: relax@crusoehotel.co.uk
dir: A92 to Kirkcaldy East, A915 to Lundin Links, then right to Lower Largo

This historic inn is located on the sea wall in Lower Largo, the birthplace of Alexander Selkirk, the real-life castaway immortalised by Daniel Defoe in his novel, Robinson Crusoe. In the past the area was also the heart of the once-thriving herring fishing industry. Today it is a charming bay ideal for a golfing break. A typical menu may include 'freshly shot' haggis, Pittenweem haddock and a variety of steaks.

Open all day all wk 11am-mdnt (Fri-Sat 11am-1am) **Bar Meals** L served all wk 11-9 D served all wk 11-9 food served all day ⊕ FREE HOUSE ◀ Belhaven 80/-, Best, Deuchars, Abbot Ale, Old Speckled Hen. **Facilities** Play area Dogs allowed Parking

MARKINCH Map 3 NO20

Balbirnie House

★★★★ COUNTRY HOUSE HOTEL

◉◉ Classic

Accomplished Scottish cuisine in imposing Georgian mansion

☎ 01592 610066 📠 01592 610529
Balbirnie Park KY7 6NE
e-mail: info@balbirnie.co.uk
web: www.balbirnie.co.uk
dir: off A92 onto B9130, entrance 0.5m on left

Dating back to 1777, Balbirnie House is one of Scotland's foremost listed buildings. The impressive Georgian mansion, set in 400 acres of stunning landscaped parkland, is now a luxurious country-house hotel. Delightful public rooms include a choice of inviting lounges. Accommodation features some splendid well-proportioned bedrooms with the best overlooking the gardens. But even the smaller standard rooms include little touches such as sherry, shortbread, fudge and mineral water. The refurbished restaurant, The Orangery, is sumptuously decorated in shades of silver, copper and chocolate with floor-to-ceiling lunette windows and a glass roof. The menu features beautifully presented classical cuisine, using the very best from Scotland's rich larder, much of it locally sourced. Expect impressive dishes such as Cullen skink or Isle of Lewis lamb shoulder pie served with the loin - pink and tender - on a bed of curly kale with potato Anna. Finish with banana parfait and peanut butter ice cream, and note the more informal Balbirnie bistro is also worth a punt.

Rooms 30 (9 fmly) (7 GF) **S** £85-£115; **D** £170-£210 (incl. bkfst)* **Facilities** ᗷ Woodland walks Jogging trails Xmas New Year Wi-fi **Conf** Class 100 Board 60 Thtr 220 **Parking** 120 **Notes** LB Civ Wed 150

Restaurant Times 12-1.30/7-9 Closed Mon-Tue

Town House

★★★★ RESTAURANT WITH ROOMS

☎ 01592 758459   🖷 01592 755039
1 High St KY7 6DQ
e-mail: townhousehotel@aol.com
web: www.townhousehotel-fife.co.uk
dir: In town centre opposite railway station

Well situated on the edge of town and close to the railway station, this friendly establishment offers well presented bedrooms with pleasant colour schemes, modern furnishings, and a good range of facilities and extras. The attractive bar-restaurant is popular with locals and serves a choice of good-value dishes.

Rooms 3 en suite (1 fmly) S £50; D £80-£90* **Facilities** FTV tea/coffee Dinner available Cen ht Wi-fi **Notes** ⊗ Closed 25-26 Dec & 1-2 Jan No coaches

---

NEWBURGH	Map 3 NO21

The Abbey Inn

★★★ INN

☎ 01337 840761   🖷 01337 840761
East Port KY14 6EZ
e-mail: wo6whiskers04@aol.com
web: www.theabbeyinn.com
dir: On A913 High St

Located at the east end of the village, the Abbey Inn offers accommodation situated on the first floor. Bedrooms are bright and well appointed with many thoughtful extras provided as standard. There is a popular public and lounge bar where meals can be provided for residents by prior arrangement.

Rooms 3 en suite (1 fmly); D £60 **Facilities** FTV tea/coffee Dinner available Cen ht Pool Table **Parking** 1 **Notes** LB No coaches

---

PEAT INN	Map 3 NO40

The Peat Inn

★★★★★ RESTAURANT WITH ROOMS

@@@ Modern British 🍴 🍃

Classy cooking using first-class local produce

☎ 01334 840206   🖷 01334 840530
KY15 5LH
e-mail: stay@thepeatinn.co.uk
dir: At junction of B940/B941, 6m SW of St Andrews

There's been no resting on their laurels for owners Geoffrey and Katherine Smeddle since they took over this 300-year-old coaching inn with a recent history as one of Scotland's top dining destinations. Pleasingly the restaurant with rooms continues to go from strength to strength. The spacious accommodation is very well appointed and all rooms have lounge areas. Public areas include a comfortable lounge, decorated in an elegant country style, and dominated by a large log fire. This leads through to three intimate dining rooms. Reflecting the natural setting, the rooms are painted in muted colours with fresh

flowers adorning the linen-clad tables. Produce comes from small local suppliers wherever possible and, with Geoffrey at the helm in the kitchen, ingredients are imaginatively paired and balanced to bring out the maximum depth and flavour. The visual impact of the food is stunning, as in a mosaic of rabbit, sweetbreads and confit duck perfectly pointed by accompanying pickled mushrooms and spiced walnuts. Perfect timing and high quality produce is evident in a John Dory main course, with fricassée of shellfish and white beans, potato gnocchi and mushroom purée. An accurately cooked mango soufflé with yogurt sorbet provides a confident close.

Rooms 8 annexe en suite (2 fmly) (8 GF) **Facilities** FTV tea/coffee Dinner available Direct Dial Cen ht **Parking** 24 **Notes** Closed 25-26 Dec & 1-3 Jan RS Sun-Mon Closed No coaches

Chef Geoffrey Smeddle **Owner** Geoffrey & Katherine Smeddle **Restaurant Times** 12.30-2/7-9.30 Closed 25-26 Dec, 1-14 Jan, Sun-Mon **Prices** Fixed L 3 course £16-£18, Fixed D 3 course fr £32, Tasting menu £50-£54, Starter £9-£15, Main £17-£25, Dessert £9-£11, Service optional **Wines** 250 bottles over £20, 9 by glass **Notes** Tasting menu 6 course, Vegetarian available **Seats** 40, Pr/dining room 14

ST ANDREWS	Map 3 NO51

The Old Course Hotel, Golf Resort & Spa

★★★★★ HOTEL

The Road Hole Restaurant

@@@ British V 🍷

Golfing views and Scottish produce

☎ 01334 474371   🖷 01334 477668
KY16 9SP
e-mail: reservations@oldcoursehotel.co.uk
dir: M90 junct 8 then A91 to St Andrews

A haven for golfers, the internationally renowned Old Course Hotel stands next to the 17th hole of the championship course. Bedrooms vary in size and style but all provide decadent levels of luxury. Day rooms include intimate lounges, a bright conservatory, a spa and a range of pro golf shops. Staff throughout are friendly and services are impeccably delivered. There are various places to eat in this elegant and modern hotel, including Sands and the Jigger Inn (see entries below) but for something a bit special go for The Road Hole. First though, have a drink in the Road Hole Bar, which offers over 200 whiskies. In the restaurant, complete with chandeliers, oak-panelled floors and crisply laid tables, the floor-to-ceiling windows offer dramatic views over the old course and sweeping coastal vista. The Road Hole Table in the corner is positioned directly over the 17th road hole of the course for those die-hard fans. For those who can take their eyes off the view, the open kitchen provides a sense of theatre indoors. There are 3 menu options available - the à la carte, eight-course tasting and vegetarian tasting menu - and each makes good use of Scottish, and often organic, ingredients. Try Severn Valley smoked eel with a crispy herb risotto, white asparagus, samphire and cockle vinaigrette, followed by cranberry and bitter chocolate granola crusted wild boar loin with haunch cottage pie, black pudding, mustard swede and Swiss pie, and leave room for rhubarb and custard jelly, sorbet and biscuit.

continued

ST ANDREWS CONTINUED
Rooms 144 (5 fmly) (1 GF) **Facilities** Spa STV FTV ⊗ ♨ 18 Putt green Gym Thermal suite Xmas New Year Wi-fi **Conf** Class 473 Board 259 Thtr 950 **Services** Lift **Parking** 125 **Notes** ⊗ Civ Wed 180

Chef Paul Hart **Owner** Kohler Company **Restaurant Times** 7-10 Closed Sun-Mon, L all week **Prices** Food prices not confirmed for 2010. Please telephone for details. **Wines** 400 bottles over £20, 11 by glass **Notes** Tasting menu & vegetarian tasting menu available, Vegetarian menu, Dress restrictions, Smart, no jeans/trainers, collared shirt req. **Seats** 70, Pr/dining room 20 **Children** Portions, Menu

Sands Restaurant

◉ International

Stylish restaurant within upmarket golf-resort hotel complex

The Sands Restaurant is the more informal of the hotel's dining options. It has a butch, rather clubby feel with black leather and dark wood - a classy look, but one that is scheduled for refurbishment in early 2010. The cooking is accurate and unfussy in style: top-drawer Scottish produce is used with a clear inclination towards brasserie-style dishes infused with a hint of the Mediterranean. Kyle of Tongue oysters with lemon, shallot and Cabernet Sauvignon vinaigrette gets things of to a classic start, then roast organic Shetland cod with chorizo, mussels and borlotti beans might follow.

Chef Simon Whitely **Owner** Kohler Company **Times** 12-6/6-10 **Prices** Food prices not confirmed for 2010. Please telephone for details. **Wines** 70 bottles over £20, 11 by glass **Notes** Vegetarian available, Dress restrictions, Smart casual **Seats** 80, Pr/dining room 40 **Children** Portions, Menu

The Jigger Inn ▼

Once the stationmaster's lodge on a railway line that disappeared many years ago, the Jigger is in the grounds of the Old Course Hotel. You won't be surprised by the golfing memorabilia, or by sharing bar space with a caddy or two, fresh in from a long game. Even Tiger Woods has been seen here. Open-hearth fires are the backdrop for a selection of Scottish beers, including St Andrew's Ale from Belhaven Brewery in Dunbar. All-day availability is one advantage of a short, simple menu that lists soup, sandwiches and barbecued chicken salad wrap with honey mustard dressing as starters, and continues with beer-battered fish and chips; sausage and mash with onion gravy; warm sunblushed tomato with goats' cheese and rocket tart, and gremolata dressing; and grilled Speyside steak with seasoned fries and onion rings.

Open all day all wk 11-11 (Sun noon-11) Closed: 25 Dec **Bar Meals** L served all wk 12-9.30 Av main course £11 food served all day **Restaurant** D served all wk 12-9.30 booking required ⊕ FREE HOUSE ◼ Guinness, St Andrews Best. ▼ 8 **Facilities** Children's menu Garden

Rufflets Country House

★★★★ HOTEL

◎◎ Modern British ▲

Scottish cuisine in friendly country-house hotel

☎ 01334 472594 📠 01334 478703
Strathkinness Low Rd KY16 9TX
e-mail: reservations@rufflets.co.uk
web: www.rufflets.co.uk
dir: 1.5m W on B939

This charming turreted mansion a few minutes' drive from the town centre was originally built in 1924 as a private home for the widow of a prominent Dundee jute baron. Located one mile west of St Andrews, the charming Edwardian country house with splendid formal gardens and woodland has been in the same family ownership since 1952. Stylish, spacious bedrooms are individually decorated, and public rooms include a well-stocked bar, a choice of inviting lounges and the Garden Room Restaurant, featuring a simple and stylish traditional décor with lots of colourful artwork that serves imaginative, carefully prepared cuisine. Service is particularly friendly and attentive making the diner feel really at ease. Cooking style is Scottish with Mediterranean influences, using fresh local produce. Typical dishes include a starter of malt whisky cured organic Scottish salmon with caper crème fraîche, followed by a main of braised Fife lamb shank with pearl barley risotto and port wine jus. Impressive conference and banqueting facilities are available in the adjacent Garden Suite.

Rooms 24 (5 annexe) (2 fmly) (3 GF) **S** £140-£155; **D** £195-£245 (incl. bkfst)* **Facilities** STV Putt green ⛳ Golf driving net Xmas New Year Wi-fi **Conf** Class 60 Board 60 Thtr 200 Del from £150 to £250* **Parking** 50 **Notes** LB ⊗ Civ Wed 130

Chef Mark Nixon **Owner** Ann Murray-Smith **Restaurant Times** 12.30-2.30/7-9 Closed L Mon-Sat **Prices** Fixed L 2 course £10.95-£20, Starter £4.75-£8.50, Main £14.95-£29.75, Dessert £6.50-£9, Service optional, Groups min 20 service 10% **Wines** 88 bottles over £20, 18 bottles under £20, 9 by glass **Notes** Sunday L, Vegetarian available, Dress restrictions, No shorts **Seats** 80, Pr/dining room 130 **Children** Portions, Menu

Macdonald Rusacks

★★★★ 73% HOTEL

◎◎ Scottish International

Fine food in world famous golf hotel

☎ 0844 879 9136 & 01334 474321 📠 01334 477896
Pilmour Links KY16 9JQ
e-mail: general.rusacks@macdonald-hotels.co.uk
web: www.macdonald-hotels.co.uk
dir: A91 W, straight over rdbt entering St Andrews. Hotel 220yds on left

The Macdonald Rusacks Hotel in St Andrews is one of the most famous golfing hotels on the planet. Bedrooms, though varying in size, are comfortably appointed and well equipped. Classically styled public rooms include an elegant reception lounge and a smart restaurant. The long-established hotel enjoys an unrivalled location close to the 18th hole with superb views across the world-famous course. Take your eyes off the green and you'll find the food up to par, served in the smart restaurant with huge windows to take in those views. The traditional Scottish and international cuisine offers a tempting range of sophisticated, contemporary, weekly-changing dishes, including the likes of foie gras terrine with Madeira jelly as a starter, or mains such as fillet of wild halibut with braised oxtail, horseradish blini, parsnip purée and port wine reduction. For those with a sweet tooth, the warm chocolate fondant with vanilla ice cream and pistachio anglaise will definitely appeal.

Rooms 68 **Facilities** STV FTV Xmas New Year Wi-fi **Conf** Class 35 Board 20 Thtr 80 Del from £95 to £365* **Services** Lift **Parking** 21 **Notes** Civ Wed 60

Chef Cameron Roberson **Owner** Macdonald Hotels **Restaurant Times** 12-2.30/6.30-9 **Prices** Food prices not confirmed for 2010. Please telephone for details. **Wines** 35 bottles over £20, 15 bottles under £20, 13 by glass **Notes** Vegetarian available, Dress restrictions, Smart casual **Seats** 70 **Children** Portions, Menu

Best Western Scores

★★★ 79% HOTEL

☎ 01334 472451 📠 01334 473947
76 The Scores KY16 9BB
e-mail: reception@scoreshotel.co.uk
web: www.scoreshotel.co.uk
dir: M90 junct 2A onto A92 E. Follow signs Glenrothes then St Andrews. Straight over at 1st two rdbts then left onto Golf Place & right onto The Scores

Enjoying views over St Andrews Bay, this well presented hotel is situated only a short pitch from the first tee of the famous Old Course. Bedrooms are impressively furnished and come in various sizes; many are quite spacious. Smart public areas include a restaurant offering food all day in addition to dinner. Alexander's Restaurant & Cocktail Bar opens during the summer months and on Friday and Saturday nights in winter.

Rooms 30 (1 fmly) **S** £84.50-£180; **D** £120-£286 (incl. bkfst)* **Facilities** FTV New Year Wi-fi **Conf** Class 60 Board 40 Thtr 180 Del from £135 to £187* **Services** Lift **Parking** 8 **Notes** ⊗ Civ Wed 100

Russell Hotel

★★ 81% HOTEL

◉ Scottish, International

Imaginative cooking in an intimate setting

☎ 01334 473447 📠 01334 478279
26 The Scores KY16 9AS
e-mail: russellhotel@talk21.com
dir: From A91 left at 2nd rdbt into Golf Place, right in 200yds into The Scores, hotel in 300yds on left

This friendly, family-run hotel on The Scores overlooking St Andrews Bay has lovely sea views and provides well appointed bedrooms in varying sizes. The restaurant is cosy and candlelit by night, creating an intimate atmosphere in which to enjoy some imaginative Scottish

cooking. Take a drink in the welcoming Victorian Lounge Bar with its roaring log fire before dinner. High-quality local ingredients appear in dishes like steamed Loch Fyne mussels in white wine and coconut milk with lime, chilli and coriander, and trio of Aberdeen Angus beef (medallion fillet, braised oxtail and tongue). Baked lemon tart with champagne sorbet and a raspberry coulis makes a fitting finale.

Rooms 10 (3 fmly) **Facilities** New Year **Notes** ⊗

Restaurant Times 12-2/6.30-9.30 Closed Xmas

St Andrews Golf

Ⓤ

◉◉ Scottish

Timeless dining with a modern Scottish accent

☎ 01334 472611 📠 01334 472188
40 The Scores KY16 9AS
e-mail: reception@standrews-golf.co.uk
web: www.standrews-golf.co.uk
dir: Follow 'Golf Course' signs into Golf Place, 200yds turn right into The Scores

Currently the rating for this establishment is not confirmed. This may be due to a change of ownership or because it has only recently joined the AA rating scheme. For further details please see the AA website: theAA.com

The superb location and spectacular views at the family-run St Andrews Golf Hotel gives it broad appeal well beyond the golfing fraternity, although the name is a bit of a giveaway. The elegant Number Forty Restaurant is decked out in muted tones of brown and cream, making for a bright modern space. Scottish ingredients are used to good effect by a kitchen which has a definite eye for presentation. Think salted-cod brandade with paprika and herb crostini, followed by braised ox cheeks with fresh buttered pasta. Desserts are quite traditional and might feature pear crumble with pouring cream or a selection of home-made sorbets such as lemon, mulled wine or orange.

Rooms 22 **Facilities** New Year Wi-fi **Conf** Class 80 Board 20 Thtr 200 **Services** Lift **Parking** 6 **Notes** LB Closed 26-28 Dec Civ Wed 180

Restaurant Times 12.30-2/7-9.30 Closed 26-28 Dec

The Paddock

★★★★★ GUEST ACCOMMODATION

☎ 01334 850888 📠 01334 850870
Sunnyside, Strathkinness KY16 9XP
e-mail: thepaddock@btinternet.com
web: www.thepadd.co.uk
dir: 3m W from St Andrews off B939. The Paddock signed from village centre

Situated in a peaceful village overlooking rolling countryside, this friendly, family-run guest house offers stylish and very well-equipped bedrooms. Superb fish tanks, one freshwater, the other salt, line the entrance hall and contain beautiful and unusual fish. The lounge-dining room in the conservatory is a lovely setting for the delicious

continued

breakfasts.

Rooms 4 en suite (1 fmly) (2 GF) **Facilities** tea/coffee Cen ht Wi-fi
Parking 8 **Notes** ⊗ Closed 1-27 Dec

Glenderran

★★★★ GUEST HOUSE

☎ 01334 477951 📄 01334 477908
9 Murray Park KY16 9AW
e-mail: info@glenderran.com
web: www.glenderran.com
dir: In town centre. Off North St onto Murray Place & Murray Park

This smart terrace house has a super location just minutes from the
town centre, seafront, West Sands beach and the Old Course.
Aviation-theme pictures and memorabilia decorate the public rooms.
Well-equipped bedrooms come in a variety of sizes, and carefully
prepared breakfasts are enjoyed in the ground-floor dining room.

Rooms 5 rms (4 en suite) (1 pri facs) S £35-£47; D £70-£100*
Facilities FTV TVL tea/coffee Cen ht Wi-fi **Notes** LB ⊗ No Children
12yrs Closed Jan

Nethan House

★★★★ GUEST HOUSE

☎ 01334 472104 📄 01334 850870
17 Murray Park KY16 9AW
e-mail: enquiries@nethan-standrews.com
dir: A91 towards St Andrews, over 2nd rdbt onto North St, Murray
Park on left before cinema

This large Victorian terrace house is set in the heart of St Andrews; a
short walk from the main tourist attractions and the famous St
Andrews golf course. The bright bedrooms are stylish and well
appointed. The freshly cooked breakfast is a highlight and is served
in the attractive dining room.

Rooms 7 en suite (1 fmly) (1 GF) **Facilities** FTV TVL tea/coffee Cen ht
Wi-fi **Notes** ⊗ Closed 24-26 Dec

Craigmore

★★★★ GUEST HOUSE

☎ 01334 472142 📄 01334 477963
3 Murray Park KY16 9AW
e-mail: info@standrewscraigmore.com
web: www.standrewscraigmore.com
dir: In town centre. Off North St onto Murray Place & Murray Park

Lying between the town centre and the seafront, this immaculately
maintained guest house forms part of a Victorian row. Close to the
Old Course, it is adorned with lots of amusing golfing touches. The
stylish bedrooms are attractively decorated and well equipped.
Breakfast is served at individual tables in the elegant lounge-dining
room.

Rooms 7 en suite (4 fmly) (1 GF); D £72-£96 **Facilities** FTV TVL tea/
coffee Cen ht Wi-fi **Notes** LB ⊗

The Inn at Lathones

★★★★ INN

◉◉ Modern European

Creative combinations in a charming coaching inn

☎ 01334 840494 📄 01334 840694
Largoward KY9 1JE
e-mail: lathones@theinn.co.uk
web: www.theinn.co.uk
dir: 5m S of St Andrews on A915, 0.5m before village of Largoward on
left just after hidden dip

This lovely old coaching inn, parts of which are 400 years old, is full
of character and individuality. The friendly staff help to create a
relaxed atmosphere. Smart contemporary bedrooms are in two
separate wings. The colourful, cosy restaurant is the main focus,
serving modern Scottish and European food; and it's close enough to
St Andrew's for a spot of golf, too. Although tables are formally laid,
the friendly staff and colourful interior give it a relaxed vibe, enough,
hopefully, to allay any fears about meeting the resident ghost.
Imaginative flavour combinations utilise top-notch local ingredients
in dishes such as fillet of hare and fresh scallops on a salad of
rocket dressed with a blackcurrant and thyme vinaigrette. Main-
course roasted gigot of lamb comes with mutton stovies, a garlic
cream and succulent red cabbage, and end on a sweet note with
orange blossom crème brûlée with a local fruit compôte and yogurt
ice cream.

Rooms 13 annexe en suite (1 fmly) (11 GF) **Facilities** STV TVL tea/
coffee Dinner available Direct Dial Cen ht Wi-fi **Conf** Max 40 Thtr 40
Class 10 Board 20 **Parking** 35 **Notes** Closed 26 Dec & 3-16 Jan RS
24 Dec Civ Wed 45

Chef Richard Brackenbury **Owner** Mr N White **Restaurant**
Times 12-2.30/6-9.30 Closed 26 Dec, 1st 2 wks Jan, **Prices** Fixed L 2
course £15.50, Starter £3.95-£7.50, Main £16.50-£22, Dessert
£5.95-£7.50, Service optional **Wines** 89 bottles over £20, 13 bottles
under £20, 5 by glass **Notes** Sunday L, Vegetarian available, Dress
restrictions, Smart casual **Seats** 40, Pr/dining room 40
Children Menu

Spinkstown Farmhouse (NO541144)

★★★★ FARMHOUSE

☎ 01334 473475 📠 01334 473475 Mrs A E Duncan
KY16 8PN
e-mail: admin@spinkstown.com
dir: 2m E on A917 to Crail, 3rd farmhouse on right

This immaculately maintained modern farmhouse is surrounded by gently rolling countryside. Bedrooms are stylish, spacious and well-equipped. The comfortable lounge, complete with baby grand piano, overlooks the well-tended rear garden. Breakfast is served around a communal table in the dining room.

Rooms 3 en suite S £35-£40; D £62-£65* **Facilities** TVL tea/coffee Cen ht **Parking** 3 **Notes** ⊗ 250 acres arable/cattle/sheep

Lorimer House

★★★★ 🅰 GUEST HOUSE

☎ 01334 476599 📠 01334 476599
19 Murray Park KY16 9AW
e-mail: info@lorimerhouse.com
dir: A91 to St Andrews, left onto Golf Place, right onto The Scores, right onto Murray Park

Rooms 5 en suite (1 GF) S £40-£90; D £60-£120* **Facilities** STV FTV TVL tea/coffee Cen ht Wi-fi **Notes** ⊗ No Children 12yrs

Millhouse B&B

★★★★ 🅰 BED AND BREAKFAST

☎ 01334 850557
2 Cauldside Farm Steading, Strathkinness High Rd KY16 9TY
e-mail: stay@bandbinstandrews.co.uk
web: www.bandbinstandrews.co.uk
dir: B939 W of St Andrews, right onto Strathkinness High Rd. After 1m, right onto farm track

Rooms 2 en suite S £40-£50; D £60-£75* **Facilities** FTV TVL tea/coffee Cen ht Wi-fi **Parking** 3 **Notes** ⊗ No Children 12yrs

The Seafood Restaurant

◉◉◉

Modern Seafood 🍷
Superb seafood in a stunning glass building above the waves

☎ 01334 479475 📠 01334 479476
The Scores KY16 9AS
e-mail: reservations@theseafoodrestaurant.com
dir: Please telephone for directions

The glass cube perched on the sea wall above the waves certainly makes a style statement in the tweedy golfing Mecca of St Andrews. It is an elemental setting for a restaurant dealing in the ocean's bounty: look out of the floor-to-ceiling windows - that is where your food is coming from. In fact, the connection with the sea is so direct that the staff could dangle a line outside and haul fish straight from waves to pan. Inside, too, is a modishly minimalist and sleek tableau of glinting glass, metal and wood. The kitchen team have nowhere to hide in the gleaming steel theatre of their open-plan kitchen; perhaps this is why they go about their business with quiet, effortless professionalism. No tantrums or drama here, just unbeatably fresh fish and shellfish treated simply and married thoughtfully with clear, modern flavours, as in a starter of sesame seed and cumin-crusted cod served with butternut squash and pancetta velouté and sage oil. Next up, pan-seared halibut is given robust treatment with Parmentier potatoes, shiitake mushrooms, oxtail, garlic purée and red wine reduction. All that light and healthy seafood means there's no need to skip dessert: try a warm chocolate fondant with toasted marshmallow and pistachio ice cream.

Chef Craig Millar, Scott Swift **Owner** Craig Millar, Tim Butler **Times** 12-2.30/6.30-10 Closed 25-26 Dec, Jan 1, **Prices** Food prices not confirmed for 2010. Please telephone for details. **Wines** 180 bottles over £20, 5 bottles under £20, 8 by glass **Notes** Sunday L, Vegetarian available, Air con **Seats** 60 **Children** Portions **Parking** 50mtrs away

---

ST MONANS   Map 3 NO50

The Seafood Restaurant

◉◉ Modern Scottish, Seafood 🍷

Impeccably fresh seafood by the harbour

☎ 01333 730327 📠 01333 730508
16 West End KY10 2BX
e-mail: info@theseafoodrestaurant.com
dir: Take A959 from St Andrews to Anstruther, then W on A917 through Pittenweem. In St Monans to harbour then right

There is nothing that accompanies great seafood better than a great view, and this smart restaurant offers both in spades. The elder sibling of the restaurant of the same name at St Andrews (see entry) looks across the Firth of Forth towards Edinburgh from a sophisticated setting featuring light beech wood and Rennie Mackintosh-style chairs - originally an old fisherman's cottage with an 800-year-old freshwater well with mystical healing powers. What else could you ask for? Ah yes, slithery fresh fish and seafood, prepared with simplicity and a light touch. A half-dozen Kilbrandon oysters might precede sea-fresh collops of monkfish with crispy smoked haddock and leek risotto cake and cauliflower and truffle purée. Rich, grown-up puddings, such as bitter dark chocolate tart with fennel ice cream, round things off. Unrelenting carnivores are appeased by a token meat dish.

Chef Craig Millar, Roy Brown **Owner** Craig Millar, Tim Butler **Times** 12-2.30/6-9.30 Closed 25-26 Dec, 1-2 Jan, Mon-Tue (Sep-Jun) **Prices** Fixed L 2 course fr £20, Fixed D 3 course fr £37, Service optional **Wines** 40 bottles over £20, 18 bottles under £20, 6 by glass **Notes** Oct-1 Apr fixed D menu 3 course £19.95 Wed-Fri, Sunday L, Vegetarian available **Seats** 44 **Children** Portions **Parking** 10

Charing Cross, Glasgow

IN HONOUR OF
SIR CHARLES CAMERON, BART. D.L.L.L.D.
IN RECOGNITION OF
HIS MANY SERVICES TO THIS CITY

GLASGOW   Map 2 NS56

See also **Clydebank (West Dunbartonshire) & Uplawmoor (East Renfrewshire)**

Hotel du Vin at One Devonshire Gardens

★★★★ TOWN HOUSE HOTEL

◉◉◉ Modern European

Fine dining in sophisticated townhouse hotel

☎ 0141 339 2001 🖷 0141 337 1663
1 Devonshire Gardens G12 0UX
e-mail: reservations.odg@hotelduvin.com
web: www.hotelduvin.com
dir: M8 junct 17, follow signs for A82, 1.5m turn left into Hyndland Rd, 1st right, right at mini rdbt, right at end

Arguably the jewel in the Hotel du Vin crown, One Devonshire Gardens has been a destination hotel in the heart of Glasgow's West End for many a year. The fashionable hotel chain has remodelled the building, situated on a tree-lined Victorian terrace, into its own image, which is entirely in-keeping. The boutique styling makes the best of the grand original features of the building, while adding all the expected modern comforts. Stunning, individually designed bedrooms and suites have the trademark Egyptian linen and seriously good showers. Naturally, wine is an important part of the equation here, and knowledgeable staff can guide guests around the impressive wine list. Sink into a deep sofa in the bar-lounge to sip an aperitif, or head straight into one of the quartet of oak-panelled rooms that make up the bistro. The crisp linen tablecloths give a clue to the fact that this HdV leans more towards fine dining than its siblings. The kitchen's output of modern and classic dishes supports the group's philosophy - quality food cooked simply with the freshest local ingredients. But again, here they've cranked up the ante with all the extra trappings such as amuse-bouche and petits fours and some ambitious cooking supporting the classics. Dishes are constructed to deliver visual impact, as with a foie gras and guinea fowl terrine served with pain d'épice and an avante-garde sweetcorn pannacotta and sweet-and-sour reduction. Main-course butter-roasted monkfish tail with ratte potatoes and curried mussel jus might precede a perfectly risen soufflé (coffee coulant with Tokaji lollipop and crème vierge).

Rooms 49 (7 GF) **Facilities** Gym Tennis & Squash facilities at nearby club Xmas New Year Wi-fi **Conf** Class 30 Board 30 Thtr 50 **Notes** Civ Wed 70

Chef Paul Tamburrini **Owner** MWB/Hotel Du Vin **Restaurant Times** 12-2.30/6-10.30 Closed L Sat **Prices** Fixed L 2 course fr £14.50, Starter £6.50-£12, Main £14-£32, Dessert £6.75-£15, Service added but optional 10% **Wines** 600 bottles over £20, 12 bottles under £20, 12 by glass **Notes** Tasting menu 6 course, Sunday L, Vegetarian available **Seats** 78, Pr/dining room 70 **Children** Portions, Menu

Glasgow Marriott Hotel

★★★★ 78% HOTEL

☎ 0141 226 5577 🖷 0141 221 9202
500 Argyle St, Anderston G3 8RR
e-mail: london.regional.reservations@marriott.com
web: www.glasgowmarriott.co.uk
dir: M8 junct 19, turn left at lights, then left into hotel

Conveniently located for all major transport links and the city centre, this hotel benefits from extensive conference and banqueting facilities and a spacious car park. Public areas include an open-plan lounge/bar and a Mediterranean style restaurant. High quality, well-equipped bedrooms benefit from air-conditioning and generously sized beds; the suites are particularly comfortable.

Rooms 300 (89 fmly) **Facilities** ⊗ Gym Beautician Poolside steam room Sauna New Year Wi-fi **Conf** Class 300 Board 50 Thtr 800 **Services** Lift Air con **Parking** 180 **Notes** ⊗ Civ Wed 700

City Inn Glasgow

★★★★ 77% HOTEL

◉ Modern European ◖

Modern cuisine beside the Clyde

☎ 0141 227 1010 & 240 1002 🖷 0141 248 2754
Finnieston Quay G3 0HN
e-mail: glasgow.citycafe@cityinn.com
web: www.citycafe.co.uk
dir: M8 junct 19 follow signs for SECC. Hotel on left 200yds before entrance to SECC

A contemporary hotel sitting alongside the River Clyde and the 'Squinty Bridge', and ideally located for the SECC & Science Centre. Modern, well-equipped bedrooms and bathrooms have many thoughtful extras for guests. The restaurant has wonderful panoramic views of the Clyde and surrounding area. Its relaxed and informal bistro style works well, with vibrant artwork on the walls and a cosy mixture of chairs and bench-style seating. You can also eat alfresco on the riverside terrace in good weather. The well-balanced menu uses quality ingredients to good effect, producing modern cuisine that ranges from informal comfort foods to fine dining dishes, including smooth chicken liver parfait with red onion marmalade and toasted brioche, followed by Shetland cod fillet and fine French beans with hollandaise sauce.

Rooms 164 **S** £89-£195; **D** £89-£195* **Facilities** STV FTV Gym Xmas New Year Wi-fi **Conf** Class 20 Board 24 Thtr 45 Del from £125 to £270* **Services** Lift Air con **Parking** 120 **Notes** ⊗ Civ Wed 50

Chef Scott MacDonald, Charles Hilton **Owner** City Inn Limited **Restaurant Times** 12-2.30/6.30-10.30 **Prices** Fixed L 2 course £9.95, Fixed D 3 course £16.50, Starter £4.95-£6.95, Main £9.95-£19.95, Dessert £5.50-£5.95, Service optional **Wines** 36 bottles over £20, 12 bottles under £20, 29 by glass **Notes** Sunday L, Vegetarian available, Dress restrictions, Smart casual, Air con **Seats** 80, Pr/dining room 22 **Children** Portions, Menu

Abode Hotel Glasgow

★★★★ 75% HOTEL

◉◉ Modern European

High-impact cooking in former prime minister's home

☎ 0141 221 6789 & 572 6000 📠 0141 221 6777
129 Bath St G2 2SZ
e-mail: reservationsglasgow@abodehotels.co.uk
web: www.abodehotels.co.uk
dir: From S, M8 junct 19 onto Bothwell St, turn left at Hope St, left onto Bath St. Hotel 0.3m on left

In the heart of the city, this concept hotel offers rooms in a choice of sizes; all are contemporary and well appointed, including internet access and CD players. Formerly the Department of Education offices, and once the home of the Edwardian prime minister Sir Henry Campbell-Bannerman, the hotel has been transformed, yet keeps most of the grander features. The public areas include a stylish café bar, while the ABode group's expansion has done Michael Caines proud, proving that a proliferating hotel chain under a star chef's imprimatur needn't become a recipe for dull standardisation. Understated décor in the main, wood-floored dining room includes a glass-fronted wine store. There is nothing understated about the cooking, which aims for big flavour and achieves it in dishes such as crab cannelloni with langoustine mayonnaise, poached wild sea bass with scallop and truffle mousse, and Mey beef sirloin with prune purée and wild mushrooms in Madeira.

Rooms 60 (11 fmly) (5 GF) **D** £130-£245* **Facilities** STV ♬ Xmas New Year **Conf** Class 40 Board 35 Thtr 70 **Services** Lift Air con **Notes** LB ⊗ Civ Wed 100

Chef Craig Dunn **Owner** ABode Hotels **Restaurant**
Times 12-2.30/6-10 Closed 1st 2 wks Jan, 14-28 Jul, Sun-Mon
Prices Fixed L course £12.95, Fixed D 3 course £19.95, Tasting menu £55, Starter £10.50-£12.95, Main £19.50-£23.95, Dessert £7.50, Service added but optional 11% **Wines** 100 bottles over £20, 8 by glass **Notes** Tasting menu 7 course, Vegetarian available, Air con **Seats** 40, Pr/dining room 40 **Children** Portions

Thistle Glasgow

★★★★ 75% HOTEL

☎ 0871 376 9043 📠 0871 376 9143
36 Cambridge St G2 3HN
e-mail: glasgow@thistle.co.uk
web: www.thistle.com/glasgow
dir: In city centre, just off Sauchiehall St

Ideally located within the centre of Glasgow and with ample parking, this hotel is well presented with the lobby area that gives a great impression on arrival. It also benefits from having a well-presented leisure club along with the largest ballroom in Glasgow. Service is friendly and attentive.

Rooms 300 (38 fmly) (1 smoking) **S** £70-£200; **D** £70-£200*
Facilities STV ♨ Gym Sauna Steam room New Year Wi-fi
Conf Class 800 Board 15 Thtr 1000 Del from £125 to £170*
Services Lift Air con **Parking** 216 **Notes** LB Civ Wed 720

Menzies Glasgow

★★★★ 72% HOTEL

☎ 0141 222 2929 & 270 2323 📠 0141 270 2301
27 Washington St G3 8AZ
e-mail: glasgow@menzieshotels.co.uk
web: www.menzieshotels.co.uk
dir: M8 junct 19 for SECC, follow signs for Broomielaw. Left at lights

Centrally located, this modern hotel is a short drive from the airport and an even shorter walk from the centre of the city. Bedrooms are generally spacious and boast a range of facilities, including high-speed internet access. Facilities include a brasserie restaurant and an impressive indoor leisure facility.

Rooms 141 (16 fmly) (15 smoking) **S** £65-£170; **D** £65-£170*
Facilities STV ♨ supervised Gym Sauna Steam room Hair & beauty salon Xmas New Year Wi-fi **Conf** Class 60 Board 70 Thtr 160 Del from £130 to £165* **Services** Lift Air con **Parking** 50 **Notes** Civ Wed 150

Millennium Hotel Glasgow

★★★★ 72% HOTEL

☎ 0141 332 6711 📠 0141 332 4264
George Square G2 1DS
e-mail: glasgow.reservations@millenniumhotels.co.uk
web: www.millenniumhotels.co.uk
dir: From M8 junct 15 through 4 sets of lights, at 5th turn left into Hanover St. George Sq directly ahead, hotel on right

Right in the heart of the city, this hotel has pride of place overlooking George Square. Inside, the property has a contemporary air, with a spacious reception concourse and a glass veranda overlooking the square. There is a stylish brasserie and separate lounge bar, and bedrooms come in a variety of sizes.

Rooms 116 (17 fmly) **S** £70-£199; **D** £70-£199* **Facilities** STV Soul therapies Health & beauty New Year Wi-fi **Conf** Class 24 Board 32 Thtr 40 Del from £125 to £175* **Services** Lift **Notes** LB ⊗ Closed 24-26 Dec Civ Wed 120

Crowne Plaza Glasgow

★★★★ ⓐ HOTEL

☎ 0870 443 1691 📠 0141 221 2022
Congress Rd G3 8QT
e-mail: cpglasgow@qmh-hotels.com
web: www.crowneplaza.co.uk
dir: M8 junct 19, follow signs for SECC, hotel adjacent to centre

Rooms 283 (15 fmly) **Facilities** Spa STV ♨ supervised Gym Beauty salon Xmas New Year Wi-fi **Conf** Class 482 Board 68 Thtr 800 **Services** Lift Air con **Parking** 300 **Notes** ⊗ Civ Wed 120

Malmaison Glasgow

★★★ 83% HOTEL

🏵 Modern French, Scottish

Fine-dining brasserie using locally-sourced produce

☎ 0141 572 1000 📠 0141 572 1002
278 West George St G2 4LL
e-mail: glasgow@malmaison.com
web: www.malmaison.com
dir: From S & E - M8 junct 18 (Charing Cross), from W & N - M8 city centre

Far removed from its origins as a 19th-century Greek Orthodox church, this member of the boutique hotel chain is full of atmosphere and opulent décor. Smart and contemporary, it offers impressive levels of service and hospitality. Bedrooms are spacious and feature a host of modern facilities, such as CD players and mini bars. The stylish restaurant is housed in the vaulted crypt and furnished with smart leather banquettes and chairs and subtle lighting that makes for an intimate setting. First-class regional produce is used to create the traditional Scottish and French dishes on the seasonally-changing à la carte menu and the daily-changing 'home-grown and local' menu. Typical dishes include steamed Fassfern mussels with garlic and black pepper bacon, or slow-roasted shin of beef with winter vegetable cassoulet and horseradish dumplings, and smoked Finnan haddock gratin with boulangère potatoes and mustard sauce.

Rooms 72 (4 fmly) (19 GF) **Facilities** STV Gym Cardiovascular equipment New Year Wi-fi **Conf** Board 22 Thtr 30 **Services** Lift **Notes** Civ Wed 80

Chef Graham Digweed **Owner** Malmaison Hotels Ltd **Restaurant Times** 12-2.30/5.30-10.30 **Prices** Fixed L 2 course £13.50, Fixed D 3 course £15.50, Starter £4.50-£5.75, Main £9.95-£18.50, Dessert £4.95-£8.50, Service added but optional 10%, Groups min 10 service 10% **Wines** 160 bottles over £20, 20 bottles under £20, 20 by glass **Notes** Sunday L, Vegetarian available **Seats** 85, Pr/dining room 22 **Children** Portions, Menu

Holiday Inn

★★★ 81% HOTEL

🏵 French, Mediterranean

Classic French cuisine in a modern hotel

☎ 0141 352 8300 📠 0141 332 7447
161 West Nile St G1 2RL
e-mail: reservations@higlasgow.com
web: www.holidayinn.co.uk
dir: M8 junct 16, follow signs for Royal Concert Hall, hotel opposite

In the heart of the city's fashionable theatreland district and handy for the shops, on a corner site close to the Theatre Royal Concert Hall, this contemporary hotel features well equipped and comfortable bedrooms; suites are available. Staff are friendly and attentive. The popular and relaxed French brasserie-style restaurant offers a crowd-pleasing repertoire that necessarily plays to the crowds, with a wide range of accomplished, honest, French- and Mediterranean-inspired dishes. Menus take in a fixed-price pre-theatre option, while lunch might deliver simple classics like French onion soup, chargrilled rib-eye with green peppercorn sauce and French fries, or specialities like croquet-monsieur, while dinner cranks up the ante with slow-cooked belly and pan-roasted pork loin served with parsnip purée and pork jus.

Rooms 113 (20 fmly) (28 smoking) **Facilities** STV FTV Wi-fi **Conf** Class 60 Board 60 Thtr 100 **Services** Lift Air con **Notes** LB 🏵

Chef Gerry Sharkey **Owner** Chardon Leisure Ltd **Restaurant Times** 12-2.15/5-10 **Prices** Food prices not confirmed for 2010. Please telephone for details. **Wines** 26 bottles over £20, 23 bottles under £20, 8 by glass **Notes** Air con **Seats** 90, Pr/dining room 100 **Children** Portions, Menu

Novotel Glasgow Centre

★★★ 78% HOTEL

☎ 0141 222 2775 📠 0141 204 5438
181 Pitt St G2 4DT
e-mail: H3136@accor.com
web: www.novotel.com
dir: M8 junct 18 for Charing Cross. Follow to Sauchiehall St. Take 3rd street on right

Enjoying a convenient city centre location and with limited parking spaces, this hotel is ideal for both business and leisure travellers. Well-equipped bedrooms are brightly decorated and offer functional design. Modern public areas include a small fitness club and a brasserie serving a range of meals all day.

Rooms 139 (139 fmly) (12 smoking) **Facilities** Gym Pool table Playstation Sauna Steam room Xmas Wi-fi **Conf** Class 20 Board 20 Thtr 40 Del from £100 to £140* **Services** Lift Air con **Parking** 19 **Notes** LB

Best Western Glasgow City Hotel

★★★ 74% TOWN HOUSE HOTEL

☎ 0141 227 2772 & 419 1915 📠 0141 227 2774
27 Elmbank St G2 4PB
e-mail: glasgowcity@mckeverhotels.co.uk
dir: Adjacent to Kings Theatre

A new hotel in the heart of the city offers spacious and well-equipped accommodation suitable for both families and business guests. Staff are friendly and helpful, and are mindful of the needs of the modern traveller. There is a secure pay car park close to the hotel.

Rooms 53 (4 fmly) (12 GF) **S** £49-£89; **D** £59-£109* **Facilities** FTV Xmas Wi-fi **Notes** LB 🏵

continued

The Argyll Hotel

★★★ 70% HOTEL

973 Sauchiehall Street G3 7TQ

☎ 0141 337 3313 📄 0141 337 3283
e-mail: info@argyllhotelglasgow.co.uk
web: www.argyllhotelglasgow.co.uk
dir: M8 junct 18, stay in right lane & straight ahead to 2nd set of
lights. Right into Berkley St, right into Elderslie St & 1st left to
Sauchiehall St

Enjoying a prime city centre location this popular run hotel is within
easy reach of the main shopping district, the University and the
Scottish Exhibition & Conference Centre. The recently refurbished
bedrooms are all attractively presented with a good range of facilities
including flat screen TVs and free Wi-Fi. The public areas include
Sutherlands Restaurant and a cosy basement bar.

Rooms 38 en suite (8 fmly) (5 GF) S£50-£70 D £60-£90 (incl. bkfst)
Facilities FTV Wi-fi **Conf** 20 Class 16 Board Thtr 25 **Parking** 5

Campanile Glasgow

BUDGET HOTEL

☎ 0141 287 7700 📄 0141 287 7701
10 Tunnel St G3 8HL
e-mail: glasgow@campanile.com
dir: M8 junct 19, follow signs to SECC. Hotel next to SECC

This modern building offers accommodation in smart, well-equipped
bedrooms, all with en suite bathrooms. Refreshments may be taken
at the informal bistro. See also the Hotel Groups pages on theAA.com.

Rooms 106 (2 fmly) (21 GF) **Conf** Class 60 Board 90 Thtr 150
Del from £95 to £125

Express by Holiday Inn Glasgow City Centre

BUDGET HOTEL

☎ 0141 331 6800 📄 0141 331 6828
165 West Nile St G1 2RL
e-mail: express@higlasgow.com
web: www.hiexpress.com/glasgowctyct
dir: Follow signs to Royal Concert Hall

A modern hotel ideal for families and business travellers. Fresh and
uncomplicated, the spacious rooms include Sky TV, power shower
and tea and coffee-making facilities. Continental buffet breakfast is
included in the room rate; other meals may be taken at the nearby
family pub or restaurant. See also the Hotel Groups pages
on theAA.com.

Rooms 118 (34 fmly) **Conf** Board 12 Thtr 20

Express by Holiday Inn Glasgow City Riverside

BUDGET HOTEL

☎ 0141 548 5000 📄 0141 548 5048
122 Stockwell St G1 4LT
e-mail: glasgow@expressholidayinn.co.uk
web: www.hiexpress.com/glascowcityct
dir: M8 E & S junct 19 SECC, left at end of exit, follow river under
Central Station bridge to Stockwell St

Rooms 128 (79 fmly) (13 smoking) **S** £59-£149; **D** £59-£149 (incl.
bkfst)* **Conf** Class 16 Board 16 Thtr 30

Ibis Glasgow

BUDGET HOTEL

☎ 0141 225 6000 📄 0141 225 6010
220 West Regent St G2 4DQ
e-mail: H3139@accor-hotels.com
web: www.ibishotel.com

Modern, budget hotel offering comfortable accommodation in bright
and practical bedrooms. Breakfast is self-service and meals are also
available in the café-bar 24 hours. See also the Hotel Groups pages
on theAA.com.

Rooms 141

Innkeeper's Lodge Glasgow/Cumbernauld

BUDGET HOTEL

☎ 0845 112 6003 📄 0845 112 6297
1 Auchenkilns Park, Cumbernauld G68 9AT
web: www.innkeeperslodge.com/glasgowcumbernauld
dir: M80 junct 3 or M73 (N'bound), or M80 junct 4 (S'bound), take
A80 towards Cumbernauld. At Auchenkilns rdbt take B8048 signed
Kirkintilloch

Innkeeper's Lodge represents an exciting, high value concept within
the budget hotel market. Comfortable bedrooms provide excellent
facilities that include satellite TV and modem points. Options include
family rooms; and for the corporate guest, cutting edge IT includes
Wi-fi access. Food is served all day in the adjacent Country Pub. The
extensive continental breakfast is complimentary. See also the Hotel
Groups pages on theAA.com.

Rooms 57 **Conf** Thtr 28

Travelodge Glasgow Central

BUDGET HOTEL

☎ 0871 984 6141 📄 0141 333 1221
9 Hill St G3 6PR
web: www.travelodge.co.uk
dir: M8 junct 17, at lights left into West Graham St. Right into
Cowcaddens Rd. Right into Cambridge St. Right into Hill St

Travelodge offers good quality, good value, modern accommodation.
Ideal for families, the spacious en suite bedrooms include remote-
control TV, tea and coffee-making facilities and comfortable beds.

Meals can be taken at the nearby family restaurant. See also the Hotel Groups pages on theAA.com.

Rooms 95 **S** fr £29; **D** fr £29

Travelodge Glasgow Paisley Road

BUDGET HOTEL

☎ 0871 984 6142 ⬚ 0141 420 3884
251 Paisley Rd G5 8RA
web: www.travelodge.co.uk
dir: M8 westbound junct 20 , through lights, pass Saab garage. Left onto Morrison St leads onto Paisley Rd. Left directly after Harry Ramsden's

Rooms 75 **S** fr £29; **D** fr £29

The Kelvingrove

★★★★ GUEST ACCOMMODATION

☎ 0141 339 5011 ⬚ 0141 339 6566
944 Sauchiehall St G3 7TH
e-mail: info@kelvingrovehotel.com
web: www.kelvingrove-hotel.co.uk
dir: M8 junct 18 signed Charing Cross. Into right lane, through 1st lights, right at 2nd lights. Into left lane, through next lights. At bottom follow to right, at junct left into Sauchiehall St. Establishment 600yds on right

This friendly, well maintained establishment is in a terrace just west of the city centre, and is easily spotted in summer with its colourful floral displays. Bedrooms, including several rooms suitable for families, are well equipped and have smart, fully tiled en suite bathrooms. There is a bright breakfast room, and the reception lounge is open 24 hours.

Rooms 22 en suite (5 fmly) (3 GF) **Facilities** tea/coffee Direct Dial Cen ht

Argyll Guest House

★★★ GUEST ACCOMMODATION

☎ 01435 75155
960 Sauchiehall St G3 7TH
e-mail: info@argyllguesthouseglasgow.co.uk
web: www.argyllguesthouseglasgow.co.uk

A very popular guesthouse that is close to the city centre, the Scottish Conference and Exhibition centre and the University. The bedrooms have all been refurbished and each room is attractively presented, well equipped and include features like free Wi-Fi. A full hot & cold buffet breakfast is served at the adjacent Argyll Hotel.

Rooms 20 en suite (5 fmly) (5 GF) **Facilities** FTV tea/coffee Direct Dial Cen ht **Notes** ⊗

Clifton Guest House

★★★ GUEST HOUSE

☎ 0141 334 8080 ⬚ 0141 337 3468
26-27 Buckingham Ter, Great Western Rd G12 8ED
e-mail: kalam@cliftonhotelglasgow.co.uk
web: www.cliftonhotelglasgow.com
dir: 1.25m NW of city centre off A82 (Inverquhomery Rd

Located north-west of the city centre, the Clifton forms part of an elegant terrace and is ideal for business and leisure. The attractive bedrooms are spacious, and there is an elegant lounge. Hearty breakfasts are served at individual tables in the dining room.

Rooms 23 rms (17 en suite) (6 fmly) (3 GF) **Facilities** STV TVL tea/coffee Direct Dial Cen ht **Parking** 8 **Notes** ⊗

Georgian House

★★★ GUEST HOUSE

☎ 0141 339 0008 & 07973 971563
29 Buckingham Ter, Great Western Rd, Kelvinside G12 8ED
e-mail: thegeorgianhouse@yahoo.com
web: www.thegeorgianhousehotel.com
dir: M8 junct 17 towards Dumbarton, through 4 sets of lights & right onto Queen Margaret Dr, then right onto Buckingham Ter

The friendly guest house offers good value accommodation at the west end of the city in a peaceful tree-lined Victorian terrace near the Botanic Gardens. Bedrooms vary in size and are furnished in modern style. Only a continental style breakfast is served which is in the first-floor lounge dining room.

Rooms 11 rms (10 en suite) (1 pri facs) (4 fmly) (3 GF) **S** £30-£45; **D** £50-£90* **Facilities** FTV TVL tea/coffee Ccn ht Wi-fi **Parking** 7 **Notes** LB

The Kelvin

★★★ GUEST HOUSE

☎ 0141 339 7143 ⬚ 0141 339 5215
15 Buckingham Ter, Great Western Rd, Hillhead G12 8EB
e-mail: enquiries@kelvinhotel.com
web: www.kelvinhotel.com
dir: M8 junct 17, A82 Kelvinside/Dumbarton, 1m on right before Botanic Gardens

Two substantial Victorian terrace houses on the west side of the city have been combined to create this friendly establishment close to the Botanical Gardens. The attractive bedrooms are comfortably proportioned and well equipped. The dining room on the first floor is the setting for hearty traditional breakfasts served at individual tables.

Rooms 21 rms (9 en suite) (4 fmly) (2 GF) (14 smoking) **S** £30-£33; **D** £60-£66 **Facilities** FTV tea/coffee Cen ht Wi-fi **Parking** 5

Lomond

★★★ GUEST ACCOMMODATION

☎ 0141 339 2339 📄 0141 339 0477
6 Buckingham Ter, Great Western Rd, Hillhead G12 8EB
e-mail: info@lomondhotel.co.uk
web: www.lomondhotel.co.uk
dir: M8 junct 17, A82 Dumbarton, 1m on right before Botanic Gardens

Situated in the west end of the city in a tree-lined Victorian terrace, the Lomond offers well maintained, good value accommodation in a friendly environment. Bedrooms are brightly appointed and suitably equipped for leisure guests. Hearty breakfasts are served at individual tables in the bright ground-floor dining room.

Rooms 17 rms (6 en suite) (5 fmly) (3 GF) S £20–£45; D £40–£60 **Facilities** tea/coffee Direct Dial Cen ht **Notes** LB

Craigielea House B&B

★★ 🅰 BED AND BREAKFAST

☎ 0141 554 3446
35 Westercraigs G31 2HY
e-mail: craigieleahouse@yahoo.co.uk
dir: 1m E of city centre. M8 junct 15, onto A8, left onto Duke St, pass Tennents Brewery & left into road after lights into Craigpark. 3rd on left, then right into Westercraigs

Rooms 3 rms (1 GF); D £44–£46* **Facilities** tea/coffee Cen ht Wi-fi **Parking** 3 **Notes** ⊗ No Children 3yrs ✆

An Lochan

⊛ Scottish Seafood ✆

Simple café style in a trendy residential area, serving Scottish produce

☎ 0141 338 6606 📄 01700 811300
340 Crow Rd, Broomhill G11 7HT
e-mail: glasgow@anlochan.co.uk
dir: Please telephone for directions

Named after one of its restaurants that is situated by a loch, the Glasgow outpost of this select group is housed in a former bank. Step through the original door to find a lively restaurant with a cheery bistro-style décor, with blue walls adorned with local art, white leather chairs and white tablecloths. The restaurant serves modern Scottish food, simply cooked to make the most of fresh local produce. Light snacks, a blackboard tapas menu and pre-theatre dinners feature alongside the evening carte. Majoring on seafood, a sample evening menu might include smoked haddock chowder, followed by fish stew with crusty bread, or sea bass with lemon dressing, with winter berry soufflé or a plate of Scottish cheeses to finish.

Chef Claire McKie, Andrew Moss **Owner** The McKie Family
Times 12-3/6-11.30 Closed 24-26 Dec, 1-3 Jan, Mon, D Sun
Prices Fixed L 2 course £8.95–£30, Fixed D 3 course £15.95–£55.95, Starter £4.95–£8.95, Main £10.95–£26.95, Dessert £4.95–£8.95,

Service added but optional, Groups min 6 service 10% **Wines** 17 bottles over £20, 8 bottles under £20, 5 by glass **Notes** Early evening menu available Fri-Sat 5.30-7 pm, Sunday L, Vegetarian available, Air con **Seats** 40 **Children** Portions **Parking** On street

Brian Maule at Chardon d'Or

⊛ French V 📄NOTABLE WINE LIST

Confident cooking in a classy city-centre venue

☎ 0141 248 3801 📄 0141 248 3901
176 West Regent St G2 4RL
e-mail: info@brianmaule.com
dir: 10 minute walk from Glasgow central station

A Victorian townhouse in the heart of the city provides the setting for this elegant restaurant. Inside it is every inch the contemporary dining space - smart but understated, with suede and leather banquette seating, high-backed chairs and white-clothed tables set against wooden floors, cream walls and glass panels. There is a bar upstairs and an extended area downstairs with three private dining rooms. The cooking is classical French with Scottish produce to the fore: lamb (pan-fried fillet with creamed potatoes) is full of flavour, and scallops with chorizo and aubergine caviar is a well-judged starter.

Chef Brian Maule **Owner** Brian Maule at Chardon d'Or
Times 12-2/6-10 Closed 25-26 Dec, 1-2 Jan, 2 wks Jan, 2 wks Aug, BHs, Sun, L Sat **Prices** Fixed L 2 course £16.50, Fixed D 3 course £19.50, Tasting menu £55, Starter £7.20-£12, Main £21-£26.50, Dessert £8.20-£11.75, Service optional, Groups min 8 service 10% **Wines** 280 bottles over £20, 6 by glass **Notes** Tasting menu 6 course, Pre-theatre 6-6.45pm, Vegetarian menu, Dress restrictions, Smart casual, Air con **Seats** 90, Pr/dining room 60 **Children** Portions **Parking** Metered parking on street

Gamba

⊛⊛ Scottish, Seafood ✆

Well-regarded seafood restaurant in the West End

☎ 0141 572 0899 📄 0141 572 0896
225a West George St G2 2ND
e-mail: info@gamba.co.uk
dir: Please telephone for directions

A basement restaurant in the heart of the fashionable West End of Glasgow, Gamba has been serving consistently good food for over 10 years, earning it a well deserved reputation in the city as the place to go for all things fishy. Decidedly Mediterranean in feel, the décor of warm terracotta colours along with some booth seating helps create an appealing, intimate setting. Gamba is the Spanish for king prawn and paintings of seafood with their Latin names points up the food to come. There are both Mediterranean and Asian influences in dishes such as the favourite Gamba soup (still delicious), and the use of top quality ingredients, served in generous portions, means the standards remain high in the likes of mussel and onion stew with sundried tomato, basil and aged balsamic or roast monkfish with stewed red cabbage, redcurrant and rosemary.

Chef Derek Marshall **Owner** Mr A C Tomkins & Mr D Marshall
Times 12-2.30/5-10.30 Closed 25-26 Dec, 1-2 Jan, BHs, L Sun
Prices Fixed L 2 course fr £15.95, Starter £8-£12, Main £12-£30,

Dessert £6-£9, Service optional, Groups min 6 service 10% **Wines** 60 bottles over £20, 8 bottles under £20, 8 by glass **Notes** Pre-theatre £15 inc wine 5-6pm, Vegetarian available, Air con **Seats** 66 **Parking** On street

Killermont Polo Club

◉ Traditional Indian

Creative Indian cooking in a setting fit for a maharaja

☎ 0141 946 5412 📠 0141 946 0812
2002 Maryhill Rd, Maryhill Park G20 0AB
dir: Please telephone for directions or visit website

No, this is not some snooty country house hotel with starched waiters, nor is it your everyday Indian curry house either. The subcontinent's age-old fascination with polo provides the inspiration for the interior, while Dum Pukht is the culinary speciality - an esoteric cuisine that tickled the tastebuds of Indian Moghul emperors. Subtle spices are blended with others brought from the Silk Road city of Samarkand in Uzbekistan to create a new style of slow-cooked dishes. The kitchen delivers a compendious list of dishes, taking in old favourites from the tandoor oven to Dum Pukht offerings such as murgh Wajid Ali - chicken breast stuffed with fresh pomegranate, mint, cheese and onions and braised in orange and saffron juices.

Times 12-2.30/5-11.30

La Parmigiana

◉◉ Italian, Mediterranean

A taste of classical Italy in cosmopolitan Glasgow

☎ 0141 334 0686 📠 0141 357 5595
447 Great Western Rd G12 8HH
e-mail: sgiovanazzi@btclick.com
dir: Please telephone for directions

This family-run restaurant is located on the vibrant and busy Great Western Road, close to the river. It's an intimate space decked out with dark-wood panelling and deep red paint on the walls. The wonderfully friendly service is in keeping with the traditional style of the operation. The food is classical Italian, prepared with care and attention to detail. Cuttlefish pasta with shellfish, olive oil, parsley and chilli has generous amounts of seafood, while medallions of venison with porcini and Italian sausage, served on chargrilled polenta, is a hearty main course. The wine list is predominantly Italian with some interesting bottles from the less well known wine producing areas.

Chef Peppino Camilli **Owner** Sandro & Stefano Giovanazzi
Times 12-2.30/5.30-10.30 Closed 25-26 Dec, 1 Jan, Sun **Prices** Fixed D 3 course £14.40, Starter £4.20-£10.50, Main £15.30-£24, Dessert £4.95-£7.90, Service optional **Wines** 50 bottles over £20, 7 bottles under £20 **Notes** Pre-theatre 2 courses £15.70, 3 courses £17.80 5.30-7.30pm, Vegetarian available, Air con **Seats** 50
Children Portions

Rococo

◉◉ Modern European

Quality cooking in stylish city centre restaurant

☎ 0141 221 5004 📠 0141 221 5006
48 West Regent St G2 2RA
e-mail: res@rococoglasgow.co.uk
dir: City centre

Located in the heart of Glasgow's city centre, Rococo offers modern European food with a firm emphasis on top-notch seasonal, local produce. Terrine of oxtail, potato and watercress with langoustine tartare and horseradish emulsion might feature as a starter on the dinner menu, with perhaps spiced Barbary duck breast with honey-glazed shallots, salsify, minted peas and Madeira jus as a main course. Round things off with a dessert of chocolate parfait with passionfruit and sesame wafers. The more simple lunch and pre-theatre menu is excellent value for money.

Times 12-3/5-10.30 Closed 26 Dec, 1 Jan

Shish Mahal

◉ Modern Indian

Smart Indian restaurant with universal appeal

☎ 0141 339 8256 & 334 7899 📠 0141 572 0800
60-68 Park Rd G4 9JF
e-mail: reservations@shishmahal.co.uk
dir: From M8/A8 take exit towards Dumbarton. On Great Western Rd 1st left into Park Rd

Located in Kelvinbridge, a mainly residential quarter of Glasgow, Shish Mahal remains deservedly popular. Service is from a team in formal black and white, with long, brasserie-style aprons, and the inspired modern Indian food draws influences from many regions. Generously sized dishes include prawn zahrani, in a sweet-and-sour sauce with coconut, lime and fresh chillies, citrussy butter chicken finished with fresh apricot, and tender lamb cooked in fenugreek. Finish with phirnee, a Punjabi pudding of clotted cream, crushed rice and cinnamon, garnished with hazelnuts. Incidentals like naan breads and rice are all up to the mark.

Chef Mr I Humayun **Owner** Ali A Aslam, Nasim Ahmed
Times 12-2/5-11 Closed 25 Dec, L Sun **Prices** Fixed L 3 course £5.50-£7.25, Starter £2.95-£7.50, Main £6.50-£15.95, Dessert £2.50-£3.95, Service optional, Groups min 5 service 10% **Wines** 3 bottles over £20, 13 bottles under £20, 1 by glass **Notes** Fixed L 4 course, Vegetarian available, Air con **Seats** 95, Pr/dining room 14
Children Portions **Parking** Side street, Underground station car park

Stravaigin

◉◉ Modern International

The global larder comes to Glasgow

☎ 0141 334 2665 📄 0141 334 4099
28 Gibson St, Kelvinbridge G12 8NX
e-mail: stravaigin@btinternet.com
web: www.stravaigin.com
dir: Next to Glasgow University. 200yds from Kelvinbridge underground

'Not a tablecloth in sight,' proclaim the owners of this three-storey Glasgow tenement restaurant that combines an informal approach with chic décor. Eat in the bar or the restaurant - or even out on the street in clement weather - and note the same high standards apply throughout. World cuisine is the name of the game, with Far Eastern spices and seasonings especially notable. A fragrant sweet chilli and lemongrass sauce is the medium, therefore, for plump, fresh mussels and chunky bread. Continue the voyage of exploration with a main course of tamari-glazed duck breast with sesame-roast yams, kimchi (Korean preserved veg) and anise gravy, while Belgian chocolate délice with blueberry jelly will wow the chocoholics.

Chef Daniel Blencowe **Owner** Colin Clydesdale **Times** 12-3.30/5-11 Closed 25-26 Dec, 1 Jan, L Mon-Thu **Prices** Starter £5.95-£11.95, Main £12.95-£21.95, Dessert £5.95-£7.95, Service optional **Wines** 39 bottles over £20, 17 bottles under £20, 9 by glass **Notes** Sun brunch menus available, Vegetarian available, Air con **Seats** 76 **Children** Portions, Menu **Parking** On street, car park 100yds

the left bank

◉ Traditional International

Great value global food in vibrant urban setting

☎ 0141 339 5969
33-35 Gibson St, Hillhead G12 8NU
e-mail: contact@theleftbank.co.uk
dir: M8 junct 17, A82. After Kelvinbridge turn left onto Otago St, left onto Gibson St. Restaurant on right

This funky modern eatery in Glasgow's vibrant West End will sort you out with just about any meal for any time of day. Its eclectic menu ricochets around a global whirl of diverse flavours from satay skewers to Aberdeen Angus rib-eye steak, and from moules marinière to garlic masala fried fish on Goan seafood curry with Malabar garlic pickle and tomato rice - wherever the eye lands, South Asian influences are never far away. The vibe is casual, with split-level nooks and crannies to tuck yourself away from the madding crowd and admire the maverick style of local artists: the Timorous Beasties did the wallpaper and light fittings, and sculptor Chris Bannerman created the unique concrete bar.

Chef Liz McGougan **Owner** Catherine Hardy, Jacqueline Fennessy, George Swanson **Times** 9am-mdnt Closed 25 Dec, 1 Jan, **Prices** Fixed L 2 course £10.95, Fixed D 3 course £12.95, Starter £3.50-£5.95, Main £7.25-£24.95, Dessert £2.95-£4.75, Service optional, Groups min 6 service 10% **Wines** 5 bottles over £20, 17 bottles under £20, 15 by glass **Notes** Fixed D served until 7pm, Vegetarian available **Seats** 75 **Children** Portions

Ubiquitous Chip

◉◉ Traditional Scottish 🏆

Reliable Scottish cuisine in a unique setting

☎ 0141 334 5007 📄 0141 337 6417
12 Ashton Ln G12 8SJ
e-mail: mail@ubiquitouschip.co.uk
dir: In West End, off Byres Rd. Adjacent to Hillhead underground station

You might be forgiven for thinking you have taken a wrong turn and pitched up in the Glasgow Botanic Gardens on arriving at this constant of the West End dining scene. The Ubiquitous Chip has been going for nigh on forty years and the owner's drive to showcase the very finest Scottish produce remains undimmed. A glass canopy shelters a cobbled courtyard with a jungly tangle of greenery beneath a mezzanine gallery, plus there's a skylit dining room, brasserie and a trio of pubby venues. The kitchen takes a no-nonsense, fiercely Scottish line with its output and likes to throw in off-the-wall combinations - gingerbread and strawberries with sautéed duck livers - alongside Seil Island crab with salt and pepper tuiles, saffron and fennel with pastis sauce, or a game suet pudding with deep-fried cabbage and sweet potatoes.

Times 12-2.30/5.30-11 Closed 25 Dec, 1 Jan

Urban Bar and Brasserie

◉ Modern French

Contemporary bar-brasserie with food to match

☎ 0141 248 5636 📄 0141 248 5720
23/25 St Vincent Place G1 2DT
e-mail: info@urbanbrasserie.co.uk
dir: In city centre between George Sq & Buchanan St

As banks around the UK have slashed branches, many of their grandiose buildings have been recycled as characterful restaurants for lucky diners. Urban Bar and Brasserie was once a biggie: the erstwhile Scottish HQ of the Bank of England, no less, is now a stylish modern restaurant and champagne bar. Beneath soaring ceilings and a glass skylight, an imposing décor blends traditional plasterwork and wood panelling with burnished blond-wood floors, tobacco-brown banquettes and vibrant modern art on white walls. Not to be outshone by its surroundings, the kitchen team rises to the challenge with skilled cooking that delivers clearly-defined flavours from quality Scottish produce - fish soup with crabmeat, stem ginger and prawn dumplings for example, or fillet of sea bass on plum tomato, feta, prawns and basil.

Chef Derek Marshall & John Gillespie **Owner** Alan Tomkins, Derek Marshall **Times** 12-10/12-10 Closed 25-26 Dec, 1-2 Jan, **Prices** Fixed L 2 course £15.95, Fixed D 3 course £18.95, Starter £6-£10, Main £12-£22, Dessert £5.95-£7.50, Groups min 6 service 10% **Wines** 40 bottles over £20, 20 bottles under £20, 10 by glass **Notes** Pre-theatre menu 5-6pm £15, Sunday L, Vegetarian available, Air con **Seats** 110, Pr/dining room 20 **Children** Portions **Parking** NCP West Nile St

Rab Ha's

☎ 0141 572 0400 📄 0141 572 0402
83 Hutchieson St G1 1SH
e-mail: management@rabhas.com
dir: Telephone for directions

In the heart of Glasgow's revitalised Merchant City, Rab Ha's takes its name from Robert Hall, a local 19th-century character known as 'The Glasgow Glutton'. This hotel, restaurant and bar blend Victorian character with contemporary Scottish decor. Pre-theatre and set menus show extensive use of carefully sourced Scottish produce in starters like poached egg on grilled Stornoway black pudding, and pan-seared Oban scallops, followed by roast saddle of Rannoch Moor venison.

Open all day all wk noon-mdnt (Sun 12.30pm-mdnt) **Bar Meals** L served Sun-Thu 12-9, Fri-Sat 12-10 D served Sun-Thu 12-9, Fri-Sat 12-10 food served all day ⊕ FREE HOUSE ◧ Tennents.

Glen Trool, Galloway Forest Park

HIGHLAND

ABRIACHAN
Map 5 NH53

Loch Ness Lodge

★★★★★ 🏠 RESTAURANT WITH ROOMS

◉◉ French, Scottish

Stylish restaurant with stunning Loch Ness views

☎ 01456 459469 📠 01456 459439
Brachia, Loch Ness-Side IV3 8LA
e-mail: escape@lodgeatlochness.com
dir: From S on A9 to 1st rdbt. Follow signs to A82 Fort William/Loch Ness Rd. On right hand side after Clansman Hotel. From Airport take A96 to Inverness. At Raigmore Interchange join A9 north to 1st rdbt. follow signs Fort William/Loch Ness

Loch Ness Lodge is the AA's Guest Accommodation of the Year for Scotland 2009-2010. A beautifully designed, purpose-built restaurant with rooms, it enjoys spectacular views over Loch Ness from a prominent loch-side position. Money has been lavished on the interior, with bold colours and a contemporary look, yet the feel and atmosphere is more country house than designer-chic. Each of the individually designed, beautifully presented bedrooms offers a nice mix of traditional luxury and modern technology, including Wi-fi. There's a spa with a hot tub, sauna and a therapy room offering a variety of treatments, and guests have a choice of attractive lounges which feature real fires in the colder months. Original artwork, discreet music and gleaming glassware on immaculate, linen-dressed tables set the relaxed mood in the modern restaurant. Bag a window seat if you can and take in the stunning loch views over a well-executed five-course dinner prepared from quality seasonal ingredients. The kitchen displays originality, flair and good technical skills resulting in imaginative, full-flavoured dishes. Take a delicious brown crab velouté, which packs a punch with great flavours and accurate seasoning, a gamey warm salad of wood pigeon, and an impressive main course of moist and tender loin and leg of wild hare with garlic crisps and truffle oil. Dessert, perhaps a rich dark chocolate tart with prune and Armagnac parfait, follows a plate of Scottish cheeses.

Rooms 7 en suite (1 GF) S £120-£180; D £190-£280*
Facilities Dinner available Direct Dial Cen ht Wi-fi Fishing Sauna Hot tub Therapy room **Conf** Max 14 Thtr 14 Class 10 Board 14 **Parking** 10 **Notes** LB ⊗ No Children 12yrs Closed 2-31 Jan No coaches Civ Wed 24

Chef Ross Fraser **Owner** Scott & Iona Sutherland **Restaurant Times** 7-11.30 Closed 2-31 Jan, L all week (except by arrangement) **Prices** Food prices not confirmed for 2010. Please telephone for details, Service optional **Wines** 43 bottles over £20, 2 bottles under £20, 6 by glass **Notes** Fixed D 5 course £45, Dress restrictions, Smart casual **Seats** 14 **Children** Portions

ACHILTIBUIE
Map 4 NC00

The Summer Isles Hotel

◉◉ Modern British

Top-drawer Scottish produce with gorgeous sea views

☎ 01854 622282 📠 01854 622251
IV26 2YG
e-mail: info@summerisleshotel.co.uk
dir: 10m N of Ullapool. Left off A835 onto single track road. 15m to Achiltibuie. Hotel 100yds after post office on left

Terry and Irina Mackay purchased the hotel in 2008 from a family who had run it for over 40 years. They wisely left well alone when it came to the style and tone of the place, and the white-fronted house remains a haven of tranquillity with gorgeous sea views. Located in a stunningly beautiful and unspoilt landscape, Summer Isles is the perfect place in which to unwind. The bar at the side of the hotel is the original crofters' meeting place, and dates from the mid-19th century. Highland real ales and a huge selection of malt whiskies head the choice of refreshments, but wine lovers will need time to study the list too – there are over 400 to choose from. The seafood platter is the hotel's signature dish, served at lunchtime; lighter offerings include sandwiches; smoke-roasted salmon steaks; and desserts such as bannoffee pie, strawberry millefeuille, and home-made ice creams. Smart table settings in the cream-coloured dining room establish a mood of quiet refinement, and the menus deal in the top-drawer Scots produce for which Summer Isles has always been renowned. Dinner might begin with a filo parcel of monkfish, served with tamarind sauce, and go on to a pairing of langoustines and spiny lobster, served whole in the shell with hollandaise. The meat main course could be roast rib of Aberdeen Angus with wild mushrooms and red onions, sauced with red wine. Choose desserts from a trolley, and leave room for the excellent cheeses.

Times 12.30-2/8 Closed mid Oct-Etr

Open all wk ⊕ FREE HOUSE ◖ Red Cuillin, Misty Isle, Hebridean Gold, Young Pretender, IPA Deuchars. **Facilities** Dogs allowed Garden Parking

ARDELVE
Map 4 NG82

Caberfeidh House

★★★ GUEST HOUSE

☎ 01599 555293
IV40 8DY
e-mail: info@caberfeidh.plus.com
web: www.caberfeidh.plus.com
dir: A87 over Dornie Bridge into Ardelve, 1st left, 100yds on right

Set in a peaceful location overlooking Lochs Alsh and Duich, Caberfeidh House offers good value, comfortable accommodation in relaxed and friendly surroundings. Bedrooms are traditionally furnished and thoughtfully equipped, and there is a cosy lounge with a wide selection of books, games and magazines. Hearty breakfasts are served at individual tables in the dining room.

Rooms 5 rms (4 en suite) (1 pri facs) (3 fmly) S £28; D £56*
Facilities TVL tea/coffee Cen ht **Parking** 4 **Notes** ⊗ Closed 25-26 Dec

Eilean a Cheo

★★★ GUEST HOUSE

☎ 01599 555485
Dornie IV40 8DY
e-mail: stay@scothighland.com
web: www.scothighland.com
dir: A87 N of Dornie Bridge, exit for Ardelve, 110yds on right

Set in a quiet location overlooking Loch Duich and the famous Eilean Donan castle, this well maintained house offers well-equipped bedrooms some of which benefit from the view. Breakfast is freshly prepared and served in the tidy breakfast room, with a real fire burning on cooler mornings.

Rooms 5 en suite (3 GF) S £36-£50; D £50-£66 **Facilities** tea/coffee Cen ht Wi-fi **Parking** 6 **Notes** ⊗

Cnoc-na-Faire

★★★★ ⬥ INN

⊚ Modern Scottish

Local produce in a lovely setting

☎ 01687 450249   📠 01687 450249
Back of Keppoch, PH39 4NS
e-mail: cnocnafaire@googlemail.com
web: www.cnoc-na-faire.co.uk
dir: A830, onto B8008 at sign for establishment, after 1m, left into driveway

On the famous Road to the Isles, this delightful Art Deco-style white painted building overlooks the sea, with picture-postcard views down to the white sandy beach and further afield towards the islands of Skye, Eigg and Rhum. Gaelic for 'Hill of Vigil', Cnoc-na-Faire offers modern bedrooms and bathrooms that cater well for guests' needs. In the restaurant there are slate table mats on the well spaced tables while the walls are hung with local photos and artwork. Service is very relaxed and welcoming, and the menu makes the most of the wonderful local produce, with plenty of fresh fish featuring, as well as interesting game and meat dishes. You might start with curried parsnip soup, accompanied by spiced, local chutney. Follow with perfectly cooked cod that comes with a brioche crumb and locally landed langoustine, excellent smooth and creamy mashed potato, with crispy kale adding both colour and texture. End with toffee and apple crumble with homemade ice cream.

Rooms 6 en suite S £90-£110; D £90-£130 * **Facilities** STV tea/coffee Cen ht Wi-fi **Parking** 15 **Conf** Max 20 Thtr 20 Class 16 Board 16 Notes Closed 23 Dec-4 Jan

Owners D & J Sharpe **Chef** Allan Ritchie **Restaurant Times** 12-2/6-9 Closed 23-27 Dec **Prices** Starter £3.95-£6.95 Main £9.95-£20.95 Dessert £5.45-£8 Service optional **Wines** 1 bottle over £20, 13 bottles under £20, 4 by glass Notes Sunday L, Vegetarian available **Seats** 20 Children Menu, Portions

Macdonald Highlands

★★★★ 75% HOTEL

☎ 01479 815100   📠 01479 815101
Aviemore Highland Resort PH22 1PN
e-mail: general@aviemorehighlandresort.com
web: www.aviemorehighlandresort.com
dir: From N: Exit A9 to Aviemore (B970). Right at T-junct, through village. Right (2nd exit) at 1st rdbt into Macdonald Aviemore Highland Resort, follow reception signs. From S: Exit A9 to Aviemore, left at T-junct. Immediately after Esso garage, turn left into Resort

This hotel is part of the Aviemore Highland Resort which boasts a wide range of activities including a championship golf course. The modern, well-equipped bedrooms suit business, leisure guests and families, and Aspects Restaurant is the fine dining option. In addition there is a state-of-the-art gym, spa treatments and a 25-metre pool with a wave machine and flume.

Rooms 151 (10 fmly) (44 GF) **Facilities** Spa STV FTV ⓣ supervised ⅃ 18 Putt green Gym Steam room Sauna Out & indoor childrens playground Xmas New Year Wi-fi **Conf** Class 610 Board 38 Thtr 1000 **Services** Lift **Parking** 500 **Notes** LB ⊗ Civ Wed 300

The Old Minister's House

★★★★★ GUEST HOUSE

☎ 01479 812181   📠 0871 661 9324
Rothiemurchus PH22 1QH
e-mail: kate@theoldministershouse.co.uk
web: www.theoldministershouse.co.uk
dir: B970 from Aviemore signed Glenmore & Coylumbridge, establishment 0.75m at Inverdruie

Built originally as a manse in 1906, the Old Minister's House stands in well-tended grounds close to Aviemore. The house is beautifully furnished and immaculately maintained. Bedrooms are spacious, attractively decorated and thoughtfully equipped. There is an inviting lounge and a dining room where hearty breakfasts are served.

Rooms 4 en suite (1 fmly) S £50-£70; D £90-£96 **Facilities** tea/coffee Cen ht Wi-fi **Parking** 4 **Notes** ⊗ No Children 10yrs

Ravenscraig

★★★★ GUEST HOUSE

☎ 01479 810278   📠 01479 810210
Grampian Rd PH22 1RP
e-mail: info@aviemoreonline.com
web: www.aviemoreonline.com
dir: N end of main street, 250yds N of police station

This friendly, family-run guest house is on the north side of the village, a short walk from local amenities. Bedrooms vary between the traditionally styled rooms in the main house and modern

continued

spacious rooms in a brand new chalet-style annexe. There is a relaxing lounge and separate dining room, where freshly prepared breakfasts are served at individual tables.

Rooms 6 en suite 6 annexe en suite (6 fmly) (6 GF) S £30-£40; D £60-£80* **Facilities** TVL tea/coffee Cen ht Wi-fi **Parking** 15 **Notes** ⊗

Corrour House

★★★★ 🅰 GUEST HOUSE

☎ 01479 810220 📠 01479 811500
Inverdruie PH22 1QH
e-mail: enquiries@corrourhouse.co.uk
web: www.corrourhouse.co.uk
dir: From Aviemore take B970, signed Coylumbridge, entrance 0.5m on right

Rooms 8 en suite (2 fmly) S £45-£55; D £80-£90* **Facilities** tea/coffee Cen ht Licensed Wi-fi **Parking** 12 **Notes** Closed 17 Nov-29 Dec

The Old Bridge Inn ♥

☎ 01479 811137
Dalfaber Rd PH22 1PU
e-mail: nigel@oldbridgeinn.co.uk
dir: Exit A9 to Aviemore, 1st left to Ski Rd, then 1st left again 200mtrs

Set in the spectacular Scottish Highlands, in an area well-known for its outdoor pursuits, this friendly Aviemore pub overlooks the River Spey. Dine in the relaxing bars with roaring log fire, the comfortable restaurant, or in the attractive riverside garden. A tempting chargrill menu includes lamb chops in redcurrant jelly, Aberdeen Angus sirloin or rib-eye steaks, and butterflied breast of chicken marinated in yoghurt, lime and coriander. Other choices include braised guinea fowl with brandy or potato gnocchi with butternut squash in a filo basket. Fine cask ales and large selection of malt whiskies available.

Open all wk 11-11 (Fri-Sat 11am-mdnt Sun 12.30-11) **Bar Meals** L served all wk 12-2 D served all wk 6-9 **Restaurant** L served all wk 12-2 booking required D served all wk 6-9 booking required ⊕ FREE HOUSE ◀ Caledonian 80/-, Cairngorm Highland IPA, Deuchars IPA, Timothy Taylor, Atlas Avalanche. ♥ 18 **Facilities** Children's menu Play area Family room Garden Parking

The Badachro Inn ♥

☎ 01445 741255 📠 01445 741319
IV21 2AA
e-mail: Lesley@badachroinn.com
dir: From Kinlochewe A832 towards Gairloch. Onto B8056, right to Badachro after 3.25m, towards quay

Great views from one of Scotland's finest anchorages are afforded at this convivial waterside pub, with two mooring available free for visitors. Decking, with nautical-style sails and rigging, runs right down to the water overlooking Loch Gairloch. Interesting photographs and collages adorn the bar walls, where there is a dining area by a log fire. Friendly staff serve a couple of beers from the An Teallach or

Caledonian breweries and a farm cider. A further dining conservatory overlooks the bay. Excellent fresh fish is the speciality of the house, along with dishes such as local venison terrine and chicken breast on crushed haggis, neeps and tatties.

Open all wk Closed: 25 Dec **Bar Meals** L served all wk 12-3 D served all wk 6-9 **Restaurant** L served all wk 12-3 D served all wk 6-9 ⊕ FREE HOUSE ◀ Red Cullen, An Teallach, Blaven, 80/-, Guinness. ♥ 11 **Facilities** Dogs allowed Garden Parking

Priory

★★★ 74% HOTEL

☎ 01463 782309 📠 01463 782531
The Square IV4 7BX
e-mail: reservations@priory-hotel.com
web: www.priory-hotel.com
dir: Signed from A832, into Beauly, hotel in square on left

This popular hotel occupies a central location in the town square. Standard and executive rooms are on offer, both providing a good level of comfort and range of facilities. Food is served throughout the day in the open-plan public areas, with menus offering a first rate choice.

Rooms 37 (3 fmly) (1 GF) (10 smoking) S £49.50-£65; D £55-£100 (incl. bkfst) **Facilities** STV FTV Xmas New Year Wi-fi **Conf** Class 40 Board 30 Thtr 40 Del from £65 to £80 **Services** Lift **Parking** 20 **Notes** LB ⊗

Lovat Arms

★★★ 73% HOTEL

☎ 01463 782313 📠 01463 782862
IV4 7BS
e-mail: info@lovatarms.com
web: www.lovatarms.com
dir: From The Square past Royal Bank of Scotland, hotel on right

This fine family run hotel enjoys a prominent position in this charming town which is a short drive from Inverness. The bedrooms are comfortable and well appointed. The spacious foyer has a real fire and comfortable seating, while the Strubag lounge is ideal for informal dining.

Rooms 34 (12 annexe) (3 fmly) S £40-£80; D £55-£100 (incl. bkfst) **Facilities** Wi-fi **Conf** Class 18 Board 36 Thtr 60 **Parking** 15

Buachaille Etive Beag reflected in Lochan na Fola, Glen Coe

BOAT OF GARTEN — Map 5 NH91

Boat

★★★ 82% HOTEL

◉◉ Modern Scottish

Scottish cuisine with a modern twist amid beautiful Cairngorms scenery

☎ 01479 831258 & 831696 📠 01479 831414
PH24 3BH
e-mail: info@boathotel.co.uk
dir: Off A9 N of Aviemore onto A95, follow signs to Boat of Garten

You could arrive in period style by steam train on the Strathspey Railway from Aviemore at this Victorian station hotel at the heart of the Cairngorms. Individually styled bedrooms reflect the unique character of the hotel; all are comfortable, well equipped and have a host of thoughtful extras. The public areas include a choice of comfortable lounges and, as you're in Speyside, a wee dram from the bar's array of over 80 single malts wouldn't go amiss before dining in the smartly modernised intimate, restaurant, where a real fire and dark blue walls hung with striking modern artwork make for a stylish setting. The kitchen's line in Scottish cuisine takes the pick of local produce and prepares it with imagination and contemporary flair. Well-balanced combinations might begin with marinated Scottish salmon with poached West Coast oysters and basil aïoli, followed by an assiette of Spey Valley pork with buttered spinach, baby turnips and Madeira jus.

Rooms 34 (2 fmly) **Facilities** Xmas New Year Wi-fi **Conf** Class 30 Board 25 Thtr 40 **Parking** 36 **Notes** Civ Wed 40

Chef John Dale **Owner** Mr J Erasmus & Mr R Drummond **Restaurant Times** 7-9.30 Closed Dec-Feb (bookings only), L all week **Prices** Fixed D 2 course £27-£35, Service optional **Wines** 40 bottles over £20, 6 bottles under £20, 4 by glass **Notes** Tasting menu 7 course, Sunday L, Vegetarian available, Dress restrictions, No jeans **Seats** 30, Pr/dining room 40

BONAR BRIDGE — Map 5 NH69

Royal Marine Hotel, Restaurant & Spa

★★★★ 75% HOTEL

◉ Modern Scottish V

Traditional Highland hotel with reliable cooking

☎ 01408 621252 📠 01408 621181
Golf Rd KW9 6QS
e-mail: info@royalmarinebrora.com
web: www.royalmarinebrora.com
dir: Off A9 in village towards beach & golf course

With the lovely Highland village of Brora, a renowned golf course and glorious beaches on its doorstep, it's not hard to see what keeps guests coming to this distinctive Edwardian residence. Its leisure centre is popular, and a modern bedroom wing complements the original bedrooms, which retain period style. There are also luxury apartments just a short walk away. The hotel is looking sharp after a smart refurbishment, and you have a choice of 3 dining venues: a

café-bar overlooking the pool, a buzzy modern bistro and the formal Lorimer Dining Room, which serves up good wholesome cooking with clear flavours in the modern Scottish idiom. Kick off with an old favourite like Cullen skink, then move on to breast of chicken wrapped in Parma ham with wild mushrooms and asparagus, and end with blueberry and raspberry pannacotta.

Rooms 21 (1 fmly) (2 GF) **S** £89; **D** £134-£194 (incl. bkfst)*
Facilities FTV ⊗ ♨ Putt green Fishing ♨ Gym Steam room Sauna Xmas New Year Wi-fi **Conf** Class 40 Board 40 Thtr 70 **Parking** 40 **Notes** LB Civ Wed 60

Chef Steven Dalesby **Owner** Duncraggie Ltd **Restaurant Times** 12-2/6.30-8.45 Closed L (pre booking only) **Prices** Starter £4.50-£8.50, Main £16.50-£20.95, Dessert £4.95-£6.95 **Wines** 35 bottles over £20, 35 bottles under £20, 10 by glass **Notes** Sunday L, Vegetarian menu **Seats** 50, Pr/dining room 12 **Children** Portions, Menu

Kyle House

★★★ GUEST ACCOMMODATION

☎ 01863 766360 📠 01863 766360
Dornoch Rd IV24 3EB
e-mail: kylehouse360@msn.com
dir: On A949 N from village centre

A spacious house with splendid views of the Kyle of Sutherland and the hills beyond. Bedrooms are comfortably furnished in traditional style and equipped with all the expected facilities. There is a lounge and hearty breakfasts are enjoyed in the dining room.

Rooms 5 rms (3 en suite) (2 fmly) S £30; D £60* **Facilities** TVL tea/coffee Cen ht **Parking** 5 **Notes** ⊗ No Children 5yrs Closed Dec-Jan RS Oct & Apr Occasional closure (phone in advance) ☻

CARRBRIDGE — Map 5 NH92

Dalrachney Lodge

★★★ 75% SMALL HOTEL

☎ 01479 841252 📠 01479 841383
PH23 3AT
e-mail: dalrachney@aol.com
web: www.dalrachney.co.uk
dir: Follow Carrbridge signs off A9. In village on A938

A traditional Highland lodge, Dalrachney lies in grounds by the River Dulnain on the edge of the village. Spotlessly maintained public areas include a comfortable and relaxing sitting room and a cosy well-stocked bar, which has a popular menu providing an alternative to the dining room. Bedrooms are generally spacious and furnished in period style.

Rooms 11 (3 fmly) **S** £60-£90; **D** £90-£140 (incl. bkfst)*
Facilities Fishing Xmas New Year Wi-fi **Parking** 40 **Notes** LB

Craigellachie Guest House

★★★★ A GUEST HOUSE

☎ 01479 841641 📠 01479 841415
Main St PH23 3AS
e-mail: info@craigellachiehouse.co.uk
web: www.craigellachiehouse.co.uk
dir: A95 N from Aviemore, after 4m left to Carrbridge

Rooms 6 rms (4 en suite) (2 pri facs) S £27-£28; D £54-£58
Facilities TVL tea/coffee Cen ht Wi-fi **Parking** 7 **Notes** LB ⊗ No Children 4yrs

The Pines Country House

★★★ BED AND BREAKFAST

☎ 01479 841220 📠 01479 841220
Duthil PH23 3ND
e-mail: lynn@thepines-duthil.co.uk
dir: 2m E of Carrbridge in Duthil on A938

A warm welcome is assured at this comfortable home in the Cairngorms National Park. The bright bedrooms are traditionally furnished and offer good amenities. Enjoyable home-cooked fare is served around a communal table. Guests can relax in the conservatory-lounge and watch squirrels feed in the nearby wood.

Rooms 4 en suite (1 fmly) (1 GF); D £50-£55 **Facilities** STV tea/coffee Dinner available Cen ht Wi-fi **Parking** 5 **Notes** LB

The Cairn

★★★ A INN ▼

☎ 01479 841212 📠 01479 841362
Main Rd PH23 3AS
e-mail: info@cairnhotel.co.uk
web: www.cairnhotel.co.uk
dir: In village centre

The Highland village of Carrbridge and this family-run inn make the perfect base for exploring the Cairngorms, the Moray coast and the Malt Whisky Trail. In the homely, tartan-carpeted bar, you'll find cracking Isle of Skye and Cairngorm ales on handpump, blazing winter log fires, all-day sandwiches, and hearty bar meals, including sweet marinated herring with oatcakes, venison sausage casserole, and sticky toffee pudding.

Rooms 7 rms (5 en suite) (2 fmly) S £28-£56; D £56-£60
Facilities STV tea/coffee Dinner available Wi-fi Pool Table **Parking** 20 **Notes** Closed 25 Dec

Pub Open all day all wk 11-11 (Fri-Sat 11am-1am) **Bar Meals** L served all wk 12-2 D served all wk 6-8.30 Av main course £7 ⊕ FREE HOUSE ◀ Cairngorm, Orkney. ▼ 8 **Facilities** Children's menu Dogs allowed Garden Parking

CAWDOR — Map 5 NH85

Cawdor Tavern ▼

☎ 01667 404777 📠 01667 404777
The Lane IV12 5XP
e-mail: enquiries@cawdortavern.info
dir: From A96 (Inverness-Aberdeen) take B9006 & follow Cawdor Castle signs. Tavern in village centre

Standing close to the famous castle in a beautiful conservation village, the tavern was formerly a joinery workshop for the Cawdor Estate. Oak panelling from the castle, gifted by the late laird, is used to great effect in the lounge bar. Roaring log fires keep the place cosy and warm on long winter evenings, while the garden patio comes into its own in summer. A single menu is offered for both restaurant and bar, where refreshments include a choice of real ales and 100 malt whiskies. The pub's reputation for seafood draws diners from some distance for dishes like fresh Wester Ross salmon with potatoes and parsley butter. Other favourites include smooth chicken liver pâté with home-made apple jelly and crostini, a trio of Scottish puddings — black pudding, white pudding and haggis served with home-made chutney; and prime beef steak pie and mash.

Open all wk 11-3 5-11 (Sat 11am-mdnt Sun 12.30-11) Closed: 25 Dec, 1 Jan **Bar Meals** L served Mon-Sat 12-2, Sun 12.30-3 D served all wk 5.30-9 booking required Av main course £8.95 **Restaurant** D served all wk 5.30-9 booking required Av 3 course à la carte fr £18.95 ⊕ FREE HOUSE ◀ Red McGregor, 3 Sisters, Orkney Dark Island, Raven Ale, Latitude Highland Pilsner. ▼ 8 **Facilities** Children's menu Family room Dogs allowed Garden Parking

Coul House

★★★ 79% COUNTRY HOUSE HOTEL

⊚ Modern Scottish V

Georgian country-house hotel with superb views and ambitious fine dining

☎ 01997 421487 🖹 01997 421945
IV14 9ES
e-mail: stay@coulhousehotel.com
dir: Exit A9 north onto A835. Hotel on right

You can't fail to be impressed by the surroundings when you dine at this classic Georgian country house. A number of the generally spacious bedrooms have superb views of the distant mountains and all are thoughtfully equipped. The dramatic Octagonal Restaurant is the magnificent centrepiece, where the lengthy menu offers contemporary Scottish cuisine with classic French overtones, backed up by a biblical wine list. Kick off with dishes such as hickory smoked rabbit saddle, served tender and lightly cooked, with pan-fried gnocchi, before main-course pan-seared sea bass - a fine piece of fish - with a rather complex mêlée of contrasting flavours comprising three pimento mousse, lemon and spinach risotto, tomato and balsamic cappuccino and an artichoke salad with spring onion and chorizo oil.

Rooms 20 (3 fmly) (4 GF) **S** £45-£95; **D** £85-£190 (incl. bkfst)*
Facilities 9 hole pitch & putt New Year Wi-fi Child facilities
Conf Class 30 Board 30 Thtr 80 **Parking** 60 **Notes** LB Closed 24-26 Dec Civ Wed 100

Chef G Kenley **Owner** Stuart MacPherson **Restaurant Times** 12-2.30/6.30-9 Closed 24-26 Dec **Prices** Starter £4-£10.50, Main £14-£25, Dessert £4-£5.95, Service optional **Wines** 77 bottles over £20, 20 bottles under £20, 9 by glass **Notes** Sunday L, Vegetarian menu **Seats** 70, Pr/dining room 40 **Children** Portions, Menu

Achilty Hotel

★★★ 73% SMALL HOTEL

⊚ Traditional, Mediterranean

Scottish and Mediterranean flavours in former drovers' inn

☎ 01997 421355 🖹 01997 421923
IV14 9EG
e-mail: info@achiltyhotel.co.uk
web: www.achiltyhotel.co.uk
dir: A9 onto A835, hotel 6m on right

Surrounded by the stunning Scottish countryside of the north Highlands, this former drovers' inn is a warm and welcoming hotel. Friendly owners contribute to great hospitality and a relaxed atmosphere. Bedrooms are smartly furnished and cheerfully decorated, while public areas are full of interest; the lounges have books and games and the Steading bar features exposed stone walls and offers a good selection of tasty home-cooked meals. Dating back to the 1700s, the attractive open-plan restaurant features high ceilings and stone walls as well as well-appointed tables and efficient, friendly service. Expect traditional Scottish dishes combined with a Mediterranean influence. So, Cullen skink joins chicken bruschetta among starters, and main courses range from saddle of venison with a rich port and cranberry sauce to monkfish tail poached in white wine and served with spicy tomato sauce and saffron rice.

Rooms 11 (1 annexe) (3 GF) (1 smoking) **Facilities** New Year **Conf** Class 50 Board 20 Thtr 50 **Parking** 100 **Notes** ⊗ Closed 3-10 Jan

Restaurant Times 12-2/5-8.30 Closed L Mon-Tue

Tulloch Castle

★★★★ 74% HOTEL

☎ 01349 861325 🖹 01349 863993
Tulloch Castle Dr IV15 9ND
e-mail: info@tullochcastle.co.uk
web: www.oxfordhotelsandinns.com
dir: A9 N, Tore rdbt 2nd left signed Dingwall, at Dingwall turn left at 4th lights, hotel signed

Overlooking the town of Dingwall this 12th-century castle is still the gathering place of the Clan Davidson and boasts its own ghost in the shape of the Green Lady. The friendly team are very helpful and love to tell you about the history of the castle; the ghost tour after dinner is a must. The hotel has a self contained suite and a number of bedrooms with four-posters.

Rooms 20 (2 fmly) **Facilities** FTV Xmas New Year Wi-fi **Conf** Class 70 Board 70 Thtr 120 Del from £115 to £180* **Parking** 50 **Notes** ⊗ Civ Wed 110

Dornoch Castle Hotel

★★★ 74% HOTEL

◉ Scottish, Fusion

Modern Scottish brasserie food in a stylishly renovated 15th-century castle

☎ 01862 810216 📠 01862 810981
Castle St IV25 3SD
e-mail: enquiries@dornochcastlehotel.com
web: www.dornochcastlehotel.com
dir: 2m N of Dornoch Bridge on A9, turn right to Dornoch. Hotel in village centre

Built originally as the bishop's palace for the nearby 12th-century cathedral, Dornoch Castle has been restored over the last decade in a characterful blend of ancient stone walls and classy modern style which have made it a popular wedding venue. Within the original castle are some splendid themed bedrooms, and elsewhere the more modern bedrooms have all the expected facilities. The walled castle gardens make a charming backdrop for dining in the purpose-built Garden Restaurant, or the same menu is on offer in the Bishop's kitchen bar, where a roaring log fire in a huge fireplace and exposed 15th-century stone walls give a bit of ye aulde Scotland. The daily menus, however, take a modern Scottish route, offering brasserie-style dishes such as duck confit with chestnut ravioli and warm plum sauce, followed by braised oxtail with parsnip and vanilla purée, roasted shallots and wild mushrooms.

Rooms 21 (3 fmly) (4 GF) **Facilities** FTV New Year Wi-fi **Conf** Class 30 Board 30 Thtr 60 **Parking** 16 **Notes** LB Civ Wed 95

Restaurant Times 12-3/6-9.30 Closed 25-26 Dec

2 Quail Restaurant & Rooms

★★★★★ RESTAURANT WITH ROOMS

◉◉ International

Classic cooking in tiny Highland restaurant

☎ 01862 811811
Inistore House, Castle St IV25 3SN
e-mail: theaa@2quail.com
dir: On main street, 200yds from cathedral

Small is certainly beautiful at this homely restaurant with rooms in the Royal Burgh of Dornoch on the Highland coast. Set in the main street the careful renovation of its Victorian origins transports guests back in time. Cosy public rooms are ideal for conversation, while there are masses of books for those just wishing to relax. The stylish, individual bedrooms match the character of the house but are thoughtfully equipped to include DVD players. Food is the main feature however, with excellent breakfasts and set four-course dinners. With just three rooms and 12 covers in the restaurant, booking ahead is a wise move, and well worth it for the civilised ambience and accomplished cuisine. Kerensa Carr - one half of the husband-and-wife-team who run 2 Quail with hands-on hospitality - delivers efficient, cheery service in the book-lined dining room, while chef Michael makes everything in-house from the best available

locally-sourced ingredients. Three-course dinners might open with Maryland-style crab cake with a pink peppercorn beurre blanc, followed by roast best-end of Dornoch lamb with dauphinoise potatoes, Provençal vegetables and thyme jus. And for dessert, dark chocolate marquise with griottines. There's a serious approach to wine too, with a thoughtful array served by the glass or bottle.

Rooms 3 en suite (1 fmly) S £60-£100; D £80-£120* **Facilities** FTV tea/coffee Dinner available Direct Dial Cen ht Wi-fi Golf 18 **Notes** LB ⊗ No Children 8yrs Closed Xmas & 2 wks Feb/Mar RS Nov-Mar Fri-Sat only No coaches

Chef Michael Carr **Owner** Michael and Kerensa Carr **Restaurant Times** 7.30-9.30 Closed Xmas, 2 wks Feb-Mar, Sun-Mon, L all week **Prices** Fixed D 3 course £38, Service optional **Wines** 44 bottles over £20, 2 bottles under £20, 8 by glass **Notes** Vegetarian available, Dress restrictions, Smart casual **Seats** 14

Loch Ness Lodge

★★★ 🅰 HOTEL

☎ 01456 450342 📠 01456 450429
IV63 6TU
e-mail: info@lochness-hotel.com
dir: Off A82 onto A831 (Cannich road)

Rooms 50 (4 fmly) (10 GF) **Facilities** FTV Visitors centre Shops Cinema Boat cruises Hairdresser ⛱ Wi-fi **Conf** Class 40 Board 40 Thtr 150 **Parking** 80 **Notes** ⊗ Closed Nov-Feb Civ Wed 50

Ferness Cottage

★★★★ BED AND BREAKFAST

☎ 01456 450564
Lewiston IV63 6UW
e-mail: info@lochnessaccommodation.co.uk
web: www.lochnessaccommodation.co.uk
dir: A82, from Inverness turn right after Esso service station; from Fort William left before Esso service station, 100mtrs phone box on left. 100mtrs on right

This rose-covered cottage dating from the 1840s has a peaceful location and is within easy walking distance of the village centre. The two charming bedrooms are well equipped, with many thoughtful extra touches. Traditional breakfasts in the cosy lounge-dining room feature the best of local produce. Guests can use the grass area, with seating, beside the River Coiltie, where fishing is available.

Rooms 2 en suite S £40-£65; D £50-£65 **Facilities** tea/coffee Cen ht Wi-fi Fishing **Parking** 2 **Notes** LB ⊗ No Children 10yrs

DRUMNADROCHIT CONTINUED

Glen Rowan

★★★★ BED AND BREAKFAST

☎ 01456 450235
West Lewiston IV63 6UW
e-mail: info@glenrowan.co.uk
dir: From Inverness A82 to Drumnadrochit & Lewiston, right after
Esso station, Glen Rowan 600yds on left

Set in a peaceful village, this friendly family home offers attractive,
smartly furnished and well-equipped accommodation. Neat gardens
surround the house and rooms at the rear overlook the River Coiltie.
There is a choice of comfortable lounges, and a smart dining room
where delicious home-cooked fare is served at individual tables.
Bicycle storage and drying facilities are available.

Rooms 3 en suite (2 fmly) (3 GF) S £36-£46; D £52-£60*
Facilities tea/coffee Dinner available Cen ht Wi-fi Fishing **Parking** 5
Notes LB ⊗

Tigh Na Bruaich

★★★★ Ⓐ BED AND BREAKFAST

☎ 01456 459341
Glen Urquhart IV63 6TH
e-mail: stay@tigh.clara.net
web: www.tigh.clara.net
dir: 3m from Drumnadrochit on A831. Left at sign, house 50yds on
right

Rooms 2 rms (1 en suite) (1 pri facs) (2 GF) S £45-£60; D £55-£70*
Facilities TVL tea/coffee Cen ht Wi-fi **Parking** 2 **Notes** ⊗ No Children
12yrs Closed Xmas ⊜

| FORT AUGUSTUS | Map 5 NH30 |

Lovat Arms

★★★ 87% HOTEL

⊛⊛ Modern Scottish ◑

Intimate bistro-style dining with fine Highland produce and views

☎ 0845 450 1100 & 01456 459250 🗎 01320 366677
Loch Ness Side PH32 4DU
e-mail: info@lovatarms-hotel.com
web: www.lovatarms-hotel.com
dir: In town centre on A82

The Lovat Arms has much to recommend it: the friendly, family-run
Victorian hotel sits above the lochside village of Fort Augustus at the
southern point of Loch Ness, where the Caledonian Canal joins at a
daunting five-lock 'staircase' amid moody mountain scenery.
Impressively styled bedrooms offer a host of thoughtful extras, and
inviting public areas include a comfortable lounge with a log fire and
a stylish bar. The hospitality and commitment to guest care will
leave a lasting impression. While there's plenty of original period
charm, this is not a hotel that dwells in Victoriana: the contemporary
bistro-style restaurant is revamped with 21st-century style in the
form of oak floors, shiny tubular chrome seating, bold colours and
low-key lighting. The kitchen chooses carefully from the Highlands'
legendary produce - including über-fresh fish and seafood from
Mallaig - and its modern Scottish repertoire includes citrus-cured
Scottish salmon with ginger and coriander yogurt, followed with roast
haunch of venison with braised red cabbage, herb mash and port
redcurrant jus.

Rooms 29 (6 annexe) (3 fmly) (7 GF) **Facilities** FTV Xmas New Year
Wi-fi **Conf** Class 20 Board 20 Thtr 50 **Services** Lift **Parking** 30

Chef Colin Clark **Owner** David, Geraldine & Caroline Gregory
Restaurant Times 7-9 Closed Hogmanay (Jan) - guests only, Nov-
Mar, D Sun-Mon **Prices** Fixed L 3 course £15-£25, Fixed D 3 course
£30-£45, Starter £4.25-£7.95, Main £9.95-£22.50, Dessert £5.50-
£7.25, Service optional, Groups min 8 service 10% **Wines** 20 bottles
over £20, 20 bottles under £20, 10 by glass **Notes** Sunday L,
Vegetarian available **Seats** 27, Pr/dining room 50 **Children** Portions,
Menu

| FORT WILLIAM | Map 4 NN17 |

Inverlochy Castle

★★★★★ COUNTRY HOUSE HOTEL

⊛⊛⊛ Modern British Ⓥ ◮NOTABLE WINE LIST

Fine dining in opulent and historic Scottish building

☎ 01397 702177 🗎 01397 702953
Torlundy PH33 6SN
e-mail: info@inverlochy.co.uk
web: www.inverlochycastlehotel.com
dir: Accessible from either A82 (Glasgow-Fort William) or A9
(Edinburgh-Dalwhinnie). Hotel 3m N of Fort William on A82, in
Torlundy

Built in 1863 by the first Lord Abinger, near the site of the original
13th-century fortress, Inverlochy Castle sits in the foothills of Ben
Nevis amidst some of Scotland's finest scenery. This imposing and
gracious castle sits amidst extensive gardens and grounds
overlooking the hotel's own loch. Lavishly appointed in classic
country-house style, spacious bedrooms are extremely comfortable
and boast flat-screen TVs and laptops with internet access. The
sumptuous main hall and lounge provide the perfect setting for
afternoon tea or a pre-dinner cocktail. A snooker room and a DVD
library are also available. This is a truly impressive setting for fine
dining - aperitifs are taken in the sumptuous lounge or on the terrace
on warm sunny days, while dinner is an experience to savour in any
of the 3 dining rooms, each with elaborate period furniture and
stunning mountain views. Genuine comfort and luxury abound, while
service is highly professional but with a relaxed and friendly tone.
The kitchen's accomplished modern approach - underpinned by a
classical theme - suits the surroundings and makes fine use of the
abundant Highland larder, as well as produce from the estate's
walled garden, on its repertoire of daily-changing five-course dinner
and tasting menus. Expect high-level technical skill and clear
flavours in dishes like caramelised scallops with morel tortellini and
sweetcorn velouté, followed by cannon of lamb with a chicory and
goat's cheese Tatin. There's an excellent wine list, too, with an
extensive range of half-bottles to enjoy. Pack your jacket and tie
gentlemen, as they are required.

Rooms 17 (6 fmly) **S** £245-£345; **D** £380-£640 (incl. bkfst)*

Facilities STV ♨ Fishing ⚓ Fishing on loch Massage Riding Hunting Stalking Clay pigeon shooting Archery ♫ Xmas New Year Wi-fi **Conf** Class 20 Board 20 Thtr 50 **Parking** 17 **Notes** LB Civ Wed 80

Chef Matthew Gray **Owner** Inverlochy Hotel Ltd **Restaurant Times** 12.30-1.45/6.30-10 **Prices** Food prices not confirmed for 2010. Please telephone for details. **Wines** 283 bottles over £20, 8 by glass **Notes** Fixed D 4 course, Vegetarian menu, Dress restrictions, Jacket & tie for D **Seats** 40, Pr/dining room 20 **Children** Portions, Menu

Moorings

★★★ 80% HOTEL

◉ Modern, Traditional

Popular Highland hotel with contemporary cooking

☎ 01397 772797 🖹 01397 772441
Banavie PH33 7LY
e-mail: reservations@moorings-fortwilliam.co.uk
web: www.moorings-fortwilliam.co.uk
dir: take A380 (N from Fort William), cross Caledonian Canal, 1st right

The Moorings Hotel has a plum location right on the Caledonian Canal next to the daunting flight of locks known as Neptune's Staircase, with the hump of Ben Nevis as a backdrop. Catch the right time of day and you'll see the Jacobite steam train go past on the way to the fishing port of Mallaig. A dedicated team offers friendly service, while aAccommodation comes in two distinct styles - the newer rooms are particularly appealing. And at the end of a day's Highland activities, you can settle into the beamed Jacobean Restaurant with a menu of soundly-prepared British and European cuisine built on West Coast seafood and game. Start, perhaps, with West Coast hot-smoked salmon on potato and mustard salad, followed by pan-fried scallops and mallard duck in an orange and grain mustard dressing.

Rooms 27 (1 fmly) (1 GF) (1 smoking) **S** £43-£116; **D** £86-£142 (incl. bkfst)* **Facilities** STV New Year Wi-fi **Conf** Class 60 Board 40 Thtr 140 Del from £95 to £120* **Parking** 60 **Notes** LD RS 24-27 Dec Civ Wed 120

Chef Paul Smith **Owner** Mr S Leitch **Restaurant Times** 7-9.30 Closed 24-26 Dec, L all week **Prices** Starter £5.10-£8.95, Main £12.95-£21.95, Dessert £5.10-£8.95, Service optional **Wines** 17 bottles over £20, 28 bottles under £20, 4 by glass **Notes** Vegetarian available, Dress restrictions, Smart casual **Seats** 60, Pr/dining room 120 **Children** Portions

Lime Tree Hotel & Restaurant

★★★ 78% SMALL HOTEL

◉ Modern European

Stylish small hotel with art gallery and modern menu

☎ 01397 701806 🖹 01397 701806
Lime Tree Studio, Achintore Rd PH33 6RQ
e-mail: info@limetreefortwilliam.co.uk
dir: On A82 at entrance to Fort William

The Lime Tree is a charming family-owned boutique hotel with fantastic views of Loch Linnhe and the hills beyond as well as a super art gallery on the ground floor, and lots of original artwork displayed throughout. The hotel's comfortable lounges with their real fires are ideal for pre or post dinner drinks or maybe just to relax in. Individually designed bedrooms are spacious with some nice little personal touches courtesy of the artist owner. The old stone manse is fresh and contemporary thanks to the chic décor, but real fires and the clever use of natural materials remain as touchstones to the past. The menu is a blend of local ingredients and modern European ideas: Highland lamb 'osso bucco' is made using a gigot of Lochaber lamb leg, slow cooked with orange and bay leaf, served with a creamy parmesan risotto and seasonal vegetables, while local loch mussels are cooked in white wine, fresh herbs, cream and salted kale. Finish with passionfruit soufflé served with lavender ice cream.

Rooms 9 (4 fmly) (4 GF) **S** £60-£75; **D** £80-£100 (incl. bkfst)* **Facilities** New Year Wi-fi **Conf** Class 40 Board 30 Thtr 60 **Parking** 9 **Notes** Closed Nov

Chef Ross Sutherland **Owner** David Wilson & Charlotte Wright **Restaurant Times** 12-2.30/6.30-9 Closed Nov, **Prices** Starter £3.95-£5.50, Main £12.50-£30, Dessert £3.95-£5.50, Service optional **Wines** 14 bottles over £20, 17 bottles under £20, 5 by glass **Notes** Sunday L, Vegetarian available, Civ Wed 50 **Seats** 30 **Children** Portions

Alexandra

★★★ 75% HOTEL

☎ 01397 702241 🖹 01397 705554
The Parade PH33 6AZ
e-mail: salesalexandra@strathmorehotels.com
dir: Off A82. Hotel opposite railway station

This charming old hotel enjoys a prominent position in the town centre and is just a short walk from all the major attractions. Front-facing bedrooms have views over the town and the spectacular Nevis mountain range. There is a choice of restaurants, including a bistro serving meals until late, along with several stylish and very comfortable lounges.

Rooms 93 (5 fmly) **Facilities** Free use of nearby leisure club ♫ Xmas Wi-fi **Conf** Class 100 Board 40 Thtr 120 **Services** Lift **Parking** 50

Ben Nevis Hotel & Leisure Club

★★ 75% HOTEL

☎ 01397 702331 📠 01397 700132
North Rd PH33 6TG
e-mail: bennevismanager@strathmorehotels.com
dir: Off A82

This popular hotel is ideally situated on the outskirts of Fort William. It provides comfortable, well equipped bedrooms; many with views of the impressive Nevis mountains. The hotel's leisure centre is a firm favourite with guests at the hotel.

Rooms 119 (3 fmly) (30 GF) **Facilities** ⓢ supervised Gym Beauty salon ♬ Xmas New Year Wi-fi **Conf** Class 60 Board 40 Thtr 150 **Parking** 100 **Notes** Civ Wed 60

Croit Anna

★★ 67% HOTEL

☎ 01397 702268 📠 01397 704099
Achintore Rd, Drimarben PH33 6RR
e-mail: croitanna.fortwilliam@alfatravel.co.uk
dir: From Glencoe on A82 into Fort William, hotel 1st on right

Located on the edge of Loch Linnhe, just two miles out of town, this hotel offers some spacious bedrooms, many with fine views over the loch. There is a choice of two comfortable lounges and a large airy restaurant. The hotel appeals to coach parties and independent travellers alike.

Rooms 92 (5 fmly) (13 GF) **S** £37-£50; **D** £60-£86 (incl. bkfst) **Facilities** FTV Pool table ♬ Xmas New Year **Parking** 25 **Notes** LB ⊗ Closed Dec-Jan (ex Xmas) RS Nov, Feb, Mar

The Grange

★★★★★ 🏠 GUEST ACCOMMODATION

☎ 01397 705516
Grange Rd PH33 6JF
e-mail: info@thegrange-scotland.co.uk
web: www.thegrange-scotland.co.uk
dir: A82 S from Fort William, 300yds from rdbt left onto Ashburn Ln, at top on left

This lovely Victorian villa stands in immaculate gardens on an elevated position with beautiful views of Loch Linnhe. Attractive decor and pretty fabrics have been used to good effect in the charming bedrooms, two of which have loch views. There is ample provision of books and fresh flowers in the carefully furnished lounge, and the elegant dining room is a lovely setting for hearty breakfasts.

Rooms 3 en suite; D £110-£118* **Facilities** tea/coffee Cen ht Wi-fi **Parking** 4 **Notes** LB ⊗ No Children 13yrs Closed Nov-Mar

Distillery House

★★★★ GUEST HOUSE

☎ 01397 700103
Nevis Bridge, North Rd PH33 6LR
e-mail: disthouse@aol.com
dir: A82 from Fort William towards Inverness, on left after Glen Nevis rdbt

Situated in the grounds of the former Glenlochy Distillery, this friendly guest house was once the distillery manager's home. Bedrooms are attractively decorated, comfortably furnished and very well equipped. There is a relaxing lounge, which features a superb range of games, and a bright airy dining room where traditional Scottish breakfasts are served at individual tables.

Rooms 10 en suite (1 fmly) (1 GF) **Facilities** tea/coffee Cen ht Licensed **Parking** 21 **Notes** LB ⊗

Mansfield Guest House

★★★★ GUEST HOUSE

☎ 01397 772262 & 0845 6449432
Corpach PH33 7LT
e-mail: mansefield@btinternet.com
web: www.fortwilliamaccommodation.com
dir: 2m N of Fort William A82 onto A830, house 2m on A830 in Corpach

Peacefully set in its own well-tended garden this friendly, family-run guest house provides comfortable, attractively decorated and well-equipped accommodation. There is a cosy lounge, where a roaring coal fire burns on cold evenings, and an attractive dining room where delicious, home-cooked evening meals and breakfasts are served at individual tables.

Rooms 6 en suite (1 GF) S £30-£40; D £52-£70* **Facilities** TVL tea/coffee Dinner available Cen ht Wi-fi **Parking** 7 **Notes** LB ⊗ No Children 12yrs

Glenlochy

★★★ GUEST ACCOMMODATION

☎ 01397 702909
Nevis Bridge PH33 6LP
e-mail: glenlochy1@aol.com
web: www.glenlochy.co.uk
dir: A82 from Inverness, guest house on left after 2nd lights

The well-tended garden of this friendly, family-run guest house marks the end of the famous West Highland Way. Bedrooms are pleasantly decorated and well equipped. There is a comfortable first-floor lounge and a bright, airy ground-floor dining room, where hearty breakfasts are served at individual tables.

Rooms 10 en suite 1 annexe en suite (2 fmly) (7 GF) **Facilities** TVL tea/coffee Cen ht **Parking** 13 **Notes** ⊗

Stobhan B & B

★★★ BED AND BREAKFAST

☎ 01397 702790 📠 01397 702790
Fassifern Rd PH33 6BD
e-mail: boggi@supanet.com
dir: In town centre. A82 onto Victoria Rd beside St Mary's Church, right onto Fassifern Rd

Stobhan B & B occupies an elevated location overlooking Loch Linnhe and offers comfortable, good-value accommodation. Bedrooms, one of which is on the ground floor, are traditionally furnished and have en suite facilities. Breakfast is served in the ground-floor dining room, which is adjacent to the lounge.

Rooms 4 en suite (1 GF) S £30-£34; D £56-£64 **Facilities** tea/coffee Cen ht

Lochview

★★★ 🅰 GUEST HOUSE

☎ 01397 703149
Heathercroft, Argyll Rd PH33 6RE
e-mail: info@lochview.co.uk
dir: Off A82 rdbt at S end of town centre onto Lundavra Rd, left onto Argyll Ter, 1st right onto Heathercroft to top

Rooms 6 en suite S £38-£45; D £60-£70* **Facilities** tea/coffee Cen ht Wi-fi **Parking** 6 **Notes** ⊗ Closed Oct-Apr

Craigdarroch House

★★★★ 🍴 RESTAURANT WITH ROOMS

☎ 01456 486400 📠 01456 486444
IV2 6XU
e-mail: info@hotel-loch-ness.co.uk
dir: Take B862 from either end of loch, then B852 signed Foyers

Craigdarroch is located in an elevated position high above Loch Ness on the south side. Bedrooms vary in style and size but all are comfortable and well equipped; front-facing have wonderful views. Dinner should not be missed and breakfasts are also impressive.

Rooms 10 en suite **Facilities** FTV tea/coffee Dinner available Direct Dial Cen ht Wi-fi **Parking** 24 **Notes** No Children 12yrs No coaches Civ Wed 30

Foyers Bay Country House

★★★ GUEST HOUSE

☎ 01456 486624
Lochness IV2 6YB
e-mail: enquiries@foyersbay.co.uk
dir: Off B852 into Lower Foyers

Situated in sloping grounds with pines and abundant colourful rhododendrons, this delightful Victorian villa has stunning views of Loch Ness. The attractive bedrooms vary in size and are well equipped. There is a comfortable lounge next to the plant-filled conservatory-cafe, where delicious evening meals and traditional breakfasts are served.

Rooms 6 en suite (1 GF) S £45-£55; D £60-£90* **Facilities** FTV tea/coffee Dinner available Cen ht Licensed Wi-fi **Conf** Max 20 Thtr 20 Class 20 Board 20 **Parking** 6 **Notes** LB ⊗ No Children 16yrs Civ Wed 20

The Old Inn 🍷

☎ 01445 712006 📠 01445 712933
IV21 2BD
e-mail: info@theoldinn.net
dir: Just off A832, near harbour at south end of village

Gairloch's oldest hostelry enjoys a fabulous setting at the foot of the Flowerdale Valley by the harbour, looking out across Gairloch Harbour to the isles of Rona, Raasay and Skye, and was built by the estate in 1750 as a changing house for horses. On a good day, you might be able to spy the Outer Hebrides from this attractive inn, which makes a popular base for the many local activities - walking, fishing, golf, bird-watching and boat trips to see whales and bottlenose dolphins – or for simply resting and lolling about on the golden beaches. In the two bars you'll find the inn's own beer, the Blind Piper of Gairloch, which was created by the landlord and enthusiastic locals, alongside a good range of real ales, from Isle of Skye Red Cullin to

continued

GAIRLOCH CONTINUED

Wildcat, a full-bodied and strong brew from Cairngorm Brewery. If you fancy a wee dram, then you have an extensive range of Highland malts to choose from. Seafood is the main draw in an area where Gairloch lobster, Loch Ewe scallops, Minch langoustines, mussels, brown crab and fresh fish are regularly landed. Tuck into the traditional Cullen skink, a soup of smoked haddock, potato and cream, or crispy-fried squid, before launching into smoked haddock risotto; pan-seared scallops with smoked bacon mash and tamarind sauce, or Cajun-spiced cod. Carnivores will not be disappointed with pork belly served with herb-roasted vegetables, or venison steak with braised red cabbage, garlic confit, basil mash, and Highland blue cheese and whisky cream. A large grassy area by the pretty stream with picnic tables is an attractive place to eat and enjoy the views. Dogs are more than welcome, with bowls, baskets and rugs to help them feel at home.

Open all day all wk 11am-mdnt (Sun noon-mdnt) **Bar Meals** L served all wk 12-2.30 (summer 12-4.30) D served all wk 5-9.30 Av main course £9.50 food served all day **Restaurant** D served all wk 6-9.30 booking required Fixed menu price fr £25 Av 3 course à la carte fr £17.50 ⊕ FREE HOUSE ◀ Adnams Bitter, Isle of Skye Red Cullin, Blind Piper, An Teallach, Deuchars IPA, Wildcat. ♥ 8 **Facilities** Children's menu Play area Family room Dogs allowed Garden Parking

GARVE   Map 5 NH36

Inchbae Lodge Guest House

★★ INN

☎ 01997 455269   📄 01997 455207
Inchbae IV23 2PH
e-mail: contact@inchbae.co.uk
dir: On A385, past Garve towards Ullapool

You can watch stags feeding in the garden of this 19th-century hunting lodge, and residents can fish for free in the river Blackwater, which flows just outside, making it a firm favourite with fishermen and outdoor enthusiasts. Inside you'll find a bistro and a conservatory dining room with panoramic views, and a large residents' lounge warmed by a log fire on cooler days. The international menu includes hearty traditional choices such as venison casserole or liver and onions, and an extensive list of curries. Accommodation and a good selection of local ales are available. A friendly welcome is guaranteed and while bedrooms vary in size all are well equipped and comfortable.

Rooms 7 en suite (3 fmly) S £32-£35; D £53-£59.95 (room only)* **Facilities** STV FTV TVL tea/coffee Dinner available Direct Dial Cen ht Fishing Pool Table **Conf** Max 45 Thtr 45 Class 40 Board 40 **Parking** 14 **Notes** ⊗ Closed 25-30 Dec RS Nov-Mar

Pub Open all day all wk **Bar Meals** Av main course £7 food served all day **Restaurant** Fixed menu price fr £7 food served all day ⊕ FREE HOUSE ◀ Guinness, Isle of Skye Red Cullin, An Teallach Brewhouse Special. **Facilities** Garden

GLENCOE   Map 4 NN15

Scorrybreac

★★★★ GUEST ACCOMMODATION

☎ 01855 811354
PH49 4HT
e-mail: info@scorrybreac.co.uk
web: www.scorrybreac.co.uk
dir: Off A82 just outside village, 500yds from River Coe bridge

Having a stunning location above the village and overlooking the loch, this charming family-run guest house offers guests a warm welcome. Bedrooms are attractive, well equipped and comfortably furnished. There is a cosy lounge with plenty of books, board games and maps, and a bright airy dining room where delicious breakfasts are served at individual tables.

Rooms 6 en suite (6 GF) S £40-£46; D £50-£60* **Facilities** tea/coffee Cen ht **Parking** 8 **Notes** LB ⊗ Closed 25 Dec

GLENELG   Map 4 NG81

Glenelg Inn

☎ 01599 522273   📄 01599 522283
IV40 8JR
e-mail: glenelg-inn.info.com
dir: From Shiel Bridge (A87) take unclassified road to Glenelg

The inn is a conversion of 200-year-old stables set in a large garden stretching down to the sea, with stunning views across the Sound of Sleat. Musicians are frequent visitors to the bar, where at times a ceilidh atmosphere prevails. Menus offer traditional Scottish fare based on local produce, including plenty of fresh fish and seafood, hill-bred lamb, venison and seasonal vegetables. In the bar are seafood casserole and pies, while the dinner menu offers West Coast turbot with fennel and new potatoes.

Open all day all wk noon-mdnt **Bar Meals** L served all wk 12.30-2 D served all wk 6-9 ◀ Guest Ales. **Facilities** Dogs allowed Garden Parking

GLENFINNAN   Map 4 NM98

The Prince's House

★★★ 78% SMALL HOTEL

◉◉ Modern British ♨

Welcoming old coaching inn with fine Scottish produce

☎ 01397 722246   📄 01397 722323
PH37 4LT
e-mail: princeshouse@glenfinnan.co.uk
web: www.glenfinnan.co.uk
dir: on A830, 0.5m on right past Glenfinnan Monument. 200mtrs from railway station

This delightful hotel sits on the 'Road to the Isles' between Fort William and Mallaig in exactly the sort of romantic mountain and forest Highland landscape that tourists come here for, close to where 'Bonnie' Prince Charlie raised the Jacobite standard. Bedrooms are comfortably appointed and the hotel enjoys a well deserved reputation for fine food and excellent hospitality. This is the perfect locationfor sourcing the very finest fresh fish and seafood too, as well as game from surrounding estates and quality beef and lamb. The kitchen keeps things simple, leaving the standard of the produce to talk for itself. A three-course dinner might feature a pan-seared breast of Highland wood pigeon with baked Portobello mushrooms, port reduction and truffle oil, then baked turbot fillet and Arisaig scallops with braised fennel and West Coast prawn broth. The icing on the cake is the renowned welcome and service in this superbly friendly family-run hotel.

Rooms 9 (1 fmly) **S** £55-£65; **D** £95-£120 (incl. bkfst)*
Facilities Fishing New Year **Conf** Class 20 Thtr 40 **Parking** 18
Notes LB Closed Xmas & Jan-Feb (ex New Year) RS Nov-Dec & Mar

Chef Kieron Kelly **Owner** Kieron & Ina Kelly **Restaurant Times** 7-9 Closed Xmas, Jan-Feb, Low season - booking only, L all week **Prices** Fixed D 3 course £35-£38, Service included **Wines** 50 bottles over £20, 15 bottles under £20, 8 by glass **Notes** Vegetarian available **Seats** 30 **Children** Portions

GOLSPIE	Map 5 NC80

Granite Villa Guest House

★★★★ GUEST ACCOMMODATION

☎ 01408 633146
Fountain Rd KW10 6TH
e-mail: info@granite-villa.co.uk
dir: Left from A9 (N'bound) onto Fountain Rd, immediately before pedestrian crossing lights

Originally built in 1892 for a wealthy local merchant, this traditional Victorian house has been sympathetically restored in recent years. Bedrooms are comfortable and all come with a range of thoughtful extras. Guests can relax in the large lounge, with its views over the landscaped garden where complimentary tea and coffee is often served. A warm welcome is assured in this charming period house.

Rooms 5 en suite (1 fmly) (1 GF) (2 smoking) S £40-£60; D £60-£70*
Facilities FTV tea/coffee Cen ht Wi-fi Golf Free access to leisure centre **Parking** 6 **Notes** ✆

GRANTOWN-ON-SPEY	Map 5 NJ02

Grant Arms Hotel

★★★ 78% HOTEL

☎ 01479 872526 📠 01479 873589
25-27 The Square PH26 3HF
e-mail: info@grantarmshotel.com
web: www.grantarmshotel.com
dir: Exit A9 N of Aviemore & follow A95

Conveniently located in the centre of the town this fine hotel has now been refurbished and upgraded to a high standard yet its still retains its traditional character. The spacious bedrooms are all stylishly presented and very well equipped. The Garden Restaurant is a popular venue for dinner, and lighter snacks can be enjoyed in the comfortable bar. Modern conference facilities are available and the hotel is very popular with birdwatchers and wildlife enthusiasts.

Rooms 48 (4 fmly) **S** £65-£90; **D** £130-£340 (incl. bkfst & dinner)*
Facilities STV ♫ Xmas New Year Wi-fi **Conf** Class 30 Board 16 Thtr 70 **Services** Lift **Notes** LB ⊗

Culdearn House

★★ 85% SMALL HOTEL

◉ Traditional Scottish

Quality local ingredients cooked with flair in homely small hotel

☎ 01479 872106 📠 01479 873641
Woodlands Ter PH26 3JU
e-mail: enquiries@culdearn.com
web: www.culdearn.com
dir: From SW into Grantown on A95, left at 30mph sign, hotel opposite

If you're in Speyside on a malt whisky trail, this immaculately maintained small hotel has an intriguing collection of over 50 single malts to tide you over between tastings. The granite Victorian villa was once the country home of the Earl of Seafield and has a handsome interior of spacious rooms with grand fireplaces, wood panelling, fancy ceilings and classic period features. Set in well-tended gardens on the edge of town, Culdearn House offers bedrooms with quality and comfort very much to the fore. Hospitality is excellent and every effort is made to make guests feel at home. Log fires and candlelight make the dining room a cosy, romantic spot for dinner. Simple food, cooked well using fresh local ingredients is the kitchen's philosophy, so expect superbly fresh fish and meat suppliers named on the menu for full traceability. Four-course dinner starts with, perhaps, a robust game terrine with red onion marmalade, and moves on via curried parsnip soup to tender collops of venison with chocolate and red wine gravy.

Rooms 7 (1 GF) **Parking** 12 **Notes** LB ⊗ No children 12yrs Closed Feb

Restaurant Times Closed L all week

An Cala

★★★★★ GUEST HOUSE

☎ 01479 873293 📠 01479 873610
Woodlands Ter PH26 3JU
e-mail: ancala@globalnet.co.uk
web: www.ancala.info
dir: From Aviemore on A95 left onto B9102 at rdbt outside Grantown. After 400yds, 1st left, An Cala opposite

An Cala is an impressive Victorian house set in attractive gardens within easy walking distance of the town centre. Bedrooms are individually furnished with period pieces, attractively decorated and thoughtfully equipped. There is a comfortable lounge complete with log-burning stove and an elegant dining room where first class breakfasts (and dinners by arrangement) are served.

Rooms 4 en suite (1 fmly); D £74-£80* **Facilities** FTV TVL tea/coffee Dinner available Cen ht Wi-fi **Parking** 7 **Notes** LB ⊗ No Children 3yrs Closed Xmas RS Nov-Mar Phone/e-mail bookings only

Loch Morlich with the Cairngorms behind, Cairngorms National Park

Holmhill House

★★★★ GUEST ACCOMMODATION

☎ 01479 873977
Woodside Av PH26 3JR
e-mail: enquiries@holmhillhouse.co.uk
web: www.holmhillhouse.co.uk
dir: S of town centre off A939 Spey Av

Built in 1895, and situated in a large well-tended garden within walking distance of the town centre, Holmhill House combines Victorian character with modern comforts. The attractive bedrooms are well equipped, and are en suite. There is a games room suitable for all ages, and a ramp and lift is available for easier access plus a specially equipped bathroom. Children are also well catered for with games, toys, crayons and videos available.

Rooms 4 en suite (2 fmly); D £70-£80 **Facilities** tea/coffee Cen ht Lift Wi-fi **Parking** 9 **Notes** ⊗ Closed Nov-Mar

Dunallan House

★★★★ ⚠ GUEST HOUSE

☎ 01479 872140
Woodside Ave PH26 3JN
e-mail: enquiries@dunallan.com
dir: From Granton Square lights, opposite Co-op, follow Forest Rd, right into Woodside Ave

Rooms 7 rms (6 en suite) (1 pri facs) (1 fmly) (1 GF) S £35-£50; D £60-£80* **Facilities** TVL tea/coffee Cen ht Wi-fi **Parking** 8 **Notes** ⊗

Rossmor Guest House

★★★★ ⚠ GUEST HOUSE

☎ 01479 872201
Woodlands Ter PH26 3JU
e-mail: rossmorgrantown@yahoo.com
web: www.rossmor.co.uk
dir: 500yds SW of village centre on B9102

Rooms 6 en suite (1 fmly); D £60-£76* **Facilities** tea/coffee Cen ht Wi-fi **Parking** 6 **Notes** ⊗ No Children 6yrs

Willowbank Guest House

★★★ ⚠ GUEST HOUSE

☎ 01479 872089
High St PH26 3EN
e-mail: info@wbgh.co.uk
dir: 200yds SW of village centre on B9102

Rooms 9 rms (6 en suite) (2 fmly) (2 GF) S £30-£45; D £52-£59* **Facilities** tea/coffee Dinner available Cen ht Wi-fi **Parking** 8

The Glass House Restaurant

◉◉ Modern British V 🍷

Modern British cooking in conservatory setting

☎ 01479 872980
Grant Rd PH26 3LD
e-mail: info@theglasshouse-grantown.co.uk
dir: Turn off High St between the bank and Co-op into Caravan Park Rd. First left onto Grant Rd, restaurant on left

Tucked away down a quiet back street, this unique glass conservatory restaurant occupies a lovely setting overlooking landscaped gardens. The conservatory is attached to the side of a stone cottage and the light and airy space has a relaxed, informal feel with solid oak tables and chairs, wooden floors and an open fire. The modern British food is dictated by the seasons and local produce, with 4 choices per course. Start with slow-braised gammon, potato and pea terrine wrapped in Parma ham with hawthorn jelly and warm toast and follow it with peppered Highland beef with sautéed king oyster mushrooms, pak choi and new potatoes in soy sauce.

Chef Stephen Robertson **Owner** Stephen and Karen Robertson **Times** 12-1.45/7-9 Closed 2 wks Nov, 1 wk Jan, 25-26 Dec, 1-2 Jan, Mon, L Tue, D Sun **Prices** Fixed L 2 course £15, Starter £3.95-£8.50, Main £17.95-£20.75, Dessert £6.50-£8.50, Service optional **Wines** 14 bottles over £20, 15 bottles under £20, 5 by glass **Notes** Sunday L, Vegetarian menu **Seats** 30 **Children** Portions **Parking** 10

Glengarry Castle

★★★ 82% COUNTRY HOUSE HOTEL

◉ Scottish International

Country-house hotel with traditional cooking in a majestic setting

☎ 01809 501254 📠 01809 501207
PH35 4HW
e-mail: castle@glengarry.net
web: www.glengarry.net
dir: on A82 beside Loch Oich, 0.5m from A82/A87 junct

At the heart of the Great Glen in the Highlands, by the side of one of a chain of beautiful lochs, stands the ruined castle, erstwhile family seat of the MacDonell clan. This charming country-house hotel is is mid-Victorian, but that hardly matters. Just get a load of those views. The spacious day rooms include comfortable sitting rooms with lots to read and board games to play, and the smart bedrooms vary in size and style and all boast magnificent loch or woodland views. Amid the grandeur, the friendly smiles of staff come as something of a relief, and the cooking is as proudly Scottish as the setting. Start with a richly textured Highland game terrine with port sauce, pause for a soup (perhaps green bean and almond), and then prepare for the main business. Corn-fed chicken suprême with brandy peppercorn sauce is packed with flavour.

Rooms 26 (2 fmly) **S** £62-£72; **D** £88-£168 (incl. bkfst) **Facilities** FTV 🎣 Fishing Wi-fi **Parking** 32 **Notes** Closed mid Nov-mid Mar

Chef John McDonald **Owner** Mr & Mrs MacCallum **Restaurant Times** 12-1.45/7-8.30 Closed mid Nov to mid Mar, L Mon-Sun **Prices** Food prices not confirmed for 2010. Please telephone for details. **Wines** 32 bottles over £20, 20 bottles under £20, 9 by glass **Notes** Vegetarian available **Seats** 40 **Children** Portions, Menu

The Invergarry Inn

★★★★ 🅰 INN

☎ 01809 501206 📠 01809 501400
PH35 4HJ
e-mail: info@invergarryhotel.co.uk
web: www.invergarryhotel.co.uk
dir: At junct of A82 & A87

Rooms 11 en suite (1 fmly) S £55-£70; D £75-£110 **Facilities** STV tea/coffee Dinner available Direct Dial Cen ht Licensed **Parking** 50 **Notes** I B ⊗

Forest Lodge Guest House

★★★ 🅰 GUEST HOUSE

☎ 01809 501219 & 07790 907477
South Laggan PH34 4EA
e-mail: info@flgh.co.uk
web: www.flgh.co.uk
dir: 2.5m S of Invergarry. Off A82 in South Laggan

Rooms 8 rms (7 en suite) (1 pri facs) (3 fmly) (4 GF) S £35.50-£38.50; D £55-£58* **Facilities** TVL tea/coffee Dinner available Cen ht Wi-fi **Parking** 10 **Notes** LB Closed 20 Dec-7 Jan

Kincraig House

★★★★ 78% COUNTRY HOUSE HOTEL

⦿ Modern Scottish

Fine dining in a lovingly restored period house

☎ 01349 852587 📠 01349 852193
IV18 0LF
e-mail: info@kincraig-house-hotel.co.uk
web: www.kincraig-house-hotel.co.uk
dir: off A9 past Alness towards Tain. Hotel on left 0.25m past Rosskeen Church

Set in its own landscaped grounds with glorious views over the Cromarty Firth and Black Isle, this charming country-house hotel was once the seat of the MacKenzie clan. Smart well-equipped bedrooms and inviting public areas retain the original features of the house, and the friendly service and commitment to guest care will leave a lasting impression. The fine dining restaurant brims with character, featuring a lovely stone fireplace, deep red walls, immaculately dressed linen-clothed tables and superb views. Modern Scottish cooking is accurate and honest with good use of quality local produce evident in such dishes as steamed mussels and surf clams in a spicy tomato and chorizo sauce, Black Isle lamb on Puy lentils with rosemary jus, and chocolate mocha cups with Chantilly cream. Informal meals are served in the bar.

Rooms 15 (1 fmly) (1 GF) **Facilities** STV Xmas Wi-fi **Conf** Class 30 Board 24 Thtr 50 **Parking** 30 **Notes** LB Civ Wed 70

Chef Mikael Helies **Owner** Kevin Wickman **Restaurant Times** 12.30-2/6.45-9 **Prices** Fixed D 3 course £29.50, Service optional **Wines** 29 bottles over £20, 23 bottles under £20, 4 by glass **Notes** Sunday L, Dress restrictions, Smart casual **Seats** 30, Pr/dining room 40 **Children** Portions, Menu **Parking** 40

The Old Forge

☎ 01687 462267 📠 01687 462267
PH41 4PL
e-mail: info@theoldforge.co.uk
dir: From Fort William take A830 (Road to the Isles) towards Mallaig. Take ferry from Mallaig to Inverie (boat details on website)

Britain's most remote mainland pub, The Old Forge is accessible only by boat, and stands literally between heaven and hell (Loch Nevis is Gaelic for heaven and Loch Hourn is Gaelic for hell). It's popular with everyone from locals to hillwalkers, and is renowned for its impromptu ceilidhs. It is also the ideal place to sample local fish and seafood, and other specialities such as haunch of estate venison. There are nine boat moorings and a daily ferry from Mallaig.

Open all wk **Bar Meals** L served all wk 12-3 D served all wk 6-9.30 Av main course £10 food served all day **Restaurant** L served all wk 12-3 D served all wk 6-9.30 ⊕ FREE HOUSE ◖ 80 Shilling, Guinness, Red Cuillin, real ales. **Facilities** Children's menu Play area Family room Dogs allowed Garden Parking

Dunain Park

★★★★ 79% SMALL HOTEL

☎ 01463 230512 📠 01463 224532
IV3 8JN
e-mail: info@dunainparkhotel.co.uk
web: www.dunainparkhotel.co.uk
dir: On A82, 1m from Inverness town boundary

Built in the Georgian era, this fine house has undergone an extensive refurbishment and is perfectly situated within its own six acre private Highland estate. The hotel has fifteen luxurious bedrooms, four of which are in the garden suite cottages. The stylish restaurant serves the best of local produce and guests have a choice of cosy well-appointed lounges for after dinner drinks. The garden terrace is ideal for relaxing and has splendid views over the landscaped gardens towards Inverness.

Rooms 13 (2 annexe) (8 fmly) (3 GF) **Facilities** FTV Xmas New Year Wi-fi Child facilities **Conf** Class 30 Board 20 Thtr 50 Del from £165 to £185* **Parking** 50 **Notes** Civ Wed 120

Culloden House

★★★★ 78% HOTEL

◎◎ Modern Scottish

Serious Scottish cuisine in historic setting

☎ 01463 790461 📠 01463 792181
Culloden IV2 7BZ
e-mail: info@cullodenhouse.co.uk
web: www.cullodenhouse.co.uk
dir: From Inverness take A96, turn right for Culloden. After 1m after
2nd lights left at White Church

This grand Palladian mansion of brick and stone exudes a genuine
sense of occasion and history. It was, after all, where Bonnie Prince
Charlie spent the night before his hopes and ambitions were
definitively crushed at the battle of Culloden in 1745. Despite the
palatial grandeur of its crystal chandeliers and soaring ceilings,
Adam fireplaces and fancy plasterwork, amicable staff make
Culloden House an inviting place. Bedrooms come in a range of sizes
and styles, with a number situated in a separate house. Scottish
produce takes centre stage in four-course dinners amid the awe-
inspiring grandeur of the Adam dining room. Classic dishes strewn
with luxury produce kick off with lobster ravioli with truffle cream and
chervil oil; an intermediate course of chilled asparagus soup with
black truffle oil and parmesan crisp is slotted in before mains weigh
in with tournedos of Scottish beef fillet, with shin and barley
croquette and braising jus. Dessert ends with a thoroughly Scottish
Drambuie parfait, shortbread wafer and raspberry sorbet.

Rooms 28 (5 annexe) (1 fmly) **S** £85-£175; **D** £120-£375 (incl.
bkfst)* **Facilities** STV ☺ Putt green ⚑ Boules Badminton Golf
driving net Putting green ♫ New Year Wi-fi **Conf** Class 40 Board 30
Thtr 60 Del from £125 to £275* **Parking** 50 **Notes** LB No children
10yrs Closed 24-28 Dec Civ Wed 65

Chef Michael Simpson **Owner** Culloden House Ltd **Restaurant
Times** 12.30-2/7-9 Closed 25-26 Dec, **Prices** Fixed D 3 course £40,
Starter £7.50-£13.50, Main £17.50-£28.50, Dessert £7.80-£8.50,
Service optional **Wines** 76 bottles over £20, 8 by glass **Notes** Sunday
L, Vegetarian available, Dress restrictions, Smart casual **Seats** 50,
Pr/dining room 17 **Children** Portions

The New Drumossie

★★★★ 78% HOTEL

◎◎ Modern Scottish

Art deco country-house hotel producing high-quality food

☎ 01463 236451 & 0870 194 2110 📠 01463 712858
Old Perth Rd IV2 5BE
e-mail: stay@drumossiehotel.co.uk
dir: From A9 follow signs for Culloden Battlefield, hotel on left after
1m

Set in nine acres of landscaped hillside grounds south of Inverness,
and overlooking the Moray Firth, this shipshape art deco building has
a classy country-house feel blending old-style clubby refinement with
modern design. Service is friendly and attentive and the bedrooms

spacious and well presented. A large function room is popular for
weddings, while the elegant Grill Room restaurant is as well turned
out as its dinner-suited maître d' and black-aproned staff, who serve
with an edge of formality that suits the setting. The kitchen has a
serious approach to its work, starting with meticulous sourcing of
Scottish materials and excellent attention to detail in its modern
Scottish repertoire. Orkney scallops with Arbroath smokie potato cake
is a fine way to begin, then perhaps free range chicken with sun-
blushed tomato and Stornoway black pudding or, from the grill, rib-
eye steak.

Rooms 44 (10 fmly) (6 GF) **Facilities** STV Fishing New Year Wi-fi
Conf Class 200 Board 40 Thtr 500 **Services** Lift **Parking** 200
Notes ⊗ Civ Wed 400

Chef Lynsey Horne **Owner** Ness Valley Leisure **Restaurant
Times** 12.30-2/7-9.30 **Prices** Food prices not confirmed for 2010.
Please telephone for details. **Wines** 10 by glass **Notes** Vegetarian
available, Air con **Seats** 90, Pr/dining room 500 **Children** Portions,
Menu

Glenmoriston Town House Hotel

★★★★ 74% HOTEL

Abstract

◎◎◎ Modern French V ☺

Refined French dining in elegant townhouse hotel

☎ 01463 223777 📠 01463 712378
20 Ness Bank IV2 4SF
e-mail: reception@glenmoristontownhouse.com
web: www.glenmoristontownhouse.com
dir: On riverside opposite theatre

Bold contemporary designs blend seamlessly with the classical
architecture of this stylish hotel, situated on the banks of the River
Ness. Delightful day rooms include the Contrast Brasserie (see
following entry). The smart, modern bedrooms have many facilities,
including free Wi-fi, DVD players and flat-screen TVs. Abstract
occupies the ground floor of the hotel and a slick piano bar with a
mind-bending array of malts sets the tone for the smooth
contemporary look of the dining room, where moody lighting falls on
textures of wood and leather amid a scene of chic minimal elegance.
The food is inventive stuff, driven by sharp classical technique; the
finest, freshest Scottish materials get cutting-edge modern French
treatment. Unusual flavour pairings are a hallmark of the kitchen's
creative flair, but there's nothing outlandish here - just clever, well-
balanced dishes. Served only at the chef's table, the eight-course
tasting menu delivers Black Isle roe deer, served as a spring roll of
shoulder and smoked fillet with butternut squash mousse and orange
caramel. The carte might start with seared squid and pig's head
terrine with parsley froth and smoked herring caviar, followed by
halibut cooked in olive oil with parsnip and vanilla purée and razor
clams. Desserts are complex collages such as a riff on coffee
comprising coffee bean bavarois, Kahlua jelly and cappuccino foam,
and black coffee ice cream. France is foremost on an impressive wine
list.

Rooms 30 (15 annexe) (1 fmly) (6 GF) **Facilities** STV ♫ Xmas New
Year Wi-fi **Conf** Class 10 Board 10 Thtr 15 **Parking** 40 **Notes** ⊗
Closed 26-28 Dec & 4-6 Jan Civ Wed 70

Chef Geoffrey Malmedy **Owner** Larsen & Ross South **Restaurant Times** 6-10 Closed 26-28 Dec, Sun-Mon, L all week **Prices** Tasting menu £50, Starter £10-£14.50, Main £16-£25, Dessert £8-£10, Service optional, Groups min 6 service 12.5% **Wines** 90% bottles over £20, 10% bottles under £20, 11 by glass **Notes** Tasting menu 8 course served at 6-seater chef's table, Vegetarian menu **Seats** 50, Pr/dining room 15 **Children** Portions, Menu

Contrast Brasserie

◉ Modern, traditional ✿

Stylish contemporary restaurant serving imaginative dishes along the River Ness

☎ 01463 223777
Glenmoriston Town House Hotel, 20 Ness Bank, IV2 4SF
web: www.contrastbrasserie.com

The second, more informal dining option at the smart Glenmoriston Town House Hotel, the Contrast Brasserie has a relaxed, chic atmosphere and a conservatory feel, with simply appointed tables. Great views over the River Ness – try and bag a window seat if you can! There is alfesco dining in the warmer months and the imaginative menu is supported by a serious wine list. Start, perhaps, with creamy smoked mushroom soup, and very tender braised lamb shank to follow, accompanied by crushed potato, aubergine and courgette in tomato jam and aioli. Finish with deliciously light and moist carrot cake with confit of carrot and hazelnut ice cream.

Chef Geoffrey Malmedy **Owner** Barry Larsen **Times** 12-2.30/5-10 **Prices** Starter £3-£12 Main £9-£27 Dessert £3-£5 Service charge optional **Wines** 40 bottles over £20, 5 bottles under £20, 8 by glass **Notes** Vegetarian available **Seats** 70 Pr/dining 20 **Children** Portions, Menu

Bunchrew House

★★★★ 74% COUNTRY HOUSE HOTEL

◉◉ Modern, Traditional

Scottish and European cooking in beautiful setting

☎ 01463 234917 📠 01463 710620
Bunchrew IV3 8TA
e-mail: welcome@bunchrew-inverness.co.uk
web: www.bunchrew-inverness.co.uk
dir: W on A862. Hotel 2m after canal on right

On the shores of the Beauly Firth, this imposing 17th-century Scottish baronial mansion sits in 20 acres of woodland and landscaped gardens. The carefully restored and upgraded house is steeped in history and has a timeless atmosphere, with a choice of comfortable lounges complete with real fires, and the individually styled bedrooms are spacious and tastefully furnished. Its wood-panelled restaurant has magnificent views over the water to the mountains beyond - book ahead for a window table and the chance to see a stunning summer sunset. The cooking is a fusion of Scottish and European styles, using the best the Highland larder can offer, distinguished by accomplished technique. Typical dishes may include pink breast of woodland pigeon, spiced couscous with a Madeira sauce to start, with prime roast fillet of finest Scottish beef, pomme fondant, asparagus, sweet potato ribbons and wild mushroom gratin to follow.

Rooms 16 (4 fmly) (1 GF) **S** £102-£176; **D** £147-£254 (incl. bkfst)*

Facilities FTV Fishing New Year Wi-fi **Conf** Class 30 Board 30 Thtr 80 Del from £99 to £149* **Parking** 40 **Notes** LB ⊗ Closed 24-27 Dec Civ Wed 92

Chef Walter Walker **Owner** Terry & Irina Mackay **Restaurant Times** 12-1.45/7-9 Closed 23-26 Dec, **Prices** Fixed L 2 course £25.50, Fixed D 2 course £41.50, Service optional **Wines** 4 by glass **Notes** Sunday L, Vegetarian available **Seats** 32, Pr/dining room 14 **Children** Portions, Menu

Kingsmills

★★★★ 74% HOTEL

☎ 01463 237166 & 257100 📠 01463 225208
Culcabock Rd IV2 3LP
e-mail: reservations@kingsmillshotel.com
web: www.kingsmillshotel.com
dir: From A9 S, exit Culduthel/Kingsmills 5th exit at rdbt, 0.5m, over mini-rdbt past golf club. Hotel on left after lights

This manor house hotel is located just a short drive from the city, and is set in four acres of landscaped grounds. There is a range of spacious, well-equipped modern bedrooms; the rooms in newer wing are especially impressive. There is a choice of restaurants, a comfortable lounge, a leisure club and conference facilities.

Rooms 77 (5 fmly) (34 GF) (6 smoking) **S** £93-£176; **D** £93-£206 (incl. bkfst)* **Facilities** Spa STV ⊙ supervised Putt green Gym Hairdresser Sauna Steam room Pitch & putt 🎵 Xmas New Year Wi-fi **Conf** Class 34 Board 40 Thtr 100 **Services** Lift **Parking** 102 **Notes** LB Civ Wed 80

Columba

★★★★ 73% HOTEL

☎ 01463 231391 📠 01463 715526
Ness Walk IV3 5NF
e-mail: reservations.columba@ohiml.com
web: www.oxfordhotelsandinns.com
dir: From A9/A96 follow signs to town centre, past Eastgate shopping centre onto Academy St, at bottom take left to Bank St, right over bridge, hotel 1st left

Originally built in 1881 and with many original features retained, the Columba Hotel lies in the heart of Inverness overlooking the fast flowing River Ness. The bedrooms are very stylish, and public areas include a first floor restaurant and lounge. A second dining option is the ever popular McNabs bar bistro, which is ideal for less formal meals.

Rooms 76 (4 fmly) **Facilities** FTV Complimentary use of leisure facilities 0.5m away 🎵 Xmas New Year Wi-fi **Conf** Class 50 Board 60 Thtr 200 **Services** Lift **Notes** ⊗ Civ Wed 80

Royal Highland

★★★ 77% HOTEL

☎ 01463 231926 & 251451 📄 01463 710705
Station Square, Academy St IV1 1LG
e-mail: info@royalhighlandhotel.co.uk
web: www.royalhighlandhotel.co.uk
dir: From A9 into town centre. Hotel next to rail station & Eastgate Retail Centre

Built in 1858 adjacent to the railway station, this hotel has the typically grand foyer of the Victorian era with comfortable seating. The contemporary ASH Brasserie and bar offers a refreshing style for both eating and drinking throughout the day. The generally spacious bedrooms are comfortably equipped especially for the business traveller.

Rooms 85 (12 fmly) (2 GF) (25 smoking) **S** £60–£119; **D** £80–£159 (incl. bkfst) **Facilities** FTV Gym Xmas New Year Wi-fi **Conf** Class 80 Board 80 Thtr 200 Del from £88.50 to £115 **Services** Lift **Parking** 8 **Notes** LB Civ Wed 200

Best Western Palace Hotel & Spa

★★★ 75% HOTEL

☎ 01463 223243 📄 01463 236865
8 Ness Walk IV3 5NG
e-mail: palace@miltonhotels.com
web: www.bw-invernesspalace.co.uk
dir: A82 Glenurquhart Rd onto Ness Walk. Hotel 300yds on right opposite Inverness Castle

Set on the north side of the River Ness close to the Eden Court theatre and a short walk from the town, this hotel now has a contemporary look. Bedrooms offer good levels of comfort and equipment, and a smart leisure centre attracts a mixed market.

Rooms 88 (48 annexe) (4 fmly) **Facilities** Spa FTV ⏰ supervised Gym Beautician Steam room Xmas New Year Wi-fi **Conf** Class 40 Board 30 Thtr 80 **Services** Lift **Parking** 38

Ramada Encore Inverness City Centre

★★★ 75% HOTEL

☎ 0844 801 3700 📄 0844 801 3701
63 Academy St IV1 1LU
e-mail: reservations@encoreinverness.co.uk

The Ramada Encore is ideally located in the City Centre and is close to the main shopping district, railway station and the tourist attractions of Inverness. The contemporary bedrooms have a bright stylish design and all rooms are equipped with Wi-fi along with an extensive choice of TV channels and movies. Public areas include a modern restaurant and a light-filled lounge area with its comfortable seating. There is a choice of ground floor business suites and the hotel is very popular with corporate and leisure guests.

Rooms 90 (20 fmly) **S** £45–£119; **D** £45–£119* **Facilities** STV FTV Xmas New Year Wi-fi **Conf** Class 20 Board 20 Thtr 34 Del from £99 to £119* **Services** Lift **Notes** LB ⊗

Thistle Inverness

★★★ 75% HOTEL

☎ 0871 376 9023 📄 0871 376 9123
Millburn Rd IV2 3TR
e-mail: inverness@thistle.co.uk
web: www.thistlehotels.com/inverness
dir: From A9 take Raigmore Interchange exit (towards Aberdeen) then 3rd left towards centre. Hotel opposite

Well located within easy distance of the town centre. This well presented hotel offers modern bedrooms including three suites. There is a well equipped leisure centre along with an informal brasserie and open-plan bar and lounge. Ample parking is an added benefit.

Rooms 118 **Facilities** ⏰ supervised Gym Sauna Steam room Xmas New Year Wi-fi **Conf** Class 70 Board 50 Thtr 120 Del from £125 to £150* **Services** Lift **Parking** 80 **Notes** ⊗ Civ Wed 120

Glen Mhor

★★★ 70% HOTEL

☎ 01463 234308 📄 01463 218018
8-15 Ness Bank IV2 4SG
e-mail: enquires@glen-mhor.com
web: www.glen-mhor.com
dir: On east bank of River Ness, below Inverness Castle

This hotel is a short walk from the city centre and overlooks the beautiful River Ness. This fine old property offers bedrooms and several suites that are up-to-the-minute in design. The public areas include a cosy bar and a comfortable lounge with its log fire.

Rooms 52 (34 annexe) (1 fmly) (12 GF) **S** £45–£69; **D** £60–£160 (incl. bkfst)* **Facilities** FTV ♫ Xmas New Year Wi-fi **Conf** Class 30 Board 35 Thtr 60 Del from £85 to £129* **Parking** 26 **Notes** LB ⊗

Express by Holiday Inn Inverness

BUDGET HOTEL

☎ 01463 732700 📠 01463 732732
Stoneyfield IV2 7PA
e-mail: inverness@expressholidayinn.co.uk
web: www.hiexpress.com/inverness
dir: From A9 follow A96 & Inverness Airport signs, hotel on right

A modern hotel ideal for families and business travellers. Fresh and uncomplicated, the spacious rooms include Sky TV, power shower and tea and coffee-making facilities. Continental buffet breakfast is included in the room rate; other meals may be taken at the nearby family pub or restaurant. See also Hotel Groups pages on theAA.com.

Rooms 94 (43 fmly) (24 GF) (10 smoking) **S** £39-£140; **D** £39-£140 (incl. bkfst)* **Conf** Class 20 Board 15 Thtr 35 Del from £95 to £175*

Travelodge Inverness

BUDGET HOTEL

☎ 0871 984 6148 📠 01463 718152
Stoneyfield, A96 Inverness Rd IV2 7PA
web: www.travelodge.co.uk
dir: At junct of A9 & A96

Travelodge offers good quality, good value, modern accommodation. Ideal for families, the spacious en suite bedrooms include remote-control TV, tea and coffee-making facilities and comfortable beds. Meals can be taken at the nearby family restaurant. See also the Hotel Groups pages on theAA.com.

Rooms 58 **S** fr £29; **D** fr £29

Travelodge Inverness Fairways

BUDGET HOTEL

☎ 0871 984 6285 📠 01463 250703
Castle Heather IV2 6AA
web: www.travelodge.co.uk
dir: From A9 follow Raigmore Hospital signs. At 1st rdbt take 3rd exit, B8082 towards Hilton/Culduthel. 1.5m, 2nd exit at rdbt, 3rd exit at next rdbt .At 4th rdbt take 1st exit. Lodge on left

Rooms 80 **S** fr £29; **D** fr £29

Daviot Lodge

★★★★★ 🏠 GUEST ACCOMMODATION

☎ 01463 772215 📠 01463 772099
Daviot Mains IV2 5ER
e-mail: margaret.hutcheson@btopenworld.com
dir: Off A9 5m S of Inverness onto B851 signed Croy. 1m on left

Standing in 80 acres of peaceful pasture land, this impressive establishment offers attractive, well-appointed and equipped bedrooms. The master bedroom is furnished with a four-poster bed. There is a tranquil lounge with deep sofas and a real fire, and a peaceful dining room where hearty breakfasts featuring the best of local produce are served. Full disabled access for wheelchairs.

Rooms 7 en suite (1 GF) S £46-£50; D £78-£100* **Facilities** FTV TVL tea/coffee Direct Dial Cen ht Licensed Wi-fi **Parking** 10 **Notes** LB No Children 5yrs Closed 23-26 Dec

Trafford Bank

★★★★★ 🏠 GUEST HOUSE

☎ 01463 241414
96 Fairfield Rd IV3 5LL
e-mail: enquiries@invernesshotelaccommodation.co.uk
dir: Off A82 at Kenneth St, Fairfield Rd 2nd left, 600yds on right

This impressive Victorian house lies in a residential area close to the canal. Lorraine Freel has utilised her interior design skills to blend the best in contemporary styles with the house's period character and the results are simply stunning. Delightful public areas offer a choice of lounges, while breakfast is taken in a beautiful conservatory featuring eye-catching wrought-iron chairs. Each bedroom is unique in design and have TV/DVD/CDS, sherry, silent mini fridges and much more.

Rooms 5 en suite (2 fmly) S £60-£90; D £80-£120 **Facilities** STV FTV TVL tea/coffee Cen ht Wi-fi **Parking** 10 **Notes** LB ⊗

Avalon Guest House

★★★★ GUEST HOUSE

☎ 01463 239075 📠 01463 709827
79 Glenurquhart Rd IV3 5PB
e-mail: avalon@inverness-loch-ness.co.uk
web: www.inverness-loch-ness.co.uk
dir: Exit A9 at Longman rdbt, 1st exit onto A82, at Telford St rdbt, 2nd exit. Right at lights onto Tomnahurich St/Glenurquhart Rd

Avalon Guest House is just a short walk from the city centre, and five minutes drive from Loch Ness. Each bedroom has a flat-screen LCD

continued

INVERNESS CONTINUED

TV with Freeview (some with DVD), Wi-fi, fluffy white towels and complimentary toiletries; bathrobes and slippers are available on request as well as various other useful items. A delicious breakfast, freshly cooked from a varied menu, is served in the dining room; most dietary requirements can be catered for. Public areas include a guest lounge; and the owners have a range of maps, guidebooks and brochures that guests can refer to.

Rooms 6 rms (5 en suite) (1 pri facs) (4 GF) S £50-£60; D £60-£85 **Facilities** FTV TVL tea/coffee Cen ht Wi-fi **Parking** 12 **Notes** LB ⊗ No Children 12yrs

Ballifeary Guest House

★★★★ ≘ GUEST HOUSE

☎ 01463 235572 ▤ 01463 717583
10 Ballifeary Rd IV3 5PJ
e-mail: william.gilbert@btconnect.com
web: www.ballifearyguesthouse.co.uk
dir: Off A82, 0.5m from town centre, turn left onto Bishops Rd & sharp right onto Ballifeary Rd

This charming detached house has a peaceful residential location within easy walking distance of the town centre and Eden Court Theatre. The attractive bedrooms are carefully appointed and well equipped. There is an elegant ground-floor drawing room and a comfortable dining room, where delicious breakfasts, featuring the best of local produce, are served at individual tables.

Rooms 6 en suite (1 GF) S £40-£65; D £60-£80 **Facilities** FTV tea/coffee Cen ht Wi-fi **Parking** 6 **Notes** LB ⊗ No Children 15yrs Closed 24-28 Dec

The Ghillies Lodge

★★★★ ≘ BED AND BREAKFAST

☎ 01463 232137 ▤ 01463 713744
16 Island Bank Rd IV2 4QS
e-mail: info@ghillieslodge.com
dir: 1m SW from town centre on B862, pink house facing river

Situated on the banks of the River Ness not far from the city centre, Ghillies Lodge offers comfortable accommodation in a relaxed, peaceful environment. The attractive bedrooms, one of which is on the ground floor, are all en suite, and are individually styled and well equipped. There is a comfortable lounge-dining room, and a conservatory that overlooks the river.

Rooms 3 en suite (1 GF) **Facilities** STV TVL tea/coffee Cen ht Wi-fi **Parking** 4

Moyness House

★★★★ GUEST ACCOMMODATION

☎ 01463 233836 ▤ 01463 233836
6 Bruce Gardens IV3 5EN
e-mail: stay@moyness.co.uk
web: www.moyness.co.uk
dir: Off A82 (Fort William road), almost opp Highland Regional Council headquarters

Situated in a quiet residential area just a short distance from the city centre, this elegant Victorian villa dates from 1880 and offers beautifully decorated, comfortable bedrooms and well-appointed bathrooms. There is an attractive sitting room and an inviting dining room, where traditional Scottish breakfasts are served. Guests are welcome to use the secluded and well-maintained back garden.

Rooms 6 en suite (1 fmly) (2 GF) **Facilities** tea/coffee Cen ht Wi-fi **Parking** 10

The Alexander

★★★★ ≘ GUEST HOUSE

☎ 01463 231151 ▤ 01463 232220
16 Ness Bank IV2 4SF
e-mail: info@thealexander.net
web: www.thealexander.net
dir: On E bank of river, opposite cathedral

Built in 1830 this impressive house has been extensively renovated by the current owners and many of the original Georgian features have been retained. Bedrooms are simply furnished and beds have luxurious mattresses dressed in fine Egyptian cotton. Public rooms include a charming lounge with views over the River Ness and the house is a short walk from the city centre.

Rooms 7 en suite 3 annexe en suite (1 GF) S £40-£55; D £70-£90* **Facilities** tea/coffee Cen ht Wi-fi **Parking** 8 **Notes** ⊗

Lyndon Guest House

★★★★ GUEST HOUSE

☎ 01463 232551 ▤ 01463 225827
50 Telford St IV3 5LE
e-mail: lyndonguesthouse@btopenworld.com
web: www.lyndon-guest-house.co.uk
dir: From A9 onto A82 over Friars Bridge, right at rdbt onto Telford St. House on right

A warm Highland welcome awaits at this family-run accommodation close to the centre of Inverness. All rooms are en suite and are equipped with plenty of useful facilities including full internet access. Gaelic Spoken.

Rooms 6 en suite (4 fmly) (2 GF) S £25-£38; D £50-£70* **Facilities** STV FTV TVL tea/coffee Cen ht Wi-fi **Parking** 6 **Notes** ⊗ Closed 20 Dec-5 Jan

Westbourne

★★★★ GUEST ACCOMMODATION

☎ 01463 220700 ▤ 01463 220700
50 Huntly St IV3 5HS
e-mail: richard@westbourne.org.uk
dir: A9 onto A82 at football stadium over 3 rdbts, at 4th rdbt 1st left onto Wells St & Huntly St

The immaculately maintained Westbourne looks across the River Ness to the city centre. This friendly, family-run house has bright modern bedrooms of varying size, all attractively furnished in pine and very well equipped. The ground-floor bedroom has been specially furnished for easier access. A relaxing lounge with internet access, books, games and puzzles is available.

Rooms 9 en suite (2 fmly) S £45-£50; D £70-£80 **Facilities** tea/coffee Cen ht Wi-fi **Parking** 6 **Notes** LB Closed Xmas & New Year

Sunnyholm

★★★ GUEST ACCOMMODATION

☎ 01463 231336 ▤ 01463 715788
12 Mayfield Rd IV2 4AE
e-mail: sunnyholm@aol.com
web: www.invernessguesthouse.com
dir: 500yds SE of town centre. Off B861 Culduthel Rd onto Mayfield Rd

Situated in a peaceful residential area within easy walking distance of the city centre, Sunnyholm offers comfortably proportioned and well-equipped bedrooms. A spacious conservatory-lounge overlooks the rear garden, and there is a another lounge next to the bright, airy dining room.

Rooms 4 en suite (4 GF) S £40-£42; D £58-£60* **Facilities** tea/coffee Cen ht **Parking** 6 **Notes** ⊗ No Children 3yrs ⊚

Acorn House

★★★ GUEST HOUSE

☎ 01463 717021 & 240000 ▤ 01463 714236
2A Bruce Gardens IV3 5EN
e-mail: enquiries@acorn-house.freeserve.co.uk
web: www.acorn-house.freeserve.co.uk
dir: From town centre onto A82, on W side of river, right onto Bruce Gardens

This is an attractive detached house that is just a five-minute walk from the town centre. Bedrooms are smartly presented and well equipped. Breakfast and dinner are served at individual tables in the spacious dining room and can be followed by coffee served in the comfortable lounge.

Rooms 6 en suite (2 fmly) S £49.95; D £70-£79.90* **Facilities** STV TVL tea/coffee Cen ht Wi-fi Sauna Hot tub **Parking** 7 **Notes** LB Closed 25-26 Dec

Antfield House

★★★ GUEST ACCOMMODATION

☎ 07921 650444 ▤ 01463 751323
Scaniport IV2 6DN
e-mail: antfieldhouse@live.co.uk

Antfield House enjoys an idyllic location situated among mature woodland in a quiet rural retreat. The attractive bedrooms are individually styled and all rooms have views over the countryside. The house is warm and welcoming and hearty breakfasts are served in the stylish breakfast room were a real fire is a feature in the colder months. Wi-fi is available and packed lunches can be provided. The house is close to the pretty village of Dores, which provides a dramatically picturesque gateway to South Loch Ness and the Great Glen.

Rooms 4 en suite

Fraser House

★★★ GUEST ACCOMMODATION

☎ 01463 716488 ▤ 01463 716488
49 Huntly St IV3 5HS
e-mail: fraserlea@btopenworld.com
dir: A82 W over bridge, left onto Huntly St, house 100yds

Situated on the west bank of the River Ness, Fraser House has a commanding position overlooking the city, and is within easy walking distance of the central amenities. Bedrooms, all en suite, vary in size and are comfortably furnished and well equipped. The ground-floor dining room is the setting for freshly cooked Scottish breakfasts.

Rooms 5 en suite (2 fmly) S £25-£35; D £50-£60* **Facilities** tea/coffee Cen ht **Notes** ⊚

Royston Guest House

★★★ 🄰 GUEST HOUSE

☎ 01463 231243 ▤ 01463 710434
16 Mill Burn Rd IV2 3PS
e-mail: roystonguesthouse@btinternet.com

Rooms 8 en suite (2 fmly) (1 GF) S £45-£50; D £70-£80* **Facilities** FTV TVL tea/coffee Cen ht Wi-fi **Parking** 16 **Notes** LB

St Ann's House

[U]

☎ 01463 236157 📄 01463 236157
37 Harrowden Rd IV3 5QN
e-mail: stannshous@aol.com
dir: Off rdbt junct A82 & A862 on W side of bridge

Currently the rating for this establishment is not confirmed. This may be due to a change of ownership or because it has only recently joined the AA rating scheme. For up-to-date information please see the AA website: the AA.com.

Rooms 6 rms (5 en suite) (1 pri facs) (1 fmly) (1 GF) **Facilities** TVL tea/coffee Cen ht Licensed **Parking** 4 **Notes** ⊗ ⊜

Riverhouse

⊛ British

Informal dining on banks of the River Ness

☎ 01463 222033
1 Greig St IV3 5PT
e-mail: riverhouse.restaurant@unicombox.co.uk
dir: On corner of Huntly St & Greig St

Close to the city centre and the main shopping district, this intimate bistro-style restaurant occupies a lovely spot on the banks of the River Ness. The wood-panelled interior has an intimate atmosphere, and from here you can watch the chefs at work in the open kitchen. Classic dishes are simply prepared using quality produce. A starter of Orkney crab cakes with watercress salad and a lemon, dill and natural yogurt dressing might be followed by pan-seared fillet of line caught sea bass with potato, garlic and saffron broth. Finish with a classic bread-and-butter pudding.

Times 12-2.15/5.30-10 Closed Mon, L Sun

Rocpool

⊛⊛ Modern European

Sleek design and eclectic, stylish cooking

☎ 01463 717274
1 Ness Walk IV3 5NE
e-mail: info@rocpoolrestaurant.com
web: www.rocpoolrestaurant.com
dir: Please telephone for details

Since it opened in 2002, Rocpool has brought stylish modern eating to the tranquil Highland city of Inverness. Sitting on a corner site on the west bank of the Ness, the restaurant boasts sleek, smart décor and the kind of buzz that draws in an appreciative, quality-conscious crowd. Modern European cooking blends influences from all over, perhaps serving emperor prawns and calamari with pak choi, chorizo and chilli jam, or scallops with duck confit and pineapple carpaccio, to start. Presentations aren't always so involved - a main course of simply grilled turbot is a delight - but when they are, they nonetheless work well. Treat yourself at dessert stage to something like the sensuous dark chocolate tart with prune and Armagnac sorbet.

Chef Steven Devlin **Owner** Mr Devlin **Times** 12-2.30/5.45-10 Closed 25-26 Dec, 1-2 Jan, Sun Oct-Mar, L Sun Apr-Sep **Prices** Fixed L 2 course fr £10.95, Starter £3.95-£8.95, Main £8.95-£19.95, Dessert £4.95-£5.95, Service optional **Wines** 25 bottles over £20, 17 bottles under £20, 11 by glass **Notes** Early D 5.45-6.45pm 2 course £12.95, Vegetarian available, Air con **Seats** 55 **Children** Portions **Parking** On street

The Cross at Kingussie

★★★★★ ⓘ RESTAURANT WITH ROOMS

⊛⊛⊛ Modern Scottish ♦NOTABLE WINE LIST ✍

Top-notch restaurant with rooms in an idyllic setting

☎ 01540 661166 📄 01540 661080
Tweed Mill Brae, Ardbroilach Rd PH21 1LB
e-mail: relax@thecross.co.uk
dir: From lights in Kingussie centre along Ardbroilach Rd, 300yds left onto Tweed Mill Brae

The Cross at Kingussie was once a textile mill, but there's nothing tweedy about David and Katie Young's classy restaurant with rooms. Four idyllic acres of grounds and woodland are home to red squirrels, abundant birds and wild flowers, and the Gynack Burn bubbles by an alfresco terrace that is the perfect place to de-stress with a glass of bubbly before dinner. It is hard to fault the Cross: the stone building has been beautifully restored and manages to be tasteful, relaxed and utterly without pretension. Bedrooms are spacious and airy, and little touches such as fluffy towels and hand-made toiletries providing extra luxury. Rough stone walls and heavy beams blend seamlessly with modern artworks and natural wood tables with quality glassware in the spacious dining room. The food is both fabulous and unfussy in keeping with its surroundings. Wild mushrooms are foraged locally and Scotland's finest materials are showcased in compact daily-changing menus of modern Scottish dishes. A terrine of organic Highland chicken with prosciutto and fig chutney shows the kitchen's well-balanced, uncluttered approach to flavour combinations. Main courses might offer a baked whole Scrabster lemon sole with wild mushrooms, marsh samphire, spring truffle and purple eye potato cake. Dark chocolate and pear tart with liquorice ice cream makes an exemplary finale. The wine list balances serious quality with fair pricing, and the service and hospitality are a template for how things should be done. The Cross is the AA Wine Award winner for Scotland 2009-2010.

Rooms 8 en suite (1 fmly) S £130-£195; D £180-£260* (incl.dinner) **Facilities** Dinner available Direct Dial Cen ht Wi-fi Petanque **Conf** Max 20 Thtr 20 Class 20 Board 20 **Parking** 12 **Notes** LB ⊗ No Children 8yrs Closed Xmas & Jan (ex New Year) RS Sun & Mon Accommodation/dinner not available No coaches

Chef Becca Henderson, David Young **Owner** David & Katie Young **Restaurant Times** 7-8.30 Closed Xmas & Jan (excl New Year), Sun-Mon, L all week **Prices** Fixed D 4 course £50-£55, Service included, Groups min 6 service 10% **Wines** 200 bottles over £20, 20 bottles under £20, 4 by glass **Notes** Vegetarian available **Seats** 20

Allt Gynack Guest House

★★★ 🅰 GUEST HOUSE

☎ 01540 661081
Gynack Villa, 1 High St PH21 1HS
e-mail: alltgynack@tiscali.co.uk
web: www.alltgynack.com
dir: A9 onto A86 through Newtonmore, 2m to Kingussie, on left after bridge

Rooms 5 rms (3 en suite) (1 fmly) S £27; D £50-£54* **Facilities** tea/coffee Cen ht Wi-fi Golf 18 **Parking** 5 **Notes** LB

KYLE OF LOCHALSH	Map 4 NG72

The Waterside Seafood Restaurant

🏵 Modern, Traditional Seafood 🍽

Quirky setting for fresh seafood and stunning views

☎ 01599 534813 & 577230
Railway Station Buildings, Station Rd IV40 8AE
e-mail: seafoodrestaurant@btinternet.com
dir: Off A87

The view from your table is reason enough to visit the MacRae family's restaurant at the end of the pier. Housed in a former railway building, it looks out towards the Skye Bridge in one direction and up Loch Duich in the other. The interior is simply furnished and the menu follows the same, uncomplicated theme. It's all about the fruits of the local waters, cooked at their freshest and thus without the need for much in the way of embellishment. Kick off with a plate of Skye oysters or the baked crab, followed by Stromeferry queen scallops or Isle of Skye salmon fillet with a red pepper crust.

Chef Jann MacRae **Owner** Jann MacRae **Times** 11-3/5-9.30 Closed end Oct-beginning Mar, Sun (please phone to confirm opening hrs) **Prices** Food prices not confirmed for 2010. Please telephone for details. **Wines** 2 bottles over £20, 15 bottles under £20, 2 by glass **Notes** Vegetarian available **Seats** 35 **Children** Portions **Parking** 5

KYLESKU	Map 4 NC23

Kylesku Hotel

☎ 01971 502231 📠 01971 502313
IV27 4HW
e-mail: info@kyleskuhotel.co.uk
web: www.kyleskuhotel.co.uk
dir: A835, then A837 & A894 into Kylesku. Hotel at end of road at Old Ferry Pier

The Kylesku Hotel now finds itself at the centre of Scotland's first designated Global Geopark, a 2,000-square kilometre area of lochs, mountains and coastal scenery with an abundance of wildlife and a wide range of outdoor activities. On the shores of two sea lochs, Glendhu and Glencoul, it certainly is a delightful place with truly memorable views. A former coaching inn, the Kylesku dates from 1680; it stands by the former ferry slipway and the two expanses of water, which furnish the restaurant and bar with splendid vistas over to the mountains. The chef uses fresh local produce wherever possible, and with local fishing boats landing their catch regularly on the slipway beside the hotel, seafood is the mainstay – langoustines, spineys, lobster, crab, scallops, haddock and mussels don't travel far to appear on the carte. Salmon is hot- and cold-smoked on the premises, beef and lamb come from the Highlands, and wild venison is delivered in season. Bar meal alternatives to all that fish and seafood could be starters such as a ramekin of haggis topped with a whisky and onion sauce, or parfait of chicken liver with tomato and onion chutney. Non-fish main dishes are along the lines of grilled rib-eye steak with peppercorn sauce, or wild venison and root vegetable casserole with new potatoes. Puddings range from lime cheesecake to sticky toffee pudding. Dinner takes the form of a set menu at a fixed price for two or three courses. This enables the chef to use the day's fresh ingredients in dishes such as seared hand-dived scallops with garlic butter, and pan-fried fillets of Lochinver haddock with lemon butter. If a cheese platter takes your fancy, try the Isle of Mull cheddar, made by traditional methods from unpasteurised milk. To wash it all down, choose between Highland real ales, Skye Cuillin bottled beers, 40 wines and 50 malt whiskies.

Open all wk Closed: Nov-Feb 🍴 FREE HOUSE 🍺 Tennents Ember 80/-, Selection of Black Isle Brewery and Skye Cuillin bottled ales. **Facilities** Garden

---

LETTERFINLAY LODGE HOTEL	Map 4 NN29

Letterfinlay Lodge

★★★ 77% SMALL HOTEL

☎ 01397 712622 📠 01397 712687
PH34 4DZ
e-mail: info@letterfinlaylodgehotel.co.uk
web: www.letterfinlaylodgehotel.co.uk
dir: 7m N of Spean Bridge, on A82 beside Loch Lochy

This hotel sits on the banks of Loch Lochy and boasts breathtaking views over the Great Glen. Many of the bedrooms overlook the loch from where guests can watch the glorious sunsets or see the ospreys swoop over the water; two rooms feature splendid Victorian period bathrooms. Evening meals showcase the best of local produce including seafood caught locally. There are enjoyable walks along the loch.

Rooms 14 (1 annexe) (2 fmly) **S** £60-£80; **D** £65-£120 (incl. bkfst)* **Facilities** FTV Fishing Clay pigeon shooting Boat hire Speed boat trips Waterskiing Xmas New Year **Conf** Class 50 Board 50 Thtr 30 Del from £110 to £140* **Parking** 20 **Notes** LB Civ Wed 70

LOCHINVER   Map 4 NC02

Inver Lodge

★★★★ HOTEL

@@ Modern British

Relaxed, imaginative fine dining in wonderful location

☎ 01571 844496   📠 01571 844395
IV27 4LU
e-mail: stay@inverlodge.com
web: www.inverlodge.com
dir: A835 to Lochinver, through village, left after village hall, follow private road for 0.5m

Secreted away in a far corner of the Highlands, genuine hospitality is a real feature at this delightful, purpose-built hotel. Set high on the hillside above the village all the bedrooms and public rooms enjoy stunning views. There is a choice of lounges and bedrooms are spacious, stylish and come with an impressive range of accessories. (Please note: there is no night service between 11pm and 7am.) The restaurant has spectacular views over the small harbour and the ocean beyond, and, on a clear day, even the Western Isles can be seen through its big picture windows. The accomplished kitchen makes full use of the abundant local larder, including freshly landed fish, and, from the land, perhaps Highland lamb, maybe appearing on the daily-changing menu as a roast rump, served with horseradish mash, wild mushrooms and a port wine glaze. Sea bass might feature as the offering from the sea, perhaps pan-fried and teamed with courgette spaghetti and a shellfish bisque.

Rooms 20 (11 GF) **S** £110; **D** £200 (incl. bkfst) **Facilities** FTV Fishing Sauna Wi-fi **Conf** Board 20 Thtr 30 Del from £125 to £150*
Parking 30 **Notes** LB Closed Nov-Mar Civ Wed 50

Chef Peter Cullen **Owner** Robin Vestey **Restaurant Times** 7-9 Closed Nov-Mar, L Mon-Sun **Prices** Fixed D 2 course£30, Fixed D 4 course £50, Service included **Wines** 23 bottles over £20, 41 bottles under £20, 5 by glass **Notes** Vegetarian available, Dress restrictions, No jeans, shorts, tracksuit trousers **Seats** 50 **Children** Portions

LYBSTER   Map 5 ND23

Portland Arms

★★★★ 🍴 INN 🍷

☎ 01593 721721   📠 01593 721722
Main St KW3 6BS
e-mail: manager.portlandarms@ohiml.com
web: www.portlandarms.co.uk
dir: On A99, 4m N of Thurso junct

A former coaching inn, just half a mile from the North Sea coastline, the welcoming Portland Arms has evolved into a comfortable modern hotel, offering a range of stylish comfortable bedrooms (front facing rooms have wonderful sea views), as well as a very comfortable lounge where an open log fire burns brightly in the colder months. The bar and dining areas serve fresh local produce and extensive menus cater for all tastes, with everything from home-made soup with freshly baked baguette to flash-fried langoustine in garlic and brandy butter. Look out for delicious desserts and home baking with morning coffee and afternoon tea. Sunday lunch is a speciality. Take

time for a nostalgic walk around this historic fishing town and stay over in one of the bedrooms.

Rooms 22 en suite (4 fmly) (4 GF) S £50-£75; D £70-£120*
Facilities FTV tea/coffee Dinner available Direct Dial Cen ht Wi-fi
Conf Max 150 Thtr 150 Class 150 Board 50 **Parking** 22 **Notes** LB Civ Wed 100

Pub Open all day all wk 7am-11pm **Bar Meals** food served all day **Restaurant** food served all day ⊕ FREE HOUSE 🍺 McEwans 70/-, Guinness. 🍷 6 **Facilities** Children's menu

MALLAIG   Map 4 NM69

West Highland

★★ 72% HOTEL

☎ 01687 462210   📠 01687 462130
PH41 4QZ
e-mail: westhighland.hotel@virgin.net
dir: From Fort William take A830 (The Road to the Isles) to Mallaig. At rdbt before Mallaig ferry terminal turn right, then 1st right up hill (B8008)

Once the town's station hotel the original building was destroyed by fire and the current property was built on the same site in the early 20th century. Fine views over to Skye are a real feature of the public rooms which include a bright airy conservatory, whilst the attractive bedrooms are thoughtfully equipped and generally spacious.

Rooms 34 (6 fmly) **Facilities** FTV 🎵 Wi-fi **Conf** Class 80 Board 100 Thtr 100 **Parking** 40 **Notes** Closed 16 Oct-15 Mar RS 16 Mar-1 Apr

MUIR OF ORD   Map 5 NH55

Ord House

★★ 72% SMALL HOTEL

@ Traditional British, French

Country-house comforts and fresh local produce

☎ 01463 870492   📠 01463 870297
IV6 7UH
e-mail: admin@ord-house.co.uk
dir: Off A9 at Tore rdbt onto A832. 5m, through Muir of Ord. Left towards Ullapool (A832). Hotel 0.5m on left

The 17th-century seat of the Lairds of the Clan McKenzie has been well-established as a comfortable country-house hotel for 40 years, offering brightly furnished and well-proportioned accommodation. Comfortable day rooms reflect the character and charm of the house, with inviting lounges and a cosy snug bar. The estate stretches to 60 acres of gardens and woodlands - plenty of room to supply the kitchen with fresh vegetables, herbs and fruit. Husband-and-wife-team John and Eliza Allen have taken the traditional route with their elegant hotel, and the kitchen stays in step, with simple country-house classics prepared from fresh, local, seasonal produce. Pan-seared scallops with ginger, basil and lime or West Coast oysters are typical starters, with local salmon in whisky and mushroom sauce to follow. Comforting desserts include sticky gingerbread pudding with ginger wine and brandy sauce.

Rooms 12 (3 GF) **S** £55-£80; **D** £100-£140 (incl. bkfst)*

Facilities Putt green 🏌 Clay pigeon shooting Wi-fi **Parking** 30
Notes LB Closed Nov-Apr

Chef Eliza Allen **Owner** Eliza & John Allen **Restaurant Times** 7-9
Closed Nov-end Feb, **Prices** Fixed D 3 course £28, Starter £7-£12,
Main £15-£24, Dessert £4.50-£8, Service included **Wines** 14 bottles
over £20, 18 bottles under £20, 4 by glass **Notes** Vegetarian
available **Seats** 26 **Children** Portions

NAIRN	Map 5 NH85

Golf View Hotel & Leisure Club

★★★★ 74% HOTEL

◉ Modern V

Fine dining in hotel with sea views

☎ 01667 452301 📠 01667 455267
The Seafront IV12 4HD
e-mail: golfview@crerarhotels.com
dir: Off A96 into Seabank Rd, follow road to end, hotel on right

Located on the coast overlooking the Moray Firth, the Golf View will
not only satisfy lovers of the game (the championship golf course is
adjacent to the hotel); strolling along the sandy beaches and
enjoying the stunning views across to the Black Isle has universal
appeal. Bedrooms are all of a very high standard and the public
areas are charming. A well-equipped leisure complex and swimming
pool are also available. The hotel has plenty of period detail, as does
the comfortable restaurant, making a dellightful setting for some
serious fine dining. Attentive staff help set the formal tone. The
modern Scottish cooking is underpinned by traditional French
influences but local produce is the cornerstone of the kitchen; start
with pressed Roxburghshire rabbit terrine and beetroot chutney and
move on to roasted saddle of Highland venison with parsnip purée,
braised root vegetable hotpot and juniper sauce.

Rooms 42 (6 fmly) **S** £85-£120; **D** £120-£220 (incl. bkfst)*
Facilities FTV 🦊 supervised 🏊 Gym Xmas New Year Wi-fi
Conf Class 40 Board 40 Thtr 100 Del from £149 to £169*
Services Lift **Parking** 40 **Notes** LB Civ Wed 100

Chef Lee Pattie **Owner** Crerar Hotels **Restaurant Times** 6.45-9
Closed L Mon-Sat **Prices** Fixed D 3 course £29-£34.50, Service
optional **Wines** 22 bottles over £20, 23 bottles under £20, 8 by glass
Notes Sunday L, Vegetarian menu, Dress restrictions, Smart casual,
Air con **Seats** 50 **Children** Portions, Menu

Newton

★★★★ 74% HOTEL

◉ Traditional European

Enjoyable food in hotel with famous former guests

☎ 01667 453144 📠 01667 454026
Inverness Rd IV12 4RX
e-mail: reservations.newton@ohiml.com
web: www.oxfordhotelsandinns.com
dir: A96 from Inverness to Nairn. In Nairn, hotel signed on left

Once a house and farm, this former mansion house, set in 21 acres
of mature parkland, bordes Nairn's championship golf course. The
Newton Hotel dates in part from 1640 and past guests include Harold
Macmillan and Charlie Chaplin, who used to take over the entire
second floor with his family and staff for three-week holidays.
Bedrooms are of a high standard, and many of the front-facing
rooms having splendid sea views. Choose from the traditional
restaurant or the more contemporary bistro; the cooking style is
traditional, as reflected in starters like black pudding and haggis
croquettes or smoked haddock and potato soup, while main courses
feature a selection of steaks from the grill, plus something like pan-
fried venison and beef fillet on potato rösti with wild berry red wine
jus.

Rooms 56 (2 fmly) **Facilities** Xmas New Year Wi-fi **Conf** Class 220
Board 90 Thtr 400 **Services** Lift **Parking** 100 **Notes** LB Civ Wed 250

Restaurant Times 12-2.30/6-9

Boath House

★★★ HOTEL

◉◉◉◉ Modern French, Traditional Scottish

Stunning food and effortless service in small country-house hotel

☎ 01667 454896 📄 01667 455469
Auldearn IV12 5TE
e-mail: info@boath-house.com
web: www.boath-house.com
dir: 2m past Nairn on A96, E towards Forres, signed on main road

A crunchy gravel drive leads to one of Scotland's most special small hotels, a lovingly restored mansion in 20 acres of mature woodlands with an ornamental lake stocked with brown and rainbow trout - you can even have a mini safari in the grounds spotting badgers and roe deer. Hospitality is first class - the owners are passionate about what they do, and have an ability to establish a special relationship with their guests that is particularly memorable. The house itself is delightful, with inviting lounges and striking, comfortable bedrooms that include many fine antique pieces. There's a real sense of occasion when you dine here. The elegant lounges and dining room are full of colourful ceramics, sculpture and vibrant paintings - in fact Boath is designated an art gallery and showcases works by many contemporary Highland artists. In the stylish, candlelit dining room, comfy high-backed chairs look through expansive French windows over the gardens and lake - you may even see trout jumping as you settle in a the six-course dinner. After all, interior splendour aside, one of the main attractions here is Chef Charles Lockley's inspired cooking. 'Let the ingredients do the talking' is the kitchen's ethos, but top-level technical skills founded on classics, backed by lively imagination and a virtuoso grasp of what works with what, and why, doesn't go amiss either. Ingredients are sourced by from the finest Scottish producers, and the walled garden does its bit in contributing organic fruit, herbs, vegetables and honey from the hotel's own hives. Curt menu descriptions do little justice to what arrives on the plate. Cured scallops might turn up with truffles and salsify; pork belly is teamed with chorizo and apple, and John Dory is accompanied by rice, crab and crosne (Japanese artichoke). Scottish artisanal cheeses arrive the French way before pudding, which might be white chocolate and tonka mousse with madeleines. If you want to really go to town, stay over and pamper yourself with a spa treatment.

Rooms 8 (1 fmly) (1 GF) **S** £180-£250; **D** £220-£380 (incl. bkfst)*
Facilities Spa FTV Fishing ⏷ Gym Beauty salon Xmas New Year Wi-fi
Conf Board 10 **Parking** 20 **Notes** Civ Wed 30

Chef Charles Lockley **Owner** Mr & Mrs D Matheson **Restaurant Times** 12.30-1.45/7-7.30 Closed Xmas, L Mon-Wed **Prices** Fixed L 2 course £21, Service included **Wines** 153 bottles over £20, 5 bottles under £20, 7 by glass **Notes** Fixed D 6 course £65, Sunday L, Dress restrictions, Smart casual, no shorts/T-shirts/jeans **Seats** 28, Pr/dining room 8 **Children** Portions

Alton Burn Hotel

★★ 61% HOTEL

☎ 01667 452051 & 453325 📄 01667 456697
Alton Burn Rd IV12 5ND
e-mail: enquiries@altonburn.co.uk
dir: Follow signs from A96 at western boundary of Nairn

This long-established, family-run hotel is located on the western edge of town and enjoys delightful views over the Moray Firth and adjacent golf course. Bedrooms, originally furnished in the 1950s, have been thoughtfully preserved to provide a reminder of that era whilst spacious day rooms include a well-stocked bar, several comfortable lounges and a popular restaurant.

Rooms 23 (7 GF) **Facilities** ⤜ ♨ Putt green ⏷ Table tennis Pool table **Conf** Class 50 Board 40 Thtr 100 **Parking** 40 **Notes** Closed Nov-Mar

North End

★★★★ BED AND BREAKFAST

☎ 01667 456338
18 Waverley Rd IV12 4RQ
e-mail: reservations@northendnairn.co.uk
dir: On corner of A96 (Academy St) & Waverley Rd

Built in 1895, North End is a delightful Victorian villa that has been sympathetically restored in recent years. The spacious bedrooms are comfortable and well equipped. The cosy lounge has a wood-burning stove and the original features of the house are complemented by contemporary furnishings. The house is within easy walking distance of Nairn and is a 20-minute drive from Inverness.

Rooms 3 rms (2 en suite) (1 pri facs) **Facilities** TVL tea/coffee Cen ht **Parking** 4 **Notes** ⊗ ⊜

| NETHY BRIDGE | Map 5 NJ02 |

Nethybridge

★★★ 70% HOTEL

☎ 01479 821203 📄 01479 821686
PH25 3DP
e-mail: salesnethybridge@strathmorehotels.com
dir: A9 onto A95, then onto B970 to Nethy Bridge

This popular tourist and coaching hotel enjoys a central location amidst the majestic Cairngorm Mountains. Bedrooms are stylishly furnished in bold tartans whilst traditionally styled day rooms include two bars and a popular snooker room. Staff are friendly and keen to please.

Rooms 69 (3 fmly) (7 GF) **Facilities** Putt green Bowling green ♪ Xmas New Year **Conf** Thtr 100 **Services** Lift **Parking** 80 **Notes** LB

The Mountview Hotel

★★ 78% HOTEL

◉◉ Modern British 🖐

Highland retreat with scenery as appetising as the cooking

☎ 01479 821248 📠 01479 821515
Grantown Rd PH25 3EB
e-mail: info@mountviewhotel.co.uk
dir: From Aviemore follow signs through Boat of Garten to Nethy Bridge. On main road through village, hotel on right

Set amid the ravishing scenery of the Cairngorms, alongside a forest of Caledonian pines, a little to the south of the whisky town of Grantown-on-Spey, the aptly named Mountview makes the most of its location and stunning panoramic views from its elevated position. Specialising in guided holidays, it's a favoured base for birdwatching and for walking groups. Tthe interiors have bags of character - a cosy lounge has a real fire to ward off the Highland chill, and the dining room has quality table settings and a menu of fine contemporary Scottish cuisine. A twice-baked soufflé of Isle of Mull cheddar is garnished with spinach as a starter, and main-course rack of new season's lamb is pinkly roasted and bursting with flavour, served with duchess potatoes, baby carrots and garlic confit. Finish with textbook chocolate fondant, its molten centre deep and rich, alongside impressive vanilla ice cream.

Rooms 12 (1 GF) **S** £50-£85; **D** £90-£120 (incl. bkfst)* **Parking** 20 **Notes** ⊛

Chef Lee Beale **Owner** Kevin & Caryl Shaw **Restaurant Times** 12-2/6-11 Closed 25-26 Dec, Mon-Tue, L Wed-Sat **Prices** Starter £4.50-£7.50, Main £12.50-£21, Dessert £5.25-£7.50, Service optional **Wines** 4 bottles over £20, 14 bottles under £20, 4 by glass **Notes** Sunday L, Vegetarian available **Seats** 24 **Children** Portions, Menu

NEWTONMORE　　　　　　　　　**Map 5 NN79**

Ard-Na-Coille

★★★★★ 🛏 GUEST HOUSE

☎ 01540 673214 📠 01540 673214
Kingussie Rd PH20 1AY
e-mail: jacquie@ard-na-coille.co.uk
dir: Exit A9 at Newtonmore, opp Highland Folk Museum

This large period house, with landscaped grounds, is in a stunning location overlooking open fields. The spacious bedrooms are of a very high standard with a host of thoughtful extras. The public areas include a large lounge with open fires, and a light-filled dining room where delicious breakfasts are served.

Rooms 3 en suite **Facilities** STV FTV TVL tea/coffee Direct Dial Cen ht Licensed Wi-fi Golf 18 Snooker **Parking** 10 **Notes** ⊛ No Children

Crubenbeg House

★★★★ GUEST HOUSE

☎ 01540 673300
Falls of Truim PH20 1BE
e-mail: enquiries@crubenbeghouse.com
web: www.crubenbeghouse.com
dir: 4m S of Newtonmore. Off A9 for Crubenmore, over railway bridge & right, signed

Set in peaceful rural location, Crubenbeg House has stunning country views and is well located for touring the Highlands. The attractive bedrooms are individually styled and well equipped, while the ground-floor bedroom provides easier access. Guests can enjoy a dram in front of the fire in the inviting lounge, while breakfast features the best of local produce in the adjacent dining room.

Rooms 4 rms (3 en suite) (1 pri facs) (1 GF) S £30-£36; D £50-£80 **Facilities** STV tea/coffee Dinner available Cen ht Licensed Wi-fi **Parking** 10 **Notes** LB No Children

NORTH BALLACHULISH　　　　　　　**Map 4 NN06**

Loch Leven Hotel

☎ 01855 821236 📠 01855 821550
Old Ferry Rd PH33 6SA
e-mail: reception@lochlevenhotel.co.uk
dir: Off A82, N of Ballachulish Bridge

With its relaxed atmosphere, beautiful loch-side setting, and dramatic views, this privately owned hotel lies in the heart of Lochaber, 'The Outdoor Capital of the UK', and proves popular with walkers and climbers. It began life over 300 years ago, accommodating travellers using the Ballachulish Ferry. Food is available in the restaurant and the bar, both of which offer spectacular views over the fast-flowing narrows to the mountains. Home-cooked meals are built around local produce, especially fresh seafood, game and other traditional Scottish dishes.

Open 11-11 (Thu-Sat 11am-mdnt Sun 12.30-11) Closed: afternoons in winter **Bar Meals** L served all wk 12-3 D served all wk 6-9 Av main course £8.95 **Restaurant** L served all wk 12-3 D served all wk 6-9 Fixed menu price fr £12.95 Av 3 course à la carte fr £15 ⊕ FREE HOUSE ◀ John Smith's Extra Smooth, MacEwans 80%. **Facilities** Children's menu Play area Family room Dogs allowed Garden Parking

ONICH   Map 4 NN06

Onich

★★★ 79% HOTEL

⚫ Traditional Scottish

Fine Scottish food and stunning loch views

☎ 01855 821214   📄 01855 821484
PH33 6RY
e-mail: enquiries@onich-fortwilliam.co.uk
web: www.onich-fortwilliam.co.uk
dir: Beside A82, 2m N of Ballachulish Bridge

On the shores of Loch Linnhe, this friendly hotel offers wonderful views across its beautifully landscaped gardens to the loch and mountains beyond. Bedrooms, with pleasing colour schemes, are comfortably modern, and the cocktail bar, sun lounge and restaurant all enjoy panoramic views of the loch. The kitchen's style displays a lightness of touch, using local Scottish produce and herbs and salad from the hotel's own garden to good effect. West Coast seafood and Highland game regularly feature on the menu. Expect the likes of carpaccio of peppered Lochaber venison served on a bed of rocket leaves dressed with balsamic vinegar and crème fraîche, followed by poached smoked West Coast haddock fillet with chive mash, seasonal roasted vegetables and a tomato velouté.

Rooms 26 (6 fmly) **S** £49.50-£69.50; **D** £70-£199 (incl. bkfst) **Facilities** STV Games room ♬ Xmas New Year Wi-fi **Conf** Board 40 Thtr 150 Del from £110 to £189.50 **Parking** 50 **Notes** LB Civ Wed 120

Chef Graeme Kennedy **Owner** Mr S Leitch **Restaurant Times** 7-9 Closed Xmas, L all week **Prices** Fixed L 2 course £10.70-£17.50, Fixed D 3 course £25-£28, Starter £3.75-£6.95, Main £11.95-£17.95, Dessert £4.25-£6.95 **Notes** Sunday L, Vegetarian available **Seats** 50, Pr/dining room 120 **Children** Portions, Menu

PLOCKTON   Map 4 NG83

The Plockton

★★★ 75% SMALL HOTEL 🍷

☎ 01599 544274   📄 01599 544475
41 Harbour St IV52 8TN
e-mail: info@plocktonhotel.co.uk
dir: 6m from Kyle of Lochalsh. 6m from Balmacara

The Pearson family's uniquely converted inn stands on the shores of Loch Carron, with stunning views of the loch to the surrounding Applecross hills – it's a location to die for. It was built in 1827 and later became a ship's chandlery from which it was converted into a hotel in 1913 and has now been run by the Pearson family for 20 years, who are fully committed to caring for their guests with good old-fashioned Highland hospitality. Stylish bedrooms offer individual, pleasing decor and many have spacious balconies or panoramic views. The staff and owners provide a relaxed and informal style of attentive service. (In addition to the hotel a self-contained cottage is available for group bookings.) Menus are based on the very best of Highland produce, with seafood a major strength: locally caught langoustines and fresh fish landed at Gairloch and Kinlochbervie. This translates to smoked fish soup, roast monkfish wrapped in bacon, and traditional battered haddock and chips. Meat-eaters will not be disappointed with the Aberdeen Angus rib-eye steak platter served with a peppered whisky sauce. A fine range of malts is available to round off that perfect Highland day.

Rooms 15 (4 annexe) (1 fmly) (1 GF) **S** £55-£85; **D** £80-£120 (incl. bkfst) **Facilities** STV Pool table ♬ New Year Wi-fi **Notes** ⊗ Closed 25 Dec & 1 Jan

Open all day all wk 11am-mdnt (Sun 12.30pm-11pm) **Bar Meals** L served all wk 12-2.15 D served all wk 6-10 Av main course £9.75 **Restaurant** L served all wk 12-2.15 D served all wk 6-10 booking required Av 3 course à la carte fr £20 ⊕ FREE HOUSE ◀ Caledonian Deuchars IPA, Hebridean Gold - Isle of Skye Brewery, Harvieston Blonde Ale, Crags Ale. 🍷 6 **Facilities** Children's menu Family room Garden

Plockton Inn & Seafood Restaurant

☎ 01599 544222   📄 01599 544487
Innes St IV52 8TW
e-mail: info@plocktoninn.co.uk
dir: On A87 to Kyle of Lochalsh take turn at Balmacara. Plockton 7m N

Mary Gollan and her brother Kenny, the proprietors of this attractive stone-built free house, were born and bred in Plockton. Their great grandfather built this property as a manse, just 100 metres from the harbour in the fishing village where BBC Scotland's Hamish Macbeth series was filmed in the mid-1990s. Mary, Kenny and his partner, Susan Trowbridge, bought the inn over ten years ago, Mary and Susan doing the cooking, Kenny running the bar. The atmosphere is relaxed and friendly, with winter fires in both bars, and a selection of more than 50 malt whiskies. Taking pride of place on the regular and daily-changing specials menus in the dining room and the lounge bar are fresh West Coast fish and shellfish and West Highland beef, lamb and game. Starters include fish-based soup of the day; hot Plockton prawns (landed by the barman himself) with garlic butter; and roasted red pepper pâté. Haggis and clapshot is a particular speciality (including a vegetarian version), served with neeps, tatties and home-made pickled beetroot. Seafood main dishes take in creel-caught langoustines from the waters of Loch Carron, served cold with Marie Rose sauce; and hake fillet with pesto crust, as well as the famous seafood platter. The finest seafood is taken to the smokehouse on the premises and can later be enjoyed from the menu. Other dishes include braised lamb shank; venison in ale; chicken Caesar salad; and aubergine parmigiana. Among some truly mouth-watering desserts is lemon and ginger crunch pie, as well as a selection of Scottish cheeses served with Orkney oatcakes. The National Centre of Excellence in Traditional Music is based in Plockton, which is why the inn's public bar resonates with fantastic live sounds on Tuesdays and Thursdays.

Open all day all wk **Bar Meals** L served all wk 12-2.30 D served all wk 6-9 **Restaurant** D served all wk 6-9 booking required Av 3 course à la carte fr £18 ⊕ FREE HOUSE ◀ Greene King Abbot Ale, Fuller's London Pride, Isle Of Skye Blaven, Caledonian 80/-, Plockton Crag Ale. **Facilities** Children's menu Play area Dogs allowed Garden Parking

Golden Eagle, Cairngorms National Park

POOLEWE — Map 4 NG88

Pool House

★★★★★ GUEST ACCOMMODATION

☎ 01445 781272 ⌨ 01445 781403
IV22 2LD
e-mail: stay@pool-house.co.uk
dir: 6m N of Gairloch on A832 centre

Set on the shores of Loch Ewe where the river meets the bay, the understated roadside façade gives little hint of its splendid interior, nor of the views facing the bay. Memorable features are its delightful public rooms, stunningly romantic suites, each individually designed and with feature bathrooms. Pool House is run very much as a country house - the hospitality and guest care by the Harrison Family are second to none.

Rooms 5 en suite 1 annexe en suite (2 GF) S £110-£125; D £190-£220 **Facilities** tea/coffee Dinner available Direct Dial Cen ht Licensed Fishing Snooker **Parking** 12 **Notes** LB No Children 16yrs RS Mon closed

ROY BRIDGE — Map 4 NN28

Best Western Glenspean Lodge Hotel

★★★ 80% HOTEL

☎ 01397 712223 ⌨ 01397 712660
PH31 4AW
e-mail: reservations@glenspeanlodge.co.uk
web: www.glenspeanlodge.com
dir: 2m E of Roy Bridge, right off A82 at Spean Bridge onto A86

With origins as a hunting lodge dating back to the Victorian era, this hotel sits in gardens in an elevated position in the Spean Valley. Accommodation is provided in well laid out bedrooms, some suitable for families. Inviting public areas include a comfortable lounge bar and a restaurant that enjoys stunning views of the valley.

Rooms 17 (4 fmly) **Facilities** Gym Sauna Xmas New Year Wi-fi **Conf** Class 16 **Parking** 60 **Notes** Civ Wed 60

SCOURIE — Map 4 NC14

Scourie

★★★ 73% SMALL HOTEL

☎ 01971 502396 ⌨ 01971 502423
IV27 4SX
e-mail: patrick@scourie-hotel.co.uk
dir: N'bound on A894. Hotel in village on left

This well-established hotel is an angler's paradise with extensive fishing rights available on a 25,000-acre estate. Public areas include a choice of comfortable lounges, a cosy bar and a smart dining room offering wholesome fare. The bedrooms are comfortable and generally spacious. The resident proprietors and their staff create a relaxed and friendly atmosphere.

Rooms 20 (2 annexe) (2 fmly) (5 GF) **S** £62-£73; **D** £114-£134 (incl. bkfst & dinner)* **Facilities** Fishing Wi-fi **Parking** 30 **Notes** LB Closed mid Oct-end Mar RS winter evenings

SHIEL BRIDGE — Map 4 NG91

Grants at Craigellachie

★★★★ RESTAURANT WITH ROOMS

❀ Modern Scottish ♨

Beautiful setting for bold Scottish flavours

☎ 01599 511331
Craigellachie, Ratagan IV40 8HP
e-mail: info@housebytheloch.co.uk
dir: From A87 turn to Glenelg, 1st right to Ratagan, opp Youth Hostel sign

The sound of birdsong or a bit of background jazz is all you will hear out in the rural splendour of Craigellachie, while views over Loch Duich and the Five Sisters mountains are a feast for the eyes. Bedrooms are stylish and have all the creature comforts, and guests are guaranteed a warm welcome at this charming house. The dining room is in the conservatory and, although a small space, tables are smartly and rather elegantly appointed. The magnificent local larder is well used in bold, modern Scottish dishes: cannelloni is filled with shredded goose, and knuckle of veal comes with a sweet, vine-ripened tomato sauce, while hogget (year-old sheep), full of flavour, is served with fondant potato and ratatouille. Finish with crumble and full-cream custard.

Rooms 2 en suite 2 annexe en suite (3 GF); D £150-£220* **Facilities** STV tea/coffee Dinner available Cen ht Wi-fi **Parking** 8 **Notes** LB No Children 12yrs Closed Dec-mid Feb RS Oct-Apr reservation only No coaches

Chef Tony Taylor **Owner** Tony & Liz Taylor **Restaurant Times** 7-11 Closed mid Nov-mid Feb, L all week **Prices** Fixed D 4 course fr £38.50, Starter £6-£10, Main £13-£28, Dessert £6-£10, Service optional **Wines** 42 bottles over £20, 16 bottles under £20, 5 by glass **Notes** Restaurant open only by reservation, Vegetarian available **Seats** 14 **Children** Portions

SHIELDAIG — Map 4 NG85

Tigh an Eilean

★ SMALL HOTEL

❀❀ Modern Scottish

Innovative cooking in a lochside inn

☎ 01520 755251 ⌨ 01520 755321
IV54 8XN
e-mail: tighaneilean@keme.co.uk
dir: off A896 onto village road signed Shieldaig, hotel in centre

The vista alone is worth the journey to Chris and Cathryn Field's small white-painted hotel in the fishing village of Shieldaig. Sitting on the edge of Loch Torridon, the hotel, which was built around 1800, has brightly decorated, comfortable bedrooms (though don't expect television, except in one of the lounges) and there are stunning views across the water from its light and airy dining room. Chris's modern

Scottish cuisine with French and Spanish influences offers exciting, accurately prepared dishes where nothing is more important than flavour. Daily-changing dinner menus rely on local produce, including seafood delivered directly from the village jetty to the kitchen door. Start with Shieldaig spiny lobsters with a rose de mai sauce and home-made melon sorbet, following on, perhaps, with medallion of fillet of Highland beef with ceps, olive and manchego butter sauce and Pedro Ximenez. Fresh apricot tart served warm with a chilled crème anglaise makes a fitting finale. Slightly more straightforward dishes are served in the refurbished bar, now renamed the Shieldaig Bar and Coastal Kitchen (see below).

Rooms 11 (1 fmly) **Facilities** Birdwatching Kayaks Wi-fi **Parking** 15 **Notes** LB Closed late Oct-mid Mar Civ Wed 40

Restaurant Times 7-9 Closed end Oct-mid Mar (except private booking), L all week

---

Shieldaig Bar & Coastal Kitchen ☕

☎ 01520 755251 📠 01520 755321
IV54 8XN
web: www.tighaneilean.co.uk

This rustic, no-nonsense waterfront bar belongs to a rather special league, one that might be called the League of Bars with Stunning Views Across a Loch. The loch is Torridon, which leads to the open sea and it is from the first floor eating area - The Coastal Kitchen and its balcony and open decks – that you will be most impressed by these views. As part of the two-AA Rosette Tigh an Eilean Hotel next door in a charming, mostly 18th century fishing village, the bar positively jumps at weekends with live traditional Gaelic music. In fact, all over Wester Ross you are likely to find a ceilidh taking place somewhere. Throughout the day a full range of alcoholic and non-alcoholic beverages is served to suit the hour, and there's always a ready supply of newspapers and magazines to read. Bar snacks include sandwiches, home-made soups, burgers and bangers and mash, but it's for fine seafood that the bar has earned its reputation, with daily menus ensuring the freshest of catches, such as Loch Torridon spiny lobsters with lemongrass and coriander dressing, Shieldaig crab salad, fresh razor clam fritters with Romesco sauce, and the speciality Shieldaig bar seafood stew. It's all caught locally, some from local prawn-fishing grounds that have won a national fishery award. Alternatives to fish include steaks and pizzas from the Coastal Kitchen's wood-fired oven, local venison sausages with mash and red wine and onion gravy; and shallot and goats' cheese tart with salad and new potatoes. A resident pastry cook prepares superb desserts using both traditional and unusual ingredients. Food is served all day in summer, when you can also dine in the lochside courtyard and outside on the balcony and decks. A good range of real ales is on tap from the Isle of Skye Brewery and Black Isle Ales, plus malt whiskies and a choice of wines by the glass.

Open all wk ⊕ FREE HOUSE ◀ Isle of Skye Brewery Ales, Black Isle. ☕ 8 **Facilities** Dogs allowed Garden Parking

---

The Ballachulish Hotel

★★★ 77% HOTEL

☎ 0844 855 9133 📠 01855 811629
PH49 4JY
e-mail: reservations.ballachulish@foliohotels.com
web: www.foliohotels.com/ballachulish
dir: on A828, Fort William-Oban road, 3m N of Glencoe

On the shores of Loch Linnhe and at the foot of dramatic Glencoe, guests are assured of a warm welcome here. A selection of bar meals is available at lunchtime, and evening meals are served in the Bulas Bistro which overlooks the stunning mountain scenery. The tastefully decorated bedrooms include the six Chieftain Rooms which are particularly comfortable.

Rooms 53 (2 fmly) (7 GF) **Facilities** Xmas New Year Wi-fi **Conf** Board 20 **Parking** 60 **Notes** LB Civ Wed 65

The Isles of Glencoe Hotel & Leisure Centre

★★★ 71% HOTEL

☎ 0844 855 9134 📠 0871 222 3416
PH49 4HL
e-mail: reservations.glencoe@foliohotels.com
web: www.foliohotels.com/isleofglencoe
dir: A82 N, slip road on left into village, 1st right, hotel in 600yds

This hotel enjoys a spectacular setting beside Loch Leven. This friendly modern establishment has spacious bedrooms and guests have a choice of Loch or Mountain View rooms. Public areas include a popular restaurant and a family friendly leisure centre.

Rooms 59 (21 fmly) (21 GF) **Facilities** STV ⊛ Gym Hydroseat Bio-sauna ♬ Xmas New Year Wi-fi **Conf** Class 40 Board 20 Thtr 40 **Notes** LB Civ Wed 65

Craiglinnhe House

★★★★ GUEST HOUSE

☎ 01855 811270
Lettermore PH49 4JD
e-mail: info@craiglinnhe.co.uk
web: www.craiglinnhe.co.uk
dir: From village A82 onto A828, Craiglinnhe 1.5m on left

Built during the reign of Queen Victoria, Craiglinnhe House enjoys an elevated position with stunning views across Loch Linnhe to the village of Onich, and up to the Ballachulish Bridge and the Pap of Glencoe. The attractive bedrooms vary in size, are stylishly furnished, and are well equipped. There is a ground-floor lounge and a charming dining room where delicious breakfasts, and evening meals by arrangement, are served at individual tables.

Rooms 5 en suite S £42-£60; D £50-£80 **Facilities** tea/coffee Dinner available Cen ht Licensed Wi-fi **Parking** 5 **Notes** LB ⊗ No Children 13yrs Closed 24-26 Dec

Lyn-Leven

★★★★ GUEST HOUSE

☎ 01855 811392 📠 01855 811600
West Laroch PH49 4JP
e-mail: macleodcilla@aol.com
web: www.lynleven.co.uk
dir: Off A82 signed on left West Laroch

Genuine Highland hospitality and high standards are part of the appeal of this comfortable guest house. The attractive bedrooms vary in size, are well equipped, and offer many thoughtful extra touches. There is a spacious lounge and a smart dining room where delicious home-cooked evening meals and breakfasts are served at individual tables.

Rooms 8 en suite 4 annexe en suite (3 fmly) (12 GF) S £30–£45; D £50–£64 **Facilities** TVL tea/coffee Dinner available Cen ht Licensed **Parking** 12 **Notes** LB Closed Xmas

SPEAN BRIDGE	Map 4 NN28

Russell's at Smiddy House

★★★★★ 🛏 RESTAURANT WITH ROOMS

◉◉ Modern Scottish

Good cooking in friendly Highland hotel

☎ 01397 712335 📠 01397 712043
Roy Bridge Rd PH34 4EU
e-mail: enquiry@smiddyhouse.co.uk
dir: In village centre, 9m N of Fort William, on A82 towards Inverness

Spean Bridge in the Great Glen occupies pole position for taking on Ben Nevis and generally testing yourself against terrain where World War Two commandos once trained. The attractive bedrooms, all named after places in Scotland, are comfortably furnished and well equipped, and a relaxing garden room is available for guest use. All that available fresh-air exertion should sharpen the appetite for the accomplished cuisine on offer in this convivial restaurant in the 'Smiddyhouse' - once the village blacksmith's. It's an intimate spot when candlelight twinkles off the glasses, fine china and silver cutlery, and the kitchen makes sure that local ingredients are to the fore on a regularly-changing menu. Start with local peat-smoked salmon and potato pancake with lemon and chive crème fraîche dressing, then pan-fried venison with haggis, turnip and grain mustard sauce. Don't miss plum and ginger pudding with warm toffee sauce to finish.

Rooms 4 en suite (1 fmly) S £60–£85; D £70–£90* **Facilities** tea/coffee Dinner available Wi-fi **Parking** 15 **Notes** No coaches

Chef Glen Russell **Owner** Glen Russell, Robert Bryson **Restaurant Times** 6-9 Closed 2 days a week (Nov-Apr), L all week **Prices** Fixed D 3 course £29.95-£36.95, Service optional **Wines** 21 bottles over £20, 11 bottles under £20, 5 by glass **Notes** Vegetarian available, Dress restrictions, Smart casual **Seats** 38 **Children** Portions, Menu

Corriechoille Lodge

★★★★ 🛏 GUEST HOUSE

☎ 01397 712002
PH34 4EY
web: www.corriechoille.com
dir: Off A82 signed Corriechoille, 2.5m, left at fork (10mph sign). At end of tarmac, turn right up hill & left

This fine country house stands above the River Spean. There are magnificent views of the Nevis range and surrounding mountains from the comfortable first-floor lounge and some of the spacious, well-appointed bedrooms. Friendly and attentive service is provided, as are traditional breakfasts and delicious evening meals by arrangement.

Rooms 4 en suite (2 fmly) (1 GF) S £40–£46; D £60–£72* **Facilities** tea/coffee Dinner available Cen ht Licensed Wi-fi **Parking** 7 **Notes** ⊗ No Children 7yrs Closed Nov-Mar RS Sun-Mon closed

Achnabobane *(NN195811)*

★★★ FARMHOUSE

☎ 01397 712919   Mr and Mrs N Ockenden
PH34 4EX
e-mail: enquiries@achnabobane.co.uk
web: www.achnabobane.co.uk
dir: 2m S of Spean Bridge on A82

With breathtaking views of Ben Nevis, Aonach Mhor and the Grey Corries, the farmhouse offers comfortable, good-value accommodation in a friendly family environment. Bedrooms are traditional in style and well equipped. Breakfast and evening meals are served in the conservatory-dining room. Pets are welcome.

Rooms 4 rms (1 en suite) (1 fmly) (1 GF) S fr £29; D fr £58* **Facilities** TVL tea/coffee Dinner available Cen ht Wi-fi **Parking** 5 **Notes** Closed Xmas Red Deer/Woodland

STRATHPEFFER	Map 5 NH45

Inver Lodge

★★★ GUEST HOUSE

☎ 01997 421392
IV14 9DL
e-mail: derbyshire@inverlg.fsnet.co.uk
dir: A834 through Strathpeffer centre, turn beside Spa Pavilion signed Bowling Green, Inver Lodge on right

You are assured of a warm welcome at this Victorian lodge, secluded in its own tree-studded gardens yet within easy walking distance of the town centre. Bedrooms are comfortable and well equipped, and the cosy lounge is ideal for relaxation. Breakfasts, and evening meals (by arrangement), are served at a communal table.

Rooms 2 rms (1 fmly) S £30–£32.50; D £50* **Facilities** tea/coffee Dinner available Cen ht **Parking** 2 **Notes** LB ⊗ Closed Xmas & New Year 🐾

Catalina

★★★★ BED AND BREAKFAST

☎ 01641 541395 📠 0871 900 2537
Aultivullin KW14 7RY
e-mail: catalina.bandb@virgin.net
dir: A836 at Strathy onto Strathy Point Rd, 1.5m then left & 1m to
end

Having a tranquil setting close to the sea, this former croft house
provides a getaway location for those seeking relaxation. The self-
contained bedroom is in a wing that includes a dining room and a
cosy lounge. Cuisine is home-cooked and meal times are flexible.

Rooms 1 en suite (1 GF) S £37; D £56* **Facilities** STV TVL tea/coffee
Dinner available Cen ht **Parking** 2 **Notes** ⊗ No Children ⊜

Kilcamb Lodge

★★★ COUNTRY HOUSE HOTEL

⊛⊛ Modern European V 🍴

Creative cooking in peaceful lochside setting

☎ 01967 402257 📠 01967 402041
PH36 4HY
e-mail: enquiries@kilcamblodge.co.uk **web:** www.kilcamblodge.co.uk
dir: Off A861, via Corran Ferry

Whilst strolling in the peaceful 22 acres of meadow and woodland on
the shores of Loch Sunart, it's sobering to think that this tranquil
retreat was a military barracks around the time of the Jacobite
uprising. Thought to be one of the oldest stone houses in Scotland,
Kilcamb Lodge is now a luxurious country-house hotel. Bedrooms are
tastefully decorated, with high quality fabrics, and warm hospitality
is assured. The intimate restaurant in warm shades of pink and red
offers a mix of modern European dishes, with great attention shown
to clarity of flavours and constructions that show intelligent
simplicity. Fresh local produce, in particular fish and shellfish caught
at the bottom of the garden, is cooked with flair and imagination. A
four-course dinner might start with ham hough terrine with apple
compôte and rosemary brioche, before goat's cheese petits fours with
beetroot carpaccio, and then the main course, perhaps roasted fillet
of beef and braised oxtail with pickled onions and carrots, and some
farmhouse cheeses as an alternative to dessert.

Rooms 10 (2 fmly) **S** £130-£150; **D** £210-£335 (incl. bkfst & dinner)*
Facilities FTV Fishing Boating Hiking Bird, Whale & Otter watching
Island hopping Stalking Xmas New Year Wi-fi **Conf** Class 18 Board 18
Thtr 18 Del from £158 to £200* **Parking** 18 **Notes** LB No children
10yrs Closed 2 Jan-1 Feb RS Nov & Feb Civ Wed 60

Chef Tammo Siemers **Owner** Sally & David Fox **Restaurant**
Times 12-1.30/7.30-9.30 Closed 1 Jan-1 Feb, **Prices** Fixed L course
£14.75, Fixed D 4 course £48, Service optional, Groups min 10 service
10% **Wines** 45 bottles over £20, 20 bottles under £20, 10 by glass
Notes Chef's tasting menu available Fri & Sat, Sunday L, Vegetarian
menu, Dress restrictions, Smart casual, no jeans, T-shirts or trainers
Seats 26

Glenmorangie Highland Home at Cadboll

★★★ COUNTRY HOUSE HOTEL

⊛⊛ French, International

House party-style dining in Highland hideaway

☎ 01862 871671 📠 01862 871625
Cadboll, Fearn IV20 1XP
e-mail: relax@glenmorangieplc.co.uk
web: www.theglenmorangiehouse.com
dir: From A9 onto B9175 towards Nigg. Follow tourist signs

Overlooking the unspoilt shores of the Dornoch Firth, this remote
Highland home is owned by the Glenmorangie whisky company.
Formed from a 17th-century farmhouse and an 18th-century castle,
this splendid hideaway has its own beach, plus walled orchards and
gardens which provide produce for the house. Stylish bedrooms are
divided between the traditional main house and some cosy cottages
in the grounds. This is an ideal base from which to enjoy the world
famous whisky tours. Expect to dine house-party style, at one long
table, after introductions in the drawing room over drinks. Impressive
cuisine capitalises on wonderful local produce, including fresh
seafood and venison from neighbouring estates. Dinner is a six-
course meal (with just one choice at an interim course), produced by
classically trained chefs. Expect the likes of lightly-spiced local
scallops with herb potato pancake, whisky marinated smoked salmon
and pimento sauce, followed by seared breast of duck with
dauphinoise potatoes, wilted spinach, poached pear, confit of
vegetables and port wine sauce.

Rooms 9 (3 annexe) (4 fmly) (3 GF) **Facilities** Putt green 🚣 Falconry
Clay pigeon shooting Beauty treatments Archery Xmas New Year Wi-fi
Conf Board 12 **Parking** 60 **Notes** ⊗ No children 14yrs Closed 3-31
Jan Civ Wed 60

Chef David Graham **Owner** Glenmorangie Ltd **Restaurant Times** 8pm
Closed 23-26 Dec, 4-27 Jan, L except by prior arrangement
Prices Food prices not confirmed for 2010. Please telephone for
details, Service added but optional **Wines** 38 bottles over £20, 5
bottles under £20, 15 by glass **Notes** Fixed D 5 course £50, Sunday L,
Dress restrictions, Smart casual, no jeans or T-shirts **Seats** 30, Pr/
dining room 12 **Children** Portions

| THURSO | Map 5 ND16 |

Forss House

★★★★ 76% SMALL HOTEL

⊛⊛ Modern Scottish ❦

Elegant dining in spectacular Highland surroundings

☎ 01847 861201 📠 01847 861301
Forss KW14 7XY
e-mail: anne@forsshousehotel.co.uk
web: www.forsshousehotel.co.uk
dir: On A836 between Thurso & Reay

Fans of the great outdoors will find no fault with this 200 year-old shooting lodge, hidden away in a wooded glen below a waterfall. Smartly refurbished in a plush country-house style, Forss House Hotel is set in its own 20 acres of woodland is the ideal base for fishing, hunting, hiking and golfing. When the day's exertions are done, the hotel offers a choice of bedrooms, from the traditionally-styled rooms in the main house to more contemporary annexe rooms in the grounds. All rooms are very well equipped and well appointed. The romantic dining room comes complete with an elegant Adam fireplace and idyllic view of the winding River Forss. Straightforward modern Scottish dishes use top-class ingredients from the rivers, coastline and estates all around. Try the Orkney scallops with braised pork cheek, radish and apple salad and curried vinaigrette, followed by roast loin of Berriedale venison with root vegetables, fig compôte and dauphinoise potatoes.

Rooms 14 (6 annexe) (1 fmly) (1 GF) **S** £95-£110; **D** £125-£160 (incl. bkfst)* **Facilities** FTV Fishing Wi-fi **Conf** Class 12 Board 16 Thtr 20 Del from £145 to £160* **Parking** 14 **Notes** LB Closed 23 Dec-3 Jan Civ Wed 30

Chef Kevin Dalgleish, Gary Leishman **Owner** Ian & Sabine Richards **Restaurant Times** 7-9 Closed 23 Dec-4 Jan, L all week **Prices** Food prices not confirmed for 2010. Please telephone for details. **Wines** 26 bottles over £20, 9 bottles under £20, 4 by glass **Notes** Vegetarian available **Seats** 26, Pr/dining room 14 **Children** Portions

| TOMATIN | Map 5 NH82 |

Glenan Lodge

★★★★ GUEST HOUSE

☎ 01808 511217
IV13 7YT
e-mail: enquiries@glenanlodge.co.uk **web:** www.glenanlodge.co.uk
dir: Off A9 to Tomatin, signed to Lodge

Peacefully located on the edge of the village, this relaxed and homely guest house offers a warm welcome. The comfortable bedrooms are traditionally furnished and suitably equipped. An inviting lounge is available, and delicious home-cooked evening meals and breakfasts are served in the dining room. A two mile stretch of the River Findhorn is available for fly-fishing, and golfers, walkers and bird watchers are also well provided for locally.

Rooms 7 en suite (2 fmly) S £28-£30; D £56-£60* **Facilities** TVL tea/coffee Dinner available Cen ht Licensed Wi-fi Fishing **Parking** 7 **Notes** LB ⊛ No Children 5yrs

| TONGUE | Map 5 NC55 |

Ben Loyal Hotel

★★★ 70% SMALL HOTEL

⊛ Modern, Traditional

Sound Scottish cooking in magnificent location

☎ 01847 611216 📠 01847 611212
Main St IV27 4XE
e-mail: benloyalhotel@btinternet.com
web: www.benloyal.co.uk
dir: At junct of A838/A836. Hotel by Royal Bank of Scotland

Enjoying a super location close to Ben Loyal and with views of the Kyle of Tongue, this hotel enjoys outstanding views over the unspoiled Sutherland landscape and is the perfect place from which to explore the northern Highlands. Bedrooms are thoughtfully equipped and brightly decorated and staff are especially friendly and helpful, providing useful local information to guests. The relaxed restaurant has picture windows that overlook the Kyle of Tongue, Ben Loyal, Ben Hope and the ruin of Castle Varrich that sits on the hill line opposite. Alongside informal, friendly service, quality, simply prepared and presented food is offered with an emphasis on local Scottish produce, particularly seafood. A traditional starter of haggis, neeps and tatties with whisky cream sauce might be followed by pan-seared wild Alaskan salmon fillet, crushed new potatoes, thyme-infused peas and caper beurre blanc. Finish with cranachan trifle.

Rooms 11 **S** £40; **D** £70-£80 (incl. bkfst) **Facilities** FTV Fishing Fly fishing tuition and equipment **Parking** 20 **Notes** Closed 30 Nov-1 Mar

Chef Neil Keevil **Owner** Mr & Mrs P Lewis **Restaurant Times** 12-2.15/6-8.15 Closed 30 Nov -1 Mar, L all week **Prices** Starter £3.50-£11.50, Main £8.50-£16.50, Dessert £5.50, Service optional **Wines** All bottles under £20, 4 by glass **Notes** Vegetarian available **Seats** 50 **Children** Portions, Menu

Borgie Lodge Hotel

★★ 78% HOTEL

⊛ Modern British

Seasonal cooking in secluded Highland hotel

☎ 01641 521332 📠 01641 521889
Skerray KW14 7TH
e-mail: info@borgielodgehotel.co.uk
dir: A836 between Tongue & Bettyhill. 0.5m from Skerray junct

Located in a quiet, secluded Highland glen on the banks of the beautiful River Borgie in North Sutherland, this Victorian sporting lodge continues to provide a welcome retreat for today's sportsmen, particularly anglers. Whilst fishing parties predominate, those who are not anglers are made equally welcome, and indeed the friendliness and commitment to guest care is paramount. There's a relaxed and friendly atmosphere in the cosy lounge and bar, where you can settle down by the fire and listen to tales about 'the one that got away'. A skilful kitchen makes good use of local produce in modern British and Scottish dishes. The concise menu changes daily depending on what's in season, but might include pickled herring with dressed leaves and herb oil, followed by fillet of Caithness beef with rösti potato, sautéed pak choi and field mushrooms, with warm apricot and almond tart to finish.

Rooms 8 (1 GF) **Facilities** Fishing 🎣 Shooting Stalking Boating **Parking** 20

Restaurant Times 12-2/7-8.30 Closed 25 Dec

TORRIDON — Map 4 NG95

The Torridon

★★★★ COUNTRY HOUSE HOTEL

@@ Modern British

Impressive lochside location and fantastic home-grown produce

☎ 01445 791242 📠 01445 712253
By Achnasheen, Wester Ross IV22 2EY
e-mail: info@thetorridon.com
web: www.thetorridon.com
dir: From A832 at Kinlochewe, take A896 towards Torridon. (Do not turn into village) continue 1m, hotel on right

Delightfully set amidst inspiring loch and mountain scenery, this sympathetically restored, elegant Victorian shooting lodge surely has one of the most idyllic locations on the West Coast of Scotland - 58 acres of parkland at the head of a magnificent sea loch. The attractive bedrooms are all individually furnished and most enjoy stunning Highland views. Comfortable day rooms feature fine wood panelling and roaring fires in cooler months, while outdoor activities include shooting, cycling and walking (the estate also includes the Torridon Inn, see below). Two interconnecting dining rooms feature wood panelling, wood detail on the ceiling and high backed chairs, heavy drapes, oil paintings and a lovely fireplace; it's all very luxurious. The two-choice, five-course British menu with French influences uses lots of ingredients from the 2 acres of fruit and vegetable gardens, and scours the local Highland larder for most of the rest. You can even request a tour with head gardener Les Bates. Dishes might include home-tea-smoked organic salmon tartare with cress, then grilled fresh wild halibut with basil jus, and island cheeses with oat snaps and chutneys, or warm yellow polenta and chocolate soufflé with very vanilla ice cream to finish. The bar serves an impressive selection of over 320 different malt whiskies.

Rooms 19 (2 GF) **S** £150-£185; **D** £285-£485 (incl. bkfst & dinner)* **Facilities** STV Fishing 🎣 Absailing Archery Climbing Falconry Kayaking Mountain biking Xmas New Year Wi-fi **Conf** Board 16 **Services** Lift **Parking** 20 **Notes** LB ✱ Closed 3-27 Jan RS Nov-14 Mar Civ Wed 42

Restaurant Times 12-2/7-9 Closed 2 Jan for 3 wks, L bar only

The Torridon Inn

★★★ 🛏 INN ☕

☎ 01445 791242 📠 01445 712253
IV22 2EY
e-mail: inn@thetorridon.com

The Torridon Inn, the AA's Scottish Pub of the Year for 2009-2010, was once a grand shooting lodge, built for the first Earl of Lovelace in 1887, and enjoys one of the most impressive coastal positions in the Scottish Highlands. The inn was created by converting the stable block, buttery and farm buildings of nearby Ben Damph House, now known as The Torridon Hotel (see above). Whether you use it as a base to enjoy some of the many activities on offer, (there are spacious, well equipped comfortable bedrooms available) or simply want to unwind with a warm fire and relaxing pint from the good selection of local real ales after a hard day's walking, you can be sure of a memorable visit. The inn is very popular with walkers, and guests can also avail themselves of the many outdoor pursuits that are provided at The Torridon Hotel. The cosy bar offers a Highland welcome from both staff and locals: choose from a range of over 60 malt whiskies, or recount the day's adventures over a pint of local real ale. Entertainment ranges from indoor games to regular traditional live music sessions. In the restaurant you can sample high quality, locally sourced food at any time. Local produce drives menus that might feature venison, salmon, haggis and home-made specials. Dinner could begin with caramelised onion tart with fresh rocket and olive oil, or double-baked Beauly wild boar belly with Loch Fwe scallops and caramelised apple. Typical main course choices include game casserole served with creamy mashed potatoes and seasonal baby vegetables; butternut squash, ricotta and pine nut pasta parcels in a creamy pesto sauce; and whole baked trout with almond, breadcrumb and spring onion stuffing, served with new potatoes and garden salad. Tea and coffee is available throughout the day.

Rooms 12 en suite (3 fmly) (5 GF) **S** £85; **D** £85* **Facilities** STV tea/ coffee Dinner available Cen ht Wi-fi 🎣 Fishing Pool Table Outdoor activities available **Conf** Max 35 Thtr 35 Board 16 **Parking** 12 **Notes** LB Closed Nov-Feb Civ Wed 40

Open all wk Closed: Nov-27 Mar **Bar Meals** L served all wk, all day D served all wk 6-9 Av main course £13.50 food served all day **Restaurant** Av 3 course à la carte fr £22 ◼ Isle of Skye Brewery - Red Cuillin, Blaven, Torridon Ale, Cairngorm Brewery - Stag, Tradewinds. ☕ 8 **Facilities** Children's menu Play area Dogs allowed Garden

Hermitage Bridge, Falls of Braan.

The Ceilidh Place ☏

☎ 01854 612103   📠 01854 613773
14 West Argyle St IV26 2TY
e-mail: stay@theceilidhplace.com
dir: On entering Ullapool, along Shore St, pass pier, take 1st right. Hotel straight ahead at top of hill

Organic growth has seen this old boatshed café metamorphose over 37 years into an all-day bar, coffee shop, restaurant, bookshop and art gallery. The late founder Robert Urquhart had aspirations for a place for serious writing - life histories, not postcards; a place for eating, meeting, talking and singing. This all came to pass and it is now known mostly for live traditional Scottish music, although some jazz slips in. The heart of The Ceilidh Place is the café/bar, with its big open fire and solid wooden furniture. It's a place to stay all day, and some do. Simple delights conjured up by the menu include mince and tatties, kedgeree, homity pie, and bone-warming cullen skink. Among the main dishes are braised venison chop; pan-roasted whole Loch Broom prawns; and seafood platter. A specials board offering seasonally available fish, meat, vegetables and fruits complements the printed menu.

Open all wk Closed: 2wks mid-Jan ⊕ FREE HOUSE ◀ Belhaven Best, Guinness, Scottish ales. ♀ 8 **Facilities** Dogs allowed Garden Parking

Whitebridge

★★ 69% HOTEL

☎ 01456 486226   📠 01456 486413
IV2 6UN
e-mail: info@whitebridgehotel.co.uk
dir: Off A9 onto B851, follow signs to Fort Augustus. Off A82 onto B862 at Fort Augustus

Close to Loch Ness and set amid rugged mountain and moorland scenery, this hotel is popular with tourists, fishermen and deerstalkers. Guests have a choice of more formal dining in the restaurant or lighter meals in the popular cosy bar. Bedrooms are thoughtfully equipped and brightly furnished.

Rooms 12 (3 fmly) **S** £38-£42; **D** £58-£62 (incl. bkfst)*
Facilities Fishing Wi-fi **Parking** 32 **Notes** Closed 11 Dec-9 Jan

Mackay's

★★★ 75% HOTEL

☎ 01955 602323   📠 01955 605930
Union St KW1 5ED
e-mail: info@mackayshotel.co.uk
dir: opposite Caithness General Hospital

This well-established hotel is situated just outside the town centre overlooking the River Wick. MacKay's provides well-equipped, attractive accommodation, suited to both the business and leisure traveller. There is a stylish bistro offering food throughout the day and a choice of bars that also offer food.

Rooms 30 (2 fmly) **Facilities** FTV ♫ Wi-fi **Conf** Class 100 Board 60 Thtr 100 **Services** Lift **Notes** ⊗ Closed 25-26 Dec & 1-3 Jan

The Clachan

★★★★ BED AND BREAKFAST

☎ 01955 605384
13 Randolph Place, South Rd KW1 5NJ
e-mail: enquiry@theclachan.co.uk
dir: Off A99 0.5m S of town centre

A warm welcome is assured at this immaculate detached home, by the main road on the south edge of the town. The bright, airy bedrooms (all on the ground floor) though compact, are attractively furnished to make good use of available space. Breakfast offers an extensive choice and is served at individual tables in the cosy dining room.

Rooms 3 en suite (3 GF) S £45-£50; D £60-£70* **Facilities** FTV tea/coffee Cen ht Wi-fi **Parking** 3 **Notes** ⊗ No Children 12yrs Closed Xmas & New Year ⊜

INVERCLYDE

GREENOCK   Map 2 NS27

Express by Holiday Inn Greenock

BUDGET HOTEL

☎ 01475 786666 📄 01475 786777
Cartsburn PA15 1AE
e-mail: greenock@expressbyholidayinn.net
web: www.hiexpress.com/greenockscot
dir: M8 junct 31, A8 to Greenock, right at 4th rdbt, hotel on right

A modern hotel ideal for families and business travellers. Fresh and uncomplicated, the spacious rooms include Sky TV, power shower and tea and coffee-making facilities. Continental buffet breakfast is included in the room rate; other meals may be taken at the nearby family pub or restaurant. See also the Hotel Groups pages on theAA.com.

Rooms 71 (11 fmly) (6 GF) (20 smoking) **Conf** Class 48 Board 32 Thtr 70

KILMACOLM   Map 2 NS37

Windyhill Restaurant

🍴 Modern British V 🌱

Contemporary British cuisine in a relaxed setting

☎ 01505 872613
4 St James Ter, Lochwinnoch Rd PA13 4HB
e-mail: matthewscobey@hotmail.co.uk
dir: From Glasgow Airport, A737 take Bridge of Weir exit. Onto A761 to Kilmacolm. Left into High Street

Dynamic owners are constantly fine tuning the décor and menu of this smart contemporary restaurant. Inspired by the great architect Charles Rennie Mackintosh's house, Windyhill, the black shop-front façade opens into a classily casual setting with moody lighting, dark-wood furniture and modern artwork to inject splashes of colour to pristine white walls. The cooking is founded on top-drawer, locally-sourced produce, put to good use in uncomplicated but effective dishes with some interesting flavour combinations. Monthly menus offer a half-dozen choices at each stage; smoked Finnan haddock and leek risotto with lemon oil, followed by rump of lamb with sweet potato champ and roast root vegetables. Don't dodge puddings such as steamed black treacle and date pudding with walnut ice cream.

Chef Matthew Scobey **Owner** Matthew Scobey & Careen McLean
Times 12-3/6-10 Closed Xmas-New Year, last wk Jul, 1st wk Aug, Sun-Mon, L Tue-Thu & Sat **Prices** Fixed L 2 course £15-£20, Fixed D 3 course £20-£30, Starter £3.95-£6.95, Main £9.95-£18.95, Dessert £4.95-£6.50 **Wines** 5 bottles over £20, 18 bottles under £20, 6 by glass **Notes** Vegetarian menu **Seats** 45 **Children** Portions, Menu **Parking** On street, car park opposite

NORTH LANARKSHIRE

AIRDRIE   Map 3 NS76

Shawlee Cottage

★★★ GUEST HOUSE

☎ 01236 753774 📄 01236 749300
108 Lauchope St, Chapelhall ML6 8SW
e-mail: shawleecottage@blueyonder.co.uk
web: www.csaitken.fsbusiness.co.uk/index.htm
dir: M8 junct 6, A73 to Chapelhall, left onto B799, Shawlee 600yds on right

Shawlee Cottage is close to motorway and rail networks, and within easy reach of Edinburgh and Glasgow. This delightful cottage dates from the 19th century and has comfortable, well-equipped bedrooms with wide doors and a ramp at the entrance. Scottish breakfasts (and dinner by arrangement) are served in the attractive dining room.

Rooms 5 en suite (5 GF) S £30-£40; D £55-£65 **Facilities** tea/coffee Direct Dial Cen ht Wi-fi **Parking** 6 **Notes** ⊗

COATBRIDGE   Map 2 NS76

Auchenlea

★★★ GUEST HOUSE

☎ 0141 771 6870 & 07775 791381 📄 0141 771 6870
153 Langmuir Rd, Bargeddie G69 7RT
e-mail: helenbarr06@btinternet.com
dir: N off A8 onto A752 for 0.4m

Backing onto farmland, yet only a short distance from the motorway, this detached house is well placed for Glasgow and Edinburgh. Satisfying, well-cooked breakfasts are served at a communal table in the bright dining room, and there is an attractive conservatory and adjoining lounge. The bedrooms, all on the ground floor, are modern in style with one designed for easier access.

Rooms 6 en suite (1 fmly) (6 GF) S £25-£35; D £55-£60* **Facilities** FTV TVL tea/coffee Cen ht **Parking** 10 **Notes** ⊗ ⊜

CUMBERNAULD   Map 3 NS77

The Westerwood Hotel & Golf Resort

★★★★ 80% HOTEL

☎ 01236 457171 📄 01236 738478
1 St Andrews Dr, Westerwood G68 0EW
e-mail: westerwood@qhotels.co.uk
web: www.qhotels.co.uk

This stylish, contemporary hotel enjoys an elevated position within 400 acres at the foot of the Camspie Hills. Accommodation is provided in spacious, bright bedrooms, many with super bathrooms, and day rooms include sumptuous lounges and an airy restaurant; extensive golf, fitness and conference facilities are available.

Rooms 148 (15 fmly) (49 GF) **S** £65-£125; **D** £75-£135 (incl. bkfst) **Facilities** Spa 🏊 ♨ 18 ⛳ Putt green Gym Beauty salon Jacuzzi

Relaxation room Sauna Steam room Xmas New Year Wi-fi
Conf Class 120 Board 60 Thtr 400 Del from £120 to £180*
Services Lift **Parking** 250 **Notes** LB Civ Wed 400

Castlecary House

★★★ 77% HOTEL ♥

☎ 01324 840233   📠 01324 841608
Castlecary Rd, Castlecary G68 0HD
e-mail: enquiries@castlecaryhotel.com
web: www.castlecaryhotel.com
dir: off A80 onto B816 between Glasgow & Stirling. Hotel by
Castlecary Arches

Run by the same family for over 30 years, this friendly hotel is
located close to the historic Antonine Wall and Forth and Clyde
Canal, as well as being convenient for the M80. The hotel provides a
versatile range of accommodation, in purpose-built units in the
grounds and also in an extension to the original house. Meals in the
lounge bars plough a traditional furrow with options such as home-
made steak pie; oven-baked Scottish salmon fillet with a sun-dried
tomato and herb brioche crust; and a range of flame-grilled steaks.
There is an excellent selection of real ales on offer. More formal
restaurant fare is available in Camerons Restaurant.

Rooms 60 (3 fmly) (20 GF) **S** £70-£90; **D** £70-£90 (incl. bkfst)*
Facilities FTV Wi-fi **Conf** Class 120 Board 60 Thtr 140 **Services** Lift
Parking 100 **Notes** RS 1 Jan Civ Wed 90

Pub Open all wk **Bar Meals** Av main course £8.50 food served all day
Restaurant Av 3 course à la carte fr £22 ⊕ FREE HOUSE ◀ Arran
Blonde, Harviestoun Brooker's Bitter & Twisted, Inveralmond Ossian's
Ale, Housten Peter's Well, Caledonian Deuchars IPA, ♥ 8
Facilities Children's menu Dogs allowed Garden

MOTHERWELL   Map 3 NS75

Alona Hotel

★★★★ 78% HOTEL

☎ 01698 333888   📠 01698 338720
Strathclyde Country Park ML1 3RT
e-mail: keithd@alonahotel.co.uk
web: www.alonahotel.co.uk
dir: M74 junct 5, hotel approx 250yds on left

Alona is a Celtic word meaning 'exquisitely beautiful'. This hotel is
situated within the idyllic beauty of Strathclyde Country Park, with
tranquil views over the picturesque loch and surrounding forests.
There is a very contemporary feel, from the open-plan public areas to
the spacious and well-appointed bedrooms. Wi-fi is available
throughout. M&D's, Scotland's Family Theme Park, is just next door.

Rooms 51 (24 fmly) (17 GF) **Facilities** FTV ♫ Xmas New Year Wi-fi
Conf Class 100 Board 76 Thtr 140 Del from £99 to £150*
Services Lift Air con **Parking** 100 **Notes** ⊗ Civ Wed 100

Express by Holiday Inn Strathclyde Park

BUDGET HOTEL

☎ 01698 858585   📠 01698 852375
Hamilton Rd, Hamilton ML1 3RB
e-mail: isabella.little@ichotelsgroup.com
web: www.hiexpress.com/strathclyde
dir: M74 junct 5 follow signs for Strathclyde Country park

A modern hotel ideal for families and business travellers. Fresh and
uncomplicated, the spacious rooms include Sky TV, power shower
and tea and coffee-making facilities. Continental buffet breakfast is
included in the room rate; other meals may be taken at the nearby
family pub or restaurant. See also the Hotel Groups pages
on theAA.com.

Rooms 120 (58 fmly) **Conf** Class 10 Board 18 Thtr 30

Innkeeper's Lodge Glasgow/Strathclyde Park

BUDGET HOTEL

☎ 0845 112 6004   📠 0845 112 6296
Hamilton Rd ML1 3RB
web: www.innkeeperslodge.com/glasgowstrathclydepark
dir: M74 junct 5, take exit for Strathclyde Country Park. Lodge on
right, after entering park

Innkeeper's Lodge represents an exciting, high value concept within
the budget hotel market. Comfortable bedrooms provide excellent
facilities that include satellite TV and modem points. Options include
family rooms; and for the corporate guest, cutting edge IT which
includes Wi-fi access. A popular Carvery provides all-day food,
including an extensive, complimentary continental breakfast. See
also the Hotel Groups pages on theAA.com.

Rooms 28 **Conf** Thtr 20

STEPPS   Map 2 NS66

Best Western Garfield House Hotel

★★★ 83% HOTEL

☎ 0141 779 2111   📠 0141 779 9799
Cumbernauld Rd G33 6HW
e-mail: rooms@garfieldhotel.co.uk
dir: M8 junct 11 exit at Stepps/Queenslie, follow Stepps/A80 signs

Situated close to the A80, this considerably extended business hotel
is a popular venue for local conferences and functions. Public areas
include a welcoming reception lounge and the popular Distillery Bar/
Restaurant, an all-day eatery providing good value meals in an
informal setting. Smart, well-presented bedrooms come in a range of
sizes and styles. Staff are friendly and keen to please.

Rooms 45 (10 fmly) (13 GF) **S** £60-£98; **D** £72-£116 (incl. bkfst)
Facilities FTV Wi-fi **Conf** Class 40 Board 36 Thtr 100 **Parking** 90
Notes Closed 1-2 Jan Civ Wed 80

SOUTH LANARKSHIRE

ABINGTON MOTORWAY SERVICE AREA (M74) Map 3 NS92

Days Inn Abington

BUDGET HOTEL

☎ 01864 502782 📠 01864 502759
ML12 6RG
e-mail: abington.hotel@welcomebreak.co.uk
web: www.welcomebreak.co.uk
dir: M74 junct 13, accessible from N'bound and S'bound carriageways

This modern building offers accommodation in smart, spacious and well-equipped bedrooms, suitable for families and business travellers, and all with en suite bathrooms. Continental breakfast is available and other refreshments may be taken at the nearby family restaurant. See also the Hotel Groups pages on theAA.com.

Rooms 52 (50 fmly) **S** £29-£59; **D** £39-£79* **Conf** Board 10 Del from £69 to £99*

BIGGAR Map 3 NT03

Shieldhill Castle

★★★★ 70% COUNTRY HOUSE HOTEL

◉◉ Modern British, International ≜NOTABLE WINE LIST ☙

Accomplished cooking in imposing old mansion

☎ 01899 220035 📠 01899 221092
Quothquan ML12 6NA
e-mail: enquiries@shieldhill.co.uk **web:** www.shieldhill.co.uk
dir: A702 onto B7016 (Biggar to Carnwath road), after 2m left into Shieldhill Rd. Hotel 1.5m on right

Dating back almost 800 years, this fortified country mansion is surrounded by beautiful woodland and parkland and even has its own cricket pitch. A friendly welcome is assured, even from the estate's own dogs! Bedrooms, many with feature baths, are spacious and comfortable. Public rooms are atmospheric and packed with original features, from the oak-panelled lounge to the high-ceilinged Chancellors' restaurant. The kitchen delivers imaginative modern dishes with a focus on well-defined flavours conjured from local seasonal produce - including the estate game. All dishes are available as starter or main course and might include a classic fisherman's bouillabaisse or steamed steak and ale pudding with honey-roasted parsnips and spiced red cabbage. Finish with fig and ginger tart with ginger and honey ice cream. The wine list is well worth exploring.

Rooms 26 (10 annexe) (10 GF) **Facilities** FTV ⛳ Cycling Clay shoot Hot air ballooning Falconry Laser & game bird shooting Xmas New Year Wi-fi **Conf** Class 200 Board 250 Thtr 500 **Parking** 50 **Notes** Civ Wed 200

Chef Christina Lamb **Owner** Mr & Mrs R Lamb **Restaurant Times** 12-1.45/7-8.45 **Prices** Fixed L 2 course fr £15.95, Fixed D 3 course fr £19.95, Starter £6.15-£10.95, Main £9.95-£12.95, Dessert £7.45-£8.95, Service optional, Groups min 10 service 5% **Wines** 17 bottles under £20, 30 by glass **Notes** Sunday L, Vegetarian available, **Seats** 32, Pr/dining room 30 **Children** Portions

BOTHWELL Map 2 NS75

Bothwell Bridge

★★★ 79% HOTEL

☎ 01698 852246 📠 01698 854686
89 Main St G71 8EU
e-mail: enquiries@bothwellbridge-hotel.com
web: www.bothwellbridge-hotel.com
dir: M74 junct 5 & follow signs to Uddingston, right at mini-rdbt. Hotel just past shops on left

This red-sandstone mansion house is a popular business, function and conference hotel conveniently placed for the motorway. Most bedrooms are spacious and all are well equipped. The conservatory is a bright and comfortable restaurant serving an interesting variety of Italian influenced dishes. The lounge bar offers a comfortable seating area that proves popular as a stop for coffee.

Rooms 90 (14 fmly) (26 GF) **S** £64-£90; **D** £75-£120 (incl. bkfst)* **Facilities** STV ♬ Xmas New Year Wi-fi **Conf** Class 80 Board 50 Thtr 200 Del from £90 to £103* **Services** Lift **Parking** 125 **Notes** ⊗ Civ Wed 180

EAST KILBRIDE Map 2 NS65

Holiday Inn Glasgow-East Kilbride

★★★★ 75% HOTEL

☎ 01355 236300 📠 01355 233552
Stewartfield Way G74 5LA
e-mail: salesmg@hieastkilbride.com
web: www.hieastkilbride.com
dir: M74 junct 5, A725 then A726

A modern hotel located in East Kilbride but within easy striking distance of Glasgow. Bedrooms are nicely appointed and cater well for the needs of the modern traveller. Food is served in La Bonne Auberge with a definite French and Mediterranean feel. Good leisure facilities are an added bonus.

Rooms 101 (4 fmly) (26 GF) (8 smoking) **Facilities** Spa STV ⓣ Gym Aerobics studio Spin cycle studio Sauna Steam room Xmas New Year Wi-fi **Conf** Class 120 Board 60 Thtr 400 Del from £99 to £145 **Services** Lift Air con **Parking** 200 **Notes** Civ Wed 200

Macdonald Crutherland House

★★★★ 74% HOTEL

@@ Scottish, International ℃

Polished cooking in surroundings of great elegance

☎ 0844 879 9039 🖷 01355 577047
Strathaven Rd G75 0QZ
e-mail: crutherland@macdonald-hotels.co.uk
web: www.macdonaldhotels.co.uk
dir: Follow A726 signed Strathaven, straight over Torrance rdbt, hotel
on left after 250yds

Built at the beginning of the 18th century as a dower house, the
white-fronted hotel is set in 37 acres of mature parkland. Behind its
Georgian façade is a very relaxing hotel with spacious and
comfortable bedrooms and elegant public areas plus extensive
banqueting and leisure facilities, making it an ideal wedding venue,
as well as a health spa. There is a supremely elegant panelled dining
room, where restful lighting and comfortable leather chairs set the
tone. The menu has an up-market bistro feel to it, with special
dishes appearing on designated days of the week (Tuesday is beef
stroganoff day), and good Scottish produce in evidence throughout.
Start with Cullen skink, or Stornoway black pudding and egg in a
salad, before proceeding to Atholl Estate venison loin with
dauphinoise and roasted celeriac, or hake in a cockle and saffron
broth. Dark chocolate tart with vanilla ice cream is a crowd-pleasing
finale.

Rooms 75 (16 fmly) (16 GF) **D** £80-£175 (incl. bkfst)* **Facilities** Spa
STV⤓ Gym Sauna Steam room Xmas New Year Wi-fi **Conf** Class 100
Board 50 Thtr 500 Del from £115 to £155* **Services** Lift **Parking** 200
Notes LB ⊗ Civ Wed 300

Chef Kevin Hay **Owner** Macdonald Hotels **Restaurant**
Times 6.30-9.30 Closed L all week **Prices** Starter £5-£10, Main £14-
£25, Dessert £5-£9, Service optional **Wines** 62 bottles over £20, 14
bottles under £20, 14 by glass **Notes** Vegetarian available, Dress
restrictions, Smart dress, Air con **Seats** 80, Pr/dining room 300
Children Portions, Menu

HAMILTON   **Map 2 NS75**

Express by Holiday Inn Hamilton

BUDGET HOTEL

☎ 0141 419 3500 🖷 0141 419 3500
Keith St ML3 7BL
web: www.hiexpress.com/hamilton

A modern hotel ideal for families and business travellers. Fresh and
uncomplicated, the spacious rooms include Sky TV, power shower
and tea and coffee-making facilities. Continental buffet breakfast is
included in the room rate; other meals may be taken at the nearby
family pub or restaurant. See also the Hotel Groups pages
on theAA.com.

Rooms 104

LANARK   **Map 3 NS84**
See also **Biggar**

Best Western Cartland Bridge Hotel

★★★ 77% COUNTRY HOUSE HOTEL

☎ 01555 664426 🖷 01555 663773
Glasgow Rd ML11 9UF
e-mail: sales@cartlandbridge.co.uk
dir: Follow A73 through Lanark towards Carluke. Hotel in 1.25m

Situated in wooded grounds on the edge of the town, this Grade I
listed mansion continues to be popular with both business and
leisure guests. Public areas feature wood panelling, a gallery
staircase and a magnificent dining room. The well-equipped
bedrooms vary in size.

Rooms 20 (2 fmly) **Facilities** FTV Xmas New Year Wi-fi
Conf Class 180 Board 50 Thtr 250 Del from £108 to £140
Parking 120 **Notes** ⊗ Civ Wed 200

NEW LANARK   **Map 3 NS84**

New Lanark Mill Hotel

★★★ 79% HOTEL

☎ 01555 667200 🖷 01555 667222
Mill One, New Lanark Mills ML11 9DB
e-mail: hotel@newlanark.org
web: www.newlanark.org
dir: Signed from all major roads, M74 junct 7 & M8

Originally built as a cotton mill in the 18th century, this hotel forms
part of a fully restored village, now a UNESCO World Heritage Site.
There's a bright modern style throughout which contrasts nicely with
features from the original mill. There is a comfortable foyer-lounge
with a galleried restaurant above. The hotel enjoys stunning views
over the River Clyde.

Rooms 38 (5 fmly) (6 smoking) **S** £79.50; **D** £119-£144 (incl. bkfst)*
Facilities STV⤓ Gym Beauty room Steam room Sauna Aerobics
studios Xmas New Year Wi-fi **Conf** Class 60 Board 40 Thtr 200
Del from £120 to £130* **Services** Lift **Parking** 75 **Notes** LB
Civ Wed 120

Rissons at Springvale

★★★ RESTAURANT WITH ROOMS

◉ Modern Scottish ✆

Relaxed restaurant with modern Scottish cuisine

☎ 01357 520234 & 521131
18 Lethame Rd ML10 6AD
e-mail: rissons@msn.com
dir: M74 junct 8, A71, through Stonehouse to Strathaven

Husband-and-wife-team Anne and Scott Baxter have refurbished their small and friendly restaurant with rooms in a clean-cut contemporary style. The Victorian merchant's house offers stylish and well equipped bedrooms and bathrooms, and the light and airy restaurant and adjoining conservatory overlook the local park, making a relaxed setting for good food. It's an easy-going place with clued-up service, and the kitchen likes to keep things simple with a modern-bistro repertoire to match the mood. Dishes are kept unfussy and put together with attention to detail and sharp, well-balanced flavours. A starter of haggis balls with clapshot and Drambuie cream has Scotland stamped all over it, while mains might follow up with haunch of venison with sweet red cabbage and parsnip purée.

Rooms 9 en suite (1 fmly) (1 GF) S £37.50-£42.50; D £70-£75*
Facilities tea/coffee Dinner available Cen ht Wi-fi **Parking** 10
Notes ⊗ Closed 1st wk Jan No coaches

Chef Scott Baxter, Leonard Allen, Stephen Conway **Owner** Scott Baxter & Anne Baxter **Restaurant Times** 12-2.30/6-9.30 Closed New Year, 1 wk Jan, 1st wk Jul, Mon-Tue, L Sat **Prices** Fixed L 2 course £13.95, Starter £4-£8, Main £10-£16, Dessert £4.75-£6.50, Service optional **Wines** 13 bottles over £20, 23 bottles under £20, 6 by glass **Notes** Sunday L, Vegetarian available **Seats** 40 **Children** Portions, Menu

EAST LOTHIAN

The Open Arms

★★★ 79% SMALL HOTEL

☎ 01620 850241 📠 01620 850570
EH39 5EG
e-mail: openarms@clara.co.uk
web: www.openarmshotel.com
dir: From A1, follow signs for North Berwick, through Gullane, 2m on left

Long-established, this hotel lies across from the picturesque village green and Dirleton Castle. Inviting public areas include a choice of lounges and a cosy bar. Four of the garden bedrooms and the lounge provide particularly high standards. A variety of carefully prepared meals can be enjoyed in both the informal setting of Deveau's brasserie or the more intimate Library Restaurant.

Rooms 10 (1 fmly) **Facilities** Xmas **Conf** Class 150 Board 100 Thtr 200 **Parking** 30 **Notes** Closed 4-15 Jan

La Potinière

◎◎ Modern British ✆

Ambitious cooking in cottage-style restaurant

☎ 01620 843214
Main St EH31 2AA
dir: 20m SE of Edinburgh. 3m from North Berwick on A198

Keith Marley and Mary Runciman carry off their chef-proprietor double act with unfailing charm and serious skills: both are at work in the kitchen, while Keith juggles front-of-house and wine waiter duties to boot. The small cottagey dining room hardly lends itself to grand style statements, but its elegant, traditional charm and crisply-presented tables make a fine foil to the leisurely four-course dinners (three courses at lunch). Local, seasonal produce drives the cooking - suppliers are proudly named on the day's menu - in a repertoire of artfully presented modern British dishes, with two choices at each stage. Royale of foie gras with sweetcorn cream and apricot salad, precedes superbly fragrant Thai coconut soup with poached scallops, then braised halibut with crushed new potatoes in champagne and marjoram sauce. Round things off with passionfruit mousse or chocolate pudding.

Chef Mary Runciman, Keith Marley **Owner** Mary Runciman **Times** 12.30-1.30/7-8.30 Closed Xmas, Jan, Mon-Tue, D Sun (Oct-May) **Prices** Fixed L 2 course fr £18.50, Fixed D 4 course fr £40, Service optional **Wines** 28 bottles over £20, 8 bottles under £20, 5 by glass **Notes** Sunday L, Vegetarian available, Dress restrictions, Smart casual **Seats** 30 **Children** Portions **Parking** 10

HADDINGTON — Map 3 NT57

Eaglescairnie Mains

★★★★ ⒶBED AND BREAKFAST

☎ 01620 810491 📄 01620 810491
By Gifford EH41 4HN
e-mail: williams.eagles@btinternet.com
dir: 3.5m S of Haddington. B6368 from Haddington signed Humbie &
Bolton. Through Bolton, at top of hill fork left signed Eaglescairnie &
Gifford, 0.5m on left

Rooms 3 en suite S £40-£50; D £60-£75* **Facilities** TVL tea/coffee
Cen ht Wi-fi ⌾ **Parking** 10 **Notes** Closed Xmas

NORTH BERWICK — Map 3 NT58

Macdonald Marine Hotel & Spa

★★★★ 82% HOTEL

◉◉ European

Grand setting for fine dining

☎ 0870 400 8129 📄 01620 894480
Cromwell Rd EH39 4LZ
e-mail: sales.marine@macdonald-hotels.co.uk
web: www.macdonaldhotels.co.uk
dir: From A198 turn into Hamilton Rd at lights then 2nd right

Returned to its former grandeur after extensive refurbishment, this
majestic Grade II listed Victorian property is located on East
Lothian's famous championship golf course, overlooking the Firth of
Forth. Stylish public areas provide a relaxing atmosphere, and
bedrooms come in a variety of sizes and styles, all well equipped and
some impressively large. The hotel boasts extensive leisure and
conference facilities, while the recently decorated Craigleith
Restaurant sports rich red walls, deep red, gold and brown striped
curtains and lighting that is a mix of spotlights and chandeliers.
There are great views of the golf course and the coastline. The menu
features classic European cooking with some modern elements,
made using top-notch local and seasonal ingredients. Expect simply-
presented starters such as terrine of ham hock with olive oil and
plum chutney, followed by loin of venison served with sauté potatoes,
buttered greens, sticky red cabbage, parsnip purée and redcurrant
sauce. Finish with caramelised banana bavarois and banana sorbet.

Rooms 83 (4 fmly) (4 GF) **Facilities** Spa ⓠ supervised Putt green
Gym Indoor & outdoor salt water hydro pool Xmas New Year Wi-fi
Conf Class 120 Board 60 Thtr 300 **Services** Lift **Parking** 50 **Notes** LB
Civ Wed 150

Restaurant Times 12.30-2.30/6.30-9.30

WEST LOTHIAN

BATHGATE — Map 3 NS96

The Cairn Hotel

Ⓤ HOTEL

☎ 01506 633366 📄 01506 633444
Blackburn Road EH48 2EL
e-mail: cairn@mckeverhotels.co.uk
web: www.mckeverhotels.co.uk
dir: M8 junct 3A (Eastbound), at rdbt 1st left, next rdbt 2nd left,
small rdbt straight on then 1st slip road signed Blackburn, at T-junct
turn right, hotel next right

Currently the rating for this establishment is not confirmed. This may
be due to a change of ownership or because it has only recently
joined the AA rating scheme. Please see theAA.com for up-to-date
information.

Rooms 61 (2 fmly) (12 GF) S £69-£99; D £79-£120 (inl bkfst) LB
Facilities Wi-fi **Conf** Class 100 Board 50 Thtr 250 Del from £79-£89
Parking 80 **Notes** Xmas New Year Civ Wed 180

BLACKBURN — Map 3 NS96

Cruachan B & B

★★★ GUEST ACCOMMODATION

☎ 01506 655221 📄 01506 652395
78 East Main St EH47 7QS
e-mail: enquiries@cruachan.co.uk
web: www.cruachan.co.uk
dir: On A705 in Blackburn, 1m from M8 junct 4

Ideally located for both the leisure and business traveller to central
Scotland, with Edinburgh only 30 minutes away by train and Glasgow
only 35 minutes away by car. Cruachan is the comfortable, friendly
home of the Harkins family. Bedrooms are bright, attractive and very
well equipped. Breakfast, featuring the best of local produce is
served at individual tables in the ground-floor dining room.

Rooms 4 rms (3 en suite) (1 pri facs) (1 fmly) S £35-£60; D
£55-£65* **Facilities** FTV tea/coffee Cen ht Wi-fi **Parking** 5 **Notes** ⊗

EAST CALDER — Map 3 NT06

Ashcroft Farmhouse

★★★★★ GUEST HOUSE

☎ 01506 881810 📠 01506 884327
EH53 0ET
e-mail: scottashcroft7@aol.com
web: www.ashcroftfarmhouse.com
dir: On B7015, off A71, 0.5m E of East Calder, near Almondell
Country Park

With over 40 years' experience in caring for guests, Derek and
Elizabeth Scott ensure a stay at Ashcroft will be memorable. Their
modern home sits in lovely award-winning landscaped gardens and
provides attractive and well-equipped ground-floor bedrooms. The
comfortable lounge includes a video and DVD library. Breakfast,
featuring home-made sausages and the best of local produce, is
served at individual tables in the stylish dining room. Free Wi-fi is
now available, and a Park and Ride facility is nearby.

Rooms 6 en suite (2 fmly) (6 GF) S £55-£65; D £70-£80*
Facilities TVL tea/coffee Cen ht Wi-fi **Parking** 8 **Notes** ⊗ No Children
12yrs

FAULDHOUSE — Map 3 NS96

East Badallan Farm *(NS919598)*

★★★★ FARMHOUSE

☎ 01501 770251   Ms Struthers
EH47 9AG
e-mail: mary@eastbadallan.co.uk
web: www.eastbadallan.co.uk
dir: M8 junct 3 or 4 onto B7010

Equidistant between Edinburgh and Glasgow with great
transportation links this working beef farm has been in same family
since the 18th Century. Well appointed bedrooms with modern
facilities provided as standard. Hospitality is a strength as is the
breakfast with award winning local produce used.

Rooms 3 en suite (1 fmly) (1 GF) S £30-£40; D £60-£70*
Facilities FTV tea/coffee Cen ht Wi-fi **Parking** 0 **Notes** LB ⊗ ⊛ 127
acres beef

LINLITHGOW — Map 3 NS97

Arden Country House

★★★★★ 🏠 GUEST ACCOMMODATION

☎ 01506 670172 📠 01506 670172
Belsyde EH49 6QE
e-mail: info@ardencountryhouse.com
dir: 1.3m SW of Linlithgow. A706 over Union Canal, entrance 200yds
on left at Lodge Cottage

Situated in the picturesque grounds of the Belsyde Country Estate
and close to the Royal Burgh of Linlithgow, Arden Country House
offers immaculate, stylishly furnished and spacious bedrooms. There
is a cosy ground-floor lounge and a charming dining room where
delicious breakfasts feature the best of local produce. Beth
Cruickshank was a finalist for the AA Friendliest Landlady of the Year
2008 Award.

Rooms 3 en suite (1 GF) S £50-£100; D £80-£110* **Facilities** FTV
tea/coffee Cen ht Wi-fi **Parking** 4 **Notes** LB ⊗ No Children 12yrs
Closed 25-26 Dec

Belsyde House

★★★★ 🏠 GUEST ACCOMMODATION

☎ 01506 842098 📠 01506 842098
Lanark Rd EH49 6QE
e-mail: hay@belsydehouse.co.uk
web: www.belsydehouse.co.uk
dir: 1.5m SW on A706, 1st left over Union Canal

Reached by a tree-lined driveway, this welcoming farmhouse is
peacefully situated in attractive grounds close to the Union Canal.
There are well-proportioned double, twin and family rooms, and a
cosy single. All are nicely furnished and well equipped. Breakfast,
including a vegetarian menu, is served at good-sized tables in the
dining room, next to the lounge.

Rooms 3 en suite (1 fmly); D £70-£90* **Facilities** TVL tea/coffee
Cen ht Wi-fi **Parking** 10 **Notes** ⊗ No Children 12yrs Closed Xmas

Bomains Farm

★★★★ GUEST HOUSE

☎ 01506 822188 & 822861 📠 01506 824433
Bo'Ness EH49 7RQ
e-mail: bunty.kirk@onetel.net
web: www.bomains.co.uk
dir: A706, 1.5m N towards Bo Ness, left at golf course x-rds, 1st farm
on right

From its elevated location this friendly farmhouse has stunning
views of the Firth of Forth. The bedrooms which vary in size are
beautifully decorated, well equipped and enhanced by quality fabrics,
with many thoughtful extra touches. Delicious home-cooked fare
featuring the best of local produce is served a stylish lounge-dining
room.

Rooms 5 rms (4 en suite) (1 pri facs) (1 fmly) **Facilities** STV TVL tea/
coffee Cen ht Wi-fi Golf 18 Fishing **Parking** 12

Lumsdaine House

★★★★ BED AND BREAKFAST

☎ 01506 845001
Woodcockdale Farm, Lanark Rd EH49 6QE
e-mail: margaret@lumsdainehouse.co.uk
dir: 1.5m SW on A706

Just a few minutes drive from historical town of Linlithgow this purpose built property offers modern, comfortable and spacious accommodation with some wonderful views. Hospitality is very strong and the Healthy Living Award breakfast gives the guest a great start to their day. Ample parking with large gardens.

Rooms 3 en suite S £35-£40; D £55 £60* **Facilities** TVL tea/coffee Cen ht Wi-fi **Parking** 3 **Notes** ⊗ No Children 14yrs Closed 20 Dec-1 Jan

Champany Inn

◉◉ Traditional British ⚑

Fabulous, properly hung Angus beef the star of the show

☎ 01506 834532 & 834388 📄 01506 834302
Champany Corner EH49 7LU
e-mail: reception@champany.com
dir: 2m NE of Linlithgow. From M9 (N) junct 3, at top of slip road turn right. Champany 500yds on right

A short trip out from Edinburgh, a collection of buildings, partly dating back to the days of Mary, Queen of Scots, has been turned into two splendid restaurants. The more informal is the easy chair and couch-strewn Chop and Ale House bar, where your eyes will alight on the rock pond, where you'll find fresh Loch Gruinart oysters and lobsters before preparation for the pot. The Champany has long been beacon for prime Scots beef, and the rambling buildings centre on an octagonal dining room that has become a temple to the king of meats. Walking from the bar to the restaurant takes you past a chilled counter filled with a selection of steaks for the charcoal grill. You might start with giant prawns in piri-piri seasoning, or Loch Gruinart oysters, and finish with perfectly executed crème brûlée with rhubarb and ginger compôte, but the chances are that what you're mainly here for are the minimally garnished cuts of 3-week-hung Aberdeen Angus, such as charcoal-grilled half-sirloin or sauced entrecote. Other meats might include double loin chops of lamb, or breast and leg of corn-fed chicken with chorizo mousseline. Formal but friendly service gets the balance right.

Chef C Davidson, D Gibson, Liam Ginname **Owner** Mr & Mrs C Davidson **Times** 12.30-2/7-10 Closed 25-26 Dec, 1-2 Jan, Sun, L Sat **Prices** Food prices not confirmed for 2010. Please telephone for details. **Wines** 650 bottles over £20, 8 bottles under £20, 8 by glass **Notes** Vegetarian available, Dress restrictions, No jeans or T-shirts **Seats** 50, Pr/dining room 30 **Parking** 50

Open all wk noon-2 6.30-10 (Fri-Sun noon-10) Closed: 25-26 Dec, 1 Jan **Bar Meals** food served all day **Restaurant** food served all day ⊕ FREE HOUSE ◖ Belhaven. **Facilities** Children's menu Garden Parking

Livingston's Restaurant

◉◉ Modern Scottish

Traditional Scottish cooking in a charming family-run restaurant

☎ 01506 846565
52 High St EH49 7AE
e-mail: contact@livingstons-restaurant.co.uk
web: www.livingstons-restaurant.co.uk
dir: Opposite post office

Set in the shadows of Linlithgow Palace, this charming restaurant is reached through a vennel off the main street. Once the stables for Linlithgow Palace during the reign of Mary, Queen of Scots, family-run Livingston's provides an authentic Scottish experience. Set partly in a conservatory looking on to the garden with a glimpse of the loch through the trees, ruby red fabrics, tartan carpets and soft candlelight unite to create a relaxed, Caledonian atmosphere. The modern Scottish menu showcases local ingredients in dishes such as whisky and orange cured salmon with rocket, orange and shallot vinaigrette. This could be followed by roast rack of Border Blackface lamb, slow-cooked shoulder fritter, spring greens, heritage potatoes and new season garlic.

Times 12-2.30/6-9.30 Closed 1 wk Jun, 1 wk Oct, 2wks Jan, Sun (except Mothering Sun)-Mon

Ship 2 Shore 24

◉ Modern Scottish ℭ

The best of Scottish seafood

☎ 01506 840123
57 High St EH49 7ED
dir: On the High St, across road from the Palace

Located in the heart of historic Linlithgow, Ship 2 Shore 24 is a restaurant that has a clear focus: presenting the freshest fish to the customer. The menus list the names of the skippers who landed the fish, and their wares are also on display - and available to buy - at a wet fish counter. The dining room is decorated with vibrant Scottish artworks and, at weekends, tablecloths appear to create a more intimate ambience. Service is informal, the daily specials revealed with enthusiasm. The freshness and quality of the produce is the draw here, such as the smoked haddock in a Cullen skink starter, and main-course fillet of halibut with fennel, Parisienne potatoes and mussel and Pernod sauce.

Chef Douglas Elliman **Times** 12-2.15/5.30-10 Closed 25 Dec, 1 Jan, **Prices** Fixed D 3 course fr £30.50, Starter £3.50-£6.50, Main £4.95-£20, Dessert £4.90-£5.85, Service optional **Wines** 46 bottles over £20, 30 bottles under £20, 9 by glass **Notes** Early dining menu Tue-Fri 5.30-7.30, Vegetarian available, Air con **Seats** 50

LIVINGSTON
Map 3 NT06

See also **East Calder**

Travelodge Livingston

BUDGET HOTEL

☎ 0871 984 6288 📠 0121 521 6026
Almondvale Cresent EH54 6QX
web: www.travelodge.co.uk
dir: M8 junct 3 onto A899 towards Livingston. At 2nd rdbt right onto A779. At 2nd rdbt left. Lodge on left

Travelodge offers good quality, good value, modern accommodation. Ideal for families, the spacious en suite bedrooms include remote-control TV, tea and coffee-making facilities and comfortable beds. Meals can be taken at the nearby family restaurant. See also the Hotel Groups pages on theAA.com.

Rooms 60 **S** fr £29; **D** fr £29

Redcraig

★★★★ BED AND BREAKFAST

☎ 01506 884249 📠 01506 884249
Redcraig, Midcalder EH53 0JT
e-mail: jcampbelljack@aol.com
web: www.redcraigbedandbreakfast.co.uk
dir: Off A71, turn for Morton between Lizzie Brice rdbt (Livingston) & Kirknewton traffic lights

Enjoying a peaceful location within easy reach of central Scotland's major motorway and rail network, and situated half way between Edinburgh and Glasgow this friendly family home offers spotless, comfortable and stylish accommodation in a relaxed environment. Bedrooms are attractive and well equipped with two situated on the ground floor. Hearty breakfasts are served in the smart dining room.

Rooms 3 en suite (2 GF) S £40-£45; D £56-£65* **Facilities** tea/coffee Cen ht Wi-fi **Parking** 6 **Notes** ⊛ ⊜

Whitecroft

★★★★ BED AND BREAKFAST

☎ 01506 882494 📠 01506 882598
7 Raw Holdings EH53 0ET
e-mail: lornascot@aol.com
dir: A71 onto B7015, establishment on right

A relaxed and friendly atmosphere prevails at this charming modern guest house. The bedrooms, all of which are on the ground floor, are attractively colour coordinated, well-equipped and contain many thoughtful extra touches. Breakfast is served at individual tables in the smart dining room.

Rooms 3 en suite S £40-£50; D £60-£70 **Facilities** tea/coffee Cen ht Wi-fi **Parking** 5 **Notes** ⊛ No Children 12yrs

UPHALL
Map 3 NT07

Macdonald Houstoun House

★★★★ 78% HOTEL

The Tower

⦿ Traditional British

Confident cooking in historic house

☎ 0844 879 9043 📠 01506 854220
EH52 6JS
e-mail: houstoun@macdonald-hotels.co.uk
web: www.macdonaldhotels.co.uk
dir: M8 junct 3 follow Broxburn signs, straight over rdbt then at mini-rdbt turn right towards Uphall, hotel 1m on right

Once host to none other than Mary, Queen of Scots, Macdonald Houstoun House is steeped in history. This tower house lies in beautifully landscaped grounds and gardens and features a modern leisure club and spa, a choice of dining options, a vaulted cocktail bar and extensive conference and meeting facilities. Stylish bedrooms, some located around a courtyard, are comfortably furnished and well equipped. In the elegant fine-dining restaurant with garden views, the accomplished cooking is underpinned by classical techniques and quality Scottish ingredients are used. A starter of Ugie smokehouse smoked salmon, lettuce and capers might be followed by loin of Atholl estate venison, dauphinoise potatoes and roasted celeriac.

Rooms 71 (47 annexe) (12 fmly) (10 GF) **Facilities** Spa STV ⊛ ⊰ Gym Health & beauty salon Xmas New Year Wi-fi **Conf** Class 80 Board 80 Thtr 400 **Parking** 250 **Notes** ⊛ Civ Wed 200

Chef David Murray **Owner** Macdonald Hotels **Restaurant Times** -6.30-9.30 Closed L all week **Prices** Food prices not confirmed for 2010. Please telephone for details. **Wines** 74 bottles over £20, 16 bottles under £20, 13 by glass **Notes** Vegetarian available, Dress restrictions, Smart casual, no jeans or trainers, Civ Wed 200 **Seats** 65, Pr/dining room 30 **Children** Portions, Menu

WHITBURN
Map 3 NS96

Best Western Hilcroft

★★★ 79% HOTEL

☎ 01501 740818 & 743372 📠 01501 744013
East Main St EH47 0JU
e-mail: hilcroft@bestwestern.co.uk
dir: M8 junct 4 follow signs for Whitburn, hotel 0.5m on left

This purpose-built, well-established hotel is popular with business travellers and easily accessible from all major transport routes. Smart contemporary public areas feature a spacious and inviting lounge bar and restaurant. Well-equipped bedrooms come in a variety of sizes.

Rooms 32 (7 fmly) (5 GF) **Facilities** STV FTV New Year Wi-fi **Conf** Class 50 Board 30 Thtr 200 **Parking** 80 **Notes** ⊛ Civ Wed 180

MIDLOTHIAN

The Sun Inn

★★★★ INN

◉ Modern British

☎ 0131 663 2456
Lothian Bridge EH22 4TR
e-mail: thesuninn@live.co.uk
dir: On A7 towards Galashiels, opposite Newbattle Viaduct

Dating back to 1697 and situated within easy striking distance of Edinburgh. Major refurbishment has totally transformed this property and it now has boutique-style bedrooms (one featuring a copper bath) and modern bathrooms. High quality, award-winning food is served in stylish surroundings; drinks can be enjoyed in the terraced garden area.

Very popular locally (you should probably book for Friday or Saturday night) The Sun Inn describes itself as a gastro pub and you can expect fine quality local produce and an imaginative menu with contemporay, well-cooked dishes. The staff are very positive and friendly and the early bird menus go down very well. To start with you could try Thai fish cakes with bean salad, coconut and lentil broth. Keep in a far eastern mood with hoi sin marinated duck with dauphinoise potatoes and plum sauce, the potatoes balancing the dish perfectly. To finish, there's shortbread stack - crisp and buttery shortbread with a Drambuie and honeycomb cream and contrasting berry compote.

Rooms 5 en suite S £60-£65; D £80-£150* **Facilities** STV FTV tea/coffee Dinner available Cen ht Wi-fi Fishing **Parking** 50 **Notes** LB ⊗ RS Mon (ex BH) no food served in bar No coaches

Chef Ian & Craig Minto **Owner** Bernadette McCarron **Restaurant Times** 12-2/5-9 Closed L all week **Prices** Fixed L 3 courses £14.95, Fixed D 3 course £14.95, Starter £3.75-£7.25 Main £9.95-£25 Dessert £4.95-£6.25 Service optional **Wines** 27 bottles over £20, 24 bottles under £20, 13 by glass **Notes** Sunday L, Early bird menu 2 courses £10 12-2pm, Vegetarian available Dress restrictions, Smart casual **Seats** 90 **Children** Portions, Menu

Craigiebield House

★★★★ GUEST ACCOMMODATION

☎ 01968 672557
50 Bog Rd EH26 9BZ
e-mail: reservations.craigiebield@ohiml.com

Built in 1824 and set in its own well-tended grounds, this property offers comfortable modern accommodation with many thoughtful extras provided as standard. The bar and conservatory restaurant have recently enjoyed a refurbishment, and offer a relaxed and slightly more formal dining option.

Rooms 17 en suite (4 fmly) **Facilities** FTV tea/coffee Dinner available Direct Dial Cen ht Licensed Wi-fi **Conf** Max 200 Thtr 200 Class 100 Board 50 **Parking** 40 **Notes** ⊗ Civ Wed 150

The Howgate Restaurant ⚑

☎ 01968 670000 📠 01968 670000
Howgate EH26 8PY
e-mail: peter@howgate.com
dir: 10m N of Peebles. 3m E of Penicuik on A6094 between Leadburn junct & Howgate

A short drive from Edinburgh, the Howgate was once a racehorse stables and a dairy. These days this long, low building makes a warm and welcoming bar and restaurant, overseen by chefs Steven Worth and Sean Blake. There is an impressive wine list from all the corners of the world, great real ales, a regularly changing menu, and a 'dishes of the moment' selection. Options might include Borders venison and cranberry pie, pan-fried duck breast with asparagus, pan-fried trio of sea bass, salmon and king prawns, or mushroom and red pepper stroganoff.

Open all wk Closed: 25-26 Dec, 1 Jan **Bar Meals** L served all wk 12-2 D served all wk 6-9.30 Av main course £9.95 **Restaurant** L served all wk 12-2 booking required D served all wk 6-9.30 booking required Fixed menu price fr £15 Av 3 course à la carte fr £25 ⊕ FREE HOUSE ◀ Belhaven Best, Hoegaarden Wheat Biere. ⚑ 12 **Facilities** Children's menu Garden Parking

The Original Roslin Inn

★★★★ INN

☎ 0131 440 2384 📠 0131 440 2514
4 Main St EH25 9LE
e-mail: enquiries@theoriginalhotel.co.uk
dir: Off city bypass at Straiton for A703 (inn near Roslin Chapel)

Whether you find yourself on the Da Vinci Code trail or in the area on business, this property is a very short walk from the famous Roslin Chapel, which is well worth the visit. A delightful village inn, it offers well-equipped bedrooms with upgraded en suites. Four of the rooms have four-poster beds. The Grail Restaurant, the lounge and conservatory offer a comprehensive selection of dining options.

Rooms 6 en suite (2 fmly) (1 smoking) S £55-£65; D £75-£85 (room only)* **Facilities** STV tea/coffee Dinner available Cen ht Wi-fi **Conf** Max 100 Thtr 130 Class 80 Board 60 **Parking** 8 **Notes** LB Civ Wed 180

Red stag, Glengoulandie Deer Park

ARCHIESTOWN   Map 5 NJ24

Archiestown Hotel

★★★ 77% SMALL HOTEL

◉ Modern British, International

International cuisine in small Victorian country-house hotel

☎ 01340 810218 🖹 01340 810239
AB38 7QL
e-mail: jah@archiestownhotel.co.uk
web: www.archiestownhotel.co.uk
dir: A95 Craigellachie, follow B9102 to Archiestown, 4m

Set in the heart of a Speyside village, this small hotel is popular with visiting anglers while its restaurant is also much appreciated by the locals. A Victorian country house in the heart of whisky and salmon fishing country, it also has its own charming walled garden. The intimate bistro-style restaurant offers a seasonally-changing menu of dishes with an international influence. Home-smoked chicken and spicy vegetable spring rolls on herb leaf with a sweet chilli and ginger dipping sauce makes an impressive starter, followed by pan-fried breast of duck, compôte of Cognac-marinated prunes, potato rösti and red wine jus.

Rooms 11 (1 fmly) **S** £60-£75; **D** £120-£150 (incl. bkfst) **Facilities** 🏊
New Year Wi-fi **Conf** Board 12 Thtr 20 Del from £117.50 to £145
Parking 20 **Notes** LB Closed 24-27 Dec & 3 Jan-9 Feb

Restaurant Times 12-2/7-9 Closed Xmas, 3 Jan-10 Feb

CRAIGELLACHIE   Map 5 NJ24

Craigellachie

★★★ 81% HOTEL

◉ Traditional Scottish

Scottish cuisine in the heart of whisky country

☎ 01340 881204 🖹 01340 881253
AB38 9SR
e-mail: info@craigellachie.com
web: www.oxfordhotelsandinns.com
dir: On A95 between Aberdeen & Inverness

Set in a village in the heart of Speyside, Scotland's malt whisky distilling area, it will come as no surprise that this imposing Victorian hotel features almost 700 malts in its bar. Bedrooms come in various sizes but all are tastefully decorated and bathrooms are of a high specification. Speyside and the north east of Scotland are also renowned for local produce, and the Ben Aigan Restaurant makes full use of the prime Aberdeen Angus beef, Cabrach lamb and Moray Firth fish and seafood. Expect dishes such as Craigellachie smoked salmon served with a millefeuille of wholemeal bread and herb butter, and pan-fried rib of Aberdeen Angus beef with a leek and potato terrine.

Rooms 26 (1 fmly) (6 GF) **S** £85-£105; **D** £95-£185 (incl. bkfst)*
Facilities Gym Xmas New Year Wi-fi **Conf** Class 35 Board 30 Thtr 60
Del from £100 to £250* **Parking** 30 **Notes** Civ Wed 60

Restaurant Times 12-2/6-10

CULLEN   Map 5 NJ56

Cullen Bay Hotel

★★★ 75% SMALL HOTEL

◉ Traditional Scottish 🍸

Restaurant with glorious sea views and traditional Scottish fare

☎ 01542 840432 🖹 01542 840900
A98 AB56 4XA
e-mail: stay@cullenbayhotel.com
web: www.cullenbayhotel.com
dir: on A98, 1m west of Cullen

The Moray Firth is one of the UK's wildlife hotspots for sighting dolphins, porpoises and minke whales, and this small family-run hotel perched above Cullen Bay's beach gets grandstand views of their playground from many of the bedrooms as well as the public areas, which include a comfortable modern bar, a quiet lounge and a dining room where breakfasts are served. You can make the most of the splendid views through full-length picture windows in the restaurant, while tucking into traditional Scottish cooking with modern European twists in the relaxed restaurant. Local boats provide seafood, while the verdant hills of the hinterland cater for meat, game and cheese. While you're in the homeland of Cullen skink, that seems the obvious way to start, followed by grilled red mullet fillets with orange-glazed fennel, with pesto dressing.

Rooms 14 (3 fmly) **Facilities** New Year Wi-fi **Conf** Class 80 Board 80

continued

Thtr 200 **Parking** 100 **Notes** ⊗ Civ Wed 200

Chef Gail Meikle, Graham Kirby, David Allan **Owner** Mr & Mrs Tucker & Sons **Restaurant Times** 12-2/6.30-9 Closed From 2 Jan for 10 days, **Prices** Food prices not confirmed for 2010. Please telephone for details. **Wines** 6 bottles over £20, 42 bottles under £20, 8 by glass **Notes** Sunday L, Vegetarian available **Seats** 60, Pr/dining room 40 **Children** Portions, Menu

The Seafield Arms Hotel

★★★ 68% HOTEL

☎ 01542 840791 🗐 01542 840736
Seafield St AB56 4SG
e-mail: info@theseafieldarms.co.uk
dir: In village centre on A98

Centrally located and benefiting from off-road parking, this is a small but friendly hotel. Bedrooms differ in size and style but all are comfortable. The popular restaurant serves well cooked meals using the very best of Scottish produce including the famous Cullen Skink.

Rooms 23 (1 fmly) **S** £59-£63; **D** £84-£94 (incl. bkfst)* **Facilities** FTV Xmas New Year Wi-fi **Conf** Class 16 Board 16 Thtr 16 **Parking** 17 **Notes** LB Civ Wed 200

Mansion House

★★★ 74% HOTEL

☎ 01343 548811 🗐 01343 547916
The Haugh IV30 1AW
e-mail: reception@mhelgin.co.uk
web: www.mansionhousehotel.co.uk
dir: ExitA96 into Haugh Rd, then 1st left

Set in grounds by the River Lossie, this baronial mansion is popular with leisure and business guests as well as being a popular wedding venue. Bedrooms are spacious, many having views of the river. Extensive public areas include a choice of restaurants, with the bistro contrasting with the classical main restaurant. There is an indoor pool and a beauty and hair salon.

Rooms 23 (2 fmly) (5 GF) **S** £88.50-£93.50; **D** £149-£192 (incl. bkfst)* **Facilities** ⊛ supervised Fishing Gym Hair studio New Year Wi-fi **Conf** Thtr 180 Del from £128 to £144 **Parking** 50 **Notes** LB ⊗ Civ Wed 160

Gordon Arms Hotel

☎ 01343 820508 🗐 01343 829059
80 High St IV32 7DH
e-mail: gordonarmsfochabers@live.co.uk
dir: A96 approx halfway between Aberdeen & Inverness, 9m from Elgin

This 200-year-old former coaching inn, close to the River Spey and within easy reach of Speyside's whisky distilleries, is understandably popular with salmon fishers, golfers and walkers. Its public rooms have been carefully refurbished, and the hotel makes an ideal base from which to explore this scenic corner of Scotland. The cuisine makes full use of local produce: venison, lamb and game from the uplands, fish and seafood from the Moray coast, beef from Aberdeenshire and salmon from the Spey - barely a stone's throw from the kitchen!

Open all day all wk 11-11 (Thu 11-mdnt Fri-Sat 11am-12.30am) **Bar Meals** L served all wk 12-2 D served all wk 5-9 ⊕ FREE HOUSE ◀ Caledonian Deuchars IPA, John Smiths Smooth, Guest Ales. **Facilities** Dogs allowed Parking

Ramnee

★★★ 75% HOTEL

☎ 01309 672410 🗐 01309 673392
Victoria Rd IV36 3BN
e-mail: info@ramneehotel.com
dir: Off A96 at rdbt on E side of Forres, hotel 200yds on right

Genuinely friendly staff ensure this well-established hotel remains popular with business travellers. Bedrooms, including a family suite, vary in size, although all are well presented. Hearty bar food provides a less formal dining option to the imaginative restaurant menu.

Rooms 19 (4 fmly) (2 smoking) **S** £80-£120; **D** £90-£150 (incl. bkfst)* **Facilities** STV Wi-fi **Conf** Class 30 Board 45 Thtr 100 Del from £135 to £150* **Parking** 50 **Notes** LB Closed 25 Dec & 1-3 Jan Civ Wed 100

PERTH & KINROSS

ALYTH   Map 5 NO24

Tigh Na Leigh Guesthouse

★★★★★ ≜ GUEST ACCOMMODATION

☎ 01828 632372   📄 01828 632279
22-24 Airlie St PH11 8AJ
e-mail: bandcblack@yahoo.co.uk
web: www.tighnaleigh.co.uk
dir: In town centre on B952

Situated in the heart of this country town, Tigh Na Leigh is Gaelic for 'The House of the Doctor or Physician'. Its location and somewhat sombre façade are in stunning contrast to what lies inside. The house has been completely restored to blend its Victorian architecture with contemporary interior design. Bedrooms, including a superb suite, have state-of-the-art bathrooms. There are three entirely different lounges, while delicious meals are served in the conservatory/dining room overlooking a spectacular landscaped garden.

Rooms 5 en suite (1 GF) S £45; D £90-£115* **Facilities** FTV TVL tea/coffee Dinner available Cen ht Licensed Wi-fi **Parking** 5 **Notes** No Children 12yrs Closed Dec-Feb

AUCHTERARDER   Map 3 NN91

The Gleneagles Hotel

★★★★★ HOTEL

Andrew Fairlie@Gleneagles

◎◎◎◎ Modern French 🖐

Dramatic setting, inspired food

☎ 01764 662231   📄 01764 662134
PH3 1NF
e-mail: resort.sales@gleneagles.com
web: www.gleneagles.com
dir: Off A9 at exit for A823 follow signs for Gleneagles Hotel

The AA's Hotel of the Year for Scotland 2009-2010 has an international reputation for high standards, and provides something for everyone. Set in a delightful location, Gleneagles offers a peaceful retreat, as well as many sporting activities, including the famous championship golf courses. All bedrooms are appointed to a high standard and offer both traditional and contemporary styles. Stylish public areas include various dining options - see below for The Strathearn, with two AA Rosettes. Long synonymous with golf, these days, thanks to Andrew Fairlie, Gleneagles is also associated with world-class dining. Operating as an independent business on the ground floor of this imposing hotel, the restaurant, open only for dinner, produces refined, intelligent and intricate cooking. As the first ever Roux Scholarship winner, and having trained under the legendary Michel Guérard, it is perhaps not surprising that Fairlie's inspiration is the South West of France, and, of course, the superb produce of his native Scotland. The elegant dark-panelled walls, floor-to-ceiling silk drapes and banquettes sumptuously covered in rich fabrics with a stylish leaf motif, and bespoke artworks by Archie

Frost, create a smart and stylish space. Service is highly polished, the welcome warm and genuine. Menus du marché and dégustation are available if all on a table are agreed, otherwise the à la carte offers a choice of five at each course and brings plenty of pleasures along the way. Amuse-bouche such as pumpkin and hazelnut velouté with sherry and mushroom espuma reveals the sheer technical skill and deftly handled flavours that await. First-course foie gras ballotine is perfectly partnered with an almond jelly, fig purée and divinely light brioche, and main-course fillet of wild venison comes with a wintery mix of roots and fruits, including beetroot, pumpkin, salsify, apples and pears. Presentation is stunning throughout, not least at dessert, where no holds are barred in the making of a dish of caramelised banana with peanut butter mousse, with the addition of space dust bringing a tingle to the tongue. The wine list, and sommelier, do justice to the food.

Rooms 232 (115 fmly) (11 GF) **D** £305-£560 (incl. bkfst)*
Facilities Spa STV FTV ⊙ supervised ⊰ ♨ 54 ♨ Putt green Fishing ⛳ Gym Falconry Off-road driving Golf range Archery Clay target shooting Gundog School Xmas New Year Wi-fi Child facilities
Conf Class 240 Board 60 Thtr 360 **Services** Lift **Parking** 277
Notes LB Civ Wed 360

Chef Andrew Fairlie **Owner** Andrew Fairlie **Restaurant Times** 6.30-10 Closed 24-25 Dec, 3 wks Jan, Sun, L all week **Prices** Starter £25-£35, Main £36, Dessert £14, Service optional **Wines** 300 bottles over £20, 12 by glass **Notes** Dégustation 6 course £95, Du Marché 6 course £85, Dress restrictions, Smart casual, Air con **Seats** 54

The Strathearn

◎◎ Classic

Memorable food and service in ballroom-style setting

☎ 01764 694270   📄 01764 662134
The Gleneagles Hotel PH3 1NF

The Strathearn Restaurant is a truly classic dining room. The elegant ballroom-style room is huge, with high ceilings and pillars, and a pianist adds to the traditional atmosphere. Classical dishes are given a modern slant on the seasonal menu, while a whole brigade of staff provides formal but by no means stuffy service. Flambé and carving trolleys and the top-notch wine list help make the occasion memorable. Expect a choice of hot or cold starters such as seared Loch Fyne scallops with roast cauliflower and spiced lentils, or Gleneagles-style dressed crab. Main courses might include loin and shoulder of Scotch lamb, sweetbreads and bubble-and-squeak.

Chef Paul Devonshire **Owner** Diageo plc **Times** 12.30-2.30/7-10 Closed L Mon-Sat **Prices** Fixed L course £40, Fixed D 3 course £55, Service optional **Wines** 100% bottles over £20, 15 by glass **Notes** Sunday L, Vegetarian available, Dress restrictions, Smart casual **Seats** 322 **Children** Portions, Menu

BLAIR ATHOLL — Map 5 NN86

Atholl Arms Hotel

★★★ 72% HOTEL

☎ 01796 481205   🖷 01796 481550
Old North Rd PH18 5SG
e-mail: hotel@athollarms.co.uk
web: www.athollarmshotel.co.uk
dir: off A9 to B8079, 1m into Blair Atholl, hotel near entrance to Blair Castle

Situated close to Blair Castle and conveniently adjacent to the railway station, this stylish hotel has historically styled public rooms that include a choice of bars, and a splendid baronial-style dining room. Bedrooms vary in size and style. Staff throughout are friendly and very caring.

Rooms 30 (3 fmly) **S** £45-£60; **D** £75-£90 (incl. bkfst)*
Facilities Fishing Rough shooting ♬ New Year **Conf** Class 80 Board 60 Thtr 120 **Parking** 103 **Notes** Civ Wed 120

BLAIRGOWRIE — Map 3 NO14

Gilmore House

★★★★ BED AND BREAKFAST

☎ 01250 872791   🖷 01250 872791
Perth Rd PH10 6EJ
e-mail: jill@gilmorehouse.co.uk
dir: On A93 S

This Victorian villa stands in a well-tended garden on the south side of town. Sympathetically restored to enhance its period features it offers individual bedrooms tastefully furnished in antique pine, and thoughtfully equipped to include modern amenities such as Freeview TV. There are two inviting lounges, one of which has lovely views over the gardens. Hearty traditional breakfasts are served in the attractive dining room.

Rooms 3 en suite; D £56-£70 **Facilities** FTV TVL tea/coffee Cen ht Wi-fi **Parking** 3 **Notes** Closed Xmas

COMRIE — Map 3 NN72

Royal Hotel

★★★ 82% HOTEL

◉ Traditional British

Traditional food in an elegant environment

☎ 01764 679200   🖷 01764 679219
Melville Square PH6 2DN
e-mail: reception@royalhotel.co.uk
web: www.royalhotel.co.uk
dir: off A9 on A822 to Crieff, then B827 to Comrie. Hotel in main square on A85

Comrie's central square sits at the junction where the rolling lowlands climb towards the Perthshire Highlands, a great location for this well-established 18th-century coaching inn. A traditional façade gives little indication of the style and elegance inside - it's all polished-wood floors, classy fabrics and cosy log fires. Bedrooms are tastefully appointed and furnished with smart reproduction antiques. There's a choice of the clubby lounge bar, conservatory-style brasserie, and classic formal dining room when it comes to eating, as well as the lovely walled garden in the warmer months. Traditional British dishes have their roots in local materials - fillet of sea bass with potato rösti and butter sauce, or roast rack of lamb with root vegetables and dauphinoise potatoes are typical of the style.

Rooms 13 (2 annexe) **S** £85-£105; **D** £140-£180 (incl. bkfst)
Facilities STV Fishing Shooting arranged New Year Wi-fi
Conf Class 10 Board 20 Thtr 20 **Parking** 22 **Notes** LB Closed 25-26 Dec

Chef David Milsom **Owner** The Milsom family **Restaurant Times** 12-2/6.30-9 Closed Xmas, **Prices** Fixed L 2 course £13.25-£26, Fixed D 3 course £27.75-£33.65, Starter £4.75-£7.25, Main £7.45-£19.95, Dessert £5.75, Service optional **Wines** 46 bottles over £20, 47 bottles under £20, 7 by glass **Notes** Sunday L, Vegetarian available **Seats** 60 **Children** Portions

COUPAR ANGUS — Map 3 NO23

Enverdale House

★★★ GUEST HOUSE

☎ 01828 627606   🖷 01828 627239
6 Pleasure Rd PH13 9JB

Enverdale House is located on a quiet road and is a short walk from the centre of the small market town of Couper Angus. This family run guest house has attractively presented bedrooms, and public rooms include a spacious lounge bar along with large conference facilities. An extensive breakfast menu is provided and evening meals are served in the stylish restaurant.

Rooms 5 en suite (1 fmly) **Facilities** FTV tea/coffee Dinner available Cen ht Licensed Wi-fi **Notes** ⊗ Civ Wed 200

Merlindale

★★★★ BED AND BREAKFAST

Perth Rd PH7 3EQ

☎ 01764 655205 📠 01764 655205
e-mail: merlin.dale@virgin.net
web: www.merlindale.co.uk
dir: On A85, 350yds from E end of High St

Situated in a quiet residential area within walking distance of the town centre, this delightful detached house stands in well-tended grounds and offers a warm welcome. The pretty bedrooms are comfortably furnished and well equipped. There is a spacious lounge, an impressive library, and an elegant dining room where delicious evening meals and traditional breakfasts are served.

Rooms 3 en suite (1 fmly)* **Facilities** STV TVL tea/coffee Dinner available Cen ht Wi-fi **Parking** 3 **Notes** ⊗ Closed 9 Dec-10 Feb ☺

Fortingall

★★★★ 78% SMALL HOTEL

◉◉ Modern Scottish ☺

Imaginative cooking in luxurious small hotel

☎ 01887 830367 & 830368 📠 01887 830367
PH15 2NQ
e-mail: hotel@fortingallhotel.com
dir: B846 from Aberfeldy for 6m, left signed Fortingall for 3m. Hotel in village centre

The Arts and Crafts village of Fortingall is in Glen Lyon, Scotland's longest glen, and the impressively refurbished hotel has a prime position with views over wooded slopes and towering peaks. All the bedrooms are very well equipped and have an extensive range of thoughtful extras. The comfortable lounge, with its log fire, is ideal for pre-dinner drinks, and the small bar is full of character. The main dining room follows the Arts and Crafts theme with its furniture and tweed curtains, and a second slightly more informal room, the Yew dining room, has views over the garden. The daily-changing menu makes good use of regional produce in a range of modern Scottish dishes with European influences: start with sweetbread and chicken terrine with mint jelly, followed by chargrilled lamb - excellent quality - with Arran mustard rösti, root vegetables and wild mushroom sauce. Friendly service comes from a young team.

Rooms 10 (1 fmly) **S** £99-£119; **D** £148-£194 (incl. bkfst)*
Facilities STV Fishing Stalking ♪♪ Xmas New Year Wi-fi
Conf Board 16 Thtr 30 **Parking** 20 **Notes** LB Civ Wed 30

Chef Darin Campbell **Owner** Iain & Janet Wotherspoon **Restaurant Times** 12-2/6.30-9 **Prices** Starter £3.95-£6.95, Main £13.95-£21.95, Dessert £5.50-£7.95, Service optional **Wines** 42 bottles over £20, 30 bottles under £20, 4 by glass **Notes** Sunday L, Vegetarian available **Seats** 30, Pr/dining room 30 **Children** Portions, Menu

An Lochan Tormaukin

★★★★ INN

◉ Modern Scottish ☺

High quality local produce in relaxed, rustic surroundings

☎ 01259 781252
FK14 7JY
e-mail: tormaukin@anlochan.co.uk
dir: From A9 take A823 towards Dollar

A delightful country inn dating back to the 17th century, located in an idyllic, and secluded, setting not far from the famous Gleneagles Championship golf courses. The third addition to the McKie family's mini empire, this time they have taken a charming 17th-century country inn lost among the rolling Ochil hills and treated it to a tasteful modern makeover. The small team are friendly and welcoming, while crackling log fires, bare-stone walls and unclothed wooden tables contrast with vibrant artwork to set the tone in the snug and dining room, or there's a bright and airy conservatory. As in the other An Lochan properties in Glasgow and Tighnabruaich (see entries), modern Scottish menus are constructed from locally-sourced materials - Highland beef, Perthshire lamb, venison, game and seafood. Typical offerings include wild boar terrine with fig chutney and toasted brioche and roast rump of Highland beef in a herb shallot crust with dauphinoise potatoes and black cabbage.

Rooms 13 rms (12 en suite) (4 GF) S fr £85; D fr £100*
Facilities tea/coffee Dinner available Direct Dial Cen ht Wi-fi Golf 0
Conf Max 30 **Parking** 50 **Notes** LB Closed 24-25 Dec No coaches

Chef Gary Noble **Owner** Roger & Bea McKie **Restaurant Times** 12-3/5.30-9.30 Closed Please telephone for details, **Prices** Fixed L 2 course fr £10.95, Fixed D 3 course fr £19.95, Starter £3.95-£9.50, Main £7.25-£23.95, Dessert £4.25-£5.50, Service optional **Wines** 25 bottles over £20, 6 bottles under £20, 4 by glass **Notes** Early evening menu available 5.30-6.30pm, Sunday L, Vegetarian available **Seats** 40, Pr/dining room 25 **Children** Portions, Menu

Famous Bein Inn

★★ 76% SMALL HOTEL

◉ Scottish, French ☺

Traditional inn offering good Scottish food

☎ 01577 830216 📠 01577 830211
PH2 9PY
e-mail: enquiries@beininn.com
web: www.beininn.com
dir: On intersection of A912 & B996

Located in a wooded valley south of Perth, the immodest Bein Inn was originally built to accommodate those travelling between Edinburgh and the Highlands. A friendly welcome is guaranteed and there's a relaxed, informal atmosphere, with blazing log fires a

continued

GLENFARG CONTINUED

feature on colder evenings. There's a lively bar and a restaurant which delivers some sound Scottish cuisine - the dining room is comfortable in a traditional kind of way and the kitchen uses good Scottish produce to deliver the likes of Cullen skink and Highland rabbit and foie gras terrine among starters, and fish of the day - John Dory, perhaps - alongside rump of Perthshire blackface lamb served with sesame potatoes, cauliflower purée with broad beans, minted peas and a natural jus as main courses. Finish with dark chocolate and rosemary fondant with home-made white chocolate and heather honey ice cream.

Rooms 11 (4 annexe) (4 fmly) (4 GF) **S** £55-£65; **D** £75-£110 (incl. bkfst) **Facilities** FTV New Year **Conf** Class 35 Board 30 Thtr 50 Del from £75 to £100 **Parking** 26 **Notes** LB ⊗ Closed 25 Dec RS 24 & 26 Dec

Owner John & Allan MacGregor **Restaurant Times** 12-9 Closed 25 Dec, **Prices** Fixed L 2 course £15-£18, Fixed D 3 course £21.95-£26, Starter £4-£7, Main £10-£21, Dessert £4.50-£7, Service optional **Wines** 10 bottles over £20, 13 bottles under £20, 5 by glass **Notes** Sunday L, Vegetarian available **Seats** 30, Pr/dining room 30 **Children** Portions, Menu

---

GLENSHEE (SPITTAL OF) Map 3 N017

Dalmunzie Castle

★★★ 81% COUNTRY HOUSE HOTEL

◉◉ Traditional British ⬧NOTABLE WINE LIST

Cooking fit for a laird

☎ 01250 885224 📠 01250 885225
PH10 7QG
e-mail: reservations@dalmunzie.com
web: www.dalmunzie.com
dir: on A93 at Spittal of Glenshee, follow signs to hotel

Fresh Highland air and action-packed outdoor pursuits are on the doorstep of this turreted Scots baronial pile tucked away in a secretive glen. You're not going to bump into your fellow guests too often on the 6,500-acre estate, but if you're after company, the pistes of Glenshee are within easy reach for a day's skiing. Inside, it is the archetypal Laird's retreat, with antiques and log fires in comfy lounges, and Edwardian-style bedrooms, including spacious tower rooms and impressive four-poster rooms, that are furnished with antique pieces. The elegant blue and cream dining room, softly-lit at dinner, offers top-notch seasonal Scottish bounty that forms the backbone of French-tinged British dishes on a daily-changing menu featuring the likes of roasted pork tenderloin with Tuscan bean stew, parsnip purée and redcurrant jus, followed by seared Scottish

venison with celeriac pommes dauphinoise, clapshot (that's potato and swede mash to non-Scots), caramelised spiced pear and red wine sauce.

Rooms 17 (2 fmly) **S** £65-£125; **D** £140-£270 (incl. bkfst & dinner)* **Facilities** STV ⬧ 9 ⬧ Fishing ⬧ Clay pigeon shooting Estate tours Grouse shooting Hiking Mountain bikes Stalking New Year Wi-fi **Conf** Class 20 Board 20 Thtr 20 Del from £155 to £175* **Services** Lift **Parking** 43 **Notes** LB ⊗ Closed 1-28 Dec Civ Wed 70

Chef Katie Cleary **Owner** Scott & Brianna Poole **Restaurant Times** 12-2.30/7-9 Closed 1-28 Dec, **Prices** Fixed D 4 course fr £42, Service included **Wines** 45 bottles over £20, 17 bottles under £20, 4 by glass **Notes** Fixed D 4 course, Vegetarian available, Dress restrictions, Smart casual, Jacket & tie preferred **Seats** 40, Pr/dining room 18 **Children** Portions

---

Dalhenzean Lodge

★★★★ BED AND BREAKFAST

☎ 01250 885217 📠 0871 733 5419
PH10 7QD
e-mail: mikepurdie@onetel.com
dir: On A93 2m S of Spittal of Glenshee

Dalhenzean Lodge was built in 1715, and is situated in the shadow of Meall Uaine, overlooking Shee Water. Some seven miles from the ski slopes at The Cairnwell, it is well located for fishing, hill walking and climbing, with the Cateran Trail nearby. Bedrooms are beautifully decorated and have many thoughtful extras. Hearty breakfasts featuring the best of local produce are served in the ground-floor dining room.

Rooms 2 rms (1 en suite) (1 pri facs); D £55-£60* **Facilities** STV FTV tea/coffee Cen ht **Parking** 2 **Notes** LB ⊛

KENMORE Map 3 NN74

Kenmore Hotel

★★★ 77% HOTEL

Taymouth Restaurant

◉ Traditional Scottish

Historic inn with Tay views and quality Scottish cooking

☎ 01887 830205 📠 01887 830262
The Square PH15 2NU
e-mail: reception@kenmorehotel.co.uk
web: www.kenmorehotel.com
dir: off A9 at Ballinluig onto A827, through Aberfeldy to Kenmore, hotel in village centre

Built in 1572, Scotland's oldest inn, the historic Kenmore Hotel, sits on the beautiful banks of the Tay. The poet Rabbie Burns himself was so taken with the area that he composed a poem to it, written in pencil on the chimney breast of the cosy Poets' bar. But life's not all stuck in the 16th century here: the restaurant is a modern, light-and-airy conservatory-style affair with glorious views of the river and woodland. The kitchen takes the season's fresh local produce to deliver a menu of good honest, Scottish fare. Take sage and garlic-scented terrine of wild boar with toasted brioche and sloe berry jelly to start, followed by seared collops of Highland venison with Savoy cabbage, crispy pomegranate seeds and game jus.

Rooms 40 (13 annexe) (4 fmly) (7 GF) (11 smoking) **S** £64.50-£79.50; **D** £99-£129 (incl. bkfst)* **Facilities** STV Fishing Salmon fishing on River Tay Xmas New Year Wi-fi **Conf** Class 60 Board 50 Thtr 80 Del from £99 to £114* **Services** Lift **Parking** 30 **Notes** LB Civ Wed 150

Chef Duncan Shearer **Owner** Kenmore Estates Ltd **Restaurant Times** 12-6/6-9.30 **Prices** Fixed L 2 course £13.50-£18, Fixed D 3 course £22-£26.50, Starter £3.35-£5.65, Main £10.50-£22.50, Dessert £3.85-£5.25, Service optional **Wines** 14 bottles over £20, 35 bottles under £20, 11 by glass **Notes** Taste of Scotland menu £29.50, Sunday L, Vegetarian available, Air con **Seats** 140, Pr/dining room 140 **Children** Portions, Menu

---

KILLIECRANKIE Map 5 NN96

Killiecrankie House Hotel

★★★ 82% SMALL HOTEL

◉◉ Modern British

Modern cooking in a delightful small country-house hotel

☎ 01796 473220 📠 01796 472451
PH16 5LG
e-mail: enquiries@killiecrankiehotel.co.uk
dir: off A9 at Killiecrankie, hotel 3m along B8079 on right

Originally built in the 1840s, Killiecrankie is a former Victorian dower house which sits in fours acres of wooded grounds and beautifully landscaped gardens, enjoying a tranquil location facing the Pass of Killiecrankie and the River Garry. Public areas include the wood panelled bar and the cosy sitting room where original artwork and an open fire for the colder months are features. Each of the bedrooms is individually decorated, well equipped and offer wonderful views of surrounding countryside. Work up an appetite with a leg-stretcher around the lovely gardens, then take your seat for some impressive modern Scottish cooking. Fresh local ingredients including herbs and vegetables from the kitchen garden drive the four-course dinner menus, starting with the well-matched flavours of sautéed wild mushrooms, Parma ham and garlic served in puff pastry with parsley cream sauce. Main course might be pan-fried fillet of venison and wood pigeon breast with braised Savoy cabbage, chive mash and redcurrant game jus. Each dish comes matched with a wine from an excellent list, and there's an expertly-chosen array of malts to round things off.

Rooms 10 **Notes** Closed 3 Jan-12 Mar

Restaurant Times 6.30-8.30 Closed Jan- Feb, L all week

KINCLAVEN Map 3 NO13

Ballathie House Hotel

★★★★ 78% COUNTRY HOUSE HOTEL

◉◉ Modern Scottish **V**

Grand country-house by the river Tay

☎ 01250 883268 📠 01250 883396
PH1 4QN
e-mail: email@ballathiehousehotel.com
web: www.ballathiehousehotel.com
dir: From A9, 2m N of Perth, B9099 through Stanley & signed, or from A93 at Beech Hedge follow signs for Ballathie, 2.5m

Ballathie was once a railway halt on the route from Glasgow to Aberdeen, the overgrown track now half-concealing the remains of an old Episcopalian chapel. It would all be a sleepy backwater, were it not for the majestic Ballathie House, which rises in conical turrets above the surrounding green. Overlooking the River Tay, it's a popular retreat for anglers, and a perfect backdrop to a spot of high living, with its overstuffed chairs and open fires. Bedrooms range from well-proportioned master rooms to modern standard rooms, and many boast antique furniture and art deco bathrooms. It might be worth requesting one of the Riverside Rooms, which are in a purpose-built development right on the banks of the river, complete with balconies and terraces. The opulently attired dining room is the setting for some ambitious country-house cooking, which ranges from classic comforts such as chicken liver parfait with port-soaked plums and toasted brioche to startling (and successful) ideas like the salad of shredded rabbit with Puy lentils and a prune fritter. Sorbet or a soup, such as earthy mushroom and Madeira, come next on the prix-fixe menu, and are followed by multi-layered mains like roast Gressingham duck breast with creamed Savoy cabbage, fondant potato, chanterelles, parsnip, carrots and sauce moscovite. A little less complexity might sometimes help the food to even greater impact.

Rooms 41 (16 annexe) (2 fmly) (10 GF) **S** £95-£130; **D** £190-£260 (incl. bkfst) **Facilities** FTV Putt green Fishing 🛥 Xmas New Year Wi-fi **Conf** Class 20 Board 30 Thtr 50 Del from £160 to £180 **Services** Lift **Parking** 50 **Notes** LB Civ Wed 90

Chef Andrew Wilkie **Owner** Ballathie House Hotel Ltd **Restaurant Times** 12.30-2/7-9 **Prices** Fixed L 2 course £18.50, Fixed D 3 course £41.50, Service optional **Wines** 220 bottles over £20, 4 bottles under £20, 6 by glass **Notes** Sunday L, Vegetarian menu, Dress restrictions, Jacket & tie preferred, No jeans/T-shirts **Seats** 70, Pr/dining room 32 **Children** Portions

KINLOCH RANNOCH — Map 5 NN65

Dunalastair

★★★ 77% HOTEL

🏵 Modern British

Traditional Highland hotel with confidently prepared food

☎ 01882 632323 & 632218 📄 01882 632371
PH16 5PW
e-mail: robert@dunalastair.co.uk
web: www.dunalastair.co.uk
dir: A9 to Pitlochry, at northern end take B8019 to Tummel Bridge then A846 to Kinloch Rannoch

Dunalastair is a solidly traditional Highland house dating from 1770, and in its long history has served as a staging post and barracks for Jacobite troops. Standard and superior bedrooms are on offer, and the friendly, attentive service by delightful staff will leave a lasting impression. There's certainly no forgetting that you're north of the border amid the baronial oak panelling, antler chandeliers and tartan carpets in the restaurant. The kitchen takes traditional country-house cuisine built on excellent Scottish produce and gives it a modern spin, delivering accurately cooked, uncomplicated dishes with beautifully balanced flavours. Go for confit duck leg with red onion compôte and an orange reduction, and move on to chargrilled beef fillet with butternut squash purée, glazed shallots and Madeira jus.

Rooms 28 (4 fmly) (9 GF) **Facilities** Fishing 4x4 safaris Rafting Clay pigeon shooting Bike hire Archery Xmas New Year Child facilities **Conf** Class 40 Board 40 Thtr 60 **Parking** 33 **Notes** LB Civ Wed 70

Restaurant Times 12-2.30/6.30-9

Macdonald Loch Rannoch Hotel

★★★ 73% HOTEL

☎ 0844 879 9059 & 01882 632201 📄 01882 632203
PH16 5PS
e-mail: loch_rannoch@macdonald-hotels.co.uk
web: www.macdonald-hotels.co.uk
dir: Off A9 onto B847 Calvine. Follow signs to Kinloch Rannoch, hotel 1m from village

Set deep in the countryside with elevated views across Loch Rannoch, this hotel is built around a 19th-century hunting lodge and provides a great base for exploring this beautiful area. The superior bedrooms have views over the loch. There is a choice of eating options - The Ptarmigan Restaurant and the Schiehallan Bar for informal eating. The hotel provides both indoor and outdoor activities.

Rooms 44 (25 fmly) **Facilities** 🏊 Fishing Gym Xmas New Year Wi-fi **Conf** Class 80 Board 50 Thtr 160 **Services** Lift **Parking** 52 **Notes** Civ Wed 130

KINNESSWOOD — Map 3 NO10

Lomond Country Inn 🍷

☎ 01592 840253 📄 01592 840693
KY13 9HN
e-mail: info@lomondcountryinn.co.uk
dir: M90 junct 5, follow signs for Glenrothes then Scotlandwell, Kinnesswood next village

A small, privately owned hotel on the slopes of the Lomond Hills that has been entertaining guests for more than 100 years. It is the only hostelry in the area with uninterrupted views over Loch Leven to the island on which Mary Queen of Scots was imprisoned. The cosy public areas offer log fires, a friendly atmosphere, real ales and a fine collection of single malts. If you want to make the most of the loch views, choose the charming restaurant, a relaxing room freshly decorated in country house style. Now under new management, the focus is on serving well kept real ales such as Orkney Dark Island, and a mix of traditional and favourite pub dishes which are all competitively priced.

Open all day all wk 7am-1am **Bar Meals** L served all wk 7am-9pm D served all wk 5-9 Av main course £5.95 food served all day **Restaurant** L served all wk 7am-9pm D served all wk 5-9 Fixed menu price fr £9.95 Av 3 course à la carte fr £18.95 food served all day ⊕ FREE HOUSE ◖ Deuchars IPA, Calders Cream, Tetleys, Orkney Dark Island, Bitter & Twisted. 🍷 6 **Facilities** Children's menu Play area Family room Dogs allowed Garden Parking

KINROSS — Map 3 NO10

The Green Hotel

★★★★ 73% HOTEL

🏵 Modern International

Contemporary restaurant with classic-based modern cuisine

☎ 01577 863467 📄 01577 863180
2 The Muirs KY13 8AS
e-mail: reservations@green-hotel.com
web: www.green-hotel.com
dir: M90 junct 6 follow Kinross signs, onto A922 for hotel

Nothing to do with eco-friendly philosophy, the Green in this hotel's name is the type that golf balls are whacked along. It has its origins as an 18th-century staging post on the road north from Edinburgh, but the two golf courses and prospect of trout fishing on Loch Leven are just two of the pursuits that bring travellers to a halt these days. The comfortable, well-equipped bedrooms, most of which are generously proportioned, boast attractive colour schemes and smart modern furnishings. Colourful artwork and exuberant flower displays make Basil's restaurant a cheery place for tucking into the kitchen's modern interpretations of classic dishes. Look out for terrine of monkfish with foie gras, wild mushrooms and Madeira jus for starters, followed by grilled sea bass with mussel and cider broth.

Rooms 46 (3 fmly) (14 GF) **Facilities** STV 🏊 supervised 🏌 36 ⛳ Putt green Fishing 🏌 Gym Squash Petanque Curling (Sep-Apr) New Year Wi-fi **Conf** Class 75 Board 60 Thtr 130 **Parking** 60 **Notes** LB Closed 23-24 & 26-28 Dec RS 25 Dec Civ Wed 100

Restaurant Times 7-9.30

The Windlestrae Hotel & Leisure Centre

★★★ Ⓐ HOTEL

☎ 01577 863217 📠 01577 864733
The Muirs KY13 8AS
e-mail: reservations@windlestraehotel.com
web: www.windlestraehotel.com
dir: M90 junct 6 into Kinross, left at 2nd mini rdbt. Hotel 400yds on right

Rooms 45 (13 GF) **S** £60-£100; **D** £80-£140 (incl. bkfst)*
Facilities STV Ⓡ supervised ♨ 36 ⛳ Gym Beautician Steam room Toning tables Xmas New Year Wi-fi **Conf** Class 100 Board 80 Thtr 250 Del from £90 to £160* **Parking** 80 **Notes** LB Civ Wed 100

Travelodge Kinross (M90)

BUDGET HOTEL

☎ 0871 984 6241 📠 01577 861641
Kincardine Rd, Moto Service Area, Turfhill Tourist Area KY13 0NQ
web: www.travelodge.co.uk
dir: Off M90 junct 6, on A977,Turfhills Tourist Centre

Travelodge offers good quality, good value, modern accommodation. Ideal for families, the spacious en suite bedrooms include remote-control TV, tea and coffee-making facilities and comfortable beds. Meals can be taken at the nearby family restaurant. See also the Hotel Groups pages on theAA.com.

Rooms 35 **S** fr £29; **D** fr £29

Barley Bree Restaurant with Rooms

★★★★ ⊛ RESTAURANT WITH ROOMS

☎ 01764 681451 📠 01764 910055
6 Willoughby St PH5 2AB
e-mail: info@barleybree.com
dir: A9 onto A822 in centre of Muthill

Situated in the heart of the small village of Muthill, and is just a short drive from Crieff, genuine hospitality and quality food are obvious attractions at this charming restaurant with rooms. The property has been totally refurbished under its new owners, and the stylish bedrooms are appointed to a very high standard. The public areas include a cosy lounge with a log burning fire.

A charming contemporary restaurant with rooms in the centre of the village. Plain, scrubbed wooden tables, wooden floors and a double-sided wood burning stove create a cosy, welcoming atmosphere. Art work by a local artist adds interest along with the original oak beams and exposed stone walls, and the small residents' lounge is ideal for pre-dinner drinks. To start you could have clear-flavoured ham hock and pig cheek terrine, with endive marmalade and pickled cucumber; follow that, perhaps, with tender, moist guinea fowl supreme, accompanied by lentils, pancetta and baby onion - a match made in heaven with the differing textures enhancing one another. End with pineapple and rhubarb cinnamon crumble. This is simple, rustic food with a twist, and well worth a visit.

Rooms 6 en suite (1 fmly) **S** £60-£65; **D** £85-£95* **Facilities** FTV tea/coffee Dinner available Cen ht Wi-fi **Parking** 10 **Notes** LB ⊗ Closed 2wks Autumn/Jan No coaches

Restaurant Times please telephone for details

Murrayshall House Hotel & Golf Course

★★★★ 76% HOTEL

⊛⊛ Modern British V ⓒ

Fine Scottish cuisine with stunning views

☎ 01738 551171 📠 01738 552595
New Scone PH2 7PH
e-mail: info@murrayshall.co.uk
dir: From Perth take A94 (Coupar Angus), 1m from Perth, right to Murrayshall just before New Scone

Two golf courses are a major draw at this fine old mansion set in 350 acres of the Grampian Hills. Bedrooms come in two distinct styles: modern suites in a purpose-built building contrast with more classic rooms in the main building. All that fresh air out on the links should help sharpen the appetite for a session in the Old Masters restaurant, where it's a good idea to try to bag a window seat with those magnificent views. Professional, friendly staff help foster a relaxed ambience for meals built on Scotland's bounty. Classic combinations are cooked with imagination and flair. Take rabbit served in a pastry case with Madeira jus and chanterelles to start, then Isle of Skye scallops with pig's cheeks and chorizo foam, and finish with a textbook chocolate fondant that releases its molten interior to perfection.

Rooms 41 (14 annexe) (17 fmly) (4 GF) **S** £100-£210; **D** £150-£210 (incl. bkfst)* **Facilities** STV ♨ 36 ⛳ Putt green Driving range New Year Wi-fi **Conf** Class 60 Board 30 Thtr 150 **Parking** 120 **Notes** LB Civ Wed 130

Chef Jonathan Greer **Owner** Old Scone Ltd **Restaurant Times** 12-2.30/7-9.45 Closed 26 Dec, L Sat **Prices** Fixed L 2 course £12.50, Fixed D 3 course £30, Starter £6-£8.50, Main £8-£11.50, Dessert £6-£8.50, Service optional **Wines** 30 bottles over £20, 20 bottles under £20, 8 by glass **Notes** Sunday L, Vegetarian menu, Air con **Seats** 55, Pr/dining room 40 **Children** Portions, Menu

Parklands Hotel

★★★★ 73% SMALL HOTEL

@@ Modern British

Imaginative, accomplished cuisine in a Victorian setting

☎ 01738 622451 📠 01738 622046
2 St Leonards Bank PH2 8EB
e-mail: info@theparklandshotel.com
web: www.theparklandshotel.com
dir: M90 junct 10, in 1m left at lights at end of park area, hotel on
left

The former residence of the Lord Provost enjoys an impressive
location with stunning views over the South Inch, yet is within easy
reach of the town centre. The enthusiastic proprietors continue to
invest heavily in the business and the bedrooms have a smart
contemporary feel. Public areas at the Parklands Hotel include a
choice of restaurants, with the stylish Victorian Acanthus Restaurant
providing the fine-dining option. Service here is formal and a menu
of creative, well-prepared dishes features top-notch local and
seasonal ingredients. Tuck into starters such as rabbit and white
bean terrine with onion toast and pickled walnuts, perhaps followed
by pan-roasted halibut with clam and squid ink spaghetti and
vermouth sauce. For a stylish finale, perhaps warm hazelnut tart with
honeycomb and clotted cream.

Rooms 15 (3 fmly) (4 GF) **S** £89-£159; **D** £109-£199 (incl. bkfst)
Facilities STV Wi-fi **Conf** Class 18 Board 20 Thtr 24 Del from £129.50
to £145.50 **Parking** 30 **Notes** LB Closed 26 Dec-3 Jan Civ Wed 40

Chef Graeme Pallister **Owner** Scott & Penny Edwards **Restaurant**
Times 7-9 Closed 26 Dec-7 Jan, Sun-Tue, L Wed-Sat **Prices** Fixed D 3
course £29.95, Service optional, Groups min 8 service 10% **Wines** 33
bottles over £20, 55 bottles under £20, 6 by glass **Notes** Vegetarian
available, Dress restrictions, Smart casual, no shorts or jeans
Seats 36, Pr/dining room 22 **Children** Portions, Menu

The New County Hotel

★★★ 75% HOTEL

@@ Modern British

Exciting culinary developments in city-centre boutique hotel

☎ 01738 623355 📠 01738 628969
22-30 County Place PH2 8EE
e-mail: enquiries@newcountyhotel.com
web: www.newcountyhotel.com
dir: A9 junct 11 Perth. Follow signs for town centre. Hotel on right
after library

At the heart of the garden city of Perth, this white-fronted boutique
hotel is situated next to the Bell Library. Catering for a business
clientele as well as the Perthshire smart set, the emphasis is on
sleek, modern design with the minimum of flounce. Upgraded
bedrooms have a modern stylish appearance and public areas
include a contemporary lounge area. Café 22 and a bar-bistro offer
simpler food, but the main gastronomic draw is the Opus One
restaurant, where wooden floors, simply appointed bare tables,
cream walls and low lighting create a restful, and supremely cool,
ambience. Service is professionally polished but versed in the
civilities too, and Ryan Young's modern British cooking is making
waves. Constructively resisting the temptation to over complicate,
dishes achieve great resonance, as in seared king scallops bedded
on truffled mash in a foamy seafood sauce - a starter of notable
intensity. Go on perhaps to tender venison loin with duck liver ravioli
and rosemary-scented celeriac purée, sauced lightly and fragrantly
with Marsala, before finishing with something like iced hazelnut
parfait with pineapple carpaccio in a subtle syrup. This is definitely
one to watch.

Rooms 23 (4 fmly) **S** fr £45; **Facilities** New Year Wi-fi **Conf** Class 80
Board 24 Thtr 120 Del from £90 to £125* **Parking** 10 **Notes** LB ⊗

Chef Ryan Young, David Cochrane **Owner** Mr Owen Boyle, Mrs Sarah
Boyle **Restaurant Times** 12-2/6.30-9 Closed Sun-Mon **Prices** Fixed L
2 course £15.95-£17.95, Fixed D 3 course £27.95-£36.45, Service
optional **Wines** 18 bottles over £20, 11 bottles under £20
Notes Vegetarian available **Seats** 48 **Children** Portions

Best Western Huntingtower

★★★ 75% HOTEL

⊛ Traditional British

Traditional Scottish cuisine in secluded setting

☎ 01738 583771 📠 01738 583777
Crieff Rd PH1 3JT .
e-mail: reservations@huntingtowerhotel.co.uk
web: www.huntingtowerhotel.co.uk
dir: 3m W off A85

This country-house hotel on the outskirts of Perth dates back to 1892 when it was the home of a mill owner. Situated in 6 acres of secluded landscaped gardens and grounds, it mixes period features and modern facilities. The public areas are smart and comfortable and bedrooms are of a high quality. (It's worth asking for one of the executive rooms.) Lunch is served in the conservatory, while the charming oak-panelled dining room sets the scene for more formal, intimate dining. The traditional menu features British cuisine with European influences, making good use of local produce, and might include starters such as pan-fried scallops with pesto and parmesan salad, followed by roast loin of Perthshire lamb, dauphinoise potatoes, roast root vegetables and rosemary gravy.

Rooms 34 (3 annexe) (2 fmly) (8 GF) **D** £50-£140* **Facilities** STV FTV Xmas Wi-fi **Conf** Class 140 Board 30 Thtr 200 Del from £99 to £145* **Services** Lift **Parking** 150 **Notes** LB Civ Wed 200

Restaurant Times 12-2/6-9.30

Best Western Queens Hotel

★★★ 75% HOTEL

☎ 01738 442222 📠 01738 638496
Leonard St PH2 8HB
e-mail: enquiry@queensperth.co.uk
dir: From M90 follow to 2nd lights, turn left. Hotel on right, opposite railway station

This popular hotel benefits from a central location close to both the bus and rail stations. Bedrooms vary in size and style with top floor rooms offering extra space and excellent views of the town. Public rooms include a smart leisure centre and versatile conference space. A range of meals is served in both the bar and restaurant.

Rooms 50 (4 fmly) **S** £50-£110; **D** £70-£125 (incl. bkfst)* **Facilities** STV FTV ⊙ Gym Steam room Xmas New Year Wi-fi **Conf** Class 70 Board 50 Thtr 200 **Services** Lift **Parking** 50 **Notes** LB ⊗ Civ Wed 220

Lovat

★★★ 74% HOTEL

☎ 01738 636555 📠 01738 643123
90 Glasgow Rd PH2 0LT
e-mail: enquiry@lovat.co.uk
dir: From M90 follow Stirling signs to rdbt. Right into Glasgow Rd, hotel 1.5m on right

This popular and long established hotel offers good function facilities and largely attracts a business clientele. There is a bright contemporary brasserie serving a good range of meals through the day until late.

Rooms 30 (1 fmly) (9 GF) **Facilities** Use of facilities at nearby sister hotel Xmas **Conf** Class 60 Board 50 Thtr 200 **Parking** 40 **Notes** LB ⊗ Civ Wed 180

Salutation

★★★ 70% HOTEL

☎ 01738 630066 📠 01738 633598
South St PH2 8PH
e-mail: salessalutation@strathmorehotels.com
dir: At end of South St on right before River Tay

Situated in heart of Perth, the Salutation is reputed to be one of the oldest hotels in Scotland and has been welcoming guests through its doors since 1699. It offers traditional hospitality with all the modern comforts. Bedrooms vary in size and are thoughtfully equipped. An extensive menu is available in the Adam Restaurant with its impressive barrel vaulted ceiling and original features.

Rooms 84 (5 fmly) **S** £45-£100; **D** £76-£150 (incl. bkfst) **Facilities** ♫ Xmas New Year Wi-fi **Conf** Class 180 Board 60 Thtr 300 **Services** Lift **Notes** LB Civ Wed 100

Express by Holiday Inn Perth

BUDGET HOTEL

☎ 01738 636666 📠 01738 633363
200 Dunkeld Rd, Inveralmond PH1 3AQ
e-mail: info@hiexpressperth.co.uk
web: www.hiexpress.com/perthscotland
dir: Off A9 (Inverness to Stirling road) at Inveralmond rdbt onto A912 signed Perth. Right at 1st rdbt, follow signs for hotel

A modern hotel ideal for families and business travellers. Fresh and uncomplicated, the spacious rooms include Sky TV, power shower and tea and coffee-making facilities. Continental buffet breakfast is included in the room rate; other meals may be taken at the nearby family pub or restaurant. See also the Hotel Groups pages on theAA.com.

Rooms 81 (43 fmly) (19 GF) (8 smoking) **S** £49-£99; **D** £49-£99 (incl. bkfst)* **Conf** Class 15 Board 16 Thtr 30

Innkeeper's Lodge Perth A9 (Huntingtower)

BUDGET HOTEL

☎ 0845 112 6007 ⧉ 0845 112 6293
Crieff Road (A85), Huntingtower PH1 3JJ
web: www.innkeeperslodge.com/perthhuntingtower
dir: From M90 junct 1, signed Inverness over Broxden rdbt onto A9.
Left signed Perth. At rdbt onto A85. Lodge on left (shared entrance
with Dobbies Garden World)

Innkeeper's Lodge represents an exciting, high value concept within
the budget hotel market. Comfortable bedrooms provide excellent
facilities that include satellite TV and modem points. Options include
family rooms; and for the corporate guest, cutting edge IT includes
Wi-fi access. Food is served all day in the adjacent Country Pub. The
extensive continental breakfast is complimentary. See also the Hotel
Groups pages on theAA.com.

Rooms 53

Innkeeper's Lodge Perth City Centre

BUDGET HOTEL

☎ 0845 112 6008 ⧉ 0845 112 6292
18 Dundee Rd PH2 7AB
web: www.innkeeperslodge.com/perth
dir: From M90 junct 11, A85 towards Perth. 2m, follow signs for Perth
& Scone Palace. After lights at Queens Bridge (A93), turn right into
Manse Rd. Lodge on left

Rooms 41 **Conf** Class 120 Board 120 Thtr 200

Travelodge Perth Broxden Junction

BUDGET HOTEL

☎ 0871 984 6168 ⧉ 01738 444783
PH2 0PL
web: www.travelodge.co.uk
dir: At junct of A9 & M90 (Broxden rdbt). Follow signs for Broxden
Services & Perth Park & Ride

Travelodge offers good quality, good value, modern accommodation.
Ideal for families, the spacious en suite bedrooms include remote-
control TV, tea and coffee-making facilities and comfortable beds.
Meals can be taken at the nearby family restaurant. See also the
Hotel Groups pages on theAA.com.

Rooms 87 **S** fr £29; **D** fr £29

Cherrybank Guesthouse

★★★★ GUEST ACCOMMODATION

☎ 01738 451982 ⧉ 01738 561336
217-219 Glasgow Rd PH2 0NB
e-mail: m.r.cherrybank@blueyonder.co.uk
dir: 1m SW of town centre on A93

Convenient for the town and major roads, Cherrybank has been
extended and carefully refurbished to offer well equipped and
beautifully presented bedrooms, one of which is on the ground floor.
The delightful lounge is ideal for relaxation, while delicious
breakfasts are served at individual tables in the bright airy dining
room.

Rooms 5 rms (4 en suite) (1 pri facs) (2 fmly) (1 GF) **Facilities** tea/
coffee Cen ht Wi-fi **Parking** 4 **Notes** ⊗

Clunie

★★★★ GUEST HOUSE

☎ 01738 623625 ⧉ 01738 623238
12 Pitcullen Crescent PH2 7HT
e-mail: ann@clunieguesthouse.co.uk
dir: On A94 on E side of river

Lying on the north east side of town, this family-run guest house
offers a friendly welcome. The comfortable bedrooms, which vary in
size, are attractively decorated and well equipped. Breakfast is
served at individual tables in the elegant ground-floor dining room.

Rooms 7 en suite (1 fmly) S £30-£40; D £60-£70* **Facilities** tea/
coffee Cen ht Wi-fi **Parking** 8 **Notes** LB ⊗

Westview

★★★★ BED AND BREAKFAST

☎ 01738 627787 ⧉ 01738 447790
49 Dunkeld Rd PH1 5RP
e-mail: angiewestview@aol.com
dir: On A912, 0.5m NW from town centre opp Royal Bank of Scotland

Expect a warm welcome from enthusiastic owner Angie Livingstone.
She is a fan of Victoriana, and her house captures that period, one
feature being the teddies on the stairs. Best use is made of available
space in the bedrooms, which are full of character. Public areas
include an inviting lounge and a dining room.

Rooms 5 rms (3 en suite) (1 fmly) (1 GF) **Facilities** STV TVL tea/
coffee Dinner available Cen ht **Parking** 4 **Notes** ⊜

The Anglers Inn

★★★ @ INN

☎ 01821 640329
Main Rd, Guildtown PH2 6BS
e-mail: info@theanglersinn.co.uk
web: www.theanglersinn.co.uk
dir: 6m N of Perth on A93

Extensively renovated since being bought by Jeremy and Shona Wares (formerley of 63 Tay Street) the Anglers has a bright modern restaurant with plain wooden tables, while a wood burning stove adds to the cosiness during the colder months. A very popular venue for shooting and fishing parties, as well as for racegoers (Perth Racecourse is just 2 miles away). Service is relaxed, friendly and informal, and the modern Scottish food might include a starter of Anglers fishcake with herb salad and chilli jam, and main courses like grilled breast of free range chicken with boulanger potatoes, savoy cabbage and tarragon jus. For pudding, try the excellent rhubarb crème brulee. There are five tastefully styled en suite bedrooms each equipped with flat-screen televisions and complimentary Wi-fi.

Rooms 5 en suite (1 fmly) S £50; D £100* **Facilities** FTV TVL tea/coffee Dinner available Cen ht Wi-fi ☺ Pool Table **Parking** 40 **Notes** LB No Children

Restaurant Times please telephone for details

Deans@Let's Eat

@@ Modern Scottish

Modern and imaginative Scottish cooking

☎ 01738 643377 📠 01738 621464
77-79 Kinnoull St PH1 5EZ
e-mail: deans@letseatperth.co.uk
web: www.letseatperth.co.uk
dir: On corner of Kinnoull St & Atholl St, close to North Inch

The Deans' lively and welcoming corner restaurant, close to the centre of town, is housed in a converted 19th-century theatre. These days there are no dramas or tragedies being played out, simply confident, contemporary Scottish cooking. There's a cosy bar for pre-dinner drinks and a dining room decorated in warm tones with tables immaculately laid and perfectly appointed. Service is friendly and attentive. The modern Scottish cooking is strong on the nation's best produce, notably prime Scotch beef and seafood. Accurately cooked fillet of halibut is grilled in lemongrass oil and comes with cumin rice, basil purée and warm lentil dressing, and chilled orange soufflé is a perfectly executed dessert.

Chef Willie Deans, Simon Lannon **Owner** Mr & Mrs W Deans **Times** 12-2.30/6.30-10 Closed Sun-Mon **Prices** Fixed L 2 course fr £13.95, Fixed D 3 course fr £25, Starter £3.95-£8.95, Main £11.95-£17.95, Dessert £5.75-£6, Service optional **Wines** 40 bottles over £20, 23 bottles under £20, 8 by glass **Notes** Early eve supper Tue-Thu from 6pm, Vegetarian available, Dress restrictions, Smart casual **Seats** 70 **Children** Portions **Parking** Multi-storey car park (100 yds)

63 Tay Street

@@ Modern Scottish V

Modern Scottish cooking in Perth

☎ 01738 441451 📠 01738 441461
63 Tay St PH2 8NN
e-mail: info@63taystreet.com
dir: In town centre, on river

In a city centre location, this stylish modern restaurant, housed in a large period building, serves imaginative dishes with a strong emphasis on fresh local produce. Views of the River Tay make it a popular lunch venue and in the evening it's more of a formal dining atmosphere, aided by skilled waiting staff. The modern Scottish cooking might take in well-executed hand-dived scallops with Jerusalem artichoke, truffle and hazelnut dressing, or a deconstructed main course of tasting of pork, which comprises of a pudding, beetroot-glazed cheek, confit with liver and crumbed belly, accompanied by garlic potato and apple sauce. Rhubarb and almond tart with rhubarb fool and root ginger ice cream confirms the kitchen's deft handling of flavours.

Chef Graeme Pallister **Owner** Scott & Penny Edwards, Graeme Pallister **Times** 12-2/6.30-9 Closed Xmas, New Year, 1st wk Jul, Sun-Mon **Prices** Fixed L 2 course £13.95-£14.95, Fixed D 3 course £32.50-£37.95, Service optional, Groups min 6 service 10% **Wines** 65 bottles over £20, 26 bottles under £20, 9 by glass **Notes** Vegetarian menu **Seats** 35 **Children** Portions

See also **Kinloch Rannoch**

Green Park

★★★ 87% COUNTRY HOUSE HOTEL

@ Modern, Traditional Scottish ☺

Fine cuisine in a lochside country-house hotel

☎ 01796 473248 📠 01796 473520
Clunie Bridge Rd PH16 5JY
e-mail: bookings@thegreenpark.co.uk
web: www.thegreenpark.co.uk
dir: turn off A9 at Pitlochry, follow signs 0.25m through town

The sylvan shores of Loch Faskally make a superb setting for this family-run country-house hotel. Most of the thoughtfully designed bedrooms, including a splendid wing and the comfortable lounges enjoy stunning views, while the traditional dining room, decorated in soothing shades of plum and honey, looks over well-kept gardens towards the loch, providing a delightful backdrop to the classic Scottish cuisine. The kitchen works with a splendid array of Perthshire produce - seafood and game feature strongly, as well as seasonal herbs and salads from the kitchen garden - in dishes such as a baked filo parcel of chicken with oven-dried tomatoes and lovage mousse. Main courses might take in roast loin of pork with herbs and oats, poached apples, watercress and cider sauce, or roast pheasant breast filled with haggis in whisky cream sauce.

Rooms 51 (16 GF) **S** £65-£93; **D** £130-£186 (incl. bkfst & dinner)* **Facilities** Putt green New Year Wi-fi **Parking** 51 **Notes** LB

continued

PITLOCHRY CONTINUED

Chef Chris Tamblin **Owner** Green Park Ltd **Restaurant**
Times 12-2/6.30-8.30 Closed L all week (ex residents) **Prices** Fixed D
3 course £21, Service optional **Wines** 10 bottles over £20, 65 bottles
under £20, 8 by glass **Notes** Sunday L, Vegetarian available, Dress
restrictions, Reasonably smart dress **Seats** 100 **Children** Portions,
Menu

Dundarach

★★★ 77% HOTEL

☎ 01796 472862 🖷 01796 473024
Perth Rd PH16 5DJ
e-mail: inbox@dundarach.co.uk
web: www.dundarach.co.uk
dir: S of town centre on main road

This welcoming, family-run hotel stands in mature grounds at the
south end of town. Bedrooms offer a variety of styles, including a
block of large purpose-built rooms that will appeal to business
guests. Well-proportioned public areas feature inviting lounges and a
conservatory restaurant giving fine views of the Tummel Valley.

Rooms 39 (19 annexe) (7 fmly) (12 GF) **S** £68; **D** £110 (incl. bkfst)*
Facilities Wi-fi **Conf** Class 40 Board 40 Thtr 60 **Parking** 39 **Notes** LB
⊗ Closed Jan RS Dec-early Feb

Moulin Hotel

★★★ 73% HOTEL ♟

☎ 01796 472196 🖷 01796 474098
11-13 Kirkmichael Rd, Moulin PH16 5EW
e-mail: sales@moulinhotel.co.uk
web: www.moulinhotel.co.uk
dir: Off A9 take A924 signed Braemar into town centre. Moulin 0.75m
from Pitlochry

Built in 1695 at the foot of Ben Vrackie on the old drove road from
Dunkeld to Kingussie, the inn faces Moulin's square, a rewarding
three-quarters of a mile from the busy tourist centre of Pitlochry. A
great all-round inn, popular as a walking and touring base, it offers
comfortable, well-equipped accommodation, extensive menus, and
conference and function room facilities. Locals are drawn to the bar
for the excellent home-brewed beers, with Ale of Atholl, Braveheart,
Moulin Light, and Old Remedial served on handpump. A major
refurbishment of the building in the 1990s opened up old fireplaces
and beautiful stone walls that had been hidden for many years, and
lots of cosy niches were created using timbers from the old Coach
House (now the brewery). The courtyard garden is lovely in summer,
while blazing log fires warm the Moulin's rambling interior in winter.
Menus partly reflect the inn's Highlands location, and although more
familiar dishes are available such as seafood pancake, lamb shank
and fish and chips, you also have the opportunity to try something
more local, such as haggis, neeps and tatties; venison Braveheart;
Scotsman's bunnet, which is a meat and vegetable stew-filled batter
pudding; or game casserole. You might then round off your meal with
ice cream with Highland toffee sauce, or bread-and-butter pudding.
A specials board broadens the choice further. Around 20 wines by the
glass and more than 30 malt whiskies are available. Moulin may look
like a French word but it is actually derived from the Gaelic
'maohlinn', meaning either smooth rocks or calm water.

Rooms 15 (3 fmly) **S** £50-£75; **D** £65-£90 (incl. bkfst) **Facilities** New
Year Wi-fi **Conf** Class 12 Board 10 Thtr 15 Del from £85 to £110
Parking 30 **Notes** LB ⊗

Open all day all wk 11-11 (Fri-Sat 11am-11.45pm Sun noon-11) **Bar**
Meals L served all wk 12-9.30 D served all wk 12-9.30 Av main
course £9.50 food served all day **Restaurant** D served all wk 6-9
booking required Fixed menu price fr £23.50 Av 3 course à la carte fr
£27 ⊕ FREE HOUSE ◪ Moulin Braveheart, Old Remedial, Ale of
Atholl, Moulin Light. ♟ 20 **Facilities** Children's menu Garden

Easter Dunfallandy House

★★★★★ BED AND BREAKFAST

☎ 01796 474128
Logierait Rd PH16 5NA
e-mail: sue@dunfallandy.co.uk
web: www.dunfallandy.co.uk
dir: 1m S of Pitlochry. Off A924 Perth Rd in town onto Bridge Rd, fork
left, house 1m on right

A splendid country house, Dunfallandy lies peacefully in an elevated
position on the western side of the Tummel Valley. Immaculately
maintained, it retains many original features including fine
woodwork. The lounge is very relaxing, and the dining room, with its
magnificent wood-panelled ceiling, is the setting for breakfast
served to one large table. Bedrooms are well proportioned and
thoughtfully equipped.

Rooms 3 en suite (1 GF) S fr £40; D fr £80 **Facilities** STV TVL tea/
coffee Cen ht Wi-fi **Parking** 10 **Notes** LB Closed Xmas

Craigroyston House

★★★★ GUEST HOUSE

☎ 01796 472053 🖷 01796 472053
2 Lower Oakfield PH16 5HQ
e-mail: reservations@craigroyston.co.uk
web: www.craigroyston.co.uk
dir: In town centre near information centre car park

The Maxwell family delight in welcoming you to their home, an
impressive detached Victorian villa set in a colourful garden. The
bedrooms have pretty colour schemes and are comfortably furnished
in period style. There is an inviting sitting room, complete with deep
sofas for those wishing to relax and enjoy the tranquillity. Scottish
breakfasts are served at individual tables in the attractive dining
room.

Rooms 8 en suite (1 fmly) (1 GF) D £60-£80 **Facilities** tea/coffee
Cen ht Wi-fi **Parking** 9 **Notes** LB ⊗ 🖃

Torrdarach House

★★★★ GUEST HOUSE

☎ 01796 472136 📠 01796 472136
Golf Course Rd PH16 5AU
e-mail: torrdarach@msn.com
dir: In town centre. Off A924 Atholl Rd onto Larchwood Rd to top of hill, left, red house on right

Torrdarach House enjoys an elevated position overlooking the Tummel Valley and the pretty town of Pitlochry. This impressive Victorian villa stands in its own secluded landscaped gardens and ample secure parking is available.The stylish bedrooms are comfortably furnished and well equipped.The lounge is spacious, very comfortable and this charming house has lots of period features.

Rooms 7 rms (6 en suite) (1 pri facs) (1 GF) S £25-£35; D £50-£70*
Facilities TVL tea/coffee Cen ht Licensed Wi-fi **Parking** 7 **Notes** ⊗

Wellwood House

★★★★ GUEST HOUSE

☎ 01796 474288 📠 01796 474299
13 West Moulin Rd PH16 5EA
e-mail: wellwoodhouse@aol.com
web: www.wellwoodhouse.com
dir: In town centre opp town hall

Set in lovely grounds on an elevated position overlooking the town, Wellwood House has stunning views of the Vale of Atholl and the surrounding countryside. The comfortably proportioned bedrooms are attractively decorated and well equipped. The elegant lounge has an honesty bar and a fire on cooler evenings, and the spacious dining room is the setting for hearty breakfasts served at individual tables.

Rooms 10 rms (8 en suite) (2 pri facs) (1 fmly) (1 GF) S £40-£50; D £66-£80* **Facilities** FTV TVL tea/coffee Cen ht Licensed Wi-fi **Parking** 20 **Notes** ⊗ Closed 10 Nov-14 Feb

The Old Armoury Restaurant

❀ Modern British

Modern Scottish cooking in a historic old house

☎ 01796 474281
Armoury Rd PH16 5AP
e-mail: info@theoldarmouryrestaurant.com
dir: Turn off main street onto Rieachan Rd & follow signs for Fishladder. Restaurant on left

The Old Armoury is a charming old stone-built house just off Pitlochry's main street, yet surrounded by woodlands near to Loch Faskally; the name derives from its associations with the Black Watch regiment. Inside, several connecting dining rooms have a light and airy ambience with wooden floors, heaps of artwork on tongue-and-groove panelled walls, and huge French doors opening onto a delightful garden. The cooking is modern British fare that picks the best of Perthshire produce in a menu of traditional favourites with some innovative flourishes. Start with a simply-grilled young goat's cheese crottin with apple chutney, followed by grilled organic salmon with steamed asparagus, creamy mash and chive and caper butter.

And who could turn down a steamed marmalade pudding with brown bread ice cream to finish?

Chef Angus McNab **Owner** Angus McNab **Times** 12-2.30/5.30-8.30 Closed Xmas, Jan-Feb, Mon-Wed (Nov-Dec), D Sun (Nov-Dec) **Prices** Starter £3.25-£6.60, Main £10.15-£17.65, Dessert £5.65, Service optional **Wines** 3 by glass **Notes** Pre-theatre menu available, Sunday L, Vegetarian available **Seats** 54, Pr/dining room 22 **Children** Portions **Parking** 8, On street

---

ST FILLANS   Map 2 NN62

The Four Seasons Hotel

★★★ 83% HOTEL

◉◉ Modern British V

Breathtaking lochside scenery and bold cuisine

☎ 01764 685333 📠 01764 685444
Loch Earn PH6 2NF
e-mail: info@thefourseasonshotel.co.uk
web: www.thefourseasonshotel.co.uk
dir: on A85, towards W of village

Originally built in the early 19th century for the manager of the local limekilns, this lochside lodge served as a schoolmaster's house before becoming a romantic small hotel. Take the dog if you like - pets are welcome - since its location, tucked beneath steep forested hillsides on the edge of Loch Earn, is perfect for striding into the great outdoors of Perthshire. Sublime views come as standard from many bedrooms, as well as amid the contemporary style of the waterside Meall Reamhar fine-dining restaurant. Cracking Scottish produce is used to great effect in modern British dishes with well-layered flavours and creative pairings. Pan-seared hand-dived Scrabster scallops with Aberdeenshire black pudding and asparagus cream start things off, then roast rack of Perthshire lamb with dauphinoise potatoes and braised red cabbage.

Rooms 18 (6 annexe) (7 fmly) **S** £55-£90; **D** £110-£130 (incl. bkfst)* **Facilities** Xmas New Year Wi-fi **Conf** Class 45 Board 38 Thtr 95 Del from £104 to £124 **Parking** 40 **Notes** LB Closed 2 Jan-Feb RS Nov, Dec, Mar Civ Wed 80

Chef Peter Woods **Owner** Andrew Low **Restaurant** **Times** 12-2.30/6-9.30 Closed Jan-Feb & some wkdays Mar, Nov & Dec, **Prices** Fixed L 2 course fr £9.99, Fixed D 4 course £35, Service optional **Wines** 71 bottles over £20, 29 bottles under £20, 416 by glass **Notes** Sunday L, Vegetarian menu **Seats** 60, Pr/dining room 20 **Children** Portions, Menu

Achray House Hotel

★★★ 74% SMALL HOTEL

🌸 Traditional British

Family-run hotel, loch views and traditional cooking

☎ 01764 685231   📠 01764 685320
PH6 2NF
e-mail: info@achray-house.co.uk
web: www.achray-house.co.uk
dir: Follow A85 towards Crainlarich, from Stirling follow A9 then B822 at Braco, B827 to Comrie. Turn left onto A85 to St Fillans

Achray House sits in lovely gardens in a serene spot on the shores of Loch Earn at the gateway to the Highlands in the Loch Lomond and Trossachs National Park. It's a welcoming and friendly, family-run place with a homely feel you can slide into like a comfy pair of shoes. Bedrooms are smart, attractive and well-equipped, and you get glorious views over the loch to go with aperitifs in the conservatory-style bar, before moving into the restaurant for confidently-cooked, straightforward dishes that showcase splendid Scottish ingredients. Daily-changing menus might start with mallard duck terrine with plum chutney before salmon fillet with an oatmeal, herb and lemon crust and Arran mustard cream. End with the comfort of an apple and cinnamon crumble.

Rooms 10 (2 annexe) (2 fmly) (3 GF) **S** £40-£95; **D** £80-£150 (incl. bkfst)* **Facilities** Xmas New Year Wi-fi **Conf** Class 20 Board 20 Del from £70 to £110* **Parking** 30 **Notes** Closed 3-24 Jan Civ Wed 40

Chef Andrew J Scott **Owner** Andrew J Scott **Restaurant Times** 12-2.30/6-8.30 Closed 3-31 Jan, **Prices** Fixed L 2 course fr £15.95, Starter £3.95-£6.95, Main £9.95-£17.95, Dessert £3.95-£4.95, Service optional **Wines** 11 bottles over £20, 24 bottles under £20, 9 by glass **Notes** Sunday L, Vegetarian available **Seats** 70, Pr/dining room 30 **Children** Portions, Menu **Parking** 20

RENFREWSHIRE

GLASGOW AIRPORT — Map 2 NS46

Holiday Inn Glasgow Airport

★★★ 75% HOTEL

☎ 0870 400 9031 & 0141 887 1266   📠 0141 887 3738
Abbotsinch PA3 2TR
e-mail: operations-glasgow@ihg.com
web: www.holidayinn.co.uk
dir: From E: M8 junct 28, follow hotel signs. From W: M8 junct 29, airport slip road to hotel

Located within the airport grounds and within walking distance of the terminal. Bedrooms are well appointed and cater for the needs of the modern traveller. The open-plan public areas are relaxing as is the restaurant which offers a carvary and a carte menu. Wi-fi is available in the public areas with LAN in all bedrooms.

Rooms 300 (6 fmly) (54 smoking) **S** £49-£189; **D** £55-£199* **Facilities** STV Wi-fi **Conf** Class 150 Board 75 Thtr 300 Del from £89 to £199* **Services** Lift Air con **Parking** 56 **Notes** LB Civ Wed 250

Express by Holiday Inn Glasgow Airport

BUDGET HOTEL

☎ 0141 842 1100   📠 0141 842 1122
St Andrews Dr PA3 2TJ
e-mail: glasgowairport@expressholidayinn.co.uk
web: www.hiexpress.com/ex-glasgow
dir: M8 junct 28, at 1st rdbt turn right, hotel on right

A modern hotel ideal for families and business travellers. Fresh and uncomplicated, the spacious rooms include Sky TV, power shower and tea and coffee-making facilities. Continental buffet breakfast is included in the room rate; other meals may be taken at the nearby family pub or restaurant. See also the Hotel Groups pages on theAA.com.

Rooms 141 (63 fmly) **Conf** Class 20 Board 30 Thtr 70

Travelodge Glasgow Airport

BUDGET HOTEL

☎ 0871 984 6335   📠 0141 889 0583
Marchburn Dr, Glasgow Airport Business Park, Paisley PA3 2AR
web: www.travelodge.co.uk
dir: M8 junct 28, 0.5m from Glasgow Airport

Travelodge offers good quality, good value, modern accommodation. Ideal for families, the spacious en suite bedrooms include remote-control TV, tea and coffee-making facilities and comfortable beds. Meals can be taken at the nearby family restaurant. See also the Hotel Groups pages on theAA.com.

Rooms 98 (40 fmly) **S** fr £29; **D** fr £29

Travelodge Glasgow Braehead

BUDGET HOTEL

☎ 0871 984 6372 📠 0141 885 1862
150 Kings Inch Rd PA4 8XQ
web: www.travelodge.co.uk
dir: From W: M8 junct 26, (from E: junct 25a) follow Braehead Arena
& Xscape signs. Left at 1st lights, right at 2nd lights follow Braehead
Arena & Xscape signs. Pass Sainsbury's on right. Straight ahead 1st
rdbt. Lodge 200yds on right

Rooms 99 **S** fr £29; **D** fr £29

HOUSTON	Map 2 NS46

Fox & Hounds ☞

☎ 01505 612448 & 612991 📠 01505 614133
South St PA6 7EN
e-mail: jonathon.wengel@btconnect.com
dir: A737, W from Glasgow. Take Johnstone Bridge off Weir exit,
follow signs for Houston. Pub in village centre

Run by the same family for over thirty years, this charming 18th-
century village inn is home to the award-winning Houston Brewing
Company. Sample a pint of Jock Frost or Warlock Stout in one of the
three bars. There is a micro-brewery malt of the month, wine of the
week to sample too. From the appealing bar or restaurant menus,
choose from charred sausage du jour with creamy mash and onion
gravy, tagliatelle with fresh peas and courgette, Houston ale-
battered haddock, or slow braised game casserole. Look out for
gourmet evenings and live music nights.

Open all day all wk 11am-mdnt (Fri-Sat 11am-1am Sun from 12.30)
Bar Meals Av main course £8 food served all day **Restaurant** Av 3
course à la carte fr £25 food served all day ⊕ FREE HOUSE
◀ Killelan, Warlock Stout, Texas, Jock Frost, Peter's Well. ☞ 10
Facilities Children's menu Dogs allowed Garden Parking

HOWWOOD	Map 2 NS36

Bowfield Hotel & Country Club

★★★ 81% HOTEL

◉ Modern British

Converted mill serving seasonal Scottish cuisine

☎ 01505 705225 📠 01505 705230
PA9 1DZ
e-mail: enquiries@bowfieldhotel.co.uk
web: www.bowfieldhotel.co.uk
dir: M8 junct 28a/29, onto A737 for 6m, left onto B787, right after
2m, follow for 1m to hotel

Surrounded by farmland and the rolling hills of Renfrewshire, this
hotel is a convenient stopover for travellers using Glasgow Airport.
Located in a converted 17th-century bleaching mill, it combines the
traditional character of beamed ceilings, brick and white-painted
walls and open fires with modern leisure club facilities. Bedrooms
are housed in a separate wing and offer good modern comforts and
facilities. Seasonal Scottish produce, especially fish, shellfish and
game, is cooked with skill and well presented. Expect the likes of

West Coast scallops with Ayrshire bacon and crushed new potatoes,
followed by medallion of Aberdeen Angus beef fillet with cabbage and
celeriac, potato cake and onion confit and jus. Finish with cranachan
mousse with raspberry sorbet and oatmeal praline.

Rooms 23 (3 fmly) (7 GF) **S** £40-£95; **D** £60-£130 (incl. bkfst)*
Facilities Spa FTV ☉ supervised ↥ 18 Gym Squash Children's soft
play Aerobics studio Health & beauty Xmas New Year Wi-fi
Conf Class 60 Board 40 Thtr 100 Del from £95 to £120* **Parking** 120
Notes LB ⊗ Civ Wed 80

Chef Ronnie McAdam **Owner** Bowfield Hotel & Country Club Ltd
Restaurant Times -6.30-9 Closed L all week **Prices** Food prices not
confirmed for 2010. Please telephone for details. **Wines** 8 bottles over
£20, 21 bottles under £20, 7 by glass **Notes** Sunday L, Vegetarian
available, Dress restrictions, Smart casual **Seats** 40, Pr/dining room
20 **Children** Portions, Menu

LANGBANK	Map 2 NS37

Best Western Gleddoch House

★★★ 81% HOTEL

☎ 01475 540711 📠 01475 540201
PA14 6YE
e-mail: sales.gleddochhouse@ohiml.com
web: www.oxfordhotelsandinns.com
dir: M8 to Greenock, onto A8, left at rdbt onto A789, follow for 0.5m,
turn right, 2nd on left

This hotel is set in spacious, landscaped grounds high above the
River Clyde with fine views. The period house is appointed to a very
high standard. The modern extension remains impressive and offers
spacious and very comfortable bedrooms. Warm hospitality and
attentive service are noteworthy along with the hotel's parkland golf
course and leisure club.

Rooms 70 (20 fmly) (8 GF) **Facilities** ☉ ↥ 18 Putt green Xmas New
Year **Conf** Class 70 Board 40 Thtr 150 **Parking** 150 **Notes** LB ⊗
Civ Wed 120

EAST RENFREWSHIRE

UPLAWMOOR
Map 2 NS45

Uplawmoor Hotel

★★★ 79% HOTEL

⊛ Modern Scottish

Good Scottish cuisine in former smugglers' haunt

☎ 01505 850565   📠 01505 850689
Neilston Rd G78 4AF
e-mail: info@uplawmoor.co.uk
web: www.uplawmoor.co.uk
dir: M77 junct 2, A736 signed Barrhead & Irvine. Hotel 4m beyond Barrhead

Tucked away in a tranquil village only minutes from Glasgow, this one-time coaching inn used to be frequented by smugglers travelling between Glasgow and the coast. Extensive renovation in the 1950s by architect James Gray added the Charles Rennie Mackintosh-inspired exterior. The modern bedrooms are both comfortable and well equipped. The beamed restaurant, formerly the barn, now has rich furnishings and subtle lighting; there's a cocktail bar, too, with a large copper canopied fireplace and displays of modern art. A choice of menus offers a good range of Scottish dishes, including prime beef from 5 local farms. Expect starters such as seared West Coast king scallops, Stornoway black pudding, crispy bacon and balsamic dressing, and a main course of peppered fillet, flamed in brandy and finished with cream.

Rooms 14 (1 fmly) (3 smoking) **S** £55-£70; **D** £95 (incl. bkfst)*
Facilities STV Wi-fi **Conf** Class 12 Board 20 Thtr 40 Del from £90 to £109* **Parking** 40 **Notes** LB ⊗ Closed 26 Dec & 1 Jan

Chef Barry Liversidge **Owner** Stuart & Emma Peacock **Restaurant Times** 12-3/6-9.30 Closed 26 Dec, 1 Jan, L Mon-Sat **Prices** Fixed L 2 course £15-£18, Fixed D 3 course £25-£27.50, Starter £5-£9.50, Main £13-£23, Dessert £4.50-£6.50, Service optional **Wines** 7 bottles over £20, 19 bottles under £20, 9 by glass **Notes** Early evening menu available 5.30-7 Sun-Fri, Sunday L, Vegetarian available, Dress restrictions, Smart casual **Seats** 30 **Children** Portions, Menu

SCOTTISH BORDERS

ALLANTON
Map 3 NT85

Allanton Inn

☎ 01890 818260
TD11 3JZ
e-mail: info@allantoninn.co.uk
dir: From A1 at Berwick take A6105 for Chirnside (5m). At Chirnside Inn take Coldstream Rd for 1m to Allanton

Highly acclaimed for its food, this award-winning establishment is housed in an 18th-century coaching inn. Outside is a large lawned area with fruit trees overlooking open countryside. Inside are two restaurants and a cosy bar serving real ales and a range of malt whiskies. Daily changing menus may offer braised beef and Guinness casserole with a puff pastry crust at lunch, and monkfish tail sautéed onto a risotto of asparagus, mussels and rocket for dinner.

Open 6pm-10.30pm (Sat-Sun noon-2) Closed: Mon **Bar Meals** L served Sat-Sun 12-2 D served Tue-Sat 6.30-8 booking required **Restaurant** L served Sat-Sun 12-2 D served Tue-Sat 6.30-8 booking required ⊕ FREE HOUSE ◀ Ossian, Trade Winds, Pentland IPA. **Facilities** Dogs allowed Garden Parking

BROUGHTON
Map 3 NT13

The Glenholm Centre

★★★ ⌂ GUEST ACCOMMODATION

☎ 01899 830408
ML12 6JF
e-mail: info@glenholm.co.uk
dir: 1m S of Broughton. Off A701 to Glenholm

Surrounded by peaceful farmland, this former schoolhouse has a distinct African theme. The home-cooked meals and baking have received much praise and are served in the spacious lounge-dining room. The bright airy bedrooms are thoughtfully equipped, and the service is friendly and attentive. Computer courses are available.

Rooms 3 en suite 1 annexe en suite (1 fmly) (2 GF) **Facilities** TVL tea/coffee Dinner available Cen ht Licensed Wi-fi ♿ **Conf** Max 24 Thtr 24 Class 24 Board 24 **Parking** 14 **Notes** Closed 20 Dec-1 Feb

CRAILING
Map 3 NT62

Crailing Old School

★★★★ ⌂ ⊜ GUEST HOUSE

☎ 01835 850382
TD8 6TL
e-mail: jean.player@virgin.net
web: www.crailingoldschool.co.uk
dir: A698 onto B6400 signed Nisbet, Crailing Old School also signed

This delightful rural retreat, built in 1887 as the village school, has been imaginatively renovated to combine Victorian features with modern comforts. The spacious bedrooms are beautifully maintained and decorated, and filled with homely extras. The lodge annexe suite located 10 yards from the house offers easier ground-floor access.

The best of local produce produces tasty breakfasts, served in the stylish lounge-dining room (evening meals by arrangement).

Rooms 3 rms (1 en suite) (1 pri facs) 1 annexe en suite (1 GF) S £38.50-£40; D £60-£80* **Facilities** FTV TVL tea/coffee Dinner available Cen ht Wi-fi **Parking** 7 **Notes** No Children 9yrs Closed 24 Dec-2 Jan, 1wk Feb & 2wks Autumn

The Horseshoe Inn

★★★★ RESTAURANT WITH ROOMS

◉◉◉　Modern French

Refined French cuisine on the Scottish borders

☎ 01721 730225　🖷 01721 730268
EH45 8QP
e-mail: reservations@horseshoeinn.co.uk
web: www.horseshoeinn.co.uk
dir: A703, 5m N of Peebles

Once the home of the village blacksmith, hence the name, the inn enjoys a tranquil location not far from Peebles in the majestic Scottish border country. Within an ambience of classical elegance - the pillared dining room has high-backed chairs, smart table settings and gilt-framed mirrors - some kind of celebration of the Auld Alliance is going on. Patrick Bardoulet brings the modern culinary techniques of his native France to bear on quality Scots produce, resulting in such dishes as dill-cured salmon with horseradish ice cream and toasted brioche, monkfish tail with leeks and butternut fondant in shallot and champagne sauce, and braised oxtail with Jerusalem artichoke and pied blue mushrooms. The intensity and creativity of the flavour combinations win many converts, and any lingering doubt that the chef has not been fully converted to Scottish traditions is dispelled in a serving of loin of lamb, with its tongue, liver and haggis, alongside turnip purée (the French idea of 'bashed neeps') and pearl barley. Cheeses and oatcakes are the alternative to sweet things such as pear parfait with liquorice cream and honey syrup. There are eight luxuriously appointed and individually designed bedrooms available.

Rooms 8 en suite (1 fmly) (6 GF) **Facilities** tea/coffee Dinner available Direct Dial Cen ht Wi-fi **Parking** 20 **Notes** Closed 25 Dec & Mon

Chef Patrick Bardoulet **Owner** Border Steelwork Structures Ltd **Restaurant Times** 12-2.30/7-9 Closed 25 Dec, early Jan, mid Oct, Mon, D Sun **Prices** Fixed L course £19.50, Tasting menu fr £60, Starter £9-£14, Main £15-£25, Dessert £7-£9, Service optional **Wines** 71 bottles over £20, 31 bottles under £20 **Notes** Sunday L, Vegetarian available, Dress restrictions, Smart casual, Jackets for men preferred **Seats** 40

Tushielaw Inn

☎ 01750 62205　🖷 01750 62205
TD7 5HT
e-mail: robin@tushielaw-inn.co.uk
dir: At junct of B709 & B711(W of Hawick)

An 18th-century former toll house and drovers' halt on the banks of Ettrick Water, making a good base for touring the Borders, trout fishing (salmon fishing can be arranged) and those tackling the Southern Upland Way. An extensive menu is always available with daily-changing specials. Fresh produce is used according to season, with local lamb and Aberdeen Angus beef regular specialities. Home-made steak and stout pie and sticky toffee pudding are popular choices.

Open all wk **Bar Meals** Av main course £10 ⊕ FREE HOUSE **Facilities** Children's menu Dogs allowed Parking

Kingsknowes

★★★　75%　HOTEL

☎ 01896 758375　🖷 01896 750377
Selkirk Rd TD1 3HY
e-mail: enq@kingsknowes.co.uk
web: www.kingsknowes.co.uk
dir: Off A7 at Galashiels/Selkirk rdbt

In over three acres of grounds on the banks of the Tweed, this splendid turreted, baronial mansion was built in 1869 for a textile magnate. It boasts elegant public areas and many spacious bedrooms, some with excellent views of the Eildon Hills and Abbotsford House, Sir Walter Scott's ancestral home. Meals are served in two restaurants and the Courtyard Bar, where fresh local or regional produce is used as much as possible. The impressive glass conservatory is the ideal place to enjoy a drink.

Rooms 12 (2 fmly) **S** fr £69; **D** fr £99 (incl. bkfst)* **Facilities** Wi-fi **Conf** Class 40 Board 30 Thtr 60 **Parking** 65 **Notes** LB Civ Wed 75

Pub Open all wk ⊕ FREE HOUSE ◀ McEwans 80/-, John Smiths. **Facilities** Play area Dogs allowed Garden Parking

Kelso Abbey

GALASHIELS CONTINUED

Over Langshaw (NT524400)

★★★ FARMHOUSE

☎ 01896 860244 🖶 01896 860668 Mrs S Bergius
Langshaw TD1 2PE
e-mail: overlangshaw@btconnect.com
dir: 3m N of Galashiels. A7 N from Galashiels, 1m right signed
Langshaw, right at T-junct into Langshaw, left signed Earlston, Over
Langshaw 1m, signed

There are fine panoramic views from this organic hillside farm. It
offers two comfortable and spacious bedrooms. Hearty breakfasts are
provided at individual tables in the lounge and a friendly welcome is
guaranteed.

Rooms 2 en suite (1 fmly) (1 GF) **Facilities** TVL tea/coffee Cen ht
Parking 4 **Notes** ⊛ 500 acres dairy/sheep/organic

JEDBURGH   Map 3 NT62

Ferniehirst Mill Lodge

★★ GUEST HOUSE

☎ 01835 863279
TD8 6PQ
e-mail: ferniehirstmill@aol.com
web: www.ferniehirstmill.co.uk
dir: 2.5m S on A68, onto private track to end

Reached by a narrow farm track and a rustic wooden bridge, this
chalet-style house has a secluded setting by the River Jed. Bedrooms
are small and functional but there is a comfortable lounge in which
to relax. Home-cooked dinners are available by arrangement, and
hearty breakfasts are served in the cosy dining room.

Rooms 7 en suite (1 GF) S £28; D £56* **Facilities** TVL tea/coffee
Dinner available Direct Dial Cen ht Fishing Riding **Parking** 10

KELSO   Map 3 NT73

The Roxburghe Hotel & Golf Course

★★★ 85% COUNTRY HOUSE HOTEL

◉ Modern, Traditional ◔

Scottish country-house sporting destination with fine dining

☎ 01573 450331 🖶 01573 450611
Heiton TD5 8JZ

e-mail: hotel@roxburghe.net
web: www.roxburghe.net
dir: From A68 Jedburgh take A698 to Heiton, 3m SW of Kelso

The Duke of Roxburghe certainly has plenty of space on his 54,000
acre estate, where this grand Jacobean country-house hotel is
secreted among woodlands in vast grounds encompassing a
championship golf course. Make no mistake, this is a seriously
upmarket stately home of a hotel, with gracious public areas, the
perfect setting for afternoon tea, and elegant bedrooms that have
been individually designed, some by the Duchess herself, and include
superior rooms, some with four posters and log fires. It offers a
dining experience to match. The Scottish Borders are prime huntin'
shootin' fishin' territory, renowned for top-notch fish, meat and game
which the kitchen puts to good use, together with wild mushrooms
from the estate and herbs from the garden, in menus of French-
influenced modern country-house cuisine. Expect starters like
pressed ham hock and foie gras with fig and apple chutney to
precede roast breast and confit leg of duck with fondant potato and
smoked butternut squash. The Duke's cellar is a treasure trove of
bottles for all occasions.

Rooms 22 (6 annexe) (3 fmly) (3 GF) **Facilities** Spa STV ⅃ 18 Putt
green Fishing ⤵ Clay shooting Health & beauty salon Mountain bike
hire Falconry Archery Xmas New Year **Conf** Class 20 Board 20 Thtr 50
Parking 150 **Notes** ⊗ Civ Wed 60

Chef Alasdair Stewart **Owner** Duke of Roxburghe **Restaurant
Times** 12-2/7.30-9.45 **Prices** Fixed L 2 course fr £15, Fixed D 3
course fr £39.95, Service optional **Wines** 80 bottles over £20, 8
bottles under £20, 10 by glass **Notes** Sunday L, Vegetarian available,
Dress restrictions, No jeans, trainers or T-shirts **Seats** 40, Pr/dining
room 18 **Children** Portions, Menu

Ednam House

★★★ 77% HOTEL

☎ 01573 224168 🖶 01573 226319
Bridge St TD5 7HT
e-mail: contact@ednamhouse.com
web: www.ednamhouse.com
dir: 50mtrs from town square

Overlooking a wide expanse of the River Tweed, this fine Georgian
mansion has been under the Brooks family ownership for over 75
years. Accommodation styles range from standard to grand, plus The
Orangerie, situated in the grounds, that has been converted into a
gracious two-bedroom apartment. Public areas include a choice of
lounges and an elegant dining room that has views over the gardens.

Rooms 32 (2 annexe) (4 fmly) (3 GF) **S** £75-£84.50; **D** £111-£155
(incl. bkfst)* **Facilities** FTV ⤵ Free access to Abbey Fitness Centre
Wi-fi **Conf** Board 200 Thtr 250 **Parking** 60 **Notes** Closed 24 Dec-6 Jan
Civ Wed 100

LAUDER — Map 3 NT54

Lauderdale

★★ 74% HOTEL

☎ 01578 722231 📠 01578 718642
1 Edinburgh Rd TD2 6TW
e-mail: enquiries@lauderdalehotel.co.uk
web: www.lauderdalehotel.co.uk
dir: on A68 from S, through Lauder centre, hotel on right. From Edinburgh, hotel on left at 1st bend after passing Lauder sign

Lying on the north side of the village with spacious gardens to the side and rear, this friendly hotel is ideally placed for those who don't want to stay in Edinburgh itself. The well-equipped bedrooms come in a variety of sizes, and a good range of meals is served in both the bar and the restaurant.

Rooms 10 (1 fmly) **S** £50; **D** £80 (incl. bkfst)* **Facilities** STV FTV 🎵 Xmas New Year Wi-fi Child facilities **Conf** Class 200 Board 100 Thtr 200 **Parking** 200 **Notes** Civ Wed 180

The Black Bull

★★★★ INN ☻

☎ 01578 722208 📠 01578 722419
Market Place TD2 6SR
e-mail: enquiries@blackbull-lauder.com
dir: On A68 in village centre

Just twenty minutes from Edinburgh, the Black Bull nestles in the heart of the Scottish Borders. This dazzling white, three-storey coaching inn dates from 1750: now, as an independent family-owned business, the hotel's dining rooms and Harness Room bar are open to residents and non-residents alike. Priding itself on a warm and welcoming atmosphere, great food and comfortable accommodation, the Black Bull makes an ideal country retreat. Whatever your passions – country sports, walking, golfing, shopping, or the arts – there are all sorts of wonderful places to visit nearby. While you're working up an appetite, the kitchen brigade will be busy preparing flavoursome, seasonal dishes for you to enjoy. Choose between the informal surroundings of the Harness Room bar for a gastro-pub lunch, or get around a table in the cosy lounge bar after a day on the hills. Either way, you can choose from the same seasonal menu, prepared to order from the best quality local meat, fish and seasonal game. A light lunch menu of snacks and sandwiches is served from midday, whilst a typical supper menu might start with deep-fried mushrooms in sweet potato and coriander butter, or chicken liver and cognac pâté with gooseberry jelly and Scottish oatcakes. Follow with venison bourguignon with highland burgundy mash, or mushroom

risotto cakes with sun-dried tomato, pine nuts, Parmesan shavings and side salad. Round off, perhaps, with sticky toffee pudding and cream, or baked lemon and raspberry cheesecake with winter berry salad. Alternatively, if you're staying in one of the lovely bedrooms, furnished in the period character and thoughtfully equipped with modern amenities, and have a successful day on the river, the kitchen will happily prepare your catch for dinner while you put your feet up in the cosy bar.

Rooms 8 en suite (2 fmly) S £80-£110; D £120-£150 **Facilities** FTV tea/coffee Dinner available Direct Dial Cen ht Wi-fi **Conf** Max 40 **Parking** 8 **Notes** LB Civ Wed 40

Open all day all wk 🍺 PERTHSHIRE TAVERNS LTD 🍺 Broughton Ales, Guinness, Worthington, Caffreys, Landlord Tetley. ☻ 16

LEITHOLM — Map 3 NT74

The Plough Hotel ☻

☎ 01890 840252 📠 01890 840252
Main St TD12 4JN
e-mail: theplough@leitholm.wanadoo.co.uk
dir: 5m N of Coldstream on A697. Take B6461, Leitholm in 1m

The only pub remaining in this small border village (there were originally two), the Plough dates from the 17th century and was once a coaching inn. Food is traditional with the likes of parsnip soup or pâté and Melba toast followed steak and Guinness pie; home-made lasagne; or local sausages with Yorkshire pudding. Tuesdays and Fridays are fish and chip nights.

Open all day all wk noon-mdnt **Bar Meals** Av main course £12 food served all day **Restaurant** food served all day 🍺 FREE HOUSE 🍺 Guinness. ☻ 8 **Facilities** Children's menu Garden Parking

MELROSE — Map 3 NT53

The Townhouse Hotel

★★★ 81% HOTEL

☎ 01896 822645 📠 01896 823474
3 Market Square TD6 9PQ
e-mail: info@thetownhousemelrose.co.uk
web: www.thetownhousemelrose.co.uk
dir: From A68 into Melrose. Hotel in town square

Situated on the square this smart hotel, as the name suggests, has the typical style of a Scottish town house. Bedrooms vary in size and some have views of the hills but all are well equipped and beautifully decorated - it's worth requesting one of two superior rooms. Guests can eat in either the brasserie or more traditional restaurant - both offer the same menu.

Rooms 11 (1 fmly) (1 GF) **S** £75-£116; **D** £116-£128 (incl. bkfst) **Facilities** FTV New Year Wi-fi **Conf** Class 30 Board 40 Thtr 70 Del from £100 to £150 **Notes** LB ⊗ Closed 26-27 Dec & 4-12 Jan

Burt's

★★★ 77% HOTEL

@@ Modern Scottish 🏆 ♨

Friendly, family-run Borders hotel with modern Scottish menu

☎ 01896 822285 📄 01896 822870
Market Square TD6 9PL
e-mail: enquiries@burtshotel.co.uk
web: www.burtshotel.co.uk
dir: A6091, 2m from A68 3m S of Earlston

The Henderson family have run this smart townhouse hotel for the best part of 4 decades. Built on the market square in 1722, it is rooted into the heart of life in the quiet Borders town of Melrose. It's run well by cheery, nattily-uniformed staff and, for dining, there's a choice of a traditional clubby restaurant, with green Regency-striped walls, sporting prints and high-backed chairs, or a more pubby-feeling bistro bar. Seasonally-driven menus revolve around modern Scottish dishes built on quality local produce. An assiette of Eyemouth crab comes as crab cake, tian, and spring roll with chilli and lime crème fraîche to start; you might follow with pan-fried Highland venison, fondant potato, Scottish winter chanterelles and truffle jus, and end on a thoroughly Scottish note with a duo of cranachan - mousse and brûlée - with honey and Drambuie ice cream.

Rooms 20 **S** £70; **D** £130 (incl. bkfst)* **Facilities** STV FTV Salmon fishing Shooting New Year Wi-fi **Conf** Class 20 Board 20 Thtr 38 Del from £110 to £130* **Parking** 40 **Notes** Closed 24-26 Dec & 2-3 Jan

Chef Trevor Williams **Owner** The Henderson family **Restaurant Times** 12-2/7-9 Closed 26 Dec, 2-3 Jan, **Prices** Fixed L 2 course £22-£29.50, Fixed D 3 course £35-£39, Service optional **Wines** 40 bottles over £20, 20 bottles under £20, 7 by glass **Notes** Sunday L, Vegetarian available, Dress restrictions, Jacket & tie preferred **Seats** 50, Pr/dining room 25 **Children** Portions

Fauhope House

★★★★★ 🏛 GUEST HOUSE

☎ 01896 823184 📄 01896 823184
Gattonside TD6 9LU
e-mail: fauhope@bordernet.co.uk
dir: 0.7m N of Melrose over River Tweed. N off B6360 at Gattonside 30mph sign (E) up long driveway

It's hard to imagine a more complete experience than a stay at Fauhope, set high on a hillside on the north-east edge of the village. Hospitality is first class, breakfasts are excellent, and the delightful country house has a splendid interior. Bedrooms are luxurious, each individual and superbly equipped. Public areas are elegantly decorated and furnished, and enhanced by beautiful floral arrangements; the dining room is particularly stunning.

Rooms 3 en suite **Facilities** tea/coffee Dinner available Cen ht 🐎 Riding **Parking** 10 **Notes** LB ⊗

Liddesdale

★★★★ INN

☎ 01387 375255 📄 01387 752577
Douglas Sq TD9 0QD
e-mail: reception@theliddesdalehotel.co.uk

Located in the peaceful 17th century village of Newcastleton overlooking the village square. Quality well appointed bedrooms and bathrooms and public areas offering various locations to dine. The welcoming public bar is well used by locals and residents alike. Relaxed and informal menus use the best local produce available.

Rooms 6 en suite (2 fmly) S fr £40; D £60-£70 **Facilities** STV FTV TVL tea/coffee Dinner available Direct Dial Cen ht Wi-fi 🐎 Golf 9 Fishing Pool Table **Conf** Max 60 Thtr 40 Class 40 Board 40 **Notes** LB

Cringletie House

★★★★ COUNTRY HOUSE HOTEL

◉◉ Modern British

Imaginative modern Scottish cooking in a magisterial Victorian house

☎ 01721 725750 ▤ 01721 725751
Edinburgh Rd EH45 8PL
e-mail: enquiries@cringletie.com
web: www.cringletie.com
dir: 2m N on A703

The house rises above the 28 acres of gardens and woodland that surround it, a masterpiece of Victorian Scots baronial architecture. Interiors are as elegant as is expected, easy on the eye, with an effective trompe l'oeil ceiling in the dining room, offset with contemporary fabrics and furniture. Much of the kitchen's fresh produce is grown in the grounds, and the up-to-date cooking style draws on a bedrock of established national tradition. Seared scallops are served with Jersey Royals in season - the pots come diced in a stack anointed with foam, as well as a vivid, smooth watercress purée. Proceed, perhaps, to corn-fed chicken breast, intelligently teamed with crayfish cannelloni and an array of colourful seasonal vegetables, while dessert might bring a set of strawberry variations, including a terrine and ice cream. There a stunning views from all the rooms, which include a cocktail lounge with adjoining conservatory, as well as attractively furnished bedrooms, many of which are particularly spacious.

Rooms 13 (2 GF) **Facilities** STV Putt green ⚓ Petanque Giant chess & draughts In-room spa Xmas New Year Wi fi **Conf** Class 20 Board 24 Thtr 45 Del from £200* **Services** Lift **Parking** 30 **Notes** Civ Wed 65

Restaurant Times 7-9 Closed L Mon-Sat

Macdonald Cardrona Hotel

★★★★ 76% HOTEL

Renwicks

◉ British

Accomplished cooking with stunning views

☎ 01896 833600 ▤ 01896 831166
Cardrona Mains EH45 6LZ
e-mail: general.cardrona@macdonald-hotels.co.uk
web: www.macdonald-hotels.co.uk/cardrona
dir: On A72 between Peebles & Innerleithen, 3m S of Peebles

Golf is firmly on the agenda at this smart modern hotel on the banks of the River Tweed, but you don't have to swing a niblick to fit in here. After a day's mountain biking or hiking in the Borders hills, the classy spa facilities or a dip in the huge pool will probably hit the spot. Spacious bedrooms are traditional in style, equipped with a range of extras, and most enjoy fantastic countryside views. Then, there's the food which comes with glorious views from vast picture windows in the second-floor Renwicks restaurant. The kitchen's set-

price menus aim to offer quality seasonal Scottish produce such as fresh seafood and well-hung game in unaffected, well-balanced dishes, with delightful service from a strong, professional team. Meals might start with sun-blushed tomato and basil pannacotta with chargrilled artichoke and feta cheese salad, then move on to a seared Highland venison steak with braised red cabbage, plum compôte and juniper berry jus.

Rooms 99 (24 fmly) (16 GF) **S** £82-£169; **D** £92-£179 (incl. bkfst) **Facilities** Spa STV ☜ ♨ 18 Putt green Gym Sauna Steam room Xmas New Year Wi-fi **Conf** Class 120 Board 90 Thtr 250 Del from £130 to £160 **Services** Lift **Parking** 200 **Notes** LB Civ Wed 200

Chef Ivor Clark **Owner** Macdonald Hotels **Restaurant Times** 12-2.30/6.30-9.45 Closed Please telephone for details, **Prices** Fixed L 2 course £27.50 £32.50, Service included **Wines** 70 bottles over £20, 12 bottles under £20, 18 by glass **Notes** Sunday L, Vegetarian available, Dress restrictions, Smart casual, Air con **Seats** 70, Pr/dining room 200 **Children** Portions, Menu

Peebles Hotel Hydro

★★★★ 75% HOTEL

☎ 01721 720602 ▤ 01721 722999
EH45 8LX
e-mail: info@peebleshydro.co.uk
dir: On A702, 0.3m from town

A majestic building, this resort hotel sits in grounds on the edge of the town, its elevated position giving striking views across the valley. The range of indoor and outdoor leisure activities is second to none and makes the hotel a favourite with both families and conference delegates. Accommodation comes in a range of styles and includes a number of family rooms.

Rooms 132 (24 fmly) (15 GF) **S** £105-£115; **D** £210-£230 (incl. bkfst & dinner)* **Facilities** Spa STV ☜ supervised ♨ Putt green ⚓ Gym Badminton Beautician Hairdressing Giant chess/draughts Pitch & putt ♫ Xmas New Year Wi-fi Child facilities **Conf** Class 200 Board 74 Thtr 450 Del from £140 to £150 **Services** Lift **Parking** 200 **Notes** LB ⊗ Civ Wed 200

Tontine

★★★ 81% HOTEL

☎ 01721 720892 ▤ 01721 729732
High St EH45 8AJ
e-mail: info@tontinehotel.com
web: www.tontinehotel.com
dir: In town centre

Conveniently situated in the main street, this long-established hotel offers comfortable public rooms including an elegant Adam restaurant, inviting lounge and 'clubby' bar. Bedrooms, contained in the original house and the river-facing wing, offer a smart, classical style of accommodation. The lasting impression is of the excellent level of hospitality and guest care.

Rooms 36 (3 fmly) **S** £45-£65; **D** £65-£95 (incl. bkfst)* **Facilities** STV FTV Xmas New Year Wi-fi Child facilities **Conf** Class 24 Board 24 Thtr 40 Del from £85 to £115* **Parking** 24

Park

★★★ 75% HOTEL

☎ 01721 720451 📄 01721 723510
Innerleithen Rd EH45 8BA
e-mail: reserve@parkpeebles.co.uk
dir: In town centre opposite filling station

This hotel offers pleasant, well-equipped bedrooms of various sizes - those in the original house are particularly spacious. Public areas enjoy views of the gardens and include a tartan-clad bar, a relaxing lounge and a spacious wood-panelled restaurant, open for lunch and early-bird suppers

Rooms 24 **Facilities** STV Putt green Use of facilities at Peebles Hotel Hydro Xmas New Year Wi-fi **Conf** Class 15 Board 18 Thtr 30 Del from £50 to £160* **Services** Lift **Parking** 50

ST BOSWELLS   **Map 3 NT53**

Dryburgh Abbey Hotel

★★★★ 73% COUNTRY HOUSE HOTEL

◉◉ Scottish

Impressive modern Scottish cuisine in a grand Victorian country house

☎ 01835 822261 📄 01835 823945
TD6 0RQ
e-mail: enquiries@dryburgh.co.uk **web:** www.dryburgh.co.uk
dir: B6356 signed Scott's View & Earlston. Through Clintmains, 1.8m to hotel

Dryburgh Abbey Hotel is a baronial red-brick Victorian mansion next to the romantically-ruined abbey in acres of sprawling grounds on the banks of the River Tweed. There's an array of bedrooms and suites, each displaying original features, and the classic interior sports the high ceilings and fancy plasterwork you expect in such a grandiose pile. The first-floor Tweed Restaurant lives up to its name with sweeping views over the river and glorious Borders scenery. Done out in elegant hues of claret and cream, it is a smart traditional setting for Scottish cuisine that shows a skilled hand at work in the kitchen, turning out well-balanced flavours with obvious technical flair. Ballotine of partridge with smoked mushrooms, hot mulled wine jelly and carrot and star anise purée shows a splendid array of flavours at work; a main course of monkfish wrapped in Parma ham with parsnip purée, tempura clams, haricot blanc cassoulet and mustard foam has real visual impact and an arsenal of textures.

Rooms 38 (31 fmly) (8 GF) **S** £63-£205; **D** £126-£350 (incl. bkfst & dinner)* **Facilities** FTV ⊗ Putt green Fishing ⤴ Sauna Xmas New Year Wi-fi **Conf** Class 80 Board 60 Thtr 150 Del from £140 to £200* **Services** Lift **Parking** 70 **Notes** LB Civ Wed 120

Chef Mark Greenaway **Owner** John Wallis **Restaurant Times** -7.30-9 Closed L all week **Prices** Food prices not confirmed for 2010. Please telephone for details, Service included **Wines** 52 bottles over £20, 28 bottles under £20, 11 by glass **Notes** Fixed menu 8 courses £35, Vegetarian available, Dress restrictions, No jeans or sportswear **Seats** 78, Pr/dining room 40 **Children** Portions, Menu

Buccleuch Arms Hotel ♥

☎ 01835 822243 📄 01835 823965
The Green TD6 0EW
e-mail: info@buccleucharms.com
dir: On A68, 10m N of Jedburgh. Hotel on village green

This smart and friendly country-house hotel, dating from the 16th century, sits next to the village cricket pitch. There is a large and comfortable, log fire-warmed lounge to enjoy in winter, and a spacious, enclosed garden for the warmer months. Food plays a pivotal role, from breakfast through award-winning bar meals to dinner. Menus change seasonally, but the specials may well change twice daily to reflect the availability of local ingredients from the Scottish Borders countryside, such as the beef, which is sourced from the Buccleuch estates and then hung for a minimum of 21 days. Burnside Farm Foods in Rutherford three miles away supply other meats including poultry and game, and when it comes to fish, it falls to a fishmonger in Eyemouth, who delivers six days a week, to decide on the roll-call. With the provenance outlined, here are examples of what to expect: steak, ale and mushroom pie, using slowly braised prime beef from Craig Douglas in the village; chargrilled gammon steak; breaded scampi tails; and home-made nut loaf.

Open all day all wk 7am-11pm Closed: 25 Dec **Bar Meals** L served all wk 12-2 D served all wk 6-9 Av main course £8 food served all day **Restaurant** D served all wk 6-9 booking required ⊕ FREE HOUSE ◼ John Smiths, Guinness, Broughton, guest ales. ♥ 8 **Facilities** Play area Dogs allowed Garden Parking

---

SELKIRK   **Map 3 NT42**

Best Western Philipburn Country House

★★★★ Ⓐ COUNTRY HOUSE HOTEL

☎ 01750 20747 📄 01750 21690
Linglie Rd TD7 5LS
e-mail: info@philipburnhousehotel.co.uk
dir: From A7 follow signs for A72/A707 Peebles/Moffat. Hotel 1m from town centre

Rooms 12 (2 fmly) **S** £105-£135; **D** £125-£175 (incl. bkfst)* **Facilities** FTV ⤴ Xmas New Year Wi-fi **Conf** Class 12 Board 24 Thtr 40 Del from £145 to £175* **Parking** 25 **Notes** LB ⊗ Closed 11-25 Jan Civ Wed 85

SWINTON — Map 3 NT84

Wheatsheaf at Swinton

★★★★ RESTAURANT WITH ROOMS

◉◉ Modern British **V** ❁

Confident cooking in the heart of the Borders

☎ 01890 860257   ▤ 01890 860688
TD11 3JJ
e-mail: reception@wheatsheaf-swinton.co.uk
dir: In village centre on A6112

In the heart of the Scottish Borders, in the sleepy village of Swinton, The Wheatsheaf is very much the hub of the community. A stone-built country inn with stylishly furnished bedrooms (the largest of which feature bath and separate shower). The executive bedrooms are of a very high standard. The inn has developed a formidable local reputation for its food, enjoyed in the bright and airy pine-clad conservatory, the more traditional dining room or the cosy bar lounge with its open fire. Local produce is the cornerstone of the appealing menus, with seafood landed at Eyemouth harbour, just twelve miles away, and all meat coming from local butchers. Wild salmon, venison and birds dominate the menu in their seasons and such fine provenance is clear in dishes like breast of wood pigeon and black pudding on celeriac with orange and redcurrant sauce, and main-course chargrilled sirloin of Scotch beef with a three peppercorn and brandy sauce.

Rooms 10 en suite (2 fmly) (1 GF) S £65-£95; D £98-£148
Facilities FTV tea/coffee Dinner available Direct Dial Cen ht Wi-fi
Conf Max 18 Thtr 18 Class 18 Board 12 **Parking** 7 **Notes** LB ⊗
Closed 25-26 Dec, 31 Jan Civ Wed 50

Owner Mr & Mrs Chris Winson **Restaurant Times** 12-2/6-9
Closed 25-27 Dec, **Prices** Starter £4.25-£6.95, Main £14.95-£19.95, Dessert £5.45-£7.95, Service optional, Groups min 12 service 10%
Wines 84 bottles over £20, 34 bottles under £20, 12 by glass
Notes Sunday L, Vegetarian menu **Seats** 45, Pr/dining room 29
Children Portions, Menu

TIBBIE SHIELS INN — Map 3 NT22

Tibbie Shiels Inn

☎ 01750 42231   ▤ 01750 42302
St Mary's Loch TD7 5LH
dir: From Moffat take A708. Inn 14m on right

On the isthmus between St Mary's Loch and the Loch of the Lowes, this waterside hostelry is named after the woman who first opened it in 1826. Isabella 'Tibbie' Shiels expanded the inn from a small cottage to a hostelry capable of sleeping around 35 people, many of them on the floor! Famous visitors during her time included Walter Scott, Thomas Carlyle and Robert Louis Stevenson. Tibbie Shiels herself is rumoured to keep watch over the bar, where the selection of over 50 malt whiskies helps sustain long periods of ghost watching. Now under new ownership, meals can be enjoyed in either the bar or the dining room. The inn will also prepare packed lunches for your chosen activity – be it walking (the inn now lies on the coast-to-coast Southern Upland Way walking trail), windsurfing or fishing (residents fish free of charge).

Open all day all wk 9am-mdnt **Bar Meals** Av main course £10 food served all day **Restaurant** Fixed menu price fr £16 Av 3 course à la carte fr £20 food served all day ⊕ FREE HOUSE ◀ Broughton Greenmantle Ale, Belhaven 80/- ⬠ Stowford Press.
Facilities Children's menu Play area Dogs allowed Garden Parking

WEST LINTON — Map 3 NT15

The Gordon Arms ♥

☎ 01968 660208   ▤ 01968 661852
Dolphinton Rd EH46 7DR
e-mail: info@thegordon.co.uk

Set in the pretty village of West Linton but within easy reach of the M74, this 17th-century inn has a real log fire in the cosy lounge bar, and a lovely sun-trap beer garden. Enjoy a local ale alongside your meal, which may start with feta cheese and cous cous fritters with a spicy red schoog, or cullen skink; continue with steak and ale pie, haggis, or collops of venison with a rustic butternut squash and sweet potato purée; and finish with sticky toffee pudding.

Open all day all wk 11-11 (Fri-Sat 11-1am Tue 11-mdnt) **Bar Meals** L served Mon-Fri 12-3, Sat-Sun all day D served Mon-Fri 6-9, Sat-Sun all day **Restaurant** L served Mon-Fri 12-3, Sat-Sun all day D served Mon-Fri 6-9, Sat-Sun all day ⊕ SCOTTISH & NEWCASTLE ◀ John Smiths, Guinness, real ales. ♥ 7 **Facilities** Children's menu Play area Dogs allowed Garden Parking

STIRLING

ABERFOYLE
Map 2 NN50

Macdonald Forest Hills Hotel & Resort

★★★★ 75% HOTEL

☎ 0844 879 9057 & 01877 389500 📠 01877 387307
Kinlochard FK8 3TL
e-mail: forest_hills@macdonald-hotels.co.uk
web: www.macdonald-hotels.co.uk/foresthills
dir: A84/A873/A81 to Aberfoyle onto B829 along lochside to hotel

Situated in the heart of The Trossachs with wonderful views of Loch Ard, this popular hotel forms part of a resort complex offering a range of indoor and outdoor facilities. The main hotel has relaxing lounges and a restaurant that overlook the landscaped gardens. A separate building houses the refurbished leisure centre, lounge bar and bistro.

Rooms 49 (16 fmly) (12 GF) **S** £94-£196; **D** £104-£206 (incl. bkfst)* **Facilities** Spa STV FTV 🕙 ♨ Gym Children's club Snooker Watersports Quad biking Archery Clay pigeon shooting 🎵 Xmas New Year Wi-fi **Conf** Class 60 Board 45 Thtr 150 Del from £130 to £165* **Services** Lift **Parking** 100 **Notes** LB ⊛ Civ Wed 100

ARDEONAIG
Map 2 NN63

The Ardeonaig Hotel 🍸

☎ 01567 820400 📠 01567 820282
South Lock Tay Side FK21 8SU
e-mail: info@ardeonaighotel.co.uk
dir: In Kenmore take road to S of Loch Tay signed Acharn. 6m. Or from Killin, next Falls of Dochart, take South Rd through Achmore & on to Ardeonaig, 6m

A romantic retreat with a difference, on the south shore of Loch Tay with views of the Ben Lawers mountains. The difference is that chef/owner Pete Gottgens has totally refurbished the inn and introduced many elements dear to his heart from his native Southern Africa. Developments include a new kitchen; five thatched colonial-style garden lodges (called rondawels); a fine dining wine cellar which houses Europe's largest collection of South African wines; a new dining room called the Study, where light lunches or afternoon teas are served; and the landscaping of 13 acres of grounds. African influences notwithstanding, the Ardeonaig has a solid reputation for using the best of seasonal Scottish produce in the kitchen. A typical dinner selection could start with poached Loch Tarbet lobster salad; continue with a main course of Ardtalnaig Estate hare fillets with caramelised onions, Puy lentils and seasonal vegetables.

Open all day all wk 11-10 (Fri-Sat 11-11) **Bar Meals** Av main course £8 food served all day **Restaurant** L served all wk 12-6 D served all wk from 7pm booking required Fixed menu price fr £26.50 Av 3 course à la carte fr £32 ⊕ FREE HOUSE ◀ Arran Blonde, Tusker, Castle Lager, Windhoek Lager. 🍸 10 **Facilities** Family room Dogs allowed Garden Parking

BALMAHA
Map 2 NS49

Oak Tree Inn

★★★ INN

☎ 01360 870357 📠 01360 870350
G63 0JQ
e-mail: info@oak-tree-inn.co.uk
dir: A811 onto B837 to Balmaha

Standing in the shade of a magnificent 500-year-old oak tree on the quiet eastern shore of Loch Lomond, this friendly family-run inn is a great base for exploring the surrounding countryside. The attractive bedrooms have been refurbished to a high standard and are individually styled and well equipped. The rustic bar is complete with beams, a roaring log fire and local memorabilia, while the dining room serves delicious home-cooked fare.

Rooms 9 en suite (1 fmly) S £75; D £75-£100* **Facilities** tea/coffee Dinner available Cen ht **Parking** 6 **Notes** ⊛ Closed 25 Dec, 1 Jan No coaches

CALLANDER
Map 2 NN60

Roman Camp Country House

★★★ 86% COUNTRY HOUSE HOTEL

⊚⊚⊚ Modern French ▼

Innovative French-influenced cooking in luxurious manor house

☎ 01877 330003 📠 01877 331533
FK17 8BG
e-mail: mail@romancamphotel.co.uk
web: www.romancamphotel.co.uk
dir: N on A84, left at east end of High Street. 300yds to hotel

So named, at the outbreak of World War II, for its proximity to one of the Romans' more northerly encampments, the hotel has been lavishly appointed. 20 acres of gardens and grounds lead down to the River Teith, and the town centre is only a short walk away. Real fires warm the atmospheric public areas and service is friendly yet professional. The interiors, indeed, are a sight for sore eyes, with their positively rococo colour schemes, fabrics and tapestries. The expansive, elliptical dining room is softly candlelit, the tables decorated with ornamental flower features that nearly reach the low ceiling. The strongly Francophile cooking revolves around thrilling combinations, with prime seasonal Scottish produce underpinning it. Curry-dusted scallops are a well-judged opener, served with puréed celeriac and raw apple, and then comes an intermediate soup course, perhaps white bean infused with Périgord black truffle. Roe deer is a majestic main course, the loin wrapped in pancetta, sweetly set off with honey-roasted parsnips, puréed beetroot and a 'cigarette' of dates. Only an overwhelming coffee foam upsets the balance of the dish. An ingenious dessert is the dark chocolate délice, which oozes forth pistachio cream, fondant-fashion, and comes with nicely contrasting mascarpone ice cream. With breads, canapés and extras all up to the mark, this is without doubt a destination restaurant.

Rooms 15 (4 fmly) (7 GF) **S** £85-£135; **D** £135-£185 (incl. bkfst) **Facilities** STV FTV Fishing Xmas New Year Wi-fi **Conf** Class 60 Board 30 Thtr 120 Del from £200 to £285* **Parking** 80 **Notes** LB Civ Wed 100

Chef Ian McNaught Owner Eric Brown Restaurant Times 12-2/7-9 Prices Fixed L 3 course £25-£30, Fixed D 4 course £45-£55, Starter £9.75-£19.75, Main £24.50-£35.50, Dessert £9.75-£12.75, Service optional Wines 185 bottles over £20, 15 bottles under £20, 16 by glass Notes Sunday L, Vegetarian menu, Dress restrictions, Smart casual Seats 120, Pr/dining room 36 Children Portions

Callander Meadows

★★★★ RESTAURANT WITH ROOMS

⊛ Modern British ℭ

Restaurant with rooms in historic town

☎ 01877 330181
24 Main St FK17 8BB
e-mail: mail@callandermeadows.co.uk
web: www.callandermeadows.co.uk
dir: M9 junct 10, A8 for 15m, restaurant 1m in village on left past lights

This Georgian restaurant with rooms in the centre of the town is run with a hands-on approach by a husband-and-wife-team - he does the starters and main courses, she makes the desserts and the bread. The house is impeccably maintained, with plenty of original features, and the service is refreshingly relaxed and informal. Local produce is sourced with care and attention to detail is evident throughout. Chicken liver paté is served with plum chutney and slices of toasted walnut bread as a starter, while main-course coley comes with a cheese crust, julienne of vegetables and parsley sauce. Good value lunches include the likes of shepherd's pie. The bedrooms have been appointed to a high standard, and private parking is available to the rear.

Rooms 3 en suite; D £70-£80* Facilities tea/coffee Dinner available Cen ht Wi-fi Parking 4 Notes ⊗ RS Winter Restaurant open Thu-Sun only No coaches

Chef Nick & Susannah Parkes Owner Nick & Susannah Parkes Restaurant Times 12-2.30/6-9 Closed 25-26 Dec, Tue-Wed Prices Fixed L 2 course £7.95-£10.95, Fixed D 4 course fr £25, Starter £4.50-£7.50, Main £11.95-£24.95, Dessert £4.50-£7.50 Wines 15 bottles over £20, 17 bottles under £20, 8 by glass Notes Sunday L, Vegetarian available Seats 40, Pr/dining room 16 Children Portions

Annfield Guest House

★★★★ GUEST HOUSE

☎ 01877 330204 ▤ 01877 330674
18 North Church St FK17 8EG
e-mail: reservations@annfieldguesthouse.co.uk
dir: Off A84 Main St onto North Church St, at top on right

Situated within easy reach of the town centre, this welcoming guest house offers comfortable, good-value accommodation. The spacious bedrooms are attractively decorated and well equipped. An elegant first-floor lounge is ideal for relaxation, and hearty breakfasts are served at individual tables in the pretty dining room. Self-catering accommodation is also available.

Rooms 7 rms (4 en suite) (1 pri facs) (1 fmly) S £35-£55; D £55-£65* Facilities tea/coffee Cen ht Wi-fi Parking 7 Notes LB ⊗ No Children 6yrs Closed Xmas ⊜

Arden House

★★★★ 🏠 GUEST ACCOMMODATION

☎ 01877 330235
Bracklinn Rd FK17 8EQ
e-mail: ardenhouse@onetel.com
dir: Off A84 Main St onto Bracklinn Rd, house 200yds on left

This impressive Victorian villa lies in beautiful mature grounds in a peaceful area of the town. It featured in the 1960s hit television series Dr Finlay's Casebook and is a friendly, welcoming house. The comfortable bedrooms are thoughtfully furnished and equipped. There is a stylish lounge in addition to the attractive breakfast room where delicious breakfasts are served at individual tables.

Rooms 6 en suite (2 GF) S £40; D £70-£80* Facilities tea/coffee Cen ht Wi-fi ⚡ Parking 10 Notes ⊗ No Children 14yrs Closed Nov-Mar

Lubnaig House

★★★★ GUEST HOUSE

☎ 01877 330376
Leny Feus FK17 8AS
e-mail: info@lubnaighouse.co.uk
web: www.lubnaighouse.co.uk
dir: From town centre A84 W, right onto Leny Feus. Lubnaig House after Poppies Hotel

Lubnaig House is set in a delightful tree-lined secluded garden just a 5-minute walk from the town centre. The house, built in 1864, has been modernised to provide comfortable well-appointed bedrooms. There are two cosy lounges, and an impressive dining room where hearty traditional breakfasts are served at individual tables.

Rooms 6 en suite 2 annexe en suite S £50-£60; D £70-£84* Facilities tea/coffee Cen ht Wi-fi Parking 10 Notes LB ⊗ No Children 7yrs Closed Nov-Apr

The Lade Inn ☗

☎ 01877 330152
Kilmahog FK17 8HD
e-mail: info@theladeinn.com
dir: From Stirling take A84 to Callander. 1m N of Callander, left at Kilmahog Woollen Mills onto A821 towards Aberfoyle. Pub immediately on left

First licensed in the 1960s, this family-run free house was built as a tea room in 1935. Today, it offers a friendly welcome and the highest standards of food and drink. Beside the usual range at the bar, the pub's own Scottish real ale shop stocks over 120 ales from Scotland's 26 micro-breweries. Soak them up with haggis, neeps and tatties; whole baked Trossachs trout; or penne pasta with wild mushroom sauce.

Open all day all wk noon-11 (Fri-Sat noon-1am Sun 12.30-10.30) **Bar Meals** L served May-Sep all wk, all day, Oct-Apr all wk 12-3 D served May-Sep all wk, all day, Oct-Apr Sun-Thu 5-9 Av main course £8 **Restaurant** L served May-Sep all wk, all day, Oct-Apr all wk 12-3 D served May-Sep all wk, all day, Oct-Apr all wk 5-9 booking required Fixed menu price fr £14.25 Av 3 course à la carte fr £15 ⊕ FREE HOUSE ◀ Waylade, LadeBack, LadeOut, Bellhaven Best. ☗ 9 **Facilities** Play area Family room Dogs allowed Garden Parking

The Crianlarich Hotel

★★ 79% HOTEL

☎ 01838 300272   📠 01838 300329
FK20 8RW
e-mail: info@crianlarich-hotel.co.uk
web: www.crianlarich-hotel.co.uk
dir: At junct of A85 Oban & Fort William to Perth and A82 Glasgow road, in Crianlarich

Impressive ground floor areas have benefitted from recent investment. Bedrooms & bathrooms present well offering good ease of use. Friendly relaxed service & high quality food makes for an enjoyable stay in this perfectly located hotel close to Loch Lomond and the Trossachs National Park.

Rooms 36 (1 fmly) **S** £50-£75; **D** £65-£135* **Facilities** FTV 🎵 New Year Wi-fi **Conf** Class 60 Board 40 Thtr 100 Del from £75 to £160 **Services** Lift **Parking** 30 **Notes** LB

Winnock Hotel

★★★ 75% HOTEL

☎ 01360 660245   📠 01360 660267
The Square G63 0BL
e-mail: info@winnockhotel.com
web: www.winnockhotel.com
dir: From S: M74 onto M8 junct 16b through Glasgow. Follow A809 to Aberfoyle

Occupying a prominent position overlooking the village green, this popular hotel offers well-equipped bedrooms of various sizes and styles. The public rooms include a bar, a lounge and an attractive formal dining room that serves dishes of good, locally sourced food.

Rooms 73 (18 fmly) (19 GF) **S** £34-£96; **D** £49-£129 (incl. bkfst)* **Facilities** FTV Xmas New Year Wi-fi **Conf** Class 60 Board 70 Thtr 140 Del from £59 to £109* **Parking** 60 **Notes** LB ⊗ Civ Wed 100

The Clachan Inn

☎ 01360 660824
2 Main St G63 0BG
dir: Telephone for directions

Quaint, white-painted cottage, believed to be the oldest licensed pub in Scotland, situated in a small village on the West Highland Way, and once owned by Rob Roy's sister. Locate the appealing lounge bar for freshly-made food, the varied menu listing filled baked potatoes, salads, fresh haddock in crispy breadcrumbs, spicy Malaysian lamb casserole, vegetable lasagne, a variety of steaks, and good daily specials.

Open all wk Closed: 25 Dec & 1 Jan ⊕ FREE HOUSE ◀ Caledonian Deuchars IPA, Belhaven Best, Guinness. **Facilities** Dogs allowed Parking

FINTRY — Map 2 NS68

Culcreuch Castle

★★★ 75% HOTEL

☎ 01360 860555 & 860228 📠 01360 860556
Kippen Rd G63 0LW
e-mail: info@culcreuch.com
web: www.culcreuch.com
dir: On B822, 17m W of Stirling

Peacefully located in 1,600 acres of parkland, this ancient castle dates back to 1296. Tastefully restored accommodation is in a mixture of individually themed castle rooms, some with four-poster beds, and more modern courtyard rooms which are suitable for families. Period style public rooms include a bar, serving light meals, a wood-panelled dining room and an elegant lounge.

Rooms 14 (4 annexe) (4 fmly) (4 GF) **S** £81-£115; **D** £102-£180 (incl. bkfst) **Facilities** FTV Fishing New Year Wi-fi **Conf** Class 70 Board 30 Thtr 140 Del from £119 to £129 **Parking** 100 **Notes** LB ⊗ Closed 25-26 Dec Civ Wed 110

KIPPEN — Map 2 NS69

Cross Keys Hotel

☎ 01786 870293
Main St FK8 3DN
e-mail: info@kippencrosskeys.co.uk
dir: 10m W of Stirling, 20m from Loch Lomond off A811

Refurbished by owners Debby and Brian, this cosy inn now serves food and drink all day. Nearby Burnside Wood is managed by a local community woodland group, and is perfect for walking and nature trails. The pub's interior, warmed by three log fires, is equally perfect for resting your feet afterwards. Regular events include a weekly Tuesday folk night.

Open all day noon-11 (Fri-Sat noon-1am Sun noon-11) Closed: 25 Dec, 1-2 Jan, Mon **Bar Meals** L served Tue-Sun 12-9 D served Tue-Sun 12-9 food served all day **Restaurant** L served Tue-Sun 12-9 D served Tue-Sun 12-9 food served all day ⊕ FREE HOUSE ◀ Belhaven Best, Harviestoun Bitter & Twisted, Guinness. **Facilities** Children's menu Family room Dogs allowed Garden Parking

LOCHEARNHEAD — Map 2 NN52

Mansewood Country House

★★★★ GUEST HOUSE

☎ 01567 830213
FK19 8NS
e-mail: stay@mansewoodcountryhouse.co.uk
dir: A84 N to Lochearnhead, 1st building on left; A84 S to Lochearnhead

Mansewood Country House is a spacious former manse that dates back to the 18th century and lies in a well-tended garden to the south of the village. Bedrooms are well appointed and equipped and offer high standards of comfort. Refreshments can be enjoyed in the cosy bar or the elegant lounge, and meals prepared with flair are served in the attractive restaurant. There is also a log cabin where pets are allowed.

Rooms 6 en suite (1 GF) **S** £30-£45; **D** £54-£65 **Facilities** TVL tea/coffee Dinner available Cen ht Licensed Wi-fi **Parking** 6 **Notes** LB ⊗ RS Nov-Mar Phone for advance bookings

Tigh Na Crich

★★★★ BED AND BREAKFAST

☎ 01567 830235
FK19 8PR
e-mail: johntippett2@aol.com
web: www.tighnacrich.co.uk
dir: On junct of A84 & A85, next to village shop

Located in the heart of the small village of Lochearnhead and surrounded by mountains on three sides and Loch Earn on the fourth. Very well presented accommodation with many thoughtful extras provided. The generous breakfast is served in the comfortable dining room on individual tables looking out to the front of the property.

Rooms 3 en suite (1 fmly) **S** £38-£45; **D** £56-£60* **Facilities** tea/coffee Cen ht **Parking** 3 **Notes** ⊛

STIRLING — Map 3 NS79

Barceló Stirling Highland Hotel

★★★★ 75% HOTEL

☎ 01786 272727 📠 01786 272829
Spittal St FK8 1DU
e-mail: stirling@barcelo-hotels.co.uk
web: www.barcelo-hotels.co.uk
dir: A84 into Stirling. Follow Stirling Castle signs as far as Albert Hall. Left, left again, follow Castle signs

Enjoying a location close to the castle and historic old town, this atmospheric hotel was previously the town's high school. Public rooms have been converted from the original classrooms and retain many interesting features. Bedrooms are more modern in style and comfortably equipped. Scholars Restaurant serves traditional and international dishes, and the Headmaster's Study is the ideal venue for enjoying a drink.

Rooms 96 (4 fmly) **Facilities** Spa STV ⊕ supervised Gym Squash Steam room Dance studio Beauty therapist Xmas New Year Wi-fi **Conf** Class 80 Board 60 Thtr 100 Del from £125* **Services** Lift **Parking** 96 **Notes** Civ Wed 100

Express by Holiday Inn Stirling

BUDGET HOTEL

☎ 01786 449922 📠 01786 449932
Springkerse Business Park FK7 7XH
e-mail: stirling@expressbyholidayinn.co.uk
web: www.hiexpress.com/stirling
dir: M9/M80 junct 9/A91, Stirling/St Andrews exit. 2.8m, at 4th rdbt, take 2nd exit to sports stadium, 3rd exit to hotel

A modern hotel ideal for families and business travellers. Fresh and

continued

uncomplicated, the spacious rooms include Sky TV, power shower and tea and coffee-making facilities. Continental buffet breakfast is included in the room rate; other meals may be taken at the nearby family pub or restaurant. See also the Hotel Groups pages on theAA.com.

Rooms 78 (36 fmly) **S** £69-£119; **D** £69-£119 (incl. bkfst)*
Conf Class 14 Board 18 Thtr 30

Travelodge Stirling (M80)

BUDGET HOTEL

☎ 0871 984 6178 🖷 01786 817646
Pirnhall Roundabout, Snabhead FK7 8EU
web: www.travelodge.co.uk
dir: M9/M80 junct 9

Travelodge offers good quality, good value, modern accommodation. Ideal for families, the spacious en suite bedrooms include remote-control TV, tea and coffee-making facilities and comfortable beds. Meals can be taken at the nearby family restaurant. See also the Hotel Groups pages on theAA.com.

Rooms 37 **S** fr £29; **D** fr £29

Linden Guest House

★★★★ GUEST HOUSE

☎ 01786 448850 & 07974 116573 🖷 01786 448850
22 Linden Av FK7 7PQ
e-mail: fay@lindenguesthouse.co.uk
web: www.lindenguesthouse.co.uk
dir: 0.5m SE of city centre off A9

Situated within walking distance of the town centre, this friendly guest house offers attractive and very well-equipped bedrooms, including a large family room that sleeps five comfortably. There is a bright dining room where delicious breakfasts are served at individual tables with quality Wedgwood crockery.

Rooms 4 en suite (2 fmly) (1 GF) **S** £60-£70; **D** £70-£80*
Facilities STV tea/coffee Cen ht Wi-fi **Parking** 2 **Notes** LB

Strathblane Country House

★★★ 74% COUNTRY HOUSE HOTEL

☎ 01360 770491 🖷 01360 770345
Milngavie Rd G63 9EH
e-mail: info@strathblanecountryhouse.co.uk
dir: From Glasgow city centre follow Bearsden road or Maryhill road to Canniesburn toll, then A81 (Milneavie road) to Strathblane. Hotel 0.75m past Mugdock Country Park on right

Set in 10 acres of grounds looking out on the beautiful Campsie Fells, this majestic property, built in 1874, offers a get-away-from-it-all experience, yet is just a 20 minute drive from Glasgow. Lunch and dinner are served in the relaxed Brasserie Restaurant, and guests can visit the falconry or just kick back and relax in front of the fire

with a book and a dram. Weddings are especially well catered for.

Rooms 10 (3 fmly) **S** £55-£89; **D** £90-£150 (incl. bkfst)*
Facilities FTV Falconry ♫ Xmas New Year Wi-fi **Conf** Class 60 Board 60 Thtr 180 Del from £110 to £150* **Parking** 120 **Notes** LB ⊗ Civ Wed 180

Creagan House

★★★★★ RESTAURANT WITH ROOMS

◉◉ French, Scottish ♦ᴺᴼᵀᴬᴮᴸᴱ

17th-century farmhouse with warm hospitality and good food

☎ 01877 384638 🖷 01877 384319
FK18 8ND
e-mail: eatandstay@creaganhouse.co.uk
web: www.creaganhouse.co.uk
dir: 0.25m N of village, off A84

The husband-and-wife-team who run this immaculately-restored 17th-century farmhouse put heart and soul into the place - their warm hospitality and attentive service really are the highlights of any stay. The journey itself is a real treat, and when the sun has set on the jaw-dropping Highland scenery, a baronial dining room with a grandiose stone fireplace and burnished refectory tables awaits. The kitchen delivers classical French treatment with strong Scottish flavours in accurately-cooked dishes; sticklers for food of local provenance should be reassured to know that local small-holdings grow produce specifically for Creagan House, and meat is all reared on Perthshire farms. Among starters might be truffled langoustine mousseline with hand-dived Orkney scallops in Chartreuse-scented cream sauce, followed by collops of venison with red onion marmalade and baked fig in gin and juniper berry sauce. Should the weather confine you to the house, a 100-bin wine list and 50-odd malts should keep you entertained.

Rooms 5 en suite (1 fmly) (1 GF) **S** £70-£90; **D** £120-£140
Facilities FTV tea/coffee Dinner available Cen ht Wi-fi **Conf** Max 35 Thtr 35 Class 12 Board 35 **Parking** 26 **Notes** LB Closed 4-19 Nov, Xmas & 21 Jan-5 Mar RS Wed & Thu Closed

Chef Gordon Gunn **Owner** Gordon & Cherry Gunn **Restaurant Times** 7.30-8.30 Closed 4-19 Nov, Xmas, 21 Jan-5 Mar, Wed-Thu, L all week (ex parties) **Prices** Fixed D 3 course fr £29.50, Service optional **Wines** 43 bottles over £20, 24 bottles under £20, 8 by glass **Notes** Dress restrictions, Smart casual **Seats** 15, Pr/dining room 6 **Children** Portions

The Sir Walter Scott, Loch Katrine

Cuillin Hills, looking across Loch Scavaig from Elgol, Isle of Skye

ISLE OF ARRAN

BLACKWATERFOOT   Map 2 NR92

Best Western Kinloch

★★★ 80% HOTEL

☎ 01770 860444 📄 01770 860447
KA27 8ET
e-mail: reservations@kinlochhotel.eclipse.co.uk
web: www.bw-kinlochhotel.co.uk
dir: Ferry from Ardrossan to Brodick, follow signs for Blackwaterfoot, hotel in village centre

Well known for providing an authentic island experience, this long established stylish hotel is in an idyllic location. Smart public areas include a choice of lounges, popular bars and well-presented leisure facilities. Bedrooms vary in size and style but most enjoy panoramic sea views and there are several family suites. The spacious restaurant provides a wide ranging menu, and in winter when the restaurant is closed, the bar serves a choice of creative dishes.

Rooms 37 (7 fmly) (7 GF) **S** £40-£65; **D** £80-£130 (incl. bkfst)
Facilities STV 🕲 Gym Squash Beauty therapy 🎵 New Year Wi-fi
Conf Class 20 Board 40 Thtr 120 Del from £80 to £110* **Services** Lift
Parking 2 **Notes** LB Civ Wed 60

BRODICK   Map 2 NS03

Kilmichael Country House

★★★ COUNTRY HOUSE HOTEL

◉◉ Modern British 🕲

Fine Scottish fare in historic country house

☎ 01770 302219 📄 01770 302068
Glen Cloy KA27 8BY
e-mail: enquiries@kilmichael.com
web: www.kilmichael.com
dir: From Brodick ferry terminal towards Lochranza for 1m. Left at golf course, inland between sports field & church, follow signs

This elegant, white-painted house, believed to be the oldest on the island and listed as a building of historic and architectural interest, has been lovingly restored to create a very stylish country-house hotel. Sitting in 4 acres of gardens in a peaceful glen, it has been furnished with a mix of antiques, interesting artworks and fabulous china. The delightful bedrooms are furnished in classical style; some are part of a pretty courtyard conversion. In the comfortable restaurant, the menu features first-class produce, including eggs from their own chickens and ducks, and fruit and vegetables and herbs from their own garden or the estate. Expect canapés, followed by a starter such as locally smoked salmon and prawn cheesecake (a rich mascarpone cream on an Arran oatcake and coriander base). After a sorbet follow with a main course of fillet of Scottish lamb baked with cinnamon-scented basmati rice and a rich Persian sauce.

Rooms 8 (3 annexe) (7 GF) **S** £76-£95; **D** £128-£199 (incl. bkfst)*
Facilities Wi-fi **Parking** 14 **Notes** LB No children 12yrs Closed Nov-Feb (ex for prior bookings)

Chef Antony Butterworth **Owner** G Botterill & A Butterworth
Restaurant Times -7-8.30 Closed Nov-Mar, Tue, L all week
Prices Fixed D 4 course £42, Service optional **Wines** 32 bottles over £20, 23 bottles under £20, 3 by glass **Notes** Vegetarian available, Dress restrictions, Smart casual, no T-shirts or bare feet **Seats** 18

Allandale

★★★★ GUEST HOUSE

☎ 01770 302278
KA27 8BJ
e-mail: info@allandalehouse.co.uk
dir: 500yds S of Brodick Pier, off A841 towards Lamlash, up hill 2nd left at Corriegills sign

Under enthusiastic ownership, this comfortable guest house is set in delightful gardens in beautiful countryside. Guests can relax in the lounge with its attractive garden views. Bedrooms vary in size and have pleasing colour schemes and mixed modern furnishings along with thoughtful amenities. In a peaceful location, Allandale is convenient for the CalMac ferry and Brodick centre.

Rooms 4 rms (3 en suite) (1 pri facs) 2 annexe en suite (3 fmly) (2 GF) **S** £46; **D** £74-£80 **Facilities** FTV tea/coffee Cen ht Wi-fi **Parking** 6 **Notes** LB ⊗ Closed Nov-Feb

Dunvegan House

★★★★ GUEST HOUSE

☎ 01770 302811 📄 01770 302811
Dunvegan Shore Rd KA27 8AJ
e-mail: dunveganhouse1@hotmail.com
dir: Turn right from ferry terminal, 500yds along Shore Rd

Dunvegan is a delightful detached home overlooking the bay towards Brodick Castle with Goat Fell beyond. The comfortable lounge and attractive dining room, as well as the pine-furnished bedrooms, enjoy the views. A daily-changing dinner menu and an interesting wine list encourage guests to dine in.

Rooms 9 en suite (1 fmly) (3 GF) **S** £45; **D** £80* **Facilities** tea/coffee Dinner available Cen ht Licensed **Parking** 10 **Notes** ⊗ Closed Xmas & New Year 📧

ISLE OF COLL

ARINAGOUR   **Map 4 NM25**

Coll Hotel

☎ 01879 230334 📄 01879 230317
PA78 6SZ
e-mail: info@collhotel.com
dir: Ferry from Oban. Hotel at head of Arinagour Bay, 1m from Pier
(collections by arrangement)

The Coll Hotel is the only inn on the Isle of Coll, and commands
stunning views over the sea to Jura and Mull. The island only has 170
inhabitants, so is perfect for a holiday away from it all. The hotel is a
popular rendezvous for locals, and food is served in the Gannet
Restaurant, bar or garden. Fresh produce is landed and delivered
from around the island every day and features on the specials board.
Try local seafood open sandwiches; or Coll crab and local prawn
spaghetti with chilli and parmesan at lunch, and for dinner perhaps
Argyll venison casserole with port, juniper and clove gravy; or roasted
locally caught monkfish tail with crispy Parma ham, tomato and
basil sauce, and rice. The hotel has a private helipad in the garden,
and guests are welcome to land and enjoy a meal or an overnight
stay.

Open all wk 11am-11.45pm **Bar Meals** L served all wk 12-2 D served
all wk 6-9 ⊕ FREE HOUSE ◀ Loch Fyne Ale, Pipers Gold, Guinness.
Facilities Play area Dogs allowed Garden Parking

ISLE OF HARRIS

SCARISTA   **Map 4 NG09**

Scarista House

★★★★ RESTAURANT WITH ROOMS

◉◉ Modern Scottish

Remote country house with great views and island produce

☎ 01859 550238 📄 01859 550277
HS3 3HX
e-mail: timandpatricia@scaristahouse.com
web: www.scaristahouse.com
dir: On A859 15m S of Tarbert

Picture a Georgian manse looking over three miles of golden shell
sand beach and the wild Atlantic coast of the Isle of Harris, heather-
carpeted mountains all around: that's Scarista House. The house is
run in a relaxed country-house manner by the friendly hosts - expect
wellies in the hall and masses of books and CDs in one of the two
lounges. Bedrooms are cosy, and what's more, all this natural beauty

and comfort comes with great food at the end of a day's exploration,
taken in an elegant traditional dining room. Silver cutlery and
candlesticks gleam on oak tables, original art hangs on the walls,
and open fires cast a cosy glow. The kitchen takes fish and seafood,
fruit and vegetables, fresh game and meat from the islands, going
for organic whenever possible, and transforms it all into dishes such
as velouté of Jerusalem artichokes and Puy lentils with Uist peat-
smoked scallops, followed by Harris Minch langoustines served
simply with garlic mayonnaise, crushed olive potatoes and salad
from the garden. Exquisite desserts include Cointreau baba with
caramelised blood oranges.

Rooms 3 en suite 2 annexe en suite (2 GF) S £125-£140; D
£175-£199* **Facilities** tea/coffee Dinner available Direct Dial Cen ht
Parking 12 **Notes** LB Closed Xmas, Jan & Feb No coaches Civ Wed 40

Chef Tim Martin **Owner** Tim & Patricia Martin **Restaurant**
Times 7.30-8 Closed 25 Dec, Jan-Feb, L Mon-Sat **Prices** Fixed D 3
course £39.50, Service optional **Wines** 25 bottles over £20, 25 bottles
under £20, 2 by glass **Notes** Sunday L, Vegetarian available
Seats 20, Pr/dining room 14 **Children** Portions, Menu

ISLE OF ISLAY

PORT ASKAIG   **Map 2 NR46**

Port Askaig

★★ 62% SMALL HOTEL

☎ 01496 840245 📄 01496 840295
PA46 7RD
e-mail: hotel@portaskaig.co.uk
web: www.portaskaig.co.uk
dir: At ferry terminal

This endearing family-run hotel dates back to the 18th century. The
lounge provides fine views over the Sound of Islay to Jura, and there
is a choice of bars that are popular with locals. Traditional dinners
are served in the bright restaurant and a full range of bar snacks
and meals is also available. All bedrooms are smart and comfortable,
and several rooms can sleep three people. Five bedrooms enjoy great
views over the harbour, and several also have their own private
terrace. Many bedrooms are easily accessible, having two or no
steps.

Rooms 10 (2 fmly) (10 GF) **Parking** 21 **Notes** LB

ISLE OF MULL

TOBERMORY
Map 4 NM55

Highland Cottage

★★★ SMALL HOTEL

◉◉ Modern Scottish, International ◔

Traditional Mull hotel with appealing menu jam-packed with local produce

☎ 01688 302030
Breadalbane St PA75 6PD
e-mail: davidandjo@highlandcottage.co.uk
web: www.highlandcottage.co.uk
dir: A848 Craignure/Fishnish ferry terminal, pass Tobermory signs, straight on at mini rdbt across narrow bridge, turn right. Hotel on right opposite fire station

Providing the highest level of natural and unassuming hospitality, this delightful little family-run Hebridean hotel lies high above the island's capital. 'A country house hotel in town', it is an Aladdin's Cave of collectables and treasures, as well as masses of books and magazines. There are two inviting lounges, one with an honesty bar, and bedrooms are individual; some have four-posters and all are comprehensively equipped to include TVs and music centres. If you believe in reducing food miles to a minimum, the restaurant keeps the tally impressively low. Fish and seafood are landed either round the corner on Tobermory's pier or sourced from the waters around Mull and the mainland. The cottagey dining room has a homely, welcoming atmosphere, and the food fits the bill to a tee: unfussy, skilful home cooking from a chef with the self-assurance to let the unbeatably fresh produce do the talking. Expect modern Scottish dishes with flashes of international flair, and of course, plenty of that local seafood, such as smoked Inverlussa mussels with mango mayonnaise to start, followed by seared diver-caught scallops with Argyll ham, sautéed potatoes and herb and garlic butter.

Rooms 6 (1 GF) **S** £120-£135; **D** £150-£185 (incl. bkfst) **Facilities** Wi-fi **Parking** 6 **Notes** LB No children 10yrs Closed Nov-Feb

Chef Josephine Currie **Owner** David & Josephine Currie **Restaurant Times** 7-9 Closed Nov-Feb, L all week **Prices** Fixed D 4 course £45, Service included **Wines** 33 bottles over £20, 21 bottles under £20, 11 by glass **Notes** Vegetarian available, Dress restrictions, Smart casual **Seats** 24 **Children** Portions

Western Isles Hotel

★★★ 75% HOTEL

☎ 01688 302012 📠 01688 302297
PA75 6PR
e-mail: wihotel@aol.com
web: www.mullhotel.com
dir: From ferry follow signs to Tobermory. Over 1st mini-rdbt in Tobermory, over small bridge, immediate right, to T-junct. Right, keep left, 1st left. Hotel at top of hill on right

Sitting on top of the cliffs looking over Tobermory with amazing views, this well-established hotel has benefited from a refurbishment by the new owners. Many of the spacious bedrooms and the public

areas enjoy the lovely views. Dining is in the relaxed atmosphere of the conservatory or in the traditional restaurant; menus offer fine quality food using locally sourced produce.

Rooms 26 (1 fmly) **S** £40-£60; **D** £70-£135 (incl. bkfst)* **Facilities** Xmas New Year **Conf** Class 60 Board 30 Thtr 70 **Parking** 15 **Notes** LB Civ Wed 70

Tobermory

★★ 76% HOTEL

◉ Modern Scottish ◔

Modern Scots cooking in a harbourside setting

☎ 01688 302091 📠 01688 302254
53 Main St PA75 6NT
e-mail: tobhotel@tinyworld.co.uk
web: www.thetobermoryhotel.com
dir: On waterfront

This friendly hotel, with its pretty pink frontage, sits on the seafront amid other brightly coloured, picture-postcard buildings. An amalgam of former fishermen's cottages, it fronts on to the Bay, where yachting folk and working fishing boats animate the scene. Bedrooms come in a variety of sizes; all are bright and vibrant, while the Water's Edge restaurant capitalises on the setting with both local seafood and island produce such as game and cheeses informing the menus. Begin with smoked trout seasoned with chilli and lime on sesame toasts with a salad of pickled cucumber and spring onions and, after an intervening soup or sorbet, follow on with a pairing of Glengorm beef and Ulva Bay langoustines, dressed in tequila, lime and coriander butter. A selection of steamed mini-puddings served with ice creams makes for an original finale.

Rooms 16 (3 fmly) (2 GF) **S** £38-£98; **D** £76-£122 (incl. bkfst)* **Facilities** supervised New Year Wi-fi **Notes** Closed Xmas

Chef Helen Swinbanks **Owner** Mr & Mrs I Stevens **Restaurant Times** 6-9 Closed Xmas, Jan, L all week **Prices** Fixed D 3 course £31.50, Service optional **Wines** 18 bottles over £20, 24 bottles under £20, 5 by glass **Notes** Vegetarian available **Seats** 30 **Children** Portions, Menu

ORKNEY ISLANDS

ST MARGARET'S HOPE   Map 6 ND49

Creel Restaurant

★★★★ RESTAURANT WITH ROOMS

⑧⑧ Modern, Seafood

Deserved reputation for making best of first-class Orkney produce

☎ 01856 831311
The Creel, Front Rd KW17 2SL
e-mail: alan@thecreel.freeserve.co.uk
dir: 13m S of Kirkwall on A961, on seafront in village

Situated a 20-minute drive south from Kirkwall, across the famous Churchill Barriers, the Creel restaurant and rooms occupies a stunning seafront spot in the picturesque village of St Margaret's Hope. This charming restaurant specialises in local produce, served in a relaxed dining room with local artwork on the walls and sea views. The freshest of fish is always on the menu, including unusual species such as wolf-fish, megrim, torsk and sea-witch. Hand-dived scallops, mackerel caught in a nearby bay, mussels and lobster from local creels feature when in season, as does organic salmon, prime Orkney beef and seaweed-fed lamb from North Ronaldsay. All these are accompanied by locally grown vegetables, ales from the island's award-winning brewery, and malt whiskies from the Highland Park and Scapa distilleries. Chunky fish soup is brimful with cod cheeks, haddock belly and ling roe, while seared North Sea hake comes as a main course with Orkney scallops and crushed garden peas. The stylish bedrooms have now been refurbished to a high standard and most rooms enjoy views over the bay. Breakfasts should not be missed, with local Orkney produce and freshly baked breads on the menu.

Rooms 3 en suite; D £105-£120 **Facilities** Dinner available Cen ht **Parking** 6 **Notes** ⊗ Closed mid Oct-Apr No coaches

Chef Alan Craigie **Owner** Alan & Joyce Craigie **Restaurant Times** -7-9 Closed Jan-Mar, Nov, Mon & Tue (Apr, May, Sep, Oct), L all week, D Mon **Prices** Fixed D 3 course £35-£40, Service optional **Wines** 10 bottles over £20, 18 bottles under £20, 4 by glass **Notes** Vegetarian available **Seats** 34, Pr/dining room 14 **Children** Portions

SHETLAND

LERWICK   Map 6 HU44

Shetland

★★★ 71% HOTEL

☎ 01595 695515   ▤ 01595 695828
Holmsgarth Rd ZE1 0PW
e-mail: reception@shetlandhotel.co.uk
dir: Opposite ferry terminal, on main road N from town centre

This purpose-built hotel, situated opposite the main ferry terminal, offers spacious and comfortable bedrooms on three floors. Two dining options are available, including the informal Oasis bistro and Ninians Restaurant. Service is prompt and friendly.

Rooms 64 (4 fmly) **S** £83; **D** £110 (incl. bkfst)* **Facilities** FTV Wi-fi **Conf** Class 75 Board 50 Thtr 300 **Services** Lift **Parking** 150 **Notes** LB ⊗

Glen Orchy House

★★★★ GUEST HOUSE

☎ 01595 692031   ▤ 01595 692031
20 Knab Rd ZE1 0AX
e-mail: glenorchy.house@virgin.net
dir: Next to coastguard station

This welcoming and well-presented house lies above the town with views over the Knab, and is within easy walking distance of the town centre. Bedrooms are modern in design and there is a choice of lounges with books and board games, one with an honesty bar. Substantial breakfasts are served, and the restaurant offers a delicious Thai menu.

Rooms 24 en suite (4 fmly) (4 GF) **Facilities** STV FTV TVL tea/coffee Dinner available Cen ht Licensed Wi-fi **Parking** 10

ISLE OF SKYE

ARDVASAR   Map 4 NG60

Ardvasar Hotel

★★ 74% HOTEL ☂

☎ 01471 844223   📠 01471 844495
Sleat IV45 8RS
e-mail: richard@ardvasar-hotel.demon.co.uk
web: www.ardvasarhotel.com
dir: From ferry, 500mtrs & turn left

An early 1800s white-painted cottage-style inn, the second oldest on Skye, renowned for its genuinely friendly hospitality and informal service, the hotel sits less than five minutes' drive from the Mallaig ferry and provides comfortable bedrooms and a cosy bar lounge for residents. Sea views over the Sound of Sleat reach the Knoydart Mountains beyond. Malt whiskies are plentiful, but beer drinkers will not be disappointed. Food is served in the informal lounge bar throughout the day and evening, with a sumptuous four-course dinner in the dining room during high season. Local produce figures prominently, particularly freshly-landed seafood, venison, and Aberdeen Angus beef.

Rooms 10 (4 fmly) **S** £75-£110; **D** £95-£135 (incl. bkfst)
Facilities FTV ♫ Xmas New Year Wi-fi Child facilities **Conf** Board 24 Thtr 50 Del from £105 to £160 **Parking** 30 **Notes** LB

Pub Open all day all wk 11am-mdnt (Sun noon-11pm) **Bar Meals** L served all wk 12-2.30 D served all wk 5.30-9 ⊕ FREE HOUSE ◾ IPA, Isle of Skye Red Cuillin. ☂ 6 **Facilities** Dogs allowed Garden

BROADFORD   Map 4 NG62

Broadford

★★★★ 73% SMALL HOTEL

☎ 01471 822204   📠 01471 822414
IV49 9AB
e-mail: broadford@macleodhotels.co.uk
dir: From Skye Bridge take A87 towards Portree. Hotel at end of village on left

A stylish modern hotel located in centre of the charming town of Broadford. The hotel has been refurbished to a high standard and offers all the creature comforts. Many of the spacious bedrooms **have** wonderful sea views and are attractively presented and very well equipped. Meals can be enjoyed in the fine-dining restaurant or more informal meals are served in traditional bar.

Rooms 11 (1 fmly) **S** £75-£115; **D** £88-£170 (incl. bkfst)
Facilities STV Fishing ♫ Xmas New Year Wi-fi **Conf** Class 80 Board 50 Thtr 150 Del from £120 to £200 **Parking** 20 **Notes** LB Civ Wed 100

CARBOST   Map 4 NG33

The Old Inn

☎ 01478 640205   📠 01478 640205
IV47 8SR
e-mail: reservations@oldinn.f9.co.uk

Two-hundred-year-old free house on the edge of Loch Harport with wonderful views of the Cuillin Hills from the waterside patio. Not surprisingly, the inn is popular with walkers and climbers. Open fires welcome winter visitors, and live music is a regular feature. With a great selection of real ales, the menu includes daily home-cooked specials, with numerous fresh fish dishes, including local prawns and oysters and mackerel from the loch.

Open all day all wk 11am-mdnt **Bar Meals** L served Mon-Sat 11-9, Sun 12.30-11.30 D served Mon-Sat 11-9, Sun 12.30-11.30 food served all day **Restaurant** L served Mon-Sat 11-9, Sun 12.30-11.30 D served Mon-Sat 11-9, Sun 12.30-11.30 food served all day ⊕ FREE HOUSE ◾ Red Cuillin, Black Cuillin, Hebridean ale, Cuillin Skye Ale, Pinnacle Ale. **Facilities** Children's menu Family room Dogs allowed Garden Parking

COLBOST   Map 4 NG24

The Three Chimneys

★★★★★ RESTAURANT WITH ROOMS

◉◉◉ Modern Scottish 🔥 ☺

Immaculate local cooking in a wild remote location

☎ 01470 511258   📠 01470 511358
IV55 8ZT
e-mail: eatandstay@threechimneys.co.uk
web: www.threechimneys.co.uk
dir: 5m W of Dunvegan take B884 signed Glendale. On left beside loch

In a location to restore the soul, Three Chimneys is housed in an original stone crofthouse on the shore of Loch Dunvegan, one of Skye's many almost mystical landscapes. A visit to this delightful property will make a trip to Skye even more memorable. Breakfast is an impressive array of local fish, meats and cheeses, served with fresh home baking and home-made preserves, and the stylish

continued

COLBOST CONTINUED

lounge-breakfast area has the real wow factor. Bedrooms, in the House Over-By, are creative and thoughtfully equipped - all have spacious en suites and wonderful views across Loch Dunvegan. In the little low-ceilinged dining room, simplicity is all, the bare stone walls, sturdy beamed fireplaces and polished wood tables all contributing an air of homely intimacy, while peek-a-boo views of the loch through the small windows are a delight at sunset. The produce that turns up on the fixed-price menus is never less than superb, with dishes changing daily in celebration of it, in a style that takes as its bedrock finely tuned traditional Scottish cooking, but with a modern approach. The result is skilful combinations with clear, crisply etched flavours. Seared breast of Perthshire wood pigeon comes with accompaniments of Ayrshire bacon, pearl barley, turnip, kale and game jus to make a perfectly composed first course that delivers more straightforwardly than its rollcall of ingredients might suggest. Don't miss the seafood cookery, though, on show in a brilliant main course of grilled Mallaig halibut crusted with pine nuts, teamed with flawlessly timed Sconser scallops, layered roots and a dramatically rich claret velouté. Dishes may change daily around it, but the famous hot marmalade pudding with Drambuie custard has earned its place as a long stayer, or there may be Skye whisky and lemon parfait with grapefruit, poppyseed tuiles and aniseed brittle - a complex but arresting array. When the amuse-bouche alone might be a serving of brandy-laced Skye lobster bisque, you know you're going to get looked after.

Rooms 6 (1 fmly) (6 GF) **Facilities** STV FTV Dinner available Cen ht direct dial Wf-fi tea/coffee **Parking** 8 **Notes** No dogs

Chef Michael Smith **Owner** Eddie & Shirley Spear **Restaurant Times** 12.30-2.30/6.30-10 Closed part of Jan (please telephone for details), L Nov-Mar **Prices** Fixed L 2 course £25-£35, Fixed D 3 course £55-£61, Tasting menu £70, Service optional, Groups min 8 service 10% **Notes** Tasting menu 7 course, Vegetarian tasting menu, Vegetarian available, Dress restrictions, Smart casual preferred **Seats** 38, Pr/dining room 10 **Children** Portions

---

DUNVEGAN   Map 4 NG24

Roskhill House

★★★★ GUEST HOUSE

☎ 01470 521317
Roskhill IV55 8ZD
e-mail: stay@roskhillhouse.co.uk
web: www.roskhillhouse.co.uk
dir: 3m S of Dunvegan off A863 Dunvegan

Originally built in 1890, Roskhill House was formally the village post office and general store. The house is full of character and has undergone major refurbishment under its new owners. Bedrooms are stylish, comfortable and finished to a high level of quality. Freshly cooked breakfasts are served in the cosy dining room and the lounge has traditional exposed beams and an open log fire in the cooler evenings.

Rooms 5 en suite (2 GF) S £40-£52; D £60-£78* **Facilities** TVL tea/coffee Cen ht Wi-fi **Parking** 6 **Notes** No Children 9yrs Closed Nov-mid Mar

---

EDINBANE   Map 4 NG35

Shorefield House

★★★★ GUEST HOUSE

☎ 01470 582444   🖷 01470 582414
Edinbane IV51 9PW
e-mail: stay@shorefield-house.com
dir: 12m from Portree & 8m from Dunvegan, off A850 into Edinbane, 1st on right

Shorefield stands in the village of Edinbane and looks out to Loch Greshornish. Bedrooms range from single to family, while one ground-floor room has easier access. All rooms are thoughtfully equipped and have CD players. Breakfast is an impressive choice and there is also a child-friendly garden.

Rooms 4 en suite (1 fmly) (3 GF); D £74-£98 **Facilities** TVL tea/coffee Cen ht Wi-fi **Parking** 10 **Notes** LB ⊗ Closed Xmas

Duisdale House

★★★★ 80% SMALL HOTEL

@@ Modern European ♥

Boutique-style country-house hotel dining with stunning views

☎ 01471 833202   🖷 01471 833404
IV43 8QW
e-mail: info@duisdale.com
web: www.duisdale.com
dir: 7m S of Bradford on A851 towards Armadale. 7m N of Armadale ferry

Duisdale House looks every inch the grand Victorian lodge from the outside, but inside it's clear that the old girl has had a top-to-toe chic boutique makeover. Each bedroom is individually designed and the superior rooms have four-poster beds. Classy contemporary fabrics in dramatic black and gold blend with neutral mushroom shades and period features in a décor worthy of a trendy city hotel, but relocated in the wilds of the Isle of Skye. The elegant lounge has sumptuous sofas, original artwork and blazing log fires in the colder months. Sitting in the atmospheric candlelit restaurant with sublime views across landscaped gardens to the Sound of Sleat, you realise that the beach is just a few hundred yards away. The cooking lets top-grade local produce - seafood in particular - do the talking, with simple treatment and clean-cut presentation. Local hand-dived scallops with orange and basil beurre blanc might turn up among starters, while fillet of lamb with truffle risotto and wild thyme and whisky jus is typical of main courses.

Rooms 18 (1 fmly) (1 GF) **S** £65-£150; **D** £65-£115 (incl. bkfst)*
Facilities STV Sailing on hotel's private yacht Outdoor hydropool Xmas New Year Wi-fi **Conf** Board 28 Thtr 50 Del from £90 to £125 **Parking** 30 **Notes** LB ⊗ No children 5yrs Civ Wed 58

Chef Graham Campbell **Owner** K Gunn & A Gracie **Restaurant Times** 12-2/6.30-9.30 **Prices** Fixed L 2 course £9.50-£23, Fixed D 3 course £15-£40.50, Starter £4.50-£9.50, Main £9.50-£27.50, Dessert £4.50-£7.50, Service optional **Wines** 39 bottles over £20, 11 bottles under £20, 9 by glass **Notes** Tasting menu available, Sunday L, Vegetarian available **Seats** 50 **Children** Portions

Kinloch Lodge

★★★ COUNTRY HOUSE HOTEL

@@@ French **V** ♥

The best of the Skye larder in Baronial splendour

☎ 01471 833214 & 833333   🖷 01471 833277
IV43 8QY
e-mail: reservations@kinloch-lodge.co.uk
web: www.kinloch-lodge.co.uk
dir: 6m S of Broadford on A851, 10m N of Armadale on A851

This is the home of food and cookery writer Claire Macdonald, AKA Lady Claire Macdonald, and Kinloch is the Highland pile she shares with her husband, the High Chief of Clan Donald. This seat of the clan dates from the 16th century and is idyllically situated with views over the rugged scenery of Sleat and the water of Na Dal sea loch. Bedrooms and bathrooms are well appointed and comfortable, and public areas boast open fires and relaxing seating areas. There is a cookery school run by Claire MacDonald and a shop selling her famous cookery books and produce. Portraits of Macdonalds through the centuries adorn the walls of the formal dining room, where crisp white linen-clad tables are laid with good quality crockery and vintage silver cutlery. Given Claire's devotion to regional and seasonal produce, the kitchen, under the command of Marcello Tully, uses first-class ingredients to good effect in well-balanced and imaginative modern Scottish dishes. Things start with a soup (parsnip and Pernod, perhaps), following on with an impressive construction of roast shredded duck with Stornoway black pudding, then perhaps a superb piece of halibut, and finishing with pleasingly bitter dark chocolate torte.

Rooms 14 (1 GF) **S** £130-£250; **D** £260-£360 (incl. bkfst & dinner)^
Facilities STV FTV Fishing New Year Wi-fi **Parking** 40 **Notes** LB

Chef Marcello Tully **Owner** Lord & Lady Macdonald **Restaurant Times** 12-2.30/6.30-9 Closed 1 wk Xmas, **Prices** Fixed D 4 course £52, Service optional **Notes** Fixed L 4/5 course £24.95-£27.95, Fixed D 5/6 course £55-£60, Sunday L, Vegetarian menu **Seats** 40, Pr/dining room 20 **Children** Portions

ISLEORNSAY CONTINUED

Toravaig House Hotel

★★★ 80% SMALL HOTEL

Iona Restaurant

◉◉ Modern Scottish V ◔

Stylish haven of peace serving Skye's wonderful produce

☎ 0845 055 1117 & 01471 833231 📠 01471 833231
Knock Bay IV44 8RE
e-mail: info@skyehotel.co.uk
web: www.skyehotel.co.uk
dir: From Skye Bridge, left at Broadford onto A851, hotel 11m on left. Or from ferry at Armadale take A851, hotel 4m on right

A visit to the Isle of Skye is food for the soul, so make sure you feed your inner gourmet at the same time. Toravaig House is a luxurious boutique hotel set in two acres in a jaw-dropping location overlooking the Sound of Sleat towards the Knoydart Hills on the wild mainland. Bedrooms are stylish, well-equipped and beautifully decorated. A day's sailing on the hotel's own yacht should sharpen the appetite for dinner in the classy Iona restaurant, where white-clothed tables and high-backed leather chairs set a smart tone. The island's ample larder provides peerless fish, game or lamb for daily-changing menus, thoughtfully put together by a kitchen confident enough not to mess about with produce of this class. Start with duck breast - smoked in-house over oak from Talisker casks - with brioche croûton, liver pâté and red onion marmalade, then try oven-baked pork tenderloin, sticky braised belly, parsnip purée, baby turnips and pan juices.

Rooms 9 **D** £100-£190 (incl. bkfst) **Facilities** STV Daily excursions (Apr-Sep) for residents on hotel yacht Xmas New Year Wi-fi **Conf** Board 10 Thtr 25 Del from £150 to £300 **Parking** 15 **Notes** LB ⊗ No children 12yrs Civ Wed 25

Chef Andrew Lipp **Owner** Anne Gracie & Ken Gunn **Restaurant Times** 12.30-2/6.30-9.30 **Prices** Fixed D 2 course £20-£30, Fixed D 4 course £25-£45, Starter £6-£9.95, Main £15-£29.95, Dessert £4.50-£9.95, Service optional **Wines** 20 bottles over £20, 20 bottles under £20, 6 by glass **Notes** Sunday L, Vegetarian menu, Dress restrictions, Smart casual 18 **Seats** 30

Hotel Eilean Iarmain

★★★ 77% SMALL HOTEL

◉◉ Traditional Scottish

Accomplished cooking on Skye

☎ 01471 833332 📠 01471 833275
IV43 8QR
e-mail: hotel@eileaniarmain.co.uk
web: www.eileaniarmain.co.uk
dir: A851, A852, right to Isleornsay harbour

Occupying an idyllic setting with spectacular views, this 19th-century former inn retains its old world charm and gives guests a truly genuine Highland experience. The hotel is situated on a sheltered bay in the south of Skye, with expansive views over the Sound of Sleat to the hills of Knoydart on the mainland. Bedrooms are individual and retain a traditional style, and a stable block has been converted into four delightful suites. Public rooms are cosy and inviting; take pre-dinner drinks in front of a roaring fire in the cosy lounge before moving into the elegant panelled restaurant with its view of Ornsay Lighthouse. Scottish fare prepared from high quality local ingredients is offered from a daily menu, including venison from their own estate. Specialities include pan-seared local hand-dived scallops and Loch Bracadale crab mayonnaise with guacamole and beetroot dressing, followed by roast rump of West Highland hill-reared lamb with olive oil mash, rosemary and redcurrant jus.

Rooms 16 (6 fmly) (4 GF) **Facilities** Fishing Shooting Exhibitions Whisky tasting ♪ Xmas **Conf** Class 30 Board 25 Thtr 50 **Parking** 35 **Notes** LB Civ Wed 80

Restaurant Times 12-2.30/6.30-8.45

KYLEAKIN   **Map 4 NG72**

Kings Arms Hotel

★★ 65% HOTEL

☎ 01599 534109 📠 01599 534190
King St, Kyleakin IV41 8PH
e-mail: reservations.kyleakin@ohiml.com

Overlooking the Skye Bridge and situated in the heart of the pretty village of Kyleakin the hotel boasts panoramic views across the Kyle of Lochalsh towards mainland Scotland. Bedrooms are comfortable, well equipped and front facing rooms have the super view. There is a large resident's lounge area and the public bar is popular with locals and visitors.

Rooms 81

Cuillin Hills

★★★★ 77% HOTEL

⊛⊛ Modern British

West coast ingredients in a classic country-house setting

☎ 01478 612003 🖹 01478 613092
IV51 9QU
e-mail: info@cuillinhills-hotel-skye.co.uk
web: www.cuillinhills-hotel-skye.co.uk
dir: Turn right 0.25m N of Portree off A855. Follow hotel signs

This former hunting lodge, built for the Isle of Skye's Lord MacDonald, turned country-house hotel has fantastic views overlooking Portree Bay and the Cuillin Hills. Accommodation is provided in smart, well-equipped rooms that are generally spacious, and some bedrooms are found in an adjacent building. Chic table settings in the convivial split-level restaurant, presided over by relaxed and friendly service, complement the traditional décor. West coast ingredients are used in dishes which allow them to shine. The cuisine has a distinctly Scottish influence, with Cullen skink served as an extra course, but there are also plenty of European, particularly French, influences. Start perhaps with home-cured salmon in treacle and whisky with lemon and capers and baby flowers, move on to Isle of Skye lobster with Jack Daniels and parmesan cream sauce and fancy leaf salad. Sautéed strawberries in Drambuie cream provide a boozy finish.

Rooms 26 (7 annexe) (3 fmly) (8 GF) **S** £170-£200; **D** £200-£300 (incl. bkfst)* **Facilities** STV Xmas New Year Wi-fi **Conf** Class 60 Board 40 Thtr 100 **Parking** 56 **Notes** LB ⊛ Civ Wed 45

Chef Robert Macaskill **Owner** Wickman Hotels Ltd **Restaurant Times** 12-2/6.30-9 Closed L Mon-Sat **Prices** Fixed D 3 course £35-£40, Service optional **Wines** 41 bottles over £20, 21 bottles under £20, 4 by glass **Notes** Sunday L, Vegetarian available **Seats** 48 **Children** Portions, Menu

Bosville

★★★ 81% HOTEL

⊛⊛ Modern British ❀

Superb cooking of truly local produce with great harbour views

☎ 01478 612846 🖹 01478 613434
Bosville Ter IV51 9DG
e-mail: bosville@macleodhotels.co.uk
web: www.macleodhotels.com
dir: A87 signed Portree, then A855 into town. After zebra crossing follow road to left

Set high up in the picture-postcard fishing village of Portree, with glorious views over the harbour, the Bosville is an extended fisherman's cottage with smart bedrooms, furnished to a high specification and with a fresh, contemporary feel. Then there's a popular bistro, a smart bar (formerly the village bank), and the Chandlery Restaurant. Themed around a ships' chandlery, the restaurant is stylish and modern with innovative monthly menus built around the fantastic produce to be found on Skye. Chef John Kelly's cooking is creative and focused on flavour, as seen in a

starter of langoustine tails served with slow-braised belly pork, pear and ginger purée, and a light soya and star anise jus. For main course, try guinea fowl on roast butternut squash and a light jus with chanterelles, then finish, perhaps, with a crumble rhubarb tart with Glendale mint and rhubarb salad and cardamom ice cream.

Rooms 19 (2 fmly) **S** £69-£130; **D** £88-£240 (incl. bkfst)* **Facilities** STV Use of nearby leisure club payable Xmas New Year Wi-fi **Conf** Class 20 Board 20 Thtr 20 Del from £120 to £160* **Parking** 10 **Notes** Civ Wed 80

Chef John Kelly **Owner** Donald W Macleod **Restaurant Times** 6.30-9.30 Closed L all week **Prices** Food prices not confirmed for 2010. Please telephone for details. **Wines** 20 bottles over £20, 20 bottles under £20, 12 by glass **Notes** Vegetarian available **Seats** 30 **Children** Portions

Rosedale

★★★ 73% HOTEL

⊛ Traditional Scottish ❀

Welcoming waterfront hotel with seafood a speciality

☎ 01478 613131 🖹 01478 612531
Beaumont Crescent IV51 9DB
e-mail: rosedalehotelsky@aol.com
web: www.rosedalehotelskye.co.uk
dir: Follow directions to village centre & harbour

Once a group of fishermen's cottages, this delightful, family-run waterfront hotel offers a wonderfully warm, intimate atmosphere. Modern bedrooms offer a good range of amenities, and a labyrinth of corridors and stairs connects the lounges, bar and restaurant which are set on different levels. A window seat is a must in the charming first-floor restaurant with fine views overlooking the bay and Portree's busy harbour. An inspired Scottish menu supplies local produce, including a good smattering of seafood, prepared with panache. To start try a terrine of duck, orange and brandy on dressed local leaves served with oat biscuits, followed by oven-baked fillet of sea bass on a bed of buttered leeks and spinach in a prawn bisque sauce.

Rooms 18 (1 fmly) (3 GF) **S** £30-£65; **D** £60-£150 (incl. bkfst)* **Facilities** Wi-fi **Parking** 2 **Notes** LB Closed Nov-mid Mar

Chef Kirk Moir **Owner** Mr & Mrs P Rouse **Restaurant Times** 7-8.30 Closed Nov-1 Mar, L all week **Prices** Fixed D 3 course £26-£31, Service optional **Wines** 10 bottles over £20, 20 bottles under £20, 7 by glass **Notes** Vegetarian available **Seats** 30 **Children** Portions, Menu

'Medina'

★★★★ BED AND BREAKFAST

☎ 01478 612821
Coolin Hills Gardens IV51 9NB
e-mail: medinaskye@yahoo.co.uk
web: www.medinaskye.co.uk
dir: From Portree centre, A855 to Staffin, at large sign for Cullin Hills Hotel turn right. Att 2nd large sign turn sharp left up hill

A delightful bungalow quietly located in a small residential development in the former walled gardens of the Cuillin Hills Hotel. The two ground floor bedrooms are spacious, comfortable and well equipped, and guests also have the use of an elegant and comfortable lounge, where breakfast is served around a communal table.

Rooms 2 en suite (2 GF); D £68-£80* **Facilities** TVL tea/coffee Cen ht **Parking** 2 **Notes** ⊗ No Children 14yrs Closed Nov-Feb

Skeabost Country House

★★★ COUNTRY HOUSE HOTEL

⊛ Scottish

Well executed food in a delightful loch side country house hotel

☎ 01470 532202   📠 01470 532761
By Portree IV51 9NP
e-mail: reservations.skeabost@ohiml.com
web: www.oxfordhotelsandinns.com

A country-house hotel with a superb lochside setting in mature, landscaped grounds at the edge of Loch Snizort, run by a small and very friendly team. Originally built as a hunting lodge by the MacDonalds and steeped in history, the hotel offers well appointed accommodation and the pretty grounds include a challenging 9-hole golf course. The short, well-balanced menus in the wood-panelled dining room change seasonally and make excellent use of prime local ingredients. Grilled Stornaway black pudding with new potato and poached egg might be a good place to start, followed by wild Skye venison pave, dauphinoise, braised red cabbage and red cabbage jus. A hot chocolate fondant with toasted almond ice cream rounds things off nicely.

Rooms 14 (5 GF) **Facilities** ♨ 9 holes Fishing Riding Wi-fi Ch facs **Parking** 40 **Notes** Civ Wed 80 Xmas New Year **Conf** Class 20 Board 20 Thtr 40

Flodigarry Country House

★★★ 78% COUNTRY HOUSE HOTEL

⊛ Modern Scottish **V**

Glorious views and superb fish and seafood at intimate country house

☎ 01470 552203   📠 01470 552301
IV51 9HZ
e-mail: info@flodigarry.co.uk
web: www.flodigarry.co.uk
dir: Take A855 from Portree, approx 20m, through Staffin. N to Flodigarry, signed on right

History and romance come in spades at this enchanting country house on the Isle of Skye, and its setting beneath the dramatic Trotternish Ridge with views across the sea to the mainland Torridon mountains truly deserves the over-used 'jaw-dropping' epithet. The intimate stone-walled house and neighbouring cottage were once home to Scottish heroine Flora MacDonald, and loving restoration has produced a relaxed haven of modern luxury, with great food to boot. Guests are assured of real Highland hospitality and there is an easy-going atmosphere throughout. A full range of activities is offered, with mountain walks, fishing and boat trips proving to be popular. The glorious views form a backdrop to the kitchen's modern Scottish cuisine, conjured from superb local fish, shellfish and game. Pan-fried scallops play the starring role in a beautiful starter, with honey and mustard sauce used sparingly, followed by seared line-caught sea bass with spinach and potato cake and lemon butter sauce.

Rooms 18 (7 annexe) (3 fmly) (4 GF) **S** £80-£130; **D** £80-£200 (incl. bkfst) **Facilities** FTV Xmas New Year Wi-fi **Parking** 40 **Notes** LB Closed Nov-15 Dec & Jan Civ Wed 80

Chef Joseph Miko **Owner** Robin Collins **Restaurant Times** 12-2.30/7-9.30 Closed Nov & Jan, **Prices** Starter £6.95-£16.75, Main £18-£32, Dessert £5.95-£8, Service included **Wines** 4 by glass **Notes** Sunday L, Vegetarian menu **Seats** 30, Pr/dining room 24 **Children** Portions, Menu

The Glenview

★★★ RESTAURANT WITH ROOMS

⊛ British, French ♥

Accomplished cooking in a friendly restaurant with rooms

☎ 01470 562248
Culnacnoc IV51 9JH
e-mail: enquiries@glenviewskye.co.uk
dir: 12m N of Portree on A855, 4m S of Staffin

This small restaurant with rooms has a to-die-for location on the Isle of Skye's superbly-scenic Trotternish Peninsula. Youthful owners run this charming small hotel in an old whitewashed croft house with genuine friendliness, and the individually-styled bedrooms are very comfortable. Front-facing rooms enjoy the dramatic views, and a further bonus is the top-class cooking on offer. The key here is fresh, top-notch local produce that is proudly name-checked - take Orbost heather-grazed beef, for example - on the concise three-course dinner menus offering two choices at each stage. A starter of brown crab with watercress soup delivers intense flavours, then local Iron Age pork is served with Skye kale, polenta cake and turnips with apple sauce. To finish, a freshly-baked brioche with warm plum compôte and home-made ice cream makes a well-thought-out dessert.

Rooms 5 en suite (1 fmly) (1 GF) S £55-£65; D £80-£100* **Facilities** tea/coffee Dinner available Wi-fi

Chef Simon Wallwork **Owner** Kirsty Faulds **Restaurant Times** -7-8.30 Closed Jan, Mon, L all week **Prices** Fixed D 3 course £27.50, Service optional **Wines** 4 bottles over £20, 15 bottles under £20, 4 by glass **Notes** Vegetarian available **Seats** 22 **Children** Portions, Menu

STEIN	Map 4 NG25

Loch Bay Seafood Restaurant

◉ British Seafood ◔

Welcoming approach in a lochside fish restaurant

☎ 01470 592235 ▤ 01470 592235
IV55 8GA
e-mail: david@lochbay-seafood-restaurant.co.uk
dir: 4m off A850 by B886

The location, at the end of a dead-end road next to the loch on Skye, is as out-of-the-way as they come, the restaurant being a conversion of little fishermen's cottages. Expect the freshest fish and seafood from menus chalked up on boards, and a thoroughly welcoming, homely approach. Grilled razor clams in parsley butter, or a bowl of Cullen skink, might set the ball rolling, and then be followed by anything from halibut to hake, John Dory to monkfish tail, all cooked with the minimum of intervention to allow their flavours and freshness to shine forth. Finish with apple and apricot crumble.

Chef David Wilkinson **Owner** David & Alison Wilkinson **Times** 12-2/6-9 Closed Nov-Etr (excl. 1wk over Hogmanay), Sun-Mon **Prices** Fixed L 2 course £12.95, Starter £3.60-£9, Main £12.50-£20.70, Dessert £4.50-£5.20, Service optional **Wines** 15 bottles over £20, 17 bottles under £20, 5 by glass **Notes** Extensive blackboard choices **Seats** 26 **Children** Portions **Parking** 6

Stein Inn ♀

☎ 01470 592362
Macleod's Ter IV55 8GA
e-mail: angus.teresa@steininn.co.uk
dir: A87 from Portree. In 5m take A850 for 15m. Right onto B886, 3m to T-junct. Turn left

The oldest inn on the island, set in a lovely hamlet right next to the sea, the Stein Inn provides a warm welcome, fine food, and an impressive selection of drinks: fine wines, real ales and no fewer than a hundred malt whiskies. Highland meat, game and local seafood feature strongly on daily-changing menus, ranging from lunchtime haggis toastie and smoked salmon platter to West Coast moules marinière, Highland venison pie, and salmon in a vermouth and tarragon sauce.

Open all day all wk 11am-mdnt Closed: 25 Dec, 1 Jan **Bar Meals** L served all wk 12-4 D served all wk 6-9.30 Av main course £7.50 **Restaurant** D served all wk 6-9.30 Av 3 course à la carte fr £15 ⊕ FREE HOUSE ◀ Red Cuillin, Trade Winds, Reeling Deck, Deuchars IPA, Dark Island. ♀ 8 **Facilities** Family room Dogs allowed Garden Parking

STRUAN
Map 4 NG33

Ullinish Country Lodge

★★★★★ RESTAURANT WITH ROOMS

@@@ French V ♨

Culinary paradise for foodies in an idyllic Skye setting

☎ 01470 572214 📄 01470 572341
IV56 8FD
e-mail: ullinish@theisleofskye.co.uk
web: www.theisleofskye.co.uk
dir: 9m S of Dunvegan on A863

Hidden away at the end of one of Skye's less-trodden tracks, Ullinish Lodge is a tranquil bolthole with some of Scotland's most uplifting scenery on the doorstep. Bracketed by lochs on three sides and with jaw-dropping views of the Black Cuillins and MacLeod's Tables, it's no wonder literary companions Samuel Johnson and James Boswell chose to tarry a while. Hosts Brian and Pam hope to extend the same welcome to their guests today. As you would expect, all bedrooms have amazing views, and come with half-tester beds. The interior has survived the wave of makeovers sweeping country houses, remaining comfortingly traditional with calmly genteel service in the dining room, where wood-panels and a tartan carpet are a reminder of where you are - if any were needed, given the rugged romance visible through the windows. Johnson and Boswell noted in 1773 that 'there is a plentiful garden in Ullinish' - in that respect, 21st-century guests will be pleased to note that little has changed: the local larder still provides most of what turns up in the kitchen's imaginative modern output. Chef Bruce Morrison's passion for food comes through loud and clear in creative pairings, his masterful classical technique extracting big flavours and pulling off intriguing combinations and striking presentation with panache. All the stops are pulled out at dinner, starting with roasted local hand-dived scallops teamed with creamy purslane, caper and raisin purée, crispy quail's eggs and garlic foam, before a riff on a pig theme delivers braised cheek, crispy belly and croquette of trotter with cucumber relish, horseradish marshmallow and a razor clam and fennel salad. An intermediate parmesan sorbet and sweetcorn jelly fits in before a

finale of rum and raisin soufflé, crème brûlée ice cream and sea buckthorn 'caviar'. And all the bits and treats from canapés, to breads, amuse-bouche, pre-desserts and petits fours are winners, made with the same precision and attention to detail as the main events.

Rooms 6 en suite S £60-£120; D £120-£160* **Facilities** tea/coffee Dinner available Cen ht **Parking** 8 **Notes** LB ⊗ No Children 16yrs Closed Jan & 1wk Nov No coaches

Chef Craig Halliday **Owner** Brian & Pam Howard **Restaurant Times** 12-2.30/7.30-8.30 Closed Jan, 1 wk Nov, **Prices** Fixed L 2 course £20, Fixed D 4 course £49.50, Service optional **Wines** 45 bottles over £20, 10 bottles under £20 **Notes** Sunday L, Vegetarian menu, Dress restrictions, Smart casual, No T-shirts **Seats** 22

UIG
Map 4 NG36

Woodbine House

★★★ GUEST ACCOMMODATION

☎ 01470 542243
IV51 9XP
e-mail: contact@skyeactivities.co.uk
dir: From Portree into Uig Bay, pass Ferry Inn & right onto A855 Staffin Rd, house 300yds on right

Built in the late 19th century, Woodbine House occupies an elevated position overlooking Uig Bay and the surrounding countryside and is well suited for walking and bird-watching enthusiasts. The ground floor dining room has lovely sea views as do the front facing bedrooms.

Rooms 4 en suite (1 fmly) S £35-£55; D £55-£59* **Facilities** tea/coffee Dinner available Cen ht Wi-fi Archery, Mountain bike/sea kayak hire & boat trips **Parking** 4 **Notes** LB ⊗ ⊜

Ferry Inn

★★★ 🅰 INN

☎ 01478 611216 📄 01478 611224
IV51 9XP
e-mail: info@ferryinn.co.uk
web: www.ferryinn.co.uk
dir: In Uig, on a loop road off A87, 1m from ferry terminal

Rooms 6 en suite S £39-£46; D £68-£80* **Facilities** STV TVL tea/coffee Dinner available Cen ht **Parking** 10 **Notes** ⊗ No coaches

SOUTH UIST

LOCHBOISDALE   Map 4 NF71

The Polochar Inn

☎ 01878 700215   📠 01878 700768
Polochar HS8 5TT
e-mail: polocharinn@aol.com
dir: W from Lochboisdale, take B888. Hotel at end of road

Overlooking the sea towards the islands of Eriskay and Barra, this superbly situated 18th-century inn enjoys beautiful sunsets. The bar menu offers fresh seafood dishes and steaks with various sauces, while restaurant fare includes venison, fresh scallops or steak pie. There is always a great choice of guest ales.

Open all day all wk 11-11 (Fri-Sat 11am-1am Sun 12.30pm-1am) **Bar Meals** L served Mon-Sat 12.30-8.30, Sun 1-8.30 (winter all wk 12-2.30) D served Mon-Sat 12.30-8.30, Sun 1-8.30 (winter all wk 5-8.30) ⊕ FREE HOUSE 🍺 Guest Ales. **Facilities** Family room Garden Parking

Beinn Edra and Trotternish Ridge, Isle of Skye

Loch Avon and Beinn Mheadhoin, Cairngorms National Park

Location Index

Red deer near Aberfoyle, Loch Lomond and the Trossachs National Park

View from Ben Macdui, Cairngorms National Park

Establishment Index

The Automobile Association would like to thank the following photographers, companies and picture libraries for their assistance in the preparation of this book.

Abbreviations for the picture credits are as follows: (t) top; (b) bottom; (l) left; (r) right; (c) centre; (AA) AA World Travel Library.

1 AA/D W Robertson; 3 AA/L Campbell; 7 Stockbyte Royalty Free; 9 Royalty Free Photodisc; 11 Stockbyte Royalty Free; 16 AA/D W Robertson; 26/27 Jackie Bates; 36 AA/D W Robertson; 44 AA; 63 AA/S Anderson; 67 AA/K Paterson; 74/75 AA/D Corrance; 83 AA/K Paterson; 99 AA/S Whitehorne; 106 AA/S Gibson; 115 AA/S Anderson; 119 AA/J Henderson; 130/131 AA/M Hamblin; 147 AA/M Hamblin; 154 AA/S Day; 166 AA/H Williams; 186/187 AA/J Beazley; 199 AA/D W Robertson; 200/201 AA/S Whitehorne; 205 AA/S Whitehorne; 215 AA/A J Hopkins; 216/217 AA/M Hamblin; 221 AA/D W Robertson; 222/223 AA/M Hamblin

Every effort has been made to trace the copyright holders, and we apologise in advance for any accidental errors. We would be happy to apply any corrections in the following edition of this publication.

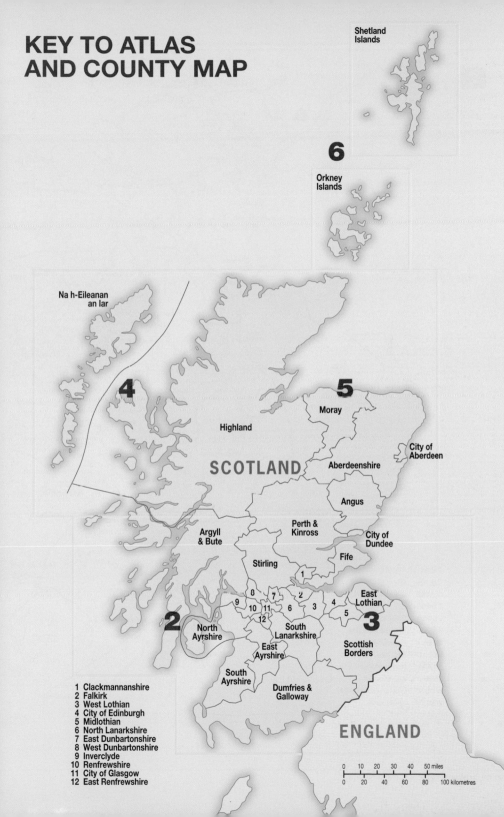

KEY TO ATLAS AND COUNTY MAP

Shetland Islands

6

Orkney Islands

Na h-Eileanan an Iar

4

5

Moray

Highland

SCOTLAND

City of Aberdeen

Aberdeenshire

Angus

Argyll & Bute

Perth & Kinross

City of Dundee

Stirling

Fife

1

East Lothian

8 7 2

9 10 11 6 3 4

12

5

2

North Ayrshire

South Lanarkshire

3

East Ayrshire

Scottish Borders

South Ayrshire

Dumfries & Galloway

ENGLAND

1 Clackmannanshire
2 Falkirk
3 West Lothian
4 City of Edinburgh
5 Midlothian
6 North Lanarkshire
7 East Dunbartonshire
8 West Dunbartonshire
9 Inverclyde
10 Renfrewshire
11 City of Glasgow
12 East Renfrewshire

0 10 20 30 40 50 miles

0 20 40 60 80 100 kilometres

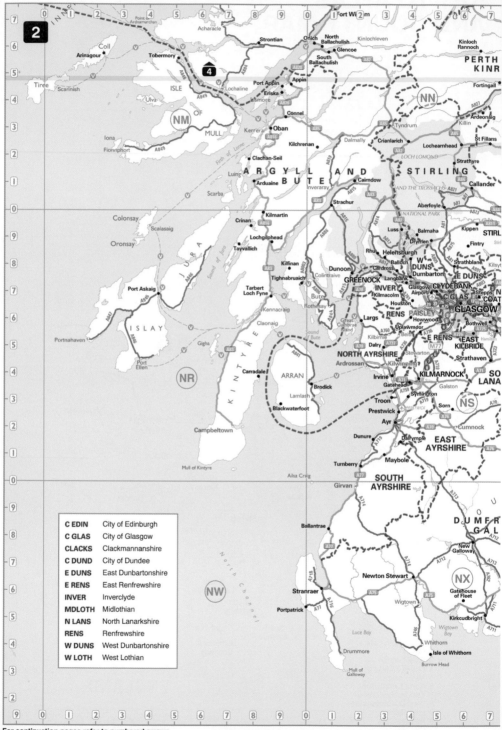

2

INN

Point Ardnamurchan

Acharacle

Fort Wim

Kinlochleven

Kinloch Rannoch

PERTH KINR

Arinagour

Coll

Tobermory

Strontian

Onich

North Ballachulish

Glencoe

South Ballachulish

Fortingall

Tiree

Scarinish

ISLE

Port Appin

Appin

Connel

Ardeonaig

Killin

St Fillans

Ulva

OF

Lochaline

Eriska

Lismore

NN

Ullva

Iona

Fionnphort

MULL

Kerrera

Oban

Kilchrenan

Dalmally

Crianlarich

Lochearnhead

Strathyre

Colonsay

Scalasaig

Clachan-Seil

Luing

ARGYLL AND BUTE

Cairndow

LOCH LOMOND

STIRLING

Callander

Oronsay

Arduaine

Inveraray

AND THE TROSSACHS

Scarba

Strachur

Aberfoyle

NATIONAL PARK

STIRL

Crinan

Kilmartin

Luss

Balmaha

Kippen

Lochgilphead

Rhu

Helensburgh

Drymen

Fintry

Stirl

Tayvallich

Kilfinan

Dunoon

Colintraive

Cardross

Ballan

Balloch

W DUNS

Strathblane

Kilsyth

Tighnabruaich

Langbank

Dumbarton

E DUNS

Tarbert Loch Fyne

Bute

GREENOCK

INVER

Glasgow Airport

CLYDEBANK

Stepps

COAT

Kennacraig

Rothesay

Kilmacolm

Houston

C GLAS

GLASGOW

Port Askaig

ISLAY

Claonaig

Great Cumbrae Island

Largs

RENS

PAISLEY

Howwood

Bothwell

Gigha

Kilbirnie

Uplawmoor

E RENS

EAST KILBRIDE

Portnahaven

Port Ellen

Dalry

Stewarton

Strathaven

NORTH AYRSHIRE

Ardrossan

Kilwinning

KILMARNOCK

SO LANA

NR

Carradale

ARRAN

Brodick

Irvine

Gatehead

Symington

Sorn

NS

KINTYRE

Lamlash

Troon

Galston

Blackwaterfoot

Prestwick

EAST AYRSHIRE

Cumnock

Campbeltown

Ayr

Dunure

Dalrymple

Mull of Kintyre

Ailsa Craig

Maybole

Turnberry

SOUTH AYRSHIRE

Girvan

North Channel

NW

Ballantrae

DUMFR GAL

New Galloway

NX

Newton Stewart

Gatehouse of Fleet

Stranraer

Wigtown

Portpatrick

Kirkcudbright

Luce Bay

Wigtown Bay

Drummore

Whithorn

Isle of Whithorn

Mull of Galloway

Burrow Head

C EDIN — City of Edinburgh
C GLAS — City of Glasgow
CLACKS — Clackmannanshire
C DUND — City of Dundee
E DUNS — East Dunbartonshire
E RENS — East Renfrewshire
INVER — Inverclyde
MDLOTH — Midlothian
N LANS — North Lanarkshire
RENS — Renfrewshire
W DUNS — West Dunbartonshire
W LOTH — West Lothian

For continuation pages refer to numbered arrows

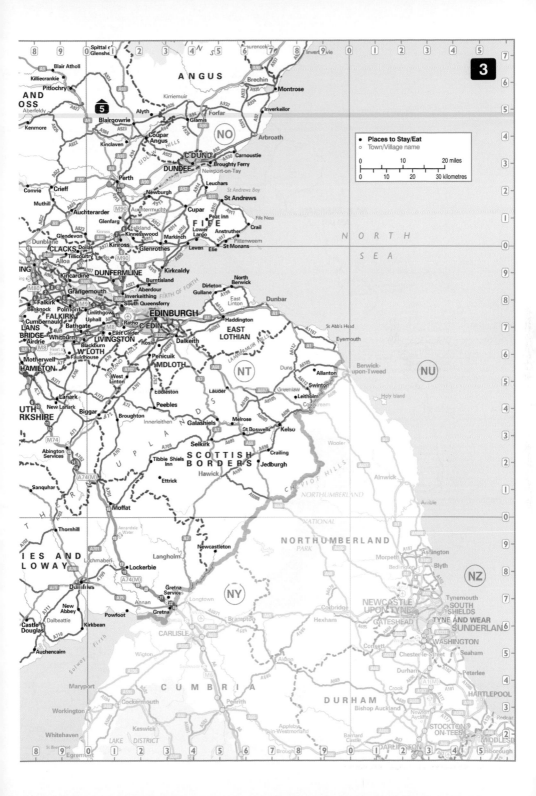

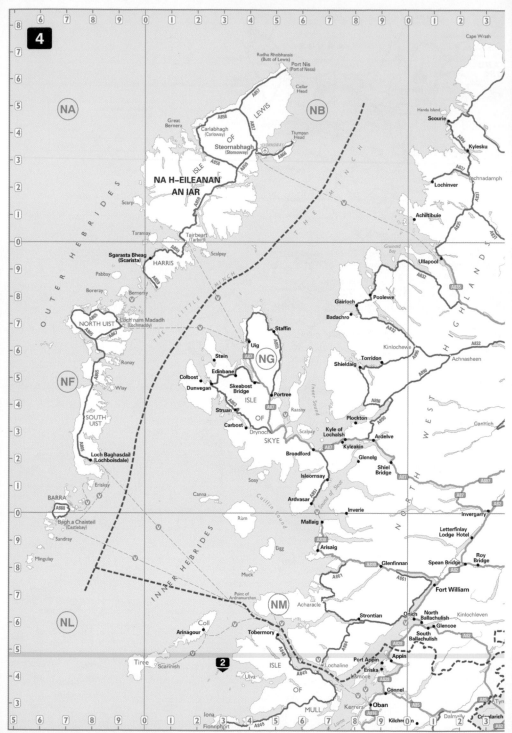

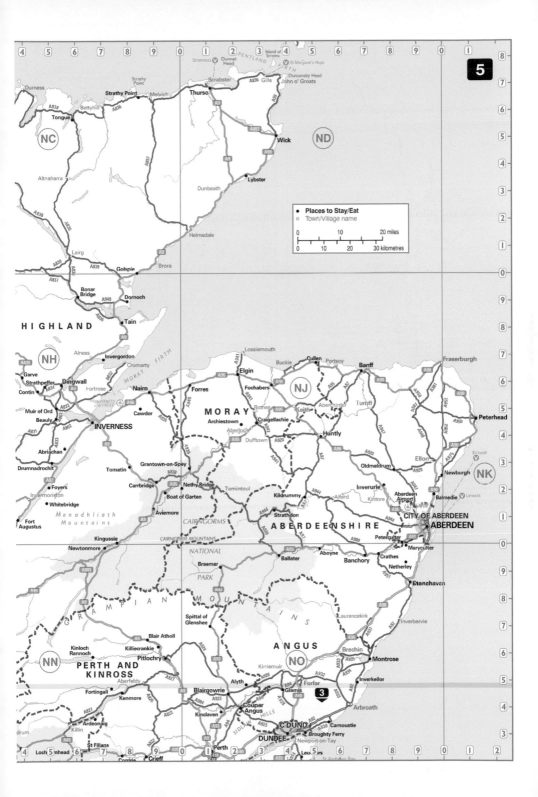

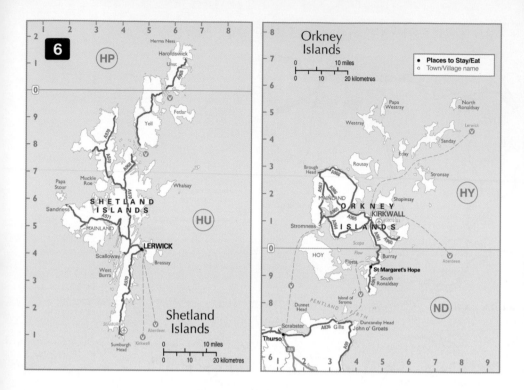

Bed & Breakfast Readers' Report Form

Please send this form to:–
Editor, The B&B Guide,
Lifestyle Guides,
AA Publishing,
Fanum House, FH13
Basingstoke RG21 4EA

or e-mail: lifestyleguides@theAA.com

Use this form to recommend any guest house, farmhouse or inn where you have stayed that is not already in the guide.

If you have any comments about your stay at an establishment listed in the Guide, please let us know, as feedback from readers helps to keep our Guide accurate and up to date. If you have a complaint during your stay, we recommend that you discuss the matter with the establishment.

Please note that the AA does not undertake to arbitrate between you and the establishment, to obtain compensation, or to engage in protracted correspondence.

Date

Your name (BLOCK CAPITALS)

Your address (BLOCK CAPITALS)

Post code

E-mail address

Name of establishment

Comments (Please include the name and address of the establishment)

(please attach a separate sheet if necessary)

Please tick here ☐ if you DO NOT wish to receive details of AA offers or products

PTO

Bed & Breakfast Readers' Report Form *continued*

Have you bought this guide before? ☐ YES ☐ NO

What other accommodation, restaurant, pub or food guides have you bought recently?

....

....

Why did you buy this guide? (tick all that apply)

Holiday ☐   Short break ☐   Business travel ☐   Special occasion ☐   Overnight stop ☐

Conference ☐   Other (please state)

How often do you stay in B&Bs? (tick one choice)

More than once a month ☐   Once a month ☐   Once in two to three months ☐

Once in six months ☐   Once a year ☐   Less than once a year ☐

Please answer these questions to help us make improvements to the guide.

Which of these factors is most important when choosing a B&B?

Price ☐   Location ☐   Awards/ratings ☐   Service ☐   Décor/surroundings ☐

Previous experience ☐   Recommendation ☐

Other (please state)

....

....

Do you read the editorial features in the guide? ☐ YES ☐ NO

Do you use the location atlas?   ☐ YES ☐ NO

What elements of the guide do you find most useful when choosing somewhere to stay?

Description ☐   Photo ☐   Advertisement ☐   Star rating ☐

Can you suggest any improvements to the guide?

....

....

....

Thank you for completing and returning this form

Bed & Breakfast Readers' Report Form

Please send this form to:–
Editor, The B&B Guide,
Lifestyle Guides,
AA Publishing,
Fanum House, FH13
Basingstoke RG21 4EA

or e-mail: lifestyleguides@theAA.com

Use this form to recommend any guest house, farmhouse or inn where you have stayed that is not already in the guide.

If you have any comments about your stay at an establishment listed in the Guide, please let us know, as feedback from readers helps to keep our Guide accurate and up to date. If you have a complaint during your stay, we recommend that you discuss the matter with the establishment.

Please note that the AA does not undertake to arbitrate between you and the establishment, to obtain compensation, or to engage in protracted correspondence.

Date

Your name (BLOCK CAPITALS)

Your address (BLOCK CAPITALS)

Post code

E-mail address

Name of establishment

Comments (Please include the name and address of the establishment)

(please attach a separate sheet if necessary)

Please tick here ☐ if you DO NOT wish to receive details of AA offers or products

Bed & Breakfast Readers' Report Form *continued*

Have you bought this guide before? ☐ YES ☐ NO

What other accommodation, restaurant, pub or food guides have you bought recently?

....

....

Why did you buy this guide? (tick all that apply)

Holiday ☐   Short break ☐   Business travel ☐   Special occasion ☐   Overnight stop ☐

Conference ☐   Other (please state)

How often do you stay in B&Bs? (tick one choice)

More than once a month ☐   Once a month ☐   Once in two to three months ☐

Once in six months ☐   Once a year ☐   Less than once a year ☐

Please answer these questions to help us make improvements to the guide.

Which of these factors is most important when choosing a B&B?

Price ☐   Location ☐   Awards/ratings ☐   Service ☐   Décor/surroundings ☐

Previous experience ☐   Recommendation ☐

Other (please state)

....

....

Do you read the editorial features in the guide? ☐ YES ☐ NO

Do you use the location atlas?   ☐ YES ☐ NO

What elements of the guide do you find most useful when choosing somewhere to stay?

Description ☐   Photo ☐   Advertisement ☐   Star rating ☐

Can you suggest any improvements to the guide?

....

....

....

....

....

Thank you for completing and returning this form

Hotel Readers' Report Form

Please send this form to:–
Editor, The Hotel Guide,
Lifestyle Guides,
AA Publishing,
Fanum House, FH13
Basingstoke RG21 4EA

or e-mail: lifestyleguides@theAA.com

Please use this form to recommend any hotel where you have stayed, whether it is included in the guide or not currently listed. You can also help us to improve the guide by completing the short questionnaire on the reverse.

The AA does not undertake to arbitrate between guide readers and hotels, or to obtain compensation or engage in protracted correspondence.

Date:

Your name (block capitals)

Your address (block capitals)

....
....
....
....
....

e-mail address:

Name of hotel:

Comments ....
....
....
....
....
....
....

(please attach a separate sheet if necessary)

Please tick here if you DO NOT wish to receive details of AA offers or products ☐

PTO

Hotel Readers' Report Form *continued*

Have you bought this guide before? ☐ YES ☐ NO

Have you bought any other accommodation, restaurant, pub or food guides recently? If yes, which ones?

....
....
....

Why did you buy this guide? (tick all that apply)

holiday ☐   short break ☐   business travel ☐   special occasion ☐

overnight stop ☐   find a venue for an event e.g. conference ☐

other ....

How often do you stay in hotels? (tick one choice)

more than once a month ☐   once a month ☐   once in 2-3 months ☐

once in six months ☐   once a year ☐   less than once a year ☐

Please answer these questions to help us make improvements to the guide:

Which of these factors are most important when choosing a hotel?

price ☐   location ☐   awards/ratings ☐   service ☐

decor/surroundings previous experience recommendation ☐

other (please state) ....

Do you read the editorial features in the guide?   Yes ☐   No ☐

Do you use the location atlas?   Yes ☐   No ☐

What elements of the guide do you find most useful when choosing a place to stay?

description ☐   photo ☐   advertisement ☐   star rating ☐

Can you suggest any improvements to the guide?

....
....
....
....

Hotel Readers' Report Form

Please send this form to:–
Editor, The Hotel Guide,
Lifestyle Guides,
AA Publishing,
Fanum House, FH13
Basingstoke RG21 4EA

or e-mail: lifestyleguides@theAA.com

Please use this form to recommend any hotel where you have stayed, whether it is included in the guide or not currently listed. You can also help us to improve the guide by completing the short questionnaire on the reverse.

The AA does not undertake to arbitrate between guide readers and hotels, or to obtain compensation or engage in protracted correspondence.

Date:

Your name (block capitals)

Your address (block capitals)

....

....

....

....

....

e-mail address:

Name of hotel:

Comments ....

....

....

....

....

....

....

(please attach a separate sheet if necessary)

Please tick here if you DO NOT wish to receive details of AA offers or products ☐

PTO

Hotel Readers' Report Form *continued*

Have you bought this guide before?   ☐ YES   ☐ NO

Have you bought any other accommodation, restaurant, pub or food guides recently? If yes, which ones?

....

....

....

Why did you buy this guide? (tick all that apply)

holiday ☐   short break ☐   business travel ☐   special occasion ☐

overnight stop ☐   find a venue for an event e.g. conference ☐

other ....

How often do you stay in hotels? (tick one choice)

more than once a month ☐   once a month ☐   once in 2-3 months ☐

once in six months ☐   once a year ☐   less than once a year ☐

Please answer these questions to help us make improvements to the guide:

Which of these factors are most important when choosing a hotel?

price ☐   location ☐   awards/ratings ☐   service ☐

decor/surroundings previous experience recommendation ☐

other (please state) ....

Do you read the editorial features in the guide?   Yes ☐   No ☐

Do you use the location atlas?   Yes ☐   No ☐

What elements of the guide do you find most useful when choosing a place to stay?

description ☐   photo ☐   advertisement ☐   star rating ☐

Can you suggest any improvements to the guide?

....

....

....

....

Pub Readers' Report Form

Please send this form to:–
Editor, The Pub Guide,
Lifestyle Guides,
AA Publishing,
13th Floor, Fanum House,
Basingstoke RG21 4EA

or fax: 01256 491647
or e-mail: lifestyleguides@theAA.com

Please use this form to tell us about any pub or inn you have visited, whether it is in the guide or not currently listed. We are interested in the quality of food, the selection of beers and the overall ambience of the establishment.

Feedback from readers helps us to keep our guide accurate and up to date. However, if you have a complaint to make during a visit, we do recommend that you discuss the matter with the pub management there and then, so that they have a chance to put things right before your visit is spoilt.

Please note that the AA does not undertake to arbitrate between you and the pub management, or to obtain compensation or engage in protracted correspondence.

Date

Your name (BLOCK CAPITALS)

Your address (BLOCK CAPITALS)

Post code

E-mail address

Name of pub

Location

Comments

(please attach a separate sheet if necessary)

Please tick here ☐ if you DO NOT wish to receive details of AA offers or products

Pub Readers' Report Form *continued*

Have you bought this guide before?   YES ☐   NO ☐

Do you regularly use any other pub,
accommodation or food guides?   YES ☐   NO ☐

If YES, which ones?

What do you find most useful about The AA Pub Guide?

Do you read the editorial features in the guide?   YES ☐   NO ☐

Do you use the location atlas?   YES ☐   NO ☐

Is there any other information you would like to see added to this guide?

What are your main reasons for visiting pubs (tick all that apply)
food ☐   business ☐   accommodation ☐   beer ☐
celebrations ☐   entertainment ☐   atmosphere ☐   leisure ☐
other

How often do you visit a pub for a meal?
more than once a week ☐   once a week ☐   once a fortnight ☐
once a month ☐   once in six months ☐

Pub Readers' Report Form

Please send this form to:–
Editor, The Pub Guide,
Lifestyle Guides,
AA Publishing,
13th Floor, Fanum House,
Basingstoke RG21 4EA

or fax: 01256 491647
or e-mail: lifestyleguides@theAA.com

Please use this form to tell us about any pub or inn you have visited, whether it is in the guide or not currently listed. We are interested in the quality of food, the selection of beers and the overall ambience of the establishment.

Feedback from readers helps us to keep our guide accurate and up to date. However, if you have a complaint to make during a visit, we do recommend that you discuss the matter with the pub management there and then, so that they have a chance to put things right before your visit is spoilt.

Please note that the AA does not undertake to arbitrate between you and the pub management, or to obtain compensation or engage in protracted correspondence.

Date

Your name (BLOCK CAPITALS)

Your address (BLOCK CAPITALS)

Post code

E-mail address

Name of pub

Location

Comments

(please attach a separate sheet if necessary)

Please tick here ☐ if you DO NOT wish to receive details of AA offers or products

PTO

Pub Readers' Report Form *continued*

Have you bought this guide before?　　　YES ☐　NO ☐

Do you regularly use any other pub,
accommodation or food guides?　　　　YES ☐　NO ☐

If YES, which ones?

What do you find most useful about The AA Pub Guide?

Do you read the editorial features in the guide?　　YES ☐　NO ☐

Do you use the location atlas?　　　　　　YES ☐　NO ☐

Is there any other information you would like to see added to this guide?

What are your main reasons for visiting pubs (tick all that apply)
food ☐　　　　　business ☐　　　　　　accommodation ☐　　beer ☐
celebrations ☐　entertainment ☐　　　atmosphere ☐　　　leisure ☐
other

How often do you visit a pub for a meal?
more than once a week ☐　　　once a week ☐　　　once a fortnight ☐
once a month ☐　　　　　　　once in six months ☐

Restaurant Readers' Report Form

Please send this form to:–
Editor, The Restaurant Guide,
Lifestyle Guides,
AA Publishing,
13th Floor, Fanum House,
Basingstoke RG21 4EA

or e-mail: lifestyleguides@theAA.com

Please use this form to tell us about any restaurant you have visited, whether it is in the guide or not currently listed. Feedback from readers helps us to keep our guide accurate and up to date. Please note, however, that if you have a complaint to make during a visit, we strongly recommend that you discuss the matter with the restaurant management there and then, so that they have a chance to put things right before your visit is spoilt. The AA does not undertake to arbitrate between you and the restaurant management, or to obtain compensation or engage in correspondence.

Date

Your name (BLOCK CAPITALS)

Your address (BLOCK CAPITALS)

Post code

E-mail address

Restaurant name and address: (If you are recommending a new restaurant please enclose a menu or note the dishes that you ate.)

Comments

(please attach a separate sheet if necessary)

We may use information we hold about you to write, e-mail or telephone you about other products and services offered by us and our carefully selected partners, but we can assure you that we will not disclose it to third parties.

Please tick here ☐ if you DO NOT wish to receive details of other products or services from the AA.

PTO

Restaurant Readers' Report Form *continued*

Have you bought this guide before?   YES ☐   NO ☐

Please list any other similar guides that you use regularly

_____

_____

What do you find most useful about The AA Restaurant Guide?

_____

_____

Please answer these questions to help us make improvements to the guide

What are your main reasons for visiting restaurants (tick all that apply)

Business entertaining ☐   Business travel ☐   Trying famous restaurants ☐

Family celebrations ☐   Leisure travel ☐   Trying new food ☐

Enjoying not having to cook yourself ☐   To eat food you couldn't cook yourself ☐

Because I enjoy eating out regularly ☐

Other (please state)

How often do you visit a restaurant for lunch or dinner? (tick one choice)

Once a week ☐   Once a fortnight ☐   Once a month ☐   Less than once a month ☐

Do you use the location atlas   ☐ YES   ☐ NO?

Do you generally agree with the Rosette ratings at the restaurants you visit in the guide?

(If not please give examples)

Who is your favourite chef?

Which is your favourite restaurant?

Which type of cuisine is your first choice e.g. French

Which of these factors is most important when choosing a restaurant?

Price ☐   Service ☐   Location ☐   Type of food ☐

Awards/ratings ☐   Décor/surroundings ☐

Other (please state)

Which elements of the guide do you find most useful when choosing a restaurant?

Description ☐   Photo ☐   Rosette rating ☐   Price ☐

Other (please state)

Restaurant Readers' Report Form

Please send this form to:–
Editor, The Restaurant Guide,
Lifestyle Guides,
AA Publishing,
13th Floor, Fanum House,
Basingstoke RG21 4EA

or e-mail: lifestyleguides@theAA.com

Please use this form to tell us about any restaurant you have visited, whether it is in the guide or not currently listed. Feedback from readers helps us to keep our guide accurate and up to date. Please note, however, that if you have a complaint to make during a visit, we strongly recommend that you discuss the matter with the restaurant management there and then, so that they have a chance to put things right before your visit is spoilt. The AA does not undertake to arbitrate between you and the restaurant management, or to obtain compensation or engage in correspondence.

Date

Your name (BLOCK CAPITALS)

Your address (BLOCK CAPITALS)

Post code

E-mail address

Restaurant name and address: (If you are recommending a new restaurant please enclose a menu or note the dishes that you ate.)

Comments

(please attach a separate sheet if necessary)

We may use information we hold about you to write, e-mail or telephone you about other products and services offered by us and our carefully selected partners, but we can assure you that we will not disclose it to third parties.

Please tick here ☐ if you DO NOT wish to receive details of other products or services from the AA.

PTO

Restaurant Readers' Report Form *continued*

Have you bought this guide before? YES ☐ NO ☐

Please list any other similar guides that you use regularly

_____

_____

What do you find most useful about The AA Restaurant Guide?

_____

_____

Please answer these questions to help us make improvements to the guide

What are your main reasons for visiting restaurants (tick all that apply)

Business entertaining ☐   Business travel ☐   Trying famous restaurants ☐

Family celebrations ☐   Leisure travel ☐   Trying new food ☐

Enjoying not having to cook yourself ☐   To eat food you couldn't cook yourself ☐

Because I enjoy eating out regularly ☐

Other (please state)

How often do you visit a restaurant for lunch or dinner? (tick one choice)

Once a week ☐   Once a fortnight ☐   Once a month ☐   Less than once a month ☐

Do you use the location atlas   ☐ YES   ☐ NO?

Do you generally agree with the Rosette ratings at the restaurants you visit in the guide?

(If not please give examples)

_____

Who is your favourite chef?

_____

Which is your favourite restaurant?

_____

Which type of cuisine is your first choice e.g. French

_____

Which of these factors is most important when choosing a restaurant?

Price ☐   Service ☐   Location ☐   Type of food ☐

Awards/ratings ☐   Décor/surroundings ☐

Other (please state)

Which elements of the guide do you find most useful when choosing a restaurant?

Description ☐   Photo ☐   Rosette rating ☐   Price ☐

Other (please state)